RADOVAN KARADŽIĆ

Radovan Karadžić, leader of the Bosnian Serb nationalists during the Bosnian War (1992–1995), stands accused of genocide and crimes against humanity before the International Criminal Tribunal for the former Yugoslavia in The Hague. This book traces the origins of the war's extreme violence against civilians to the utopian national aspirations of the Serb Democratic Party and Karadžić's personal transformation from an unremarkable family man to the powerful leader of the Bosnian Serb nationalists. Based on previously unused documents from the tribunal's archives and many hours of Karadžić's cross-examination at his trial, the author shows why and how the Bosnian Serb leader planned and directed the worst atrocities in Europe since the Second World War. This book provocatively argues that postcommunist democracy was a primary enabler of mass atrocities because it provided the means to mobilize large numbers of Bosnian Serbs for the campaign to eliminate non-Serbs from conquered land.

Robert J. Donia, an historian specializing in modern Southeast Europe, is the author or editor of six books on the history of the region, most recently *Sarajevo: A Biography*, a study of the city from its founding to the present day. He has testified as an historical expert witness at fifteen war crimes trials in The Hague, including those of former Yugoslav President Slobodan Milošević and Bosnian Serb leader Radovan Karadžić, the subject of this biography. He holds a courtesy appointment as an Associate Professor of History at the University of Sarajevo, is a corresponding member of the Academy of Sciences and the Arts of Bosnia and Herzegovina, and has been a Visiting Professor of History at the University of Michigan. He lives in San Diego, California, with his wife Jane.

Radovan Karadžić

ARCHITECT OF THE
BOSNIAN GENOCIDE

ROBERT J. DONIA

CAMBRIDGE
UNIVERSITY PRESS

CAMBRIDGE
UNIVERSITY PRESS

32 Avenue of the Americas, New York, NY 10013-2473, USA

Cambridge University Press is part of the University of Cambridge.

It furthers the University's mission by disseminating knowledge in the pursuit of
education, learning, and research at the highest international levels of excellence.

www.cambridge.org
Information on this title: www.cambridge.org/9781107423084

First published 2015

Printed in Great Britain by Clays Ltd, St Ives plc

A catalog record for this publication is available from the British Library.

Library of Congress Cataloging in Publication data
Donia, Robert J.
Radovan Karadžić, architect of the
bosnian genocide / Robert J. Donia, University of Michigan.
pages cm
Includes bibliographical references and index.
ISBN 978-1-107-07335-7 (hardback) – ISBN 978-1-107-42308-4 (paperback)
1. Karadžić, Radovan V., 1945– 2. Political leaders – Bosnia and Hercegovina – Republika
Srpska – Biography. 3. Serbs – Bosnia and Hercegovina – Biography. 4. Soldiers – Bosnia
and Hercegovina – Republika Srpska – Biography. 5. Republika Srpska
(Bosnia and Hercegovina) – Politics and government. 6. Bosnia and Hercegovina – Politics
and government – 1992– 7. Yugoslav War, 1991–1995 – Bosnia and Hercegovina. I. Title.
DR1755.K37D66 2014
949.74203–dc23   [B]
2014015583

ISBN 978-1-107-07335-7 Hardback
ISBN 978-1-107-42308-4 Paperback

For Jane,
in deep appreciation for our life together

Contents

Maps, Tables, and Illustrations

Preface

Looking gaunt and downcast, Radovan Karadžić stood for the first time in the dock of the International Criminal Tribunal for the former Yugoslavia (ICTY) on July 31, 2008, to face charges of genocide, crimes against humanity, and crimes of war. Millions of residents of the former Yugoslavia had longed for that moment to come; he himself had fervently hoped it never would. His initial appearance at the Tribunal came more than a dozen years after the end of the war in Bosnia and Herzegovina (1992–1995) and thirteen years after he was first indicted by the ICTY. He had spent the intervening years as one of the world's most successful fugitives, making dramatic escapes, devising elaborate disguises, and taunting his accusers. A week before his first appearance in court, he had been arrested in Belgrade by police of the Republic of Serbia and flown to the Scheveningen Prison in The Hague, Netherlands.

To many outside the former Yugoslavia, Radovan Karadžić is better known by his deeds and appearance than by name. Few outside his native land can pronounce, let alone remember, his name, with its two diacriticals and unfamiliar combination of two consonants (Karadžić – CAR-ahd-jich, to a speaker of English). With his craggy facial features, roughly dimpled chin, and wavy, drooping hair, he epitomizes in physical appearance the image of the archetypal Balkan atavist: coarse, volatile, and weathered by life's vicissitudes. To his circle of family, friends, and some fellow Serbs, he is a hero of mythical proportions, a valiant but persecuted champion of the Serb people against many adversaries. But to most of the global public, he is the "Butcher of Bosnia," the architect and perpetrator of genocide and other atrocities that have been the worst and most destructive in Europe since the Second World War.

Despite these divergent views of him, much about Karadžić's life is undisputed. Born in the Yugoslav Republic of Montenegro in 1945, he moved in 1960 to Sarajevo, capital of the Republic of Bosnia and Herzegovina (shortened to "Bosnia" in these pages) to attend university. While in medical school

he married a fellow student, Ljiljana Zelena, with whom he had two children. After graduating from medical school in 1971, he practiced psychiatry,
became a published poet, and worked as an advisor to two soccer teams, one
in Sarajevo and the other in Belgrade. In November 1984 he was imprisoned
(but never convicted) for almost a year on suspicion of misappropriating funds.
Upon release he returned to his staid family life and psychiatric practice, with
no profile as an ardent nationalist and no apparent predisposition for becoming a major nationalist figure in Bosnia as Yugoslavia collapsed.

His life changed abruptly in 1990, the year the ruling communists of
Yugoslavia scheduled multiparty elections and allowed rival political parties
to organize and compete for votes. In July of that year he helped found the
nationalist Serb Democratic Party (*Srpska demokratska stranka*, SDS) and was
chosen its first president. In that capacity, he led the SDS during the first half
of 1992 in seizing a large part of Bosnia by armed force and establishing a separate Bosnian Serb polity, the Republika Srpska (RS). As president of the RS
and the undisputed civilian leader of the Bosnian Serb nationalists until July
1996, he led them throughout the Bosnian war of 1992–1995 in which more
than 100,000 soldiers and civilians were killed and many mass atrocities were
committed against civilians. He was indicted by the ICTY in July 1995 and
resigned in July 1996 from his posts as president of the SDS and the RS. He
spent the next dozen years in Bosnia and Serbia as a fugitive before Serbian
police located and arrested him in Belgrade in July 2008.

I did not at first set out to write a biography of Karadžić; rather, I wanted
to understand how monstrous acts of violence could have been committed
in the Bosnian society I had come to know since 1965 from many visits and
personal acquaintances. But as I investigated and contemplated that question,
it became apparent that the answers to my inquiry lay, if anywhere, in the
ideas, plans, and deeds of Radovan Karadžić. His life was a prism through
which to view the collective behavior of himself and his followers. This book
is therefore a study both of Karadžić's life and of the internal dynamics that led
Bosnian Serb nationalists to engage collectively in mass atrocities, including
genocide.

The assessment of Radovan Karadžić that I offer in the following pages
differs both from the laudatory descriptions offered by his admirers and the
evil-from-birth portraits drawn by his detractors. I have come to see him as a
complex human being, possessed of a keen and adaptable intellect, a fertile
imagination, and a theatrical sense of human drama. He thought creatively
and acted ruthlessly in realizing, at any cost, a utopian vision of a separate
state controlled and inhabited only by Serbs. Unfortunately for his many victims, he crossed along the way several thresholds – intellectual, emotional,

and imaginative – on his way to becoming a calculating perpetrator of mass atrocities.

My view of the Bosnian Serb nationalist movement likewise departs from those who either valorize or deplore it. The movement began as a conventional political party as Yugoslavia collapsed, but it soon became a Serb national awakening with expanding ambitions and goals that could only be realized at the expense of millions of other human beings that stood in its way. In the first half of 1992, Serb nationalist ambitions shifted from claiming lands where Serbs lived to meeting the broader strategic needs of the RS. With those strategic objectives, Karadžić and his Bosnian Serb associates and followers fought the war of 1992–1995 and initiated mass atrocities to secure exclusive Serb habitation and control in the Republika Srpska.

Neither the Bosnian Serb movement nor Karadžić himself began their existence with the intent of murdering thousands of people or engaging in other mass atrocities, but both became planners and practitioners of such deeds. I have focused in this volume on their development from the relatively benign and banal to resolute perpetrators of many atrocities, in the conviction that studying them is an instructive, if deeply dismaying, undertaking. I do so in the hope that the paths they pursued may be followed by none, or at least fewer, in the future.

Acknowledgments

I can neither count nor adequately thank the many colleagues and friends in Bosnia who have shared with me their time and insights in discussing the topics in this book. But I do wish to acknowledge those who have facilitated those discussions, including Sinan Alić, Dragan Marković, Husnija Kamberović, Mirko Pejanović, and Zijad Bećirović. I am profoundly thankful to Lara Nettelfield, who offered counsel, encouragement, and assistance through all phases of the project. Victor Jackovich and Joyce Neu contributed invaluable insights and generously shared with me their personal encounters with Karadžić. Edin Hajdarpašić, Diana Cordileone, Edina Bećirović, and Jonathan Marwil read the manuscript and offered recommendations for its improvement, some of which I unwisely ignored in bringing the work to fruition. Andy Ross, an enterprising and energetic book agent, provided valuable advice and encouragement in bringing this work to its prospective readers. My thanks to Raymond Grew, John Mulder, and Susan Somers, whose generous friendship and encouragement helped sustain me through writing this work.

Special thanks to the many underappreciated attorneys and researchers at the ICTY who have been at the forefront in seeking the truth about the Bosnian war and those who fought it. They, too, are too numerous to name, but include Alan Tieger, Carolyn Edgerton, Andrew Corin, Bill Tomljanovich, Nena Tromp, and Camille Bibles.

I appreciate the unstinting and rejuvenating encouragement of John Berger at Cambridge University Press. I thank the three anonymous readers (although I now know who you are) for their kind words and gently delivered constructive criticism. This work has been edited by the intrepid Teresa Lawson with the assistance of Patricia Zerfoss, and I am pleased to acknowledge that they saved me from many embarrassments and pointed out many possible improvements. My wife, Jane Ritter, has gone over these pages repeatedly with a fine editorial eye and remarkably remained married to me throughout. I have dedicated this book to her, but that is but one reason for doing so.

Despite my arduous efforts in the preceding paragraphs to spread the blame around, I must reluctantly acknowledge that any remaining errors and faults are my own.

Introduction

I first met Radovan Karadžić in a war crimes courtroom at the International Criminal Tribunal for the Former Yugoslavia (ICTY). He was there to defend himself against a litany of accusations. I had been called by the prosecution to testify as an expert historical witness to provide background and context to wartime events, having assumed that role in a dozen previous cases before the ICTY. In most other trials, I testified for a few hours under questioning by a prosecutor and was then cross-examined for a few more hours by defense attorneys.

This case was different. In choosing to serve as his own defense attorney, Karadžić gained the opportunity to confront personally each witness, in the presence of three judges who would decide his case. Standing at the defense lectern, he cross-examined me with a barrage of barbed and loaded questions.[1] For a total of twenty-four hours, from June 1 to 10, 2010, he and I engaged in a strange kind of dialogue – testy, impassioned, or sometimes surprisingly cordial – about his rise to power and whether he had led Serb nationalists to commit mass atrocities in Bosnia during the war of 1992–95.[2] Despite the contentiousness of our encounters, with each passing day of the trial I gained new insights about him and the movement that he had led in the 1990s.

Karadžić's trial thus granted me unusual access to an accused war criminal that shaped many of the insights in this book. My encounters with him also helped me define the book's central purpose: to view, through the prism

---

[1] International Criminal Tribunal for the Former Yugoslavia (hereafter ICTY), Prosecutor v. Radovan Karadžić (IT-95-5/18-I) (hereafter PRK), Transcripts, May 31–June 10, pp. 3067–3731, accessed from //www.icty.org/case/Karadžić/4#trans, viewed December 6, 2013.

[2] Although Karadžić knows and speaks English well, and I read and speak his language, we each spoke in our native tongue – he in the language now known as BCS (Bosnian-Croatian-Serbian), I in English. Through the earphones worn by everyone in the courtroom, we each heard the translation of the other's words.

of Karadžić's biography, the causes, the course, and the consequences of the Bosnian Serb national movement in the 1990s. In examining his political career, one can identify conditions that led Karadžić and his followers to carry out mass atrocities to achieve their political ambitions. The examination of his life also suggests some lessons about nationalism, mass atrocities, and genocide in our time, to which I return in the concluding chapter.

Karadžić clearly relished his return to the global spotlight after a decade and a half in flight and seclusion. Rather than defending himself against criminal charges, he devoted his time in court to burnishing his image before history, showing no remorse for his previous actions. Three months before my testimony, in his opening statement at trial, he described himself as a martyr for the long-suffering and deeply-misunderstood Serb people. "I stand here before you not to defend the mere mortal that I am," he told the judges, "but to defend the greatness of a small nation in Bosnia-Herzegovina which, for 500 years, has had to suffer and has demonstrated a great deal of modesty and perseverance to survive in freedom."[3] He claimed that defending his own actions was synonymous with justifying the conduct of the Bosnian Serbs. "I will defend that nation of ours and their cause, which is just and holy," he said, "and in that way I shall be able to defend myself, too, and my nation, because we have a good case."

On hearing his opening statement in March, 2010, I thought it was merely a prelude to a conventional criminal defense. But by the end of my two weeks in the courtroom with him, I had concluded that he was utterly sincere in identifying his personal fate with that of the Bosnian Serbs. He saw himself as their champion and savior. From the day in July 1990 that he became president of the SDS, he believed that he bore their burdens and shared their destiny. He even viewed his ascent to the leadership of the SDS as a sacrificial act, since he relinquished his comfortable life as a Sarajevo professional to lead the nationalists' cause. His stature as their martyr-in-chief, in his view, gave him license to speak not only *for* the Serbs of Bosnia, but *as* the Serbs of Bosnia. His arguments in court were meant both to define his personal legacy and to justify the actions of those he called collectively the "Serb people."

In court, my recollections of the documentary record helped me to craft careful and sometimes extensive responses to Karadžić, despite the vehemence with which he pressed some of his questions. On occasion he would select passages from a document in BCS to prove his point, reading them into

---

[3] Opening Statement of Radovan Karadžić, March 1, 2010, ICTY, PRK, p. 808, www.icty.org/case/Karadžić/4#trans, viewed July 4, 2010.

ILLUSTRATION A.1. Radovan Karadžić in his first appearance at the ICTY, July 31, 2008. Getty Images.

the record or offering an English translation of only the excerpts favorable to the point he was making. Often I was able to contest his interpretation by explaining the context that surrounded his self-serving soliloquies. But when he cross-examined other witnesses who did not know BCS, he often used similar tactics to gain their assent to the accuracy of a misquotation and thus to distort its meaning. Even when he won a witness's concurrence, he rarely took "yes" for an answer but insisted on reiterating his point before moving on.

As a questioner, he relied on tenacity, conviction, and energy rather than finesse. Whenever he failed to win assent from me on the first try, he would press the same question relentlessly, perhaps with a slightly different wording each time. He could be adept at crafting specific questions, but in his eagerness to make a point, he often elaborated a simple question into a complex and open-ended one. Sometimes he lost track of his intended point as a well-conceived question turned into a monologue resembling testimony. These are the traits of a man accustomed to success in persuading those around him and wearing down those who refuse to agree: a bully with a brilliant

ILLUSTRATION A.2. Headquarters of the International Criminal Tribunal for the Former Yugoslavia, The Hague, Netherlands. Photograph by author.

mind, a sharp tongue, and great dexterity in exercising his impressive skills of persuasion.

Karadžić regularly employed the royal "we" in his questions and pronouncements, but in so doing he seemed to refer to different groups. Occasionally, Karadžić's "we" referred to a small cadre of senior SDS leaders; sometimes, it referred to the party as a whole; or most frequently, to all Bosnian Serbs. In what seemed to be an effort to put himself at the heart of the Bosnian Serb nationalist movement, he often referred to himself in the third person. "We're going to have to throw light on the conduct and mind set of Radovan Karadžić first of all, and then his conduct and behavior, and then the conduct of the whole SDS party and other Serb parties," he stated, emphasizing his self-identification with the Serb cause.[4]

Karadžić used documents extensively in cross-examining me, and he questioned me about each one, always with the aim of exonerating himself and the Bosnian Serbs from blame for war or war crimes. To the judges' dismay, he often read verbatim and at length from documents he hoped to put into evidence. Karadžić thus revealed a command of the written and printed records he had reviewed in preparation for the case. This was unusual: few other ICTY indictees had availed themselves of the right to review the reams of documentation pertinent to their cases.

[4]   Karadžić, cross-examination of Donia, June 9, 2010, ICTY, PRK, p. 3,533.

He revealed himself in court as a man of rage. His wrath typically rose slowly and simmered long, rather than exploding unexpectedly, but its arrival was unmistakable. Sometimes I could hear it building from the lectern to my left. His questions would become more penetrating and accusatory. His distinctive, even-toned voice gave way to a resounding bellow that scorched the ears even through the earphones I was wearing. Anger seemed to transform him into a larger, more dominant physical being. I became convinced that his anger was genuine most of the time, but Karadžić also seemed able to modulate and channel his rage, selectively employing it as a tool of persuasion or domination.

As we sparred verbally in the courtroom, I came to understand how he had used his wrath to dominate and humiliate adversaries on several occasions in his political career. I watched him repeatedly reach a crescendo of anger in an effort to get the answers he wanted from me. Occasionally, his anger seemed to flare out of control. Working himself into a volcanic rage, he would lose focus on his line of questioning, reverting instead to a topic where he seemed more confident. But such disabling anger got the best of him only a few times during our encounters. Most of the time, he was able to modulate and harness his own anger, an ability that was one of his assets as a leader.

As an interlocutor, he proved swiftly adaptive, seamlessly shifting among moods and types of behavior. As the days of my cross-examination wore on, the judges asked Karadžić to ask only relevant questions and to end his cross-examination soon. After one such admonition, he feigned shock. "It was a real surprise when I heard that I won't even have 20 of the 40 hours I had initially asked for," he said. When Presiding Judge Kwon informed him on June 10 that he had only fifteen minutes more for cross-examination, he turned sarcastic. "Our 40 hours was a conservative estimate," he told the judges. "So I am giving this time back as a present."[5] Presiding Judge Kwon, taking him literally, asked, "Dr. Karadžić, do you need that fifteen minutes at all?" Karadžić instantly became despondent. "No," he said, "it is pointless for me to raise any subjects without dealing with them properly." Then, after pausing a few seconds, he changed his mind. "Actually, I can ask him," he said, casting off his subdued persona to became again an animated and pugnacious questioner.

I came to see this as Radovan Karadžić's signature character trait: he could instantly mutate his personality and mood to suit the needs of the moment. When I returned to my research of his life in documents, I found such shifts

---

[5] Ibid., p. 3701, for quotations in this paragraph.

again and again, lasting anywhere from a minute to a month. Karadžić was a chameleon, adaptable in ways that would be comedic had not his words and deeds proven so consequential for so many human lives. Nothing would be more important in understanding him than appreciating his capacity for instant transformation for maximum effect.

At times in court, when we found ourselves concurring on some aspect of his life experiences, he would briefly flash a slight smile and nod of approval. To be sure, we did not bond. I could not forget the atrocities over which he had presided in the 1990s. He displayed unalloyed disdain for most of my testimony, and his contempt seemed to grow with each court session. However, we communicated and understood one another more than I had anticipated. Hoping to understand but with little expectation of agreeing, I listened attentively to his views of his own life and deeds.

As he questioned me, Karadžić confirmed my earlier impression that he possessed a formidable and wide-ranging intellect, and I learned that his intelligence was imaginative as well as analytical. From twenty-four hours in dialogue with him, I saw how his brilliant mind, intellectual versatility, carefully-modulated rage, and instant adaptability were enlisted to justify his every act, magnify the historical significance of his deeds, and promote his utopian vision for the Bosnian Serb nationalists. A narcissist in the courtroom no less than in public life, he projected his own personality and behavior onto those for whom he presumed to speak. According to his narrative, he had lived, acted, and fought for the Serb people, and he would suffer in their name as well. He believed passionately in his cause and in himself as its primary protagonist.

We found surprising agreement on one issue: the nature of his life in prewar Sarajevo. He sought confirmation that neither he nor his family had shown malice toward those of other nationalities before the war began. I readily concurred. In one of his many attestations that masqueraded as a question, Karadžić boasted that he had selected his barber, a man called Meho, regardless of the fact that he was a Bosniak, simply because he was reputed to be the best barber in town. From all the information I had acquired about Karadžić, it appeared that in the first decades of his life he had enjoyed good relations with Bosniaks, Croats, Jews, and others in Bosnia. Examining his life prior to his entry into politics in 1990, I found no significant nationalist leanings in either his writings or his conduct. His rhetorical question about his barber Meho suggested his vanity – he required the best barber in town to trim the unruly mane that he tossed back so ostentatiously – and further confirmed my sense that he showed a Sarajevan's typical pride in associating with those of other ethnicities and faiths. If he harbored any hatred or resentment against non-Serbs prior to the dawn of the democratic era in Bosnia, he had not shown it publicly. However, he also contended in court that he had never abandoned his positive prewar feelings toward members of other groups. I expressly disagreed with that proposition, since I had observed in the documentary record his evolution into a Serb nationalist with low regard for the Bosniaks and their political leaders.

Karadžić was not alone in devoting himself to the Serb nationalist cause in the 1990s. He had a wide following among Serbs in Bosnia, many of whom fought as soldiers in the war, and some of whom participated in organizing and leading the SDS and the Republika Srpska. One of those was Nikola Koljević, whom I too had known, many years before my courtroom encounter with Karadžić. A professor of communications at the University of Sarajevo, Nick (as he was known to his American friends and colleagues) spent the academic year 1972–73 teaching at my alma mater, Hope College, in Holland, Michigan. He loved the place; there he was known to students as a devoted teacher and to colleagues as an able Shakespeare scholar and speaker. I met him soon after, during my one-year stay in Sarajevo on a Fulbright scholarship doing historical research in 1974–75. We shared our memories of Michigan and reviewed our common acquaintances. In Sarajevo, I saw that Nick was esteemed at the university there no less than he had been at Hope College. A warm, caring person and a marvelous teacher, the Nick I knew in those days was widely liked and admired.

To my surprise, Nick later became one of the founders of the SDS in 1990 and vice president of the Republika Srpska in 1992. Like Karadžić, with whom he had become close, he had not previously expressed an interest in politics or political nationalism, although he had always been an admirer of folk culture and a rural lifestyle. His life trajectory, from compassionate literature professor to key leader of a nationalist party that sanctioned mass atrocities, suggests that Karadžić was not alone in making the leap from political indifference to impassioned nationalist conviction. In this biography, I seek to understand how that could happen. I cannot ask Nick himself, since he committed suicide in a hotel room in Banja Luka in January 1997. I mourn the loss. I found some comfort in discovering during my research a few occasions when he tried to curb some of the extreme measures of the Bosnian Serb nationalists, but I wish he had done more to restrain them. From what I have learned of his political career, he underwent much the same transition as Karadžić from national indifference to avid proponent of the utopian nationalist dream.

THE MAKING OF A FRAGILE FEDERATION

Radovan Karadžić is a South Slav, meaning he belongs to one of several different Slavic peoples inhabiting much of southeastern Europe (an area often called the Balkans after a small mountain range there). Migrations, religious conversions, and linguistic differentiation have defined and shaped the identities of South Slavs for more than a millennium. In the fifth through eighth centuries, several tribes of Slavic speakers migrated from a part of what is now Poland to Southeast Europe. These settlers were preliterate polytheists when they migrated, but toward the end of the first millennium CE they were Christianized by missionaries from Rome to the west and from Constantinople to the east.

With the Great Schism that split the Christian world in 1054, the South Slavs divided into Catholics and Orthodox. Catholicism and the Latin alphabet prevailed among most South Slavs in western lands (present-day Slovenia, Croatia, and much of Bosnia), while Orthodoxy and the Cyrillic alphabet took hold mainly in the east (present-day Serbia, Montenegro, Macedonia, and Bulgaria). However, the Orthodox and Catholics mingled in many central parts of the region, most notably in Bosnia, which was also home to its own independent Christian group called the Bosnian Church. After the Muslim-led Ottoman Empire conquered much of the area in the fourteenth through sixteenth centuries, some Catholics and Orthodox voluntarily converted to Islam, adding a third religious community to the area. A fourth religious group appeared when Jews, fleeing oppression in Europe's Iberian Peninsula (today's Portugal and Spain), migrated to the relatively tolerant havens of Ottoman cities in the fifteenth and sixteenth centuries.

For many centuries after these conversions, religion was the most important differentiator among groups in the region. But whereas most national movements in Eastern Europe distinguished among peoples primarily based on language differences, the national identities of the South Slavs were shaped by a lattice of both language and religion. As national movements took hold between the 1770s and the 1960s, groups of South Slavs came to be differentiated by secular national consciousness and minor linguistic differences as well as religious affiliation. This produced several different peoples, or nations, in the central areas of the former Yugoslavia.[6] Among these groups were the Serbs, Croats, Slovenes, Montenegrins, Macedonians,

---

[6] The term "narod" in the local language, normally rendered in the singular to denote that the group has a personality and character of its own, may be translated either as "nation" or "people" in English. I have used them both in this work.

and Bosniaks (the group known until 1993 as the Bosnian Muslims).[7] They shared, and share today, the territory of the former Yugoslavia with smaller numbers of non-Slavs, including Albanians, Hungarians, Jews, Roma, and several others.

South Slavs in the present-day areas of Croatia, Bosnia, Serbia, and Montenegro speak languages so similar that through much of the twentieth century they were commonly considered a single Slavic language, Serbo-Croatian. Today the language is identified as Bosnian-Croatian-Serbian (BCS), a term that is widely used by foreigners and international organizations but is not universally used by native speakers, many of whom refer to their language as "Serbian," "Croatian," or "Bosnian." One recent study described BCS as "the common core underlying Bosnian, Croatian, and Serbian" and concluded that "the language is simultaneously one and more than one."[8] Building on differences in religion and religious tradition, as well as minor linguistic distinctions, leading intellectuals promoted a distinction among three peoples: Serbs (Orthodox in faith and tradition, Serbian in language), Croats (Catholic in faith and tradition, Croatian in language), and Bosniaks (Islamic in faith and tradition, Bosnian in language).[9]

By the 1970s, most South Slavs in Bosnia, Croatia, and Serbia identified themselves as Serbs, Croats, or Bosniaks (at the time known as the Bosnian Muslims), but others in lesser numbers identified themselves as "Yugoslavs" to indicate their rejection of the three dominant identities.

Yugoslavism, the belief that South Slavs should unite in a single state, was a revolutionary ideal in the nineteenth century. Turning that ideal into reality would have required overthrowing or radically reorganizing the Habsburg and Ottoman Empires. The two empires thwarted Yugoslavism for all of the nineteenth century, but they were swept away when Europe's map was redrawn at the end of the First World War (1914–18). With the disappearance of Yugoslavism's primary opponents, Crown Prince Aleksandar of Serbia

---

[7] Vjekoslav Perica, *Balkan Idols: Religion and Nationalism in Yugoslav States* (New York: Oxford University Press, 2002), p. 6.

[8] Ronelle Alexander, *Bosnian, Croatian, Serbian: A Grammar with Sociolinguistic Commentary* (Madison, WI: University of Wisconsin Press, 2006), p. 379.

[9] In September 1993, during the darkest days of the Bosnian war, intellectuals and political leaders of the nation gathered in Sarajevo and voted to change their name from "Bosnian Muslims" to "Bosniaks." They did so to end the tendency of many, both within and outside their group, to dismiss them as members of a religious rather than a national community. The new name elevated the group linguistically to the same stature as Serbs and Croats. The Serbs were the secular embodiment of the religious community called the Serbian Orthodox; Croats had formerly been Croat-speaking Catholics; similarly, Bosniaks preferred that name over the Bosnian Muslim designation that had been used in federal Yugoslavia (1945–92).

proclaimed the Kingdom of Serbs, Croats, and Slovenes on December 1, 1918; in January 1929 it was renamed the Kingdom of Yugoslavia.[10] Although most political leaders of all South Slav peoples had displayed enthusiasm for that idea before Aleksandar's proclamation, the hard realities of state-making soon led to discord, particularly between Serbs and Croats. Most Croat delegates intermittently boycotted the Kingdom's assembly to protest Serb domination of the Royal Yugoslav Army and bureaucracy.

Only in August 1939 did leading Serb and Croat politicians agree to resolve their differences, chiefly by dividing the historical territory of Bosnia between them.[11] Like other nationalists in Southeast Europe, Serb and Croat leaders supported, respectively, a "Great Serbia" and a "Great Croatia," projects to expand the boundaries of their core polities to encompass all members of their nations. With the division of Bosnia in 1939, both projects partially came to fruition and would later be cited by Serb and Croat nationalists as admirable precedents to be replicated.

The agreement of 1939 came too late to save the country: the Yugoslav Kingdom had been weakened by internecine struggles and by the crippling economic crisis of the 1930s. In April 1941 German and Italian invaders conquered all of Yugoslavia in a matter of days and carved it into several occupied territories ruled by their puppets or by Germans or Italians directly. The Germans brought from exile in Italy a small group of Croatian fascists known as "Ustasha" (rebels) and helped them create a new state, the "Independent State of Croatia," that governed most of Croatia and Bosnia. Almost immediately upon assuming power, the Ustasha slaughtered thousands of Jews, hundreds of thousands of Serbs, and some Bosniaks and Croats who opposed their rule. The Ustasha recruited some Bosniaks to join their ranks, both in high leadership positions and in their armed forces, but most Bosniaks remained distant from their movement.

Ustasha atrocities spurred two movements to oppose them. Colonel (as of 1941, General) Draža Mihailović and other former Royal Yugoslav Army officers organized the Chetniks, a loosely-organized coalition of Serb nationalists who wanted to restore Royal Yugoslavia. Josip Broz, a communist organizer of mixed Croat and Slovene parentage, headed the Partisans, a group which supported national equality and a federal socialist state. After protracted fighting and much bloodshed, the Partisans emerged triumphant

[10] John R. Lampe, *Yugoslavia as History: Twice there was a Country* (New York: Cambridge University Press, 1996), tells the story of both royal and socialist Yugoslavias.
[11] Christopher Bennett, *Yugoslavia's Bloody Collapse: Causes, Course, and Consequences* (London: Hurst, 1995), pp. 39–42; and Ljubo Boban, *Sporazum Cvetković-Maček* (Zagreb: Institut društvenih nauka, 1964).

in 1945 by defeating the Chetniks and liberating much of Yugoslavia from Ustasha and foreign rule, albeit with Allied aid and support. The Ustasha and Germans had imported the Holocaust to Yugoslavia and carried out the slaughter that ended in the precipitous decline of Yugoslavia's Jews from over 80,000 before the war to fewer than 7,000 in 1948. The overwhelming majority of Jews in Bosnia, estimated variously at 10,000 to 14,000 before the war, likewise died in Nazi concentration camps; the survivors and returnees numbered fewer than a thousand in the postwar period. Yugoslav demographers showed that about a million Yugoslavs perished from violence during the fighting, much of which took place in Bosnia. Serbs, Bosniaks, and Croats perished in large numbers but in lesser percentages of their respective prewar populations than did Jews or Roma.[12] Tito's Partisan forces also committed mass atrocities against their opponents as the war was ending. The war casualties and atrocities have hung like a dark cloud over the region ever since. Leaders of every nation have contested the number of casualties, and some have manipulated the numbers to burnish claims that their people suffered the most during the war.

The victors – Tito, the Communist Party of Yugoslavia, and the Partisans – built the new Yugoslavia as a socialist federation consisting of six republics (including two autonomous regions), closely mirroring the model of Stalin's Soviet Union. (See Map A of Yugoslavia and Table A for Yugoslavia's population.) They sought to quash political nationalism, implement communist ideology, and create a fast-growing socialist economic system. (In this book, "socialist" refers to the economic and political systems of Yugoslavia from 1945 to 1990, while "communist" refers to the dominant ideology and ruling party of socialist Yugoslavia.) As of 1948, Yugoslavia had just under 16 million inhabitants; by 1991 (the last full year the country was intact) that number had grown by 47 percent to over 23 million.[13] Five of the socialist republics were named after their majority nation: Serbia, Croatia, Slovenia, Macedonia, and Montenegro. (Montenegrins were afforded a distinct identity, but most considered them, and many of them viewed themselves, as Serbs who lived in a republic with a different name and history.) Bosnia and

---

[12] Jaša Romano, *Jevreji Jugoslavije 1941–1945: Žrtve genocida i učesnici NOR* (Belgrade: Federation of Jewish communities in Yugoslavia, 1980), p. 14; Francine Friedman, personal communication, March 10, 2014; Bogoljub Kočović, *Žrtve Drugog svjetskog rata u Jugoslaviji* (London: Naše Delo, 1985); and Vladimir Žerjavić, *Gubici stanovništva Jugoslavije u drugom svjetskom ratu* (Zagreb: Jugoslavensko viktimološko društvo, 1989).

[13] Federativna Narodna Republika Jugoslavije, Savezni Zavod za Statistiku, *Konačni resultati popisa stanovništva od 15. marta 1948 godine*, vol. 9: *Stanovništvo po narodnosti*, p. xiv; and successor report for 1991.

MAP A. Federal Socialist Republic of Yugoslavia, 1990.
Original Source: Library of Congress, DI Cartography Center 753540A1
(A04846) 8–01.

Herzegovina (shortened in these pages to "Bosnia" when referring to the polity or territory as a whole) was the only republic without a majority nation and no national name. Its dual name came from a nineteenth-century union of two regional Ottoman administrative units. Herzegovina, the southern third of the triangular "Bosnia and Herzegovina," was named after a duchy ruled by Herceg – Duke, taken from "Herzog" in German – Stjepan Vukčić in the fifteenth century. Bosnia, the northern two-thirds of the triangle, was named after the Bosna River that flows north from Sarajevo and empties into the Sava River. The two autonomous regions of Kosovo (_Kosovo i metohija_ in Serbian, _Kosovë_ in Albanian) and Vojvodina, constitutionally a part of Serbia, had names that were based on historical precedents.

TABLE A. *Serbs and Majority Nations in Yugoslav Republics, 1948–1991*

Republic or Autonomous Region	1948			1991		
	Total Population	Percent of Majority Nation*	Percent Serbs	Total Population	Percent of Majority Nation*	Percent Serbs
Serbia	5,936,223	80.2%	80.2%	8,110,906	80.3%	80.3%
Croatia	3,756,807	79.2%	14.5%	4,784,265	78.1%	12.2%
Bosnia	2,565,277	n/a	44.3%	4,377,033	n/a	31.2%
Slovenia	1,391,873	97.0%	0.5%	1,913,355	88.3%	2.5%
Macedonia	1,152,986	68.5%	2.6%	2,033,964	65.3%	2.1%
Montenegro	377,189	90.7%	0.2%	615,035	61.9%	9.3%
Vojvodina	1,663,212	50.6%	50.6%	2,012,519	57.2%	57.2%
Kosovo	727,820	68.5%	23.5%	1,956,196	86.1%	9.9%
Yugoslavia, Total	15,772,098			23,229,846		

* Serbs for Serbia; Croats for Croatia; Slovenes for Slovenia; Montenegrins for Montenegro; Macedonians for Macedonia; Serbs for Vojvodina; Albanians for Kosovo. Bosnia had no nation with an absolute majority.
Sources: Federativna Narodna Republika Jugoslavije, Savezni Zavod za Statistiku, *Konačno rezultati popisa stanovništva od 15. marta 1948 godine*, vol. 9, *Stanovništvo po narodnosti*, p. xiv; and successor report for 1991.

Tito's federal system was built on the notion that those of every nation would contribute to building a unified Yugoslav state while simultaneously realizing their group's national ambitions within their respective republics. Tito contrasted the benevolent federalism he favored with both the destructive unitarism of Royal Yugoslavia and the separatism of extreme nationalists. His federal system should provide for "independence of every federal unit, full independence in the sense of free cultural and economic development," he said.[14] At the same time, he called for the "elimination of national oppression, national pressures and discrimination, and chauvinism and national hatred."[15] In outlining such an unachievably idealistic notion of a federal system, Tito omitted to mention one key element: the Communist Party held an absolute monopoly on decision-making,

[14] Esad Zgodić, *Titova nacionalna politika: temeljni pojmovi, načela i vrijednosti* (Sarajevo: Kantonalni odbor SDP BiH, 2000), p. 209.
[15] Ibid.

rendering moot whatever "free cultural and economic development" the masses might wish to pursue. The Yugoslav Constitution of 1946, like the Soviet Constitution of 1936, contained lavish guarantees of personal and group rights, making it on paper one of the most liberal and admirable constitutions in the world. However, the centralized, hierarchical rule of the Communist Party made fictive the group and individual rights guaranteed in the constitution.[16]

That began to change after June 1948, when Stalin expelled Tito's Yugoslavia from the Communist Information Bureau (Cominform), finalizing a split between the two communist leaders and forcing Tito to define a path separate from that of the Soviet Union. In the early 1950s, Tito and his associates promoted workers' self-management as the key to that separate path. Always more an ideal than reality, workers' self-management meant creating enterprise-specific workers' councils to manage economic affairs, but it also implied decentralization of government and greater popular participation in governing bodies. These principles were implemented slowly and haltingly in the ensuing decades and remained incompletely realized when Yugoslavia collapsed in the 1990s.

The erratic pace of implementation subsequently had profound consequences for relations among peoples in Yugoslavia and its successor states.

The constitutions of 1953, 1963, and 1974 were each designed to increase the rights and powers of the republics, but the constitutions of 1963 and 1974 also restored lavish promises to ethnonational groups, guaranteeing "the right of every people to self-determination, including the right to secession."[17] In guaranteeing the right of self-determination to peoples and simultaneously granting greater authority to the republics, Yugoslavia's last two constitutions set up a potential clash between the rights of national self-determination and republic secession. Those documents used ambiguity to gloss over the inherent tension between the rights of peoples and of republics, principally through the word *odnosno*, which means "that is," "in other words," or "more exactly." The historian Audrey Budding explained, "Through this formula the regime consistently and fatefully blurred the distinction between the two concepts of nationhood," namely the ethnonational concept of a people and the territorially-bounded concept of the republic. As we have seen, Serbs in particular

[16] Paul Shoup, *Communism and the Yugoslav National Question* (New York: Columbia University Press, 1968), p. 73.

[17] Quoted in Audrey Helfant Budding, "Nation/People/Republic: Self-Determination in Socialist Yugoslavia," in Lenard J. Cohen and Jasna Dragović-Soso, eds., *State Collapse in South-Eastern Europe: New Perspectives on Yugoslavia's Disintegration* (West Lafayette, IN: Purdue University Press, 2008), p. 108.

were well represented in several republics besides Serbia and therefore wished the rights of peoples to take precedence over the rights of republics. As long as the League of Communists remained strong and centralized, the tension between these two rights mattered little. Only when the League began to weaken and eventually to divide into its republic components was the inherent contradiction between these two principles laid bare. When the Yugoslav-wide League ceased to exist in 1990 and divided into its republic components, the Yugoslav People's Army was the only institution with sufficient power to hold Yugoslavia together.

Serb nationalists detested the 1974 constitution, believing it moved the country toward a confederation – a weakened central state containing powerful subunits, the republics and autonomous regions. In nationalist thought, even in an undemocratic state, demographic pre-eminence is the key to political domination, and Serbs made up the most numerous nation in Yugoslavia. Additionally, Serbs also had the most members living outside their homeland republic of Serbia, most significantly in Croatia and Bosnia, so Serb leaders opposed changes that would disperse their political influence among several different polities. (See Table A.) Speaking in wartime a year after Yugoslavia's collapse, Radovan Karadžić blamed the 1974 constitution for destroying Yugoslavia. "The basic difference between a federation and confederation – I studied this myself – lies in who owns the executive organs,"[18] he told the Bosnian Serb Assembly in 1993. Under the 1974 federal constitution, he opined, "the executive function was left to the republics." With power decentralized, he concluded, "a confederation was created at that time and Yugoslavia collapsed." In his view and that of other like-minded nationalists, Serb national interests had been best served in a strong, centralized Yugoslavia, in which Serbs enjoyed an overall plurality and had their rights guaranteed in the constitutions of both the federation and individual republics.

Bosnia, the only republic with no majority nation, benefited from the decentralization embedded in the 1974 constitution, as long as the Bosnian League of Communists was able to prevent the republic's three primary nations from coming into conflict. After 1974, leaders of the Bosnian League of Communists became particularly vigilant against both national division within their own ranks and nationalist influences from neighboring republics. They treasured their shared commitment to national impartiality and made sure to choose office-holders from all nations in roughly equal proportions. National identity was therefore a factor in choosing the decision-makers for all

[18] BSA, 34th Session, August 27, 1993, Karadžić, BCS 0215–0530.

governing bodies, but those decision-makers were expected to build socialism and work for the interests of all citizens regardless of their identity. They were not expected to *represent* their group in the sense of advocating primarily for the interests of their ethnic brethren. Each nation thereby participated in governance without being separately and explicitly represented. "Leaders in this period had different ethnic backgrounds, but were not 'ethnic leaders'," wrote the journalist and scholar Neven Andjelic. "Cosmopolitanism was one of their main characteristics and they were always the first to criticize the appearance of nationalism in each of their respective groups."[19] Raif Dizdarević, one of the perennial leaders of the republic in the 1970s, summed up the leaders' approach. "We always tried to have our own views on things, our own perspective," he said.[20]

Members of the Bosnian League of Communists gained a reputation for communist orthodoxy and earned the scorn of nationalists, particularly Serb nationalists, for their monolithic makeup and independent views. They also engaged periodically in repression of those whom they believed to be national extremists. In the late 1980s, they suffered assaults from detractors in Serbia and a series of scandals at home (discussed in Chapter 1). In Bosnia, the principles of self-determination and republic rights were in direct conflict, and League leaders asserted the rights of their republic over notions of sovereignty and self-determination for Bosniaks, Croats, or Serbs. In 1990, they led the Bosnian Parliament in passing several constitutional amendments that superseded the 1974 constitution with provisions assigning sovereignty to the Republic of Bosnia but not to its constituent peoples. Article I of the 1974 constitution, which referred to the *"sovereignty and equality of the nations* of Bosnia and members of other nations and nationalities that live in it," was replaced with a provision referring to the Republic of Bosnia as a "democratic *sovereign state* of equal citizens, peoples of Bosnia."[21] (Emphasis added.) Serb nationalists denounced the amendment as contrary to the federally-guaranteed right of peoples to secede; they argued that a part of the constitution was itself unconstitutional. But as of July 30, 1990, it was the law of the land in Bosnia.

In many countries, such discordant constitutional provisions would be resolved by a system of courts, with a supreme court being the ultimate authority on the law. But Yugoslavia's court system was not empowered to

[19] Neven Andjelic, *Bosnia-Herzegovina: The End of a Legacy* (London: Frank Cass, 2003), p. 39.

[20] Author's interview with Raif Dizdarević, Sarajevo, May 11, 2004.

[21] Suad Arnautović, *Izbori u Bosni i Hercegovini '90: Analiza izbornog procesa* (Elections in Bosnia and Herzegovina 1990: Analysis of electoral processes) (Sarajevo: Promocult, 1996), p. 179.

issue binding judgments. Each republic and the Yugoslav federation had a constitutional court, but those courts were rarely consulted prior to the last few years of socialism. Furthermore, constitutional court judgments were only advisory. The courts forwarded their judgments to the appropriate legislative body to take whatever action the legislators deemed appropriate, rather than relying on an executive branch to enforce their judgments as in the United States and many other countries. Consequently, even when a constitutional court rendered a judgment, few felt compelled to obey it. When the Yugoslav Constitutional Court ruled that certain amendments to the Slovene constitution were incompatible with the federal constitution and therefore invalid, Slovene leaders paid little heed to the ruling.

On the eve of democracy's arrival, Yugoslavia was ill prepared to cope with a transition to multiparty democracy. The economy was in decline; political gridlock had prevented most necessary reforms; citizens were accustomed to having key decisions made for them by the League of Communists; the country had neither procedures nor a culture that respected Constitutional Court decisions; the ruling League of Communists was discredited and weakened by conflicts among peoples and republics, and governmental authority was widely disregarded. The bleak situation was wide open for political entrepreneurs who could mobilize constituencies in support of alternatives to socialist rule. Radovan Karadžić, intrigued with the possibilities for building something new, was ready to plunge into politics as a Serb nationalist with a dream and considerable untapped leadership ability.

THE TERMINOLOGY OF GENOCIDE AND ATROCITY

Although I have relied extensively in the following pages on the rich documentation housed at the ICTY, I have not undertaken to determine the criminal responsibility of any individual, nor have I attributed legal terms or assigned legal categories to any particular deed. That daunting task has been given to various courts in international and domestic jurisdictions, mostly to the ICTY and its neighbor in The Hague, the International Court of Justice (ICJ). I have freely judged particular deeds and acts as morally right or wrong, good or bad, but such judgments are of a different nature than an individual's innocence or guilt as determined by a court of law.

There is no doubt that many reprehensible deeds were committed against civilians during the Bosnian war. The ICTY trials of the past two decades, together with a rich collection of documents, eyewitness statements, scholarly works and journalists' accounts, erase any doubt that mass atrocities took place in a large number of municipalities in 1992 and that genocide was committed in the Srebrenica area in 1995. Even the government of Republika Srpska has issued an official report acknowledging the atrocities at Srebrenica, although without conceding that the Srebrenica killings constituted genocide. Several chambers at the ICTY have issued judgments concluding that genocide was committed around Srebrenica in July 1995, so I have applied the term "geno-cide" to those events. But I have not used that label for other mass atrocities committed during the Bosnian war, since the courts' characterization of other atrocities remains, as of this writing in 2014, unresolved or contested.

I apply the term "mass atrocities," used in its singular form by Mark Osiel in his pioneering studies, to refer to acts of physical brutality and killings com-mitted by state, political, military, or paramilitary formations of a group against substantial numbers of those belonging to another group.[22] I have avoided characterizing those acts as "ethnic cleansing," a term that first came into Western European and North American vocabularies during the 1991 war in Croatia as a direct translation of its BCS counterpart, *etničko čiščenje*. Some English language dictionaries define ethnic cleansing as including genocide; others do not.[23] Most major English-language studies consider genocide to be the most heinous form of ethnic cleansing.[24] To many of those in the former Yugoslavia, however, "ethnic cleansing" is a euphemism employed to mini-mize or deny genocide by putting a pleasant face on mass atrocities. Many in that region consider the deeds described here as mass atrocities to be genocide. The popular understanding of genocide (or *genocid*, the BCS cognate), both in Southeast Europe and elsewhere, generally includes more events of mass atrocities than the oft-changed but strictly-constructed concept of genocide as interpreted by international judicial bodies such as the ICTY. With respect for those involved in this fraught debate, I refer mainly to mass atrocities in the following pages and limit my use of the term "genocide" to the slaughter of over 7,000 Bosniaks around Srebrenica in July 1995, since there is broad judi-cial and popular agreement that the killings there constituted genocide.

---

[22] Mark Osiel, *Mass Atrocity, Collective Memory, and the Law* (New Brunswick and London: Transaction Publishers, 1997); and Mark Osiel, *Making Sense of Mass Atrocity* (Cambridge University Press, 2009).

[23] *The American Heritage Dictionary of the English Language*, 4th ed. (New York: Houghton Mifflin, 2009), defines "ethnic cleansing" as "the systematic elimination of an ethnic group or groups from a region or society, as by deportation, forced emigration, or genocide." Genocide is not mentioned, however, in the definition given by *Collins English Dictionary*, Complete and Unabridged (New York: HarperCollins, 2003).

[24] Samantha Power, *"A Problem From Hell": America and the Age of Genocide* (New York: Basic Books, 2002); Norman Naimark, *Fires of Hatred: Ethnic Cleansing in Twentieth-century Europe* (Cambridge, MA: Harvard University Press, 2001).

NOTE ON SOURCES

In writing this book I have relied substantially on documents gathered by the Office of the Prosecutor of the ICTY in preparation for bringing various cases to trial. These documents are separate from the ICTY's own work products, which include indictments, judgments, decisions, and other such material;[25] and also distinct from the testimony of witnesses in each case.[26] I became acquainted with those documents while preparing written reports and verbal testimony as an expert historical witness called by the prosecution in thirteen cases before the ICTY. While I was given access to some documents that remain under seal, in this work I have cited and relied upon only those documents that have become public through being admitted into evidence in open court, without restriction, by a Trial Chamber.[27] Documents admitted into evidence are but a small percentage of the total ICTY holdings, but they include the most significant and revealing documents in the collections. Every document cited here is in the public domain and in principle available to anyone requesting them, although the ICTY's labyrinthine procedures and dysfunctional finding aids have precluded most scholars from having meaningful access to them.[28]

Among the voluminous holdings of the ICTY archives, four document collections proved particularly valuable sources for this work. Most significant among them is a collection of minutes and verbatim transcripts of fifty-six sessions of the Bosnian Serb Assembly (here "BSA") from its founding in October 24, 1991, until February 2006. The records of all sessions were admitted in the Karadžić case upon application by prosecutors and support of the accused.[29]

---

[25] ICTY judgments and decisions are identified by name of document, date, case, and other information as required.

[26] Witness testimony is identified in footnotes as "Testimony of" followed by witness name, ICTY, case, date, and page of testimony in the online record, as referenced at www.un.org/icty/cases/indictindex-e.htm.

[27] Upon acquisition by the ICTY, each page of each document is given a unique eight digit Evidence Registration Number (ERN), consisting of four digits, a dash, and another four digits. For multipage documents, a sequence of pages is expressed as a range (eight digits for the first page and eight for the last). In this book, documents from the ICTY archives are cited by title, date, ICTY, the case in which document was admitted, exhibit number, the document's language (ENG for English, BCS for Bosnian-Croatian-Serbian, a language identified further in Chapter 1), and the ERN(s) of the relevant page(s).

[28] An important exception is Edina Bećirević, *Na Drini genocid: Istraživanje organiziranog zločina u istočnoj Bosni* (Sarajevo: Buybook, 2009), the work of an author who followed the trials and noted documents as they entered the public domain.

[29] Bosnian Serb Assembly, 34th Session, August 27, 1993, Karadžić, BCS 0215-0530-0215-0531. Transcripts and minutes of the assembly sessions from October 24, 1991, to February 21, 1996, were admitted and listed by exhibit number in PRK, "Decision on Prosecution Bar

Second in importance are the hundreds of telephone conversations recorded and transcribed by Bosnian state security services beginning in late May 1991, a time when the Bosnian government began to doubt the loyalty of Bosnian Serb political leaders. The practice of intercepting phone calls was hardly unusual at the time. Various security services in Yugoslavia engaged in the practice to track the activities and intentions of potential adversaries. Prosecutors, defense attorneys, and self-representing accused have all cited these intercepts as evidence, essentially vouching for their authenticity.[30]

Internal documents of the SDS comprise the third most important collection cited here. Many hundreds of these documents were admitted into evidence as an omnibus collection in the case of the Prosecutor v. Momčilo Krajišnik (president of the Bosnian Serb Assembly and Karadžić's primary confidant), abbreviated here PMK, as Exhibit P67A. Bosnian government security officers seized many of those documents from SDS headquarters in Sarajevo after Serb forces had abandoned the city in April 1992.

Fourth in value is the eighteen-volume collection of the diaries of General Ratko Mladić, Commander of the Main Staff of the Army of Republika Srpska (*Vojska Republike Srpske*, VRS). His detailed diaries, pulled from their hiding place in the ceiling of his Belgrade apartment by Serbian war crimes investigators in February 2010, reveal a great deal about the thinking and actions of top Bosnian Serb leaders during wartime.[31]

I also consulted the ICTY's collection of minutes and transcripts of the Supreme Defense Council of Yugoslavia but found them of limited value for this study.[32]

Table Motion for the Admission of Bosnian Serb Assembly Records," Paragraph 12, dated July 22, 2010, viewed at www.icty.org/x/cases/Karadžić/tdec/en/100722.pdf. The ICTY exhibit numbers for assembly sessions are not included in footnotes; they are identified as "BSA," followed by the session number, date, speaker or document, language, and ERN(s) for relevant pages.

[30] The telephone conversations are noted as "Intercept," followed by names of the interlocutors, the date of the call, ICTY, case in which they were admitted, exhibit number, and ERNs.

[31] (Untitled diary of Ratko Mladić), ICTY, Prosecutor v. Radovan Karadžić, Exhibits P01476—P01490. These 16 volumes contain Mladić's entries from June 29, 1991 to November 28, 1996, with some gaps and omissions. The volumes are cited in this work as "Mladić diaries," followed by the entry date and, when required, the page number in the BCS original entry.

[32] Many of the Supreme Defense Council minutes and transcripts were admitted with substantial redactions as "Vrhovni savet odbrane," ICTY, Prosecutor v. Slobodan Milošević, Exhibit P469, various tabs from 1—49. Redacted portions of the minutes and transcripts were subsequently admitted under exhibit numbers listed in Annex A of "Decision on Prosecution Request for Change in Status of Certain Exhibits Admitted under Seal, with Annex A," ICTY, Prosecutor v. Momčilo Perišić, <http://www.icty.org/x/cases/perisic/tdec/en/110324.pdf>, viewed March 22, 2014.

Other individual documents and document collections at the ICTY, in addition to a plethora of published sources and studies consulted in libraries and archives, have furthered my understanding of Karadžić and the movement he led.

When I began examining documents at the ICTY in preparation for testimony in various cases, many of the documents were in BCS (some in the Latin script used by Croats and Bosniaks, others in the Cyrillic script that many Serbs routinely use). I speak BCS well and read it with near fluency in both alphabets, and I have made it a practice to examine the original BCS even for those documents that have been translated into English by the ICTY's official translators. I have consulted the ICTY's translations into English where available to me, but before including them in this book, I reviewed all and revised most of them. The translations should therefore be considered mine unless otherwise specified.

A GUIDE TO THE CHAPTERS

This biography presents Karadžić's life approximately in chronological order. Each chapter also treats a major thematic issue regarding the Bosnian Serb national movement. Chapter 1, summarizing Karadžić's life before he entered politics in 1990, assesses the proposition that perpetrators of mass atrocity display a predisposition from birth or early childhood to kill. Chapter 2, describing Karadžić's entry into politics, addresses the origins of national movements and the methods used by Karadžić and Bosnian Serb nationalists to mobilize and politicize a relatively passive constituency. In Chapters 3 and 4, I trace the development of Karadžić's indifference and contempt for those of other ethnoreligious identities as a case study of the gradual descent of a leader and his party into murderous intent.

Chapters 5 and 6 treat Karadžić's transformation from an angry, ineffectual reactor to events into a calculating planner seeking to create an ethnonationally separate state. Chapter 7 highlights the ideological and political clash between European values and the collectivist nationalism of the Bosnian Serbs. Chapter 8 examines the shifting strategies and plans of the Bosnian Serb nationalists as they prepared a violent takeover of Bosnia in 1991 and early 1992. Chapters 9 through 13 consider how Karadžić and the Bosnian Serb nationalists progressively expanded their ambitions and sought to achieve them through war (1992–95). Chapter 14 examines the role of Karadžić and other senior leaders in carrying out the most infamous mass atrocity of the war: the murder of thousands of Bosniaks (Bosnian Muslims) around Srebrenica in July 1995. Chapter 15 tells of Karadžić's fall from favor with Milošević, his loss of influence, and his resignation from office. Chapter 16 chronicles Karadžić's evasions and deceptions during his thirteen years as a fugitive, and the story of his arrest and transfer to the ICTY prison in The Hague.

These themes converge in the conclusion to show that Karadžić's commitment to a Serb utopian ideal, combined with his ruthless pursuit of strategic goals, led him and his closest associates to adopt attitudes, ideology, and policies that propelled them into the valley of death and mass atrocities.

1

Youth of Hardship, Lands of Lore

Radovan Karadžić was born in the Yugoslav republic of Montenegro, a land of soaring mountain peaks, roaring rivers, deep ravines, and sparsely vegetated plateaus. Widely dispersed human settlements in this mostly barren land are often marked by a Serbian Orthodox church, typically a small windowless chapel made of local stone hewn from the mountains. Less conspicuous are Serbian Orthodox monasteries, isolated and remote from villages and from one another, also made mostly of gray stone from the mountains that seclude them. The landscape bears evidence of its inhabitants' struggle to wrest a living from the angular land. Sheep graze on sparse grasses and shrubs, and shepherds shelter from frequent wind, rain, and snow in tiny mountain huts. Peasants plow scattered hillside patches of fertile land in horizontal bands to minimize erosion.

Like most rural dwellers in the Montenegrin highlands, Radovan's parents led a spartan life. His mother, Jovanka, born in 1923 to the Jakić family from Dobrijeh Sela near Pljevlje, grew up a scrappy, energetic peasant girl without attending school. She helped the family eke out a living from the scarce arable land. The eldest of six children, she cared for her younger siblings after her father died when she was twelve.[1] In her late teens, Jovanka met Vuko Karadžić, a cobbler twelve years her senior, from the nearby village of Petnjica. Vuko was well known locally for his mastery of the double flute and the *gusle*, a traditional one-stringed folk instrument often played to accompany the singing of epic poems. In 1943, during World War II, Jovanka married him, both for love and from fear of being unprotected in the midst of war. She moved to the Karadžić family compound in Petnjica, and there, on June 19, 1945, she gave birth to their first child, Radovan.

[1] Ljiljana Bulatović, *Zavet majke Radovana Karadžića* (Testament of Radovan Karadžić's mother) (Belgrade: Evro, 2003), p. 34. In this chapter, titles of citations are provided in both BCS and English since they reveal much about the authors' attitudes toward Karadžić.

Montenegro makes up in legends what it lacks in inhabitants. Locals attribute animate qualities to Mount Durmitor, the forbidding massif that towers over the region where Karadžić was born and raised. Its name means "sleeping," and the eighteen glacial lakes scattered on its face are known as "eyes of the mountain" (*Gorske Oči*). The Karadžić family name is identical with that of Vuk Stefanovic Karadžić (1787–1864), a Serb linguist who collected Serb folklore and famously standardized the Serbian Cyrillic alphabet into its modern form. Radovan Karadžić, reciting a dearly-held family belief, claimed at his trial in 2010 to be Vuk's blood relative. Even if the claim is apocryphal, a mythical blood tie to the literary giant of the same name lent stature to the Karadžić family of Petnjica. Petar Petrović Njegoš, widely considered to be the greatest Serbian language poet, hailed from Montenegro and frequently evoked the wild grandeur of its mountains in his writings. Karadžić only occasionally alluded to these iconic legends during his political career, but those around him seemed fully aware that their craggy-faced, volatile leader bore the qualities of heroic figures and legendary lands.[2]

THE YUGOSLAV CONTEXT OF KARADŽIĆ'S YOUTH

Karadžić was born amid the political and social upheavals that coincided with the end of World War II and the post-war rebirth of Yugoslavia as a socialist state. Like the vast majority of Yugoslavs, Karadžić's parents were profoundly affected by the Second World War. As the family remembered it, eight Karadžić family members were killed and their bodies thrown into a well by Partisan soldiers in 1942. This drove Vuko Karadžić, along with other males of fighting age, to join the Serb nationalist Chetniks.[3] He fought with the Chetniks in eastern Bosnia, mainly against the Bosniaks among the Ustasha.[4] Toward the end of the war, as the Partisans were rolling up victories over Germans, Ustasha, and Chetniks, Vuko left the Chetniks and returned home. The Partisans drafted him when they took control of Petnjica, and at war's end he was working as a cobbler in their ranks.

Because of Vuko's time in the Chetniks, some of Radovan Karadžić's detractors later cast him as a committed Chetnik from birth, a member of a die-hard Chetnik family who unleashed his latent hatred during the wars of the

[2] Ljiljana Bulatović, "Legenda o Karadžićima" (Legends of the Karadžić's) in Ljiljana Bulatović (comp. and ed.), *Radovan* (Belgrade: Evro, 2002), p. 35.
[3] "Bratsko kazivanje Luke Karadžića" (Brotherly account of Luka Karadžić), in Bulatović, *Radovan*, p. 67.
[4] Ibid., p. 68.

1990s.[5] The historical record fails to support this myth. As noted above, his father had served with both the Chetniks and the Partisans, and his loyalties to each appear to have been transient and shallow. In any event, his mother was clearly Radovan Karadžić's most influential parent, and she came from a family whose military-age males fought with the Partisans. Such apparently contradictory participation in different armies was hardly uncommon in those parts. Many families in the region hedged against the war's uncertain outcome by sending some of their offspring to each of the forces fighting over their lands.

In adulthood Karadžić found ample reasons to detest the communist regime, but the evidence suggests he harbored neither contempt for communism nor hatred for the Partisans in his youth. As a political leader in the 1990s, Karadžić was acutely aware that Chetnik-Partisan rivalry posed a grave threat to Serb unity, something he must have first sensed as a child in relations between his parents' families, and he strove to prevent that rivalry from tearing apart the national movement of the Bosnian Serbs.

For the Karadžić family, as for many others, the traumas of war did not end with the cessation of hostilities. Tito's security forces continued to pursue collaborators and former Chetniks for trial and punishment. The new regime deemed Vuko to be an enemy of the state owing to his Chetnik past, and he was arrested at the family home in fall 1945 by two agents of the Yugoslav security forces. He barely averted death when shooting erupted while he was being led away. He was sentenced to fifteen years in prison. Jovanka, who had never attended school, taught herself to read and write so she could correspond with Vuko while he was in prison. After she appealed to local officials, prosecutors honored a provision in postwar law that gave partial amnesty to anyone who served at any time with the Partisans, and they reduced his sentence to 7 years. The authorities later reduced his sentence again and released him on September 27, 1950, after he had served fewer than five years.[6] Thus Vuko was absent from the family home until young Radovan was five years old. As a friend from his early adulthood observed, during that time young Radovan grew close to his mother and remained closer to her than to his father into adulthood.[7]

While her husband was incarcerated, Jovanka plowed the fields, planted potatoes and grain, and did various odd jobs in her struggle to provide food for her growing son. His mother believed that young Radovan understood his

---

5   For example, *Bosanski pogledi* br. 28, September 12, 1991, page number unavailable.
6   "Namučili smo se živih muka" (We went through living hells); and "Bratsko kazivanje (A brotherly testament)," in Bulatović, *Radovan*, pp. 30–31 and 69.
7   "Bratsko kazivanje," in Bulatović, *Radovan*, p. 87.

ILLUSTRATION 1.1. Šavnik, Montenegro. Photograph by author.

father's absence, and he accepted being left with his grandmother while his mother made frequent visits to the jail in nearby Šavnik. (See Illustration 1.1) According to his mother, Radovan took up adult behavior and thinking at a very young age. She recalled occasions when Radovan showed adult maturity and confidence as a child. He did not reject religion or faith, but from youth he displayed confidence in his own rational powers and possessed a driving need to understand the forces that shaped his world.

THE FAMILY'S SEARCH FOR STABLE LIVELIHOOD

After his release from prison, Vuko found he could not earn a living as a cobbler in Petnjica due to growing competition from industrially-produced shoes. He soon moved the family to the larger town of Šavnik in hope of finding better employment. (See Illustration 1.1) Young Radovan, characteristically gregarious, befriended the local school director in their new town even before he began to attend classes.[8] In 1951, Radovan's brother Luka was born in Šavnik. The brothers would remain close through many decades, even when separated by hundreds of miles and adverse circumstances. The family grew further with

[8] Ibid., p. 52.

the birth of a daughter, Ivanka, and two more sons, Ivan and Radosav.[9] In 1956, following the trend of many other rural Yugoslavs, the Karadžić family migrated from upland Montenegro to the larger, lowland city of Nikšić. Vuko found work, purchased a small run-down house, and remodeled the place to meet the family's needs. He and Jovanka lived in Nikšić for the rest of their lives.

Vuko urged his son to remain in Nikšić for his education and become a teacher, but as a precocious and much-praised child, Radovan found Nikšić too small for his aspirations. After completing middle school (*srednja škola*) in 1960 at age 15, he left home and moved two hundred miles to the northeast to Sarajevo, capital of the Republic of Bosnia and Herzegovina, to complete his education at the high school (*gimnazija*) of medical studies and enter medical school at Sarajevo University.

After leaving his native Montenegro, Karadžić continued to hold dear his family and the land of his birth. During school breaks, he frequently returned to the family home in Nikšić to spend time with his parents and younger siblings and even visited Petnjica on occasion to relive youthful memories. His father died in 1987, just a few years before his oldest son began his political career. Jovanka survived to age 83. Chain-smoking to the end of her days and adamantly insisting that her eldest son was a persecuted savior of the Serb people, she died in 2005 at a retirement home in Nikšić.

Radovan grew into a precocious, well-adjusted, and outgoing young man beloved by those who came to know him. Despite difficult conditions, particularly during his early childhood years, Radovan was described by his mother, siblings, and friends as mature beyond his years, with great intellectual curiosity and a drive to excel in school. The adults in his life showered him with admiration and did not stand in the way of his move to Sarajevo to attend the university there.

SARAJEVO STUDENT

Karadžić arrived in Sarajevo in 1960 as a young man of 15 in search of an education and a professional career. By then, both the Republic of Bosnia and its capital city, Sarajevo, were benefiting from Tito's policies of rapid industrialization, urbanization, and educational development. After the Partisans liberated Sarajevo from German rule on April 6, 1945, Tito installed a communist-led government and made Sarajevo the republic's capital. Epicenter of fighting during World War II, the republic had become one of Yugoslavia's leading

[9] "Legenda o Karadžićima," in Bulatović, *Radovan*, p. 36.

centers of industrial development. In 1949 communist officials founded the University of Sarajevo, the republic's first, and by 1962 it had an enrollment of over 11,000 students.[10] Both the republic and its capital city grew and prospered under Tito's communist rule, even though the republic never matched the republics of Slovenia and Croatia in economic achievements.[11] Karadžić was to benefit in many ways from the republic's rapid development.

The populations of Karadžić's new city and its republic were ethnically mixed. As noted in the Introduction, Bosnia was alone among Yugoslav republics in having no national name and no nation with an absolute majority, and the same held for the city of Sarajevo. Both the city and its republic consisted of Bosniaks, Serbs, Croats, Yugoslavs, Jews, Roma, and those identified in censuses as "others." (See Table 1.1) Members of each group lived throughout the republic. In the high-rise housing compounds of the republic's urban centers, they were largely integrated, but in several areas of the republic one group or another commanded an absolute majority, and in a few places single-nation dominance approached 100 percent. Even with a few ethnically monolithic areas, it was impossible to draw boundaries on a map defining contiguous territories inhabited only by members of a single group. Furthermore, none of its three major peoples lived in Bosnia alone, and two of the three peoples lived in much larger numbers in adjacent republics. In 1961, a year after Karadžić's arrival, most Croats lived in Croatia (3,339,841 of them), while only 711,665 lived in Bosnia. There were 5,704,686 Serbs living in the Republic of Serbia, whereas only 1,406,057 lived in Bosnia, where they accounted for 42.9 percent of the population. Only the Bosniaks lived mostly in Bosnia: in 1961 they numbered 842,248 there, while another 116,107 of them lived in Serbia and Montenegro combined, mostly in the Sandžak area southeast of Bosnia that straddles the border between the Republics of Montenegro and Serbia.

Bosnia was beginning to experience a long-term demographic shift about the time Karadžić arrived. The number and percentage of Bosniaks in Bosnia increased rapidly in the thirty-two years he lived in Bosnia. Croats, on the other hand, increased only slightly in number but declined in percentage terms, while Serbs declined both in number and percentage. Those declaring themselves "Yugoslavs," the favored category of those who abjured national

---

[10] Zdravko Antonić, ed., *Istorija Saveza komunista Bosne i Hercegovine (History of the League of Communists of Bosnia and Herzegovina)* (Sarajevo: Institut za istoriju, 1990), vol 2, pp. 222–223.

[11] Husnija Kamberović, *Prema modernom društvu: Bosna i Hercegovina od 1945. do 1953. godine (Toward a modern society: Bosnia and Herzegovina from 1945 to 1953)* (Tešanj: Centar za kulturu i obrazovanje, 2000), pp. 71–100; and Robert J. Donia, *Sarajevo: A Biography* (Ann Arbor: University of Michigan Press, 2006), pp. 168–203.

TABLE 1.1. *National Composition of Bosnia and Herzegovina, 1961–1991*

Year	Total Population	Serbs		Bosniaks (Bosnian Muslims)		Croats		Yugoslavs		Jews	Other
		Number	Percent	Number	Percent	Number	Percent	Number	Percent		
1961	3,277,948	1,406,057	42.9%	842,248	25.7%	711,665	21.7%	275,883	8.4%	381	41,714
1971	3,746,111	1,393,148	37.2%	1,482,430	39.6%	772,491	20.6%	43,796	1.2%	708	55,538
1981	4,124,256	1,320,738	32.0%	1,630,033	39.5%	758,140	18.4%	326,316	7.9%	434	88,686
1991	4,377,033	1,366,104	31.2%	1,902,956	43.5%	760,852	17.4%	242,682	5.5%	n/a	93,747

Source: Jakov Gelo et al. (ed.), Republika Hrvatska, Državni zavod za statistiku, *Stanovništvo Bosne i Hercegovine: Narodnosni sastav po naseljima* (Zagreb: Državni zavod za statistiku, 1995), pp. 9–10.

29

identity or minimized its significance, peaked in 1981 and declined in the ten years thereafter.

The city of Sarajevo experienced similar demographic changes, although the percentage of Croats was consistently lower and the percentage of Bosniaks consistently higher (reaching almost 50 percent in 1991) than in Bosnia as a whole.[12] In 1961, Sarajevo's population had doubled since World War II to 227,615 inhabitants, and it nearly doubled again by 1991 (to 527,049), a reflection of the Tito regime's commitment to industrialization, urbanization, and mixed urban centers. Serb and Croat nationalist leaders bemoaned all these trends when they began to organize and pursue votes in 1990. They cited the demographic stagnation of their peoples to stoke fear among their constituents and to encourage them to think in national categories when considering their political options.

Sarajevo's historic center, known as *Stari grad* (Old Town), was home to various administrative, commercial, and religious structures, while the surrounding hills alleviated the city's urban bustle and lent to it the feel of a mountain village. Sarajevans could see the mountains on three sides: the distant snow-capped peaks of Bjelašnica and the wooded slopes of Mount Igman to the west, and the high cliffs of other mountains above the city's eastern end. Just over the horizon to the east lay Romanija, a rugged mountainous area that inspired myths of stalwart, independent, and primitive rebels,[13] much like those of the Durmitor highlands of Montenegro. During his first decades in Sarajevo, Karadžić likely found them a familiar and welcoming sight.

After arriving in Sarajevo in 1960, Karadžić soon found ways to support himself. A fellow Montenegrin helped him land a job washing dishes in the student dormitory kitchen,[14] and he wrote his parents that he needed their further financial assistance only for housing. As before, he excelled in his studies and came to be regarded as a star student. He selected psychiatry as his medical specialization and began to prepare himself for a career in that field.

Karadžić soon met Ljiljana Zelen, a Sarajevo-born fellow medical student a few months younger than he. They were married in 1967, and in that year Ljiljana gave birth to Sonja, the first of their two children. Their son, Aleksandar (known by the nickname Saša), was born in 1972. Far from being a

---

[12] Data on Sarajevo are taken from Jakov Gelo (comp.), *Stanovništvo Bosne i Hercegovine; narodnosni sastav po naseljima (Population of Bosnia and Herzegovina: national composition by settlement)* (Zagreb: Republika hrvatska, Državni zavod za statistiku, 1995), pp. 9–10.

[13] Ivo Žanić, *Flag on the Mountain: A Political Anthropology of War in Croatia and Bosnia* (trans. Graham McMaster and Celia Hawkesworth) (London: Saqi, 2007), pp. 213–226.

[14] "Patnje ranog djetinstva," in Bulatović, *Radovan*, p. 55.

"serial seducer of women" as alleged in one biographical account,[15] Karadžić
became a devoted family man and replicated the familial loyalty shown by his
mother and father for one another and for their children. A friend from student days described Karadžić as a homebody. He remained committed to his
parents and siblings and became devoted to his wife and children. He strove
to provide them with the material benefits he had lacked as a child. Ljiljana's
sister later recalled that the family enjoyed summer vacations on the Adriatic
Coast, a popular destination for Sarajevans.[16] Marriage and fatherhood lent
him a sense of gravitas and stability that was often lacking in the footloose
spirits among his growing circle of aspiring literati.[17]

SARAJEVO STUDENT LEADER

Karadžić's studies did not directly prepare him for a political career. Medical
students were viewed by those in the Faculty of Philosophy (home to depart-
ments of humanities and some social sciences) as staid, conservative, and
well-connected children from Sarajevo's "better homes" with little interest in
politics or the arts.[18] Karadžić diverged from that stereotype in coming from an
impoverished rural family and having an interest in political and literary activity. In June 1968, as student uprisings took place around the world, he was the
only student from the Medical Faculty to assume a leading role in a massive
one-day student protest at the University of Sarajevo. At the demonstration, he
climbed atop the entrance portico to the faculty building to address the student crowd. "We were founders (*prvoborci*) of the 1968" student movement, a
friend of his later wrote proudly.[19]

With these student protests, Sarajevo youth joined the global protest movement against the Vietnam War and American militarism that gained momentum
after the Vietnamese communists' Tet Offensive of 1968. Far from advocating nationalism or violence, the Sarajevo students were critical of "nationalist
jargon," according to Milorad Ekmečić, Professor of Modern History at the
University of Sarajevo. They complained that Yugoslavia had become not a
"harmonious community of equal peoples, but rather a battlefield on which

[15] Robert M. Kaplan, "Dr Radovan Karadžić: psychiatrist, poet, soccer coach and genocidal
   leader," *Australasian Psychiatry*, Vol. 11, no. 1 (March 2003), p. 75.
[16] Jovanka Karadžić, "Jača je Radovanova dobrota od svakoga zla" (Radovan's goodness is stronger than all evil), in Bulatović, *Radovan*, p. 87. This chapter was related by Jovanka, Karadžić's
   mother, to Bulatović, who took down and published her words.
[17] Rajko Petrov Nogo, "Radovan najuljudniji" (Radovan is the most refined), in Bulatović,
   Radovan, p. 79.
[18] Nogo, "Radovan najuljudniji," in Bulatović, *Radovan*, p. 79.
[19] Ibid.

nationalist oligarchies fought to enhance their socialist prestige."[20] As students in Western Europe deplored capitalist ruling elites, Sarajevo's students joined those in other Yugoslav cities to denounce the hypocrisy of bureaucratic communism that prevented the emergence of the creative, spontaneous socialist man. The Sarajevo students carried posters with pictures of Tito and the South American revolutionary Che Guevara.[21] They dispersed only after a massive police assault in which both police and students were injured.

Two decades later, in the midst of war, Bosnian authorities claimed that Karadžić had spied for the federal police after the 1968 demonstrations. They supported this allegation with two single-page documents said to be from the files of the Bosnian secret police.[22] Those two documents should be treated with some skepticism. Even if authentic, they attest only to the practice widespread at the time among intellectuals in Yugoslavia of providing information to the police.[23] If Karadžić indeed joined thousands of other students in serving on two occasions as a police informant, he would have been passing along information readily available from his academic peers.

Partly owing to his participation in the demonstration, Karadžić first came into contact in 1968 with intellectuals in the humanities, and he embraced their critique of socialist Yugoslavia. That critique began with grievances against nationalism, but in the later years of late socialism its proponents in Bosnia gradually fragmented along national lines. Their critiques subtly shifted to blaming other ethnonational groups for communism's failings. A number of the 1968 critics of communism emerged in the 1990s as leaders of various nationalist movements in Yugoslavia. Slavko Leovac, a key leader of the 1968 Sarajevo student movement who was subsequently named to the Academy of Sciences and the Arts of Bosnia-Herzegovina, acted as head of the Political Council of the nationalist Serb Democratic Party (SDS) in the 1990s. Historian Milorad Ekmečić, quoted above, who became the principal ideologue of the Bosnian Serb nationalists in 1990, also became a member of the SDS Political Council.

[20] Mirko Arsić and Dragan R. Marković, *'68. Studentski bunt i društvo ('68 Student uprising and society)*. 3rd ed. (Belgrade: Istraživačko izdavački centar SSO Srbije, 1988), p. 100.

[21] Arsić and Marković, *Studentski bunt*, p. 101.

[22] "Izvještaj" (Report), dated September 6, 1969, purports to be a report on political dissidents at Sarajevo University prepared by Karadžić himself as informant no. 309. "Karakteristika za Karadžić Radovana" (Characteristics of Radovan Karadžić), dated March 3, 1973, is a report by an intelligence officer describing Karadžić's activities. Copies of both documents were provided to the author by officials of Bosnia's Agency for Information and Documentation (AID) shortly after the war.

[23] By way of example, I learned in 2013 that Slovenian police had prepared a report on my activities as an exchange student for six months in 1965, using information that could only have come from my Slovenian fellow students.

YOUTHFUL POET

Around the time of the student upheavals of 1968, Karadžić began to write poetry.[24] His dominant poetic idiom evinced a fecund but dark and pessimistic imagination. Leading members of his literary circle expressed admiration for his asceticism.[25] In both style and content, he was unconventional; his writings were unpolished, impulsive, and mystically cryptic, with vivid, crude, and violent images. His friend Nogo commented that Karadžić's early poems had an "unfermented, rebellious, hazy, disorderly" quality, which he attributed to Karadžić's lack of formal literary instruction.[26]

Most of his poems conveyed a sense that indistinct, mystical forces lurking beyond human cognition were coalescing to wreak havoc on the world. He made oblique references to inchoate, ominous forces that defied human understanding and evoke foreboding. His poetry displayed, in the words of his friend and fellow writer Gojko Djogo, "an improbable poetic foresight."[27]

Certain of his poems – such as "Kalemagdan" and "Princip" – are meditations on historical events. Others – "Petnjica," "Šavnik," "Nikšić," "Durmitor" – are impressionistic, image-laden portraits of areas where he had lived. Such poems address nature's force and triumphs over man. Far from evincing a nostalgia for his boyhood homes in Montenegro, the stark, vivid images and ominous inferences evoke a dark mood. The few humans in his poems appear as soulless ciphers, inconsequential and impotent before nature. Many are dead or dying; few have discernible individual qualities. With the benefit of hindsight, we can see that his treatment of people in his poetry might have prefigured the callous indifference with which he came to regard non-Serbs during his political career. There is no causal linearity between his poetic imagination and his later resort to mass atrocities – not all dark poets become mass killers – but the dehumanized characters of his early poetry suggest an imaginative ability to objectify and dehumanize others.

His obscure, cryptic phrases and ascetic idiom seem calculated to repel rather than attract, and won Karadžić few readers outside his intimate circle of literati. Nevertheless, reviewers and his fellow creative writers praised his work, and the prestigious publishing house *Svjetlost* (Enlightenment) published two volumes of his poetry during his student years. Few others came to

[24] Radovan Karadžić, *Ludo Koplje* (Sarajevo: Svjetlost, 1968).
[25] Marko Vešović, "Estetizam percepcije," Afterword, in Radovan Karadžić, *Pamtivek* (Sarajevo: Svjetlost, 1971), pp. 75–80.
[26] Nogo, "Radovan najuljudniji," in Bulatović, *Radovan*, p. 79.
[27] Gojko Djogo, "Vunena vremena Radovanova" (Radovan's woollen times), in Bulatović, *Radovan*, p. 110.

appreciate Karadžić as a writer, but he would return repeatedly, later in life, to writing poetry, as well as essays, a comedic play, and even children's books.

In 1970 Karadžić published "Sarajevo," a poem that acquired notoriety later in his life for its apparent prescience. Like some of his other works, "Sarajevo" contains forebodings of imminent turbulence and human devastation. Verses two and three of this four-verse poem, among the least cryptic of his early writings, display his brooding negative imagination:

> The city burns as an incense stick,
> in that smoke our consciousness meanders.
> Empty suits glide through town. A crimson
> stone dies, built in houses. Plague!
> The calm. A company of armored poplars
> marches up within. Aggressor
> air runs through our souls
> and one moment you're a man, another an airy thing.[28]

In the 1990s, as Karadžić viewed besieged Sarajevo from the Serb lines south of the city with a visitor, he drew attention to these verses and claimed they foretold the violent siege he was then commanding. Except in the most general sense, however, this must be seen as disingenuous. He might equally have claimed prescience had a hurricane, earthquake, flood, or other calamity beset the city. "Sarajevo" belongs to the same poetic idiom as his other poems and vaguely foreshadowed physical destruction by an indeterminate cause, but it was hardly a forecast of the Sarajevo siege of the 1990s.

RESTIVE PSYCHIATRIST

In the twenty-nine years after receiving his medical degree in 1971, Karadžić's life was driven by his desire to earn a living as a psychiatrist and by his intellectual and literary ambitions. After six years (1971–77) as an organizer of cultural events in the employ of the Workers' University (an adult educational institution) in Sarajevo, he joined the staff of the Psychiatric Clinic of Koševo Hospital, a university-affiliated institution and the largest hospital in the city. He treated patients there from his appointment in April 1977 at age 31 until he left Sarajevo in April 1992 as war began. His employment at the Workers' University and the Koševo clinic was supplemented and interrupted by lengthy trips outside Bosnia, further poetry writing, and work in the private practice that he established. As a practicing psychiatrist, he reportedly issued

---

[28] Translated by Daniela Valenta and Robert Donia.

false medical reports to exempt some patients from military service, qualify other patients for early pensions, and assist accused criminals mounting insanity defenses.[29]

His work away from practicing psychiatry consisted mainly of applying his academic training to other fields of human endeavor. Sometime in the 1970s, he began to pursue a grand intellectual synthesis of group psychology and "our folk poetics,"[30] as his friend Rajko Petrov Nogo put it. Hoping to synthesize his far-ranging intellectual comprehension and his literary imagination, Karadžić applied for fellowships to study outside Bosnia and contemplated seeking a Ph.D. to supplement his medical degree. Although his yearning for such a grand synthesis never came to fruition, he increased his earnings and his academic credentials through study and practical endeavors, particularly in the field of professional soccer. While maintaining his work at the Koševo clinic, Karadžić worked intermittently as a coach and team psychiatrist to "Sarajevo," one of the town's two major soccer teams, to help build team morale and work with players who underperformed under pressure.

In 1974–75, Karadžić won a fellowship from the International Research and Exchanges Board for a year of advanced study at Columbia University in the United States.[31] His aim was to study psychological interpretations of American poetry, another manifestation of his quest to synthesize psychology and folk motifs. While in the United States, he learned near-flawless English and acquired an understanding of American politics; both would serve him well during his political career and later before the ICTY.

Karadžić's American interlude and his work advising athletes whetted his appetite for similar activities outside Sarajevo. In 1983, at age 38, he moved to Belgrade, the capital city of Yugoslavia and of the Republic of Serbia, where he worked for a time as a counselor to a premier soccer team, "Red Star" (*Crvena zvezda*). Karadžić took a tenth-floor apartment on Juri Gagarin Street in the high-rise suburb of New Belgrade, apparently unaware until later that one of his friends, Gojko Djogo (discussed later in this chapter), lived two floors below.[32] After a year in Belgrade, Karadžić returned to Sarajevo and resumed work at the Koševo clinic.[33] Some friends attributed his return to Sarajevo to his wife Ljiljana's reluctance to leave her home town of Sarajevo, and Karadžić's aversion to living apart from his family.

[29] Chuck Sudetic, *Blood and Vengeance: One Family's Story of the War in Bosnia* (New York: Penguin, 1998), p. 83.
[30] Nogo, "Radovan najuljudniji," in Bulatović, *Radovan*, p. 80.
[31] Bulatović, *Zavet majke Radovana Karadžića*, p. 41.
[32] Djogo, "Vunena vremena Radovanova," p. 106.
[33] Ibid.

ASSOCIATES AND FRIENDS

Karadžić's sociability was apparent from early childhood, and as a student he exuded a sense of confidence and stability that helped him make friends easily. He gravitated toward other intellectuals, particularly other creative writers. Many of his friends were fellow Serbs, but he mixed freely with people of all ethnic backgrounds, as most Sarajevans did at that time: few paid much attention to the national identities of their friends and neighbors. Although some important Serb intellectuals lived and worked in Sarajevo, Belgrade was the true capital of Serbdom and home to most of its leading lights, such as Dobrica Ćosić, a prolific novelist and leader of the prestigious Serbian Academy of Sciences and the Arts.

The writer and dissident Gojko Djogo became one of Karadžić's most valued friends. They met while Karadžić was organizing cultural programs for the Workers' University in Sarajevo. A Serb originally from Bosnia, Djogo served as editor of the literary program of the Youth Center in Belgrade in the early 1970s. He invited Karadžić to read some of his poems at a cultural event in Belgrade, and Karadžić reciprocated by arranging for Djogo to speak in a lecture series at the Workers' University in Sarajevo. According to Djogo, the two became friends and found common ground in discussing literary and national views that "openly emerged on the Yugoslav scene after 1968."[34]

Djogo introduced Karadžić to the Belgrade community of intellectuals, dissidents, and creative writers. In June 1981 Djogo was sentenced to two years in jail (of which he eventually served only a few months) for publishing a volume of his own poems entitled *Vunena vremena* (Woollen times) and became for many Serbs a symbolic victim of the communist regime's repression of budding Serb nationalist writers.[35] In the 1990s, as head of the "Society of Serbs from Bosnia in Belgrade," he became an avid political supporter and confidant of Karadžić as well as his friend.

Another Karadžić friend of the 1970s was Nikola Koljević (discussed in the Introduction), a professor of communications at the Philosophical Faculty of the University of Sarajevo. Nikola's older brother, Svetozar, a literature professor of international repute, owned a weekend home in the hills above Sarajevo, and Karadžić appears to have been an occasional visitor there. He gave Nikola Koljević a copy of his first book of poems (published in 1968) and

---

[34] Djogo, "Vunena vremena Radovanova," in Bulatović, *Radovan*, p. 105.
[35] Jasna Dragović-Soso, *"Saviours of the Nation": Serbia's Intellectual Opposition and the Rise of Nationalism* (London: Hurst, 2006), pp. 55–57.

wrote in it, "To Nikola Koljević, with sincere respect and friendship."[36] In a video made by Koljević in the 1980s, Karadžić appears alone in a mountain field in traditional attire playing the gusle. As previously noted, Karadžić parlayed their personal friendship into a useful political partnership: Nikola Koljević in 1990 became Vice President of the SDS and in 1992 of the RS. Koljević's excellent command of English made him indispensable in dealing with international officials.

Karadžić also found friends among his fellow psychiatrists. He met Jovan Rašković, a charismatic speaker and psychiatrist from Šibenik in Croatia, while attending a professional conference of psychiatrists from across Yugoslavia. They shared an interest in group psychology, and became friends as well as professional colleagues. Rašković had a private practice and maintained relationships with leading intellectuals there. He was admitted to the Serbian Academy of Sciences and the Arts, the most prestigious honor a Serb intellectual could receive (one never accorded to Karadžić). Rašković, too, later proved important in Karadžić's rise to political leadership of the Bosnian Serbs.

KARADŽIĆ IN THE ERA OF DECENTRALIZED SOCIALISM, 1974–90

Unabashed by his humble origins, Karadžić invited upwardly mobile urbanite friends and associates to the modest family home in Nikšić, where he proudly introduced them to his parents. His mother was awestruck by the famed literati visiting her modest dwelling. Reserved at first, she came to mix gamely with her son's companions: "I found Ćosić to be the most impressive," she later recalled, but she appears to have appreciated and admired them all.[37] Karadžić's friends reciprocated, delighted to share vicariously in the humble life of an authentic village family. When his mother visited Sarajevo, Karadžić hosted writer friends at his apartment to meet the diminutive and energetic peasant woman who had raised him. As he had in youth, Karadžić charmed and became friends with others from all walks of life. Many of them subsequently became his political associates and lifelong defenders as well.

Beginning in the 1970s, the young intellectuals' idealistic grievances against bureaucratic authority gradually turned into a Serb nationalist critique of

---

[36] Karadžić, *Ludo Koplje*. The book was retrieved from Koljević's office at the University of Sarajevo after he left the city in 1992 and is now in the Harvard University library.

[37] "Jača je Radovanova dobrota," in Bulatović, *Radovan*, p. 86. Her enthusiasm was apparently not reciprocated: Ćosić visited the Karadžić family home at Nikšić but apparently found the young poet less than impressive. Their relations remained distant, if correct, even when both had achieved political prominence.

communist authority in Yugoslavia and in Bosnia-Herzegovina. The leader of this change in thinking was the revered writer and academician Dobrica Ćosić. His writings began to display a distinctly Serb-nationalist viewpoint about 1966, the time that Tito purged his chief of intelligence, Aleksandar Ranković, accusing him of using the Serbian secret police for private advancement.[38] Ranković's fall marked the beginning of the end of centralized power in communist Yugoslavia. The essence of the new critique adopted by Karadžić and his intellectual associates was that Serbs were being victimized in socialist Yugoslavia just as they had been at the hands of the Croatian Ustasha and the Germans in World War II. In 1986, several intellectuals from the Serbian Academy of Sciences and the Arts in Belgrade prepared a memorandum reciting Serb grievances in stark, accusatory language. The document found its way into publication and became a rallying point for Serbs who felt aggrieved.[39] It frightened non-Serbs in Yugoslavia who saw in it an attempt to justify Serb domination of Yugoslavia.

Although Bosnian Serb activists adopted much of the Serb national ideology being trumpeted by some media in Serbia, they adapted their complaints to the specific circumstances of Bosnia. Leading Bosnian Serb nationalists voiced grievances about their home republic based partly on personal experience – most had remained under scrutiny by the Bosnian secret police after their participation in the 1968 student demonstrations – and based partly on speculation that the republic's authorities were biased against Serbs. Some Sarajevo-based Serb intellectuals complained that Bosnia was run by oligarchs from politically prominent Bosniak families. They alleged that the oligarchs neglected Serbs while allocating state resources and services disproportionately to Bosniaks and Croats. They further accused the Bosnian authorities of deliberately setting municipal boundaries that divided Serbs so as to deny them a majority in all but the most impoverished municipalities. There was scant evidence to support those allegations: Bosnia's communist authorities in those days were nationally neutral and wanted above all to avoid favoring any one ethnonational group over another. But some Serbs embraced the grievances and faulted the communist authorities for neglecting their interests.

Karadžić himself "had no public profile as a nationalist" prior to 1990, according to a contemporary.[40] Judging by associates' accounts, he came to share their

---

[38] Dragović-Soso, *"Saviours of the Nation,"* pp. 28–46; and Nick Miller, *The Nonconformists: Culture, Politics, and Nationalism in a Serbian Intellectual Circle, 1944–1991* (New York and Budapest: Central European University Press, 2007), pp. 177–203.

[39] Miroslav Pantić, ed., "Memorandum of the Serbian Academy of Sciences and Arts: Answers to Criticisms" (Belgrade: Serbian Academy of Sciences and Arts [SANU], 1995), pp. 95–140.

[40] Author's interview with Josip Istik, Ljubljana, November 9, 2007.

negative assessment of socialism, but he was not an originator of Serb nationalist ideology. His loyalties lay, if anywhere, with his Montenegrin origins: according to his associate Josip Istik, Karadžić believed that Montenegrins were physically superior (Dinaric types who were taller and more robust than other South Slavs); that the Montenegrin state was much older than Serbia; that Montenegro had a greater poet in Petar Petrović Njegoš than any among the Serbs; and that Montenegrins were psychologically more stable than Serbs from Serbia.[41]

These beliefs reflect a provincial variant of Montenegrin patriotism that, while distinct from Serb nationalism, was compatible with it. As a newcomer to Sarajevo, Karadžić had probably been the object of some good-natured ribbing for his rural Montenegrin origins. He and his friends drew on the unforgiving stereotypes rampant in socialist Yugoslavia that typically assigned pejorative traits by republic rather than nationality. In this stock of satirical insults, Yugoslavs portrayed Montenegrin men as lazy, oversexed country bumpkins; Montenegrins reciprocated by claiming to be better than all other Serbs. Karadžić turned to his childhood in the rugged highlands for his belief in Montenegrins as "super-Serbs," but there is no evidence to suggest that Karadžić as a student and young professional was a serious Serb nationalist.

In the 1970s, while Karadžić was seeking new jobs and new experiences, Yugoslavia was becoming more and more decentralized. In 1974, following Tito's wishes, communist lawmakers promulgated new federal and republic constitutions by which substantial power devolved from the federal state to each of the six republics and two autonomous regions. Tito and his successors would, as a result, confront a many-sided rivalry among these eight entities. In Bosnia, leaders of the League of Communists hewed to communist orthodoxy, but fought for an independent course.

In the 1980s, Karadžić's restless spirit led him into private business. As an entrepreneur, he engaged in petty corruption, but never accumulated great wealth. In 1981, he and a friend, Sarajevo native Momčilo Krajišnik, built homes for themselves in Pale (pronounced "Paah-lay"), a tiny village with a ski resort in the mountains east of Sarajevo.[42] Karadžić seems to have spent much of his income on housing: besides the house in Pale, he merged two

---

[41] Ibid.

[42] They became good friends and collaborators on the building project and later in prison, and Krajišnik later became Karadžić's most important ally among key Bosnian Serb nationalist leaders. Coming from a small rural settlement on Sarajevo's west side, Krajišnik often took the lead in organizing Sarajevo Serbs for nationalist activities. With Karadžić's support, he became in 1990 the first president of the post-socialist Bosnian Parliament and in 1991 the first president of the breakaway Bosnian Serb Assembly, positions in which he proved to be a skilled and effective parliamentarian.

ILLUSTRATION 1.2. Karadžić in a police photo at the time of his arrest in Sarajevo, November 1984. Bosnian police booking photograph.

flats into a single large two-story apartment in a fashionable area of Sarajevo. With this exception, at no time during his life did he appear to have accumulated great wealth. But the building project sparked an investigation into the sources of their funds. In November 1984, the Bosnian police imprisoned Karadžić, Krajišnik, and an associate from Karadžić's boyhood home of Šavnik on suspicion that they had misappropriated funds from Energoinvest, a large Sarajevo-based firm.[43]

The police may legitimately have suspected Karadžić of fraud, but he was also under scrutiny for his activities as a writer and traveler abroad. In 1983 and 1984, the Bosnian police arrested and imprisoned numerous suspected nationalist dissidents, perhaps hoping to repress political discord that might otherwise distract attention from the 1984 Winter Olympic Games. In October 1985, after almost a year of investigation, the authorities released Karadžić and his associates without charging them.[44] Karadžić emerged from prison pale and embittered. While in jail, he sharpened his political critique of socialist Yugoslavia. Although he had been little known as a political figure prior to his time in prison, it subsequently lent him credibility as a Serb dissident, and he became a national martyr in the eyes of some Serbs.

He returned to an appointment at the Koševo hospital clinic and a private practice that was soon thriving again. He remained aloof from politics throughout the tumultuous events of the late 1980s. Contention and controversies swirled around him, and he no doubt followed them with interest,

43 Sekretarijat za unutrašnje poslove grada Sarajevo (Secretariat for Internal Affairs of the City of Sarajevo), br. 2/1–2-KU-4865/84, "Krivična prijava" (Criminal charge), November 1, 1984. Document provided to the author by officials of Bosnia's (now-defunct) Agency for Information and Documentation.

44 "Legenda o Karadžićima," in Bulatović, *Radovan*, pp. 38–39.

but for the most part he remained disengaged. His family life was stable, his children were growing up in his adopted city, and he enjoyed the company of many friends, colleagues, and associates. Although too bright and ambitious to be called "normal," Karadžić in youth showed no predisposition toward violence, sadism, spite, or national prejudice. Nothing in his early years foreshadowed his later involvement in politics, let alone a willingness to engage in mass atrocities.[45] And once in Sarajevo, he appears to have been a responsible, well-adjusted, and compassionate young man devoted to his family.

During his cross-examination of me at trial in 2010, Karadžić described himself in the pre-1990 period as a "silent dissident who was involved in psychiatry first and foremost, but then also literature and sports as well."[46] It seemed an apt summary of his life before the commencement of his political career. But the staid, self-centered tranquility did not last. The lives of Karadžić and hundreds of thousands of others in Bosnia were about to be transformed by an unexpectedly powerful enabler of ethnonational conflict: democracy.

[45] Carole Rogel, *The Breakup of Yugoslavia and the War in Bosnia* (Westport, CT: Greenwood Press, 1998), p. 89.
[46] Karadžić cross-examination of Donia, ICTY, PRK, June 1, 2010, p. 3203.

2

Sacrificial Founder

"For us Serbs, he was and remains a messenger of Serb freedom. He appeared as a complete surprise in a moment when the Serb people were thirsty for a new life, a new heaven and a new earth that will unite us rather than divide us."

Kosta Čavoški[1]

In 1990 Radovan Karadžić rose from political obscurity to become one of several improbable novices to attain high office as Yugoslavia collapsed. He did so in the aftermath of far-reaching and fast-moving changes that led to the end of socialist governance. The precipitous rise of political nationalism, particularly in Serbia, fueled propaganda assaults on Bosnia's communist rulers from without, while scandals and contention threatened the existing order from within Bosnia. The Bosnian communists paved the way for their own departure from power when the Bosnian parliament voted to allow formation of new political parties and to hold free, multiparty elections during 1990. Although reluctant at first to plunge into politics, Karadžić was selected as the first president of the Serb Democratic Party (SDS) at its founding assembly on July 12, 1990. He immediately began to weave a narrative of himself as the sacrificial founder of the SDS who answered the Serb people's cry for leadership at the expense of his comfortable personal life. This chapter describes the upheavals of the late 1980s that made a Bosnian Serb nationalist party possible, then recounts how Karadžić helped launch the SDS during 1990.

---

[1]   Kosta Čavoški, "Branimo svjetlost istine i njen neugašlivi sjaj" (We defend the enlightenment of truth and its inextinguishable dream), in Bulatović, *Radovan*, p. 58.

SERBS BEFORE KARADŽIĆ I: MILOŠEVIĆ AND THE
ANTI-BUREAUCRATIC REVOLUTION

Until 1990, no centrally organized Serb national movement existed in post–World War II Bosnia,[2] but in the last three years of the 1980s, conditions rapidly evolved to make the rise of national movements more likely. Nationalism had never completely vanished from socialist Yugoslavia, and after Tito's death in 1980 it revived with a vengeance in republics outside Bosnia to threaten Yugoslavia's existence.[3] Competing national movements emerged into open conflict in 1987, exacerbated by the growing economic crisis and increasingly dysfunctional political system.[4] By mid-1989, Bosnia, too, was succumbing to the movements of national revival sweeping the land, and nationalist incidents had become a part of life in provincial towns.[5]

Raif Dizdarević, president of Yugoslavia's federal presidency from May 1988 to May 1989 and a citizen of Bosnia who identified himself ethnically as "Yugoslav," categorized Yugoslavia's resurgent nationalists as either "separatists" or "hegemonists."[6] He regarded both with apprehension. In his view, "separatists" included the Albanians of Kosovo and nationalist Slovenes, Croats, and Macedonians, while Serb nationalists in Serbia, Montenegro, Bosnia, Croatia, and Macedonia were "hegemonists." Perversely (from Dizdarević's viewpoint as a devotee of Titoist Yugoslavia), the two types of nationalism nourished one another: separatists provoked the hegemonists to demand greater centralization of Yugoslavia, while hegemonists contested the moves of individual republics toward greater autonomy and thereby stoked separatists' fears of recentralization. Although all national movements posed a danger to socialist Yugoslavia, the greatest imminent threat to stability in Bosnia came from the Serb nationalists in the Republics of Serbia and Montenegro and from the president of Serbia's League of Communists, Slobodan Milošević.

---

[2] Neven Andjelic, *Bosnia-Herzegovina: The End of a Legacy* (London: Frank Cass, 2003), p. 100.

[3] Ibid.; Aleksandar Pavković, *The Fragmentation of Yugoslavia: Nationalism in a Multinational State* (New York: St. Martin's Press, 1997), pp. 85–121; Sabrina P. Ramet, *Nationalism and Federalism in Yugoslavia, 1962–1991*, 2nd ed. (Bloomington: Indiana University Press, 1992), pp. 214–251.

[4] Mihailo Crnobrnja, *The Yugoslav Drama*, 2nd ed. (Montreal: McGill–Queen's University Press, 1996), p. 93.

[5] Andjelic, *Bosnia-Herzegovina*, p. 100.

[6] Raif Dizdarević, *Od smrti Tita do smrti Jugoslavije. Svjedočenja* (Sarajevo: Biblioteka Svjedok, 1999), p. 295.

Milošević was born in Požarevac, Serbia, in 1941.[7] As a member of the League of Communists with both business and political acumen, he rose to political prominence under the mentorship of Serbian LC party leader Ivan Stambolić.[8] In April 1987, Stambolić dispatched his trusted associate to the Albanian-majority Autonomous Region of Kosovo with the delicate mission of subduing nationalist passions among Serbs there.[9] But once in Kosovo, Milošević betrayed his mentor and boss by fanning the flames of Serb nationalism rather than extinguishing them. On April 17, 1987, Milošević sided with Serb demonstrators against the police by telling them, "No one has a right to beat you."[10] With this seemingly minor but well-publicized tilt toward Serb nationalism, Milošević released what his biographer Lenard Cohen called the "serpent in the bosom," the dangerous nationalism lying dormant within the Serb body politic. That evening he was hailed as a Serb national hero on Belgrade television.[11] Six months later, in September 1987, Milošević ousted his mentor Ivan Stambolić at two meetings of the League of Communists of Serbia, allowing him to gain full control in the Republic of Serbia.[12]

In 1988, organizers loyal to Milošević launched a series of demonstrations in Montenegro, Vojvodina, Kosovo, and Serbia, allegedly to protest abuses against Serbs in Kosovo at the hands of its Albanian majority. The campaign was labeled the "anti-bureaucratic revolution" because it demanded the removal of communist office-holders, who were vilified as lazy, self-indulgent bureaucrats.[13] With Milošević's backing, the anti-bureaucratic revolution drew tens of thousands of Serbs into the streets. Many were brought by bus from various republics to join the demonstrations. Intimidated by the crowds that grew more aggressive with each occurrence, incumbent communists were forced from office in Vojvodina, Montenegro, and Kosovo; each was replaced by a Milošević loyalist. On June 28, 1989, Milosevic triumphantly addressed hundreds of thousands of Serbs at a rally in Kosovo to commemorate the 600th anniversary of the Battle of Kosovo, which Serbs view as the fateful battlefield defeat of the medieval Serbian state.

---

[7] Adam LeBor, *Milošević: A Biography* (New Haven, CT: Yale University Press, 2004), p. 1.

[8] On the rise of Milošević, see Louis Sell, *Slobodan Milošević and the Destruction of Yugoslavia* (Durham NC: Duke University Press, 2002), pp. 11–64.

[9] Dusko Doder and Louise Branson, *Milošević: Portrait of a Tyrant* (New York: The Free Press, 1999), p. 43.

[10] Lenard Cohen, *Serpent in the Bosom: The Rise and Fall of Slobodan Milošević* (Boulder, CO: Westview, 2001), pp. 62–64.

[11] Slavoljub Djukić, *Milošević and Marković: A Lust for Power* (trans. Alex Dubinsky) (Montreal: McGill–Queen's University Press, 2001), p. 17. Djukić was a veteran journalist who covered Milošević's rise to power for the Belgrade newspaper *Politika*.

[12] Crnobrnja, *The Yugoslav Drama*, p. 101; and Laura Silber and Allan Little, *Yugoslavia: Death of a Nation* (New York: Penguin, 1997), pp. 42–47.

[13] Ramet, *Nationalism and Federalism in Yugoslavia*, p. 231.

Milošević's anti-bureaucratic revolution produced personnel changes only in the Republic of Montenegro and in the two autonomous regions of Vojvodina and Kosovo, all located east of the Drina River. (The Drina is both a physical and a political landmark. For much of its length, it defines the boundary between Serbia to the east and Bosnia to the west, and it also serves as a convenient if approximate separator between eastern and western Yugoslavia.) Since Milošević already held power in Serbia, he ended up with control of four of the eight votes (one for each republic and autonomous region) in the Yugoslav federal presidency. Not so in the republics of Bosnia, Croatia, and Slovenia west of the Drina, where organizers based in Serbia found it difficult to mount sustained protests.

Milošević's organizers were less effective west of the Drina also because Serbs there were less captivated by the myth of the 1389 Battle of Kosovo than those living closer to Kosovo. Some events in Slovenia, Croatia, and Bosnia drew few demonstrators; some were put down by ruling LC leaders; and some were met with counter-demonstrations supporting Tito's vision of a socialist Yugoslavia based on national equality. Some Serbs west of the Drina, however, rode buses to participate in demonstrations. Milošević's former mentor Ivan Stambolić explained the strategy: "Milošević did not aggravate the Kosovo question just for the sake of the Serbs in Kosovo," he stated. "At first he barely knew about the Serbs on the other side [west] of the Drina and then he suddenly realized that inducing them to revolt was the way to seize Yugoslavia."[14]

Milošević's organizers targeted Bosnia in the early months of the movement. Yugoslav security services, learning that organizers had scheduled a rally in the Bosnian town of Jajce for September 10, 1988, reported these plans to Raif Dizdarević, then the president of the Yugoslav federal presidency.[15] He read to other members of the federal presidency a telegram he had sent to Bosnian officials, urging them to prevent the planned gathering. Bosnian officials dissuaded Serbs in Jajce from participating, prompting organizers to cancel the gathering.[16] On August 13, 1989, Milošević lieutenants again targeted Bosnia and dispatched Serb-filled buses to Knežina, near Sarajevo, ostensibly for the consecration of a Serbian Orthodox monastery.[17] Despite a ban by

[14] Cohen, *Serpent in the Bosom*, p. 75, citing the Slovenian weekly magazine *Mladina*, August 6, 1996, pp. 34–39.
[15] The constitutions of 1974 provided for an eight-person collective presidency after Tito's death. In the late 1980s the federal Yugoslav presidency consisted of one representative from each of the six republics and two autonomous regions. The head of that body was called its president – yes, a president of the presidency – and that office rotated annually among the members.
[16] Dizdarević, *Od smrti Tita*, p. 210.
[17] Knežina, Reuters, August 13, 1989, Radio Free Europe (RFE) Press Archive, Munich (now in Budapest).

Bosnian authorities on displaying Serb nationalist symbols, the police allowed the event to proceed. As one small group assembled to display pro-Milošević nationalist placards, another group responded with pro-Titoist signs. Mihailo Crnobrnja, then Yugoslavia's Ambassador to the European Community, noted later that, "By and large the leaders of the Bosnian Serbs were still not ready to disturb the centuries-old tranquility of coexistence with the Muslims and the Croats."[18]

Milošević supporters also sought unsuccessfully to extend the anti-bureaucratic revolution to Croatia. On February 27, 1989, workers in the Serb-majority town of Knin took to the streets to display solidarity with Serbs of Kosovo. They were joined by workers chanting Milošević's name and slogans from the anti-bureaucratic revolution, but the rallies produced no changes in leadership or policy in Croatia.[19] At a second rally in Knin, the Serb economist Jovan Opačić attempted to reactivate the long-banned cultural society *Zora* (dawn). His speech turned the rally from a workers' protest to a Serb nationalist rally when he described alleged wrongs done to Serbs in Croatia. That claim earned him cheers from the crowd and a 3-month jail sentence from Croatia's socialist authorities. As in Bosnia, the Serb demonstrators failed to force leadership changes in either the local or republic governments in Croatia.

In Slovenia, officials of the League of Communists similarly withstood Milošević-inspired initiatives to discredit them. Milošević lieutenants made plans to send Serbs by train and bus to Slovenia's capital city of Ljubljana (where few Serbs lived) on December 1, 1989, but the government of Slovenia intervened by banning the meeting and cancelling train service for that day. The Serbian government retaliated by imposing an economic boycott on Slovene goods, but sanctions by underdeveloped Serbia on the economically advanced Republic of Slovenia had little practical effect. The Slovene version of the anti-bureaucratic revolution not only failed to induce official resignations, it aroused sympathy for Slovene nationalists eager to weaken their ties with Milošević-dominated Yugoslavia.

SERBS BEFORE KARADŽIĆ II: SERB NATIONALIST PRESSURE ON BOSNIAN SOCIALISM

In addition to backing the anti-bureaucratic revolution, during the late 1980s Milošević and other political and intellectual leaders in Serbia conducted a massive campaign to broadcast Serb nationalist propaganda in newspapers,

---

[18] Crnobrnja, *The Yugoslav Drama*, p. 142.
[19] Srdjan Radulović, *Sudbina Krajine* (Belgrade: Dan Graf, 1996), p. 11.

periodicals, and literature of the republics of Serbia and Montenegro.[20] First directed against the Albanians of Kosovo, the campaign expanded with vile slurs against Islam, Bosniaks, and the Republic of Bosnia.[21] Such propaganda found its way into Bosnia via print media, radio, and television. The campaign traded in grotesque stereotypes of Muslims, Sarajevo, and Bosnia, the latter referred to ominously as a "dark vilayet," in reference to the centuries of Ottoman administration.

Serb nationalists contended that Serbs should be united in a single state; they resented Yugoslavia's growing decentralization and denounced demands in Croatia and Slovenia for greater autonomy and republic sovereignty. Their slogan "All Serbs in One State," appealed to many nationally-conscious Serbs, but others saw it as a provocative endorsement of "Great Serbia," the dream of some Serbs to create through annexation or merger a unified large Serb state in Southeast Europe. Members of the Serbian Academy of Sciences and the Arts (*Srpska akademija nauka i umetnost,* SANU) composed a lengthy memorandum enumerating a host of Serb grievances. The "SANU Memorandum" was only a draft that the academy did not approve for publication until 1993, and then only together with responses to its critics.[22] The draft, however, shocked non-Serbs and League of Communist officials with its bitter allegations of systematic abuses and rampant discrimination.

Promoters of Great Serb ideology staged symbol-laden public ceremonies to revive popular awareness of Serb national myths. Serbian Orthodox Church leaders unearthed the remains of Prince Lazar, hero of the battle of Kosovo, and ceremoniously escorted them to various monasteries in Bosnia and elsewhere in a procession through Serb-inhabited areas of Yugoslavia.[23] Serbs also disinterred anonymous World War II victims of Ustasha slaughter from caves in Herzegovina.[24] In summer 1991 many of the remains were transported to

[20] For a summary of the ideological content of the campaign, see David Bruce MacDonald, *Balkan Holocausts? Serbian and Croatian Victim-Centered Propaganda and the War in Yugoslavia* (Manchester: Manchester University Press, 2003), pp. 63–97.

[21] Norman Cigar, *Genocide in Bosnia: The Policy of "Ethnic Cleansing"* (College Station, TX: Texas A&M University Press, 1995).

[22] Pantić, ed., "Memorandum of the Serbian Academy of Sciences and Arts, pp. 95–140; and Paul Mojzes, *The Yugoslav Inferno: Ethnoreligious Warfare in the Balkans* (New York: Continuum Publishing, 1994), pp. 161–162.

[23] Tim Judah, *The Serbs: History, Myth and the Destruction of Yugoslavia* (New Haven: Yale University Press, 1997), p. 39; and Katherine Verdery, *The Political Lives of Dead Bodies* (New York: Columbia University Press, 1999), p. 18.

[24] Instances of such events in Bosnia are reported in *Oslobodjenje,* August 30, 1990, p. 4; and December 16, 1990, p. 3.

Belgrade and reburied in a common grave,[25] underlining the centrality of Belgrade for Serbs wherever they lived. These movements of dead martyrs were symbolic reminders of the former greatness of the Serb people and their centuries-long oppression at the hands of their enemies.[26]

The Bosnian League of Communists' grasp on power in Bosnia and its popularity were further weakened by a succession of scandals within the republic. The scandals included cases alleging financial malfeasance (such as the charges against Karadžić and Krajišnik described in Chapter 1), displays of private wealth by high government and party officials, and government mistreatment of nationalist dissidents. Even scandals with no particular ethnonational component were distorted by media outlets to fit one or another of the nationalist narratives. Media in Serbia were particularly vitriolic in attacking the Bosnian government, accusing it of oppressing Serbs and harboring corrupt Bosniak officials. Officials of the Bosnian League of Communists suspected that many of the scandals had been drummed up by Great Serb proponents in Belgrade and Great Croat conspirators in Zagreb. In the most far-reaching controversy, the large agricultural processing firm Agrokomerc and its leading figure, Fikret Abdić, were accused of fraudulently issuing unsecured promissory notes. The alleged wrong-doing eventually brought down Hamdija Pozderac, a prominent communist politician of Bosniak identity. Forced to resign from his powerful post as president of the Federal Commission for Constitutional Change, Pozderac never returned to public life.

EXPLOITING DEMOCRACY

In January 1990 at its Fourteenth Extraordinary Congress, the faction-ridden LC of Yugoslavia, once the primary guardian of socialist unity and federalism, adjourned indefinitely and broke into its republic components. This spelled the end of LC influence at the federal level. Popular demand for democratic elections was sweeping Yugoslavia, as in other East European countries after the November 1989 fall of the Berlin Wall. The country's feuding leaders failed to agree on a single country-wide election, but in each republic, communist legislators peacefully relinquished their monopoly on power by agreeing to hold multiparty democratic elections. In a reflection of the country's

[25] Robert M. Hayden, "Recounting the Dead: The Rediscovery and Redefinition of Wartime Massacres in Late– and Post–Communist Yugoslavia," in Rubie S. Watson, ed., _Memory, History, and Opposition under State Socialism_ (Santa Fe, NM: SAR Press, 1994), p. 179.

[26] For other Serbian Orthodox commemorative events of that period, see Vjekoslav Perica, _Balkan Idols: Religion and Nationalism in Yugoslav States_ (New York: Oxford University Press, 2002), pp. 123–132.

decentralization, each republic selected a different date and adopted a different system of balloting.

The republics of Croatia and Slovenia were the first to hold democratic multiparty elections in April 1990; other republics followed in November and December. Croatia's Serb nationalists, led by a well-known psychiatrist, Karadžić's friend Jovan Rašković, took early advantage of enabling legislation by convening a gathering of several thousand to form the Serb Democratic Party (*Srpska demokratska stranka*, SDS) of Croatia on February 17, 1990.[27] Kosta Čavoški, a leader of the Democratic Party (*Demokratska stranka*, DS) of Serbia that he had helped found only two months before,[28] attended the rally as a gesture of endorsement of the new party.[29] In contrast to the sparsely attended Milošević-sponsored rallies of only a few months before, the SDS founding rally organized by indigenous Croatian Serbs drew a large crowd. Rašković stirred the assembled Serbs with his charismatic rhetoric and basked in the crowd's approval. Indigenous Serb leaders had succeeded in drawing crowds to rallies where the anti-bureaucratic revolution had failed, and Croatia's Serbs became engaged politically in much greater numbers than a year earlier.

However, despite an aggressive campaign, Serb nationalists were trounced in Croatia's elections of April 1990. The civic-oriented social democrats (the renamed and rebranded League of Communists), garnered Serb votes in substantial numbers. (I refer to the party's members and supporters from 1990 onward, in both Croatia and Bosnia, as social democrats; in fact the one-time League of Communists went through two name changes in each republic in the course of becoming social democratic parties in 1990–91. The SDS acquired only five seats in parliament, while another 24 Serbs were elected on the social democratic slate.[30] Although the social democrats did well among Croatia's Serbs, they overestimated their support among Croats in Croatia. With the benefit of a winner-take-all system in each electoral district, the nationalist Croat Democratic Union (*Hrvatska demokratska zajednica*, HDZ) won an absolute majority of seats (206 out of 356, or 58 percent) in the tricameral Croatian parliament while receiving only 41.5 percent of votes cast in the republic. The HDZ candidate Franjo Tudjman, a former Partisan general, dissident, and nationalist historian, was elected president of the republic with the benefit of a similar system. The HDZ and Tudjman set the Republic of

---

[27] Radulović, *Sudbina Krajine*, pp. 15–16.
[28] Robert Thomas, *The Politics of Serbia in the 1990s* (New York: Columbia University Press, 1999), pp. 59–62.
[29] Testimony of Milan Babić, ICTY, Prosecutor v. Slobodan Milošević (hereafter "PSM"), November 18, 2002, pp. 12,881–12,883.
[30] Radulović, *Sudbina Krajine*, p. 16.

Croatia on the path toward a declaration of sovereignty and eventual independence from Yugoslavia.

KARADŽIĆ AS BOSNIAN SERB NATIONALIST

Karadžić was intrigued by the political opportunities that arose as communist
rule disintegrated, but he was uncertain how to exploit them. In late 1989 he
attended a meeting of a group in Sarajevo that aspired to form a Green party.
According to the meeting's chair, law professor Zdravko Grebo, Karadžić sat
quietly without participating in the discussion.[31] Later at his trial, however,
Karadžić claimed to have led several meetings of Green activists, a claim
that finds no support in other sources. In any case, his interest in joining the
Greens waned and he turned to exploring other options. In January 1990 he
gathered a group of fellow writers, intellectuals, and friends in Sarajevo and
led them in forming an initiating committee, an informal organization commonly used at the time by aspiring politicians to explore creation of a political
party. The group promptly elected him president of the committee. For the
next few months, Karadžić showed considerable uncertainty about what direction to lead this nascent group of anti-communist Serb intellectuals. He and
his small circle of friends in Sarajevo knew that they wanted to advance Serb
interests in some way, but they vacillated among several possible courses of
action to pursue their goals. The election results in Croatia exerted particular
influence on Karadžić; he admired several of the leading Serb nationalists in
Croatia and was determined to learn from both their mistakes and their successes, especially Rašković's mastery of political oratory.

Karadžić and his coterie of Sarajevo Serb intellectuals were in a position
to capitalize on the widespread disillusionment with Bosnia's communists
following the scandals of the late 1980s. But they faced many obstacles in
establishing a Serb national movement in Bosnia. Some of those obstacles
were legal in nature. Delegates in Bosnia's communist-dominated parliament
presciently feared that nationalists would seek to divide the republic. When
the parliament approved legislation on February 6, 1990, allowing non-com-
munist parties to organize, the law specifically forbade Bosnians from establishing parties with "national or religious foundations."[32] For several months,
Karadžić and his group cloaked their activities in various subterfuges to avoid

---

[31] Author interview with Zdravko Grebo, April 25, 2012. Karadžić referred to his brief flirtation
with Green politics in his testimony at the ICTY; Karadžić cross-examination of Donia, ICTY,
PRK, June 1, 2010, pp. 3,208–09.

[32] Socijalistička Republika Bosne i Hercegovine, *Službeni list* (Official gazette), February
21, 1990.

arrest. They considered building their movement around the cultural association *Prosvjeta* (Enlightenment) rather than forming a political party. But *Prosvjeta* was unsuited for political activities, so Serb activists met discreetly to advance party formation in defiance of the law. Similarly, proponents of Bosnia's Croatian Democratic Union (*Hrvatska demokratska zajednica*, HDZ) conducted their activities in secret. Bosnia's leading Bosniak party, the Party of Democratic Action (*Stranka demokratske akcije*, SDA), was especially creative at circumventing the February law. Under the leadership of former dissident Alija Izetbegović, the SDA defined itself nebulously as "a political alliance of citizens of Yugoslavia who belong to the Muslim cultural-historical circle" and adopted the name "Party of Democratic Action," thus defining itself as cultural rather than national or religious in orientation.[33] Tolerating the subterfuge, the Bosnian authorities allowed the SDA to organize freely but enforced the ban on explicitly nationalist parties, including the SDS.

Since nationalists flourished and even governed in other republics well before they did in Bosnia, Serb nationalists in other republics paid close attention to Karadžić and his associates as they formed a party in Bosnia. Bosnian Serbs briefly considered forming an affiliate of an existing party in Serbia. But in the end, Karadžić's group heeded the advice of Dobrica Ćosić. Fearing interparty squabbles among Serbs, Ćosić advised Serb organizers in republics west of the Drina to refrain from becoming a subordinate unit of any party in Serbia. He encouraged them instead to create separate parties, one party in Croatia and another in Bosnia, each named the Serb Democratic Party. In promoting separate Serb parties with the same name, Ćosić prefigured Milošević's later insistence on two separate Serb statelets in Croatia and Bosnia.

Bosnian Serb nationalists, who were still not organized as a single cohesive political party, were alarmed by the SDS defeat and the HDZ victory in the election in Croatia. As Karadžić and his group in Sarajevo struggled to agree on a suitable name, structure, and program for their party, Serb leaders in other regions of Bosnia prepared to organize parties of their own. In addition to these regional efforts, another group of Serbs in Sarajevo formed an organizing committee, while Karadžić and his associates were preoccupied with internal issues of party program and organization. Karadžić learned with dismay that Rašković was triumphantly touring Serb-inhabited regions outside Sarajevo with the hope of extending the Croatian-based SDS to Bosnia. With this proliferation of other initiatives, Karadžić was under mounting pressure to organize a republic-wide Serb party or risk forfeiting leadership to others.

---

[33] Maid Hadžiomeragić, *Stranka demokratske akcije i stvarnost* (Sarajevo: Unikopis, 1991), p. 132, ICTY, Prosecutor v. Jadranko Prlić et al., Exhibit P09536, BCS 0357-3599.

Ćosić intervened to mediate among the Serb contenders in Bosnia. He asked Rašković to relinquish his plans to expand the Croatian SDS into Bosnia. Rašković complied and lent his considerable charisma to support Karadžić and the SDS, mainly by speaking at their rallies. The Sarajevo intellectuals worked to persuade restive Serbs elsewhere in Bosnia to coordinate their regional initiatives and support the formation of a single republic-wide Serb party. With Ćosić's guidance, Karadžić soon found himself the top leader of Bosnia's Serb nationalists.

COMPETITORS AND THE FREEDOM TO ORGANIZE

To the nationalists' relief, the Constitutional Court of Bosnia ruled on June 11, 1990, that the February legislative ban on religious and ethnic parties was unconstitutional. Without waiting for the Bosnian Parliament to bring the law into accord with the court's ruling, Karadžić and other nationalists took the court's ruling as a green light to move their meetings from cellars and cafes into the public arena. But they remained wary, as Karadžić later reported. "Before St. Peter's Day last year [July 12, 1990], when the Initiating Committee was working with over 2,000 people participating from Sarajevo and Bosnia, it was prohibited to form parties with the name of a people," he recalled. "At that time it wasn't known whether they would arrest us or allow us to work."[34] Despite the legal ambiguity, Serb and Croat nationalists scheduled their parties' founding assemblies, the SDS for July 12 and the HDZ for August 18.

On July 31, 1990, the Bosnian Parliament removed the final barriers to electoral democracy by defining the structure of Bosnia's post-electoral governing bodies and explicitly permitting religious and national parties to organize. The legislation further provided for elections to the republic's presidency and parliament, and to assemblies in each of the republic's 109 municipalities (*opštine*).[35] Officials authorized the electoral campaign to begin formally on September 15 and scheduled Bosnia's free multiparty elections for November 18, 1990.

The dozens of parties that competed in the November 1990 elections may be categorized as either "civic" or "ethnonational" in orientation.[36] Civic parties

---

[34] "Stenografske bilješke sa Skupštine SDS Bosne i Hercegovine održane na Petrov dan 12.VII. 91. g. u Sarajevu," ICTY, Prosecutor v. Momčilo Krajišnik (hereafter PMK), Exhibit P67A, BCS 0027–0628–0027–0639.

[35] The term *opština* is conventionally translated into English as "municipality," but many *opštine* (the plural form) consisted of agricultural and forest land and villages as well as a town that served as the seat of government and had the same name as the municipality. Thus some *opštine* were truly urban aggregations, while others were largely rural.

[36] Mirko Pejanović, *The Political Development of Bosnia and Herzegovina in the Post–Dayton Period*, trans. Borislav Radović (Sarajevo: Šahinpašić, 2007), p. 73.

sought to appeal to all voters regardless of national identity and argued that such identity had cultural significance but should not be politically salient. The largest civic party was the Social Democratic Party, the rebranded and renamed former League of Communists. The party sought to erase its association with the authoritarian methods of its predecessor, but it staunchly stood by Titoist principles of multiethnicity and advocated a cautious and partial transition from a socialist to a capitalist economy. As is the case with Croatia, I refer to the party's members and supporters from 1990 onward as social democrats; they should not be confused with the Reformists, to be discussed next.

The second major civic party was the Alliance of Reformist Forces of Yugoslavia (*Savez reformskih snage Jugoslavije*), popularly known at the time (and in this volume) as the Reformists. Led by Federal Prime Minister Ante Marković, the Reformists favored privatization, a market economy, and support for economic development. Civic party candidates hoped to capitalize on widespread public fear of national division by warning that the nationalists harbored ominous plans to carve up Bosnia.

Ethnic parties, by contrast, urged voters to cast their ballots for candidates of their own ethnicity and no one else. Realizing that voters might opt for civic-party candidates of nationalities other than their own group, leaders of all three parties urged their followers to cast only two votes, for their party's own nominees, out of their possible seven. Voters were told that casting ballots for those of other groups represented unacceptable interference in the affairs of another group. This strategy succeeded at preventing civic-option parties from winning any seats on the presidency. In the final vote tally, the SDS, HDZ, and SDA candidates received majority support within their respective ethnonational groups, but very few votes from others.

FALTERING NOVICE

Karadžić continued to display political naiveté by advancing flawed proposals for structuring the party. After first suggesting that the party should have a "left-center" orientation, he proposed dividing the party into two wings. "I personally supported creating, in the strictest sense, a party of the democratic center," he recalled a year later, "or that in addition to a left-center, social democratic wing, it should have a right-center, or national, wing."[37] Such an organizational structure would likely have ended with the party fracturing, but Karadžić held to his notion for several months, envisioning himself as head of the party's national wing.

---

[37] Karadžić, "Rašković: Borac za srpstvo i demokratiju," in Bulatović, *Radovan*, p. 126.

To complicate matters, Karadžić declared in April 1990 that neither he nor his fellow Sarajevo Serb intellectuals wished to lead the party. "Being that we were deep in our professional lives, none of us wanted to dedicate himself completely to politics," he later wrote.[38] Ćosić and other Belgrade nationalists sifted through a short list of other candidates to lead the Bosnian SDS. Ćosić first offered the party presidency to Nenad Kecmanović, a popular former rector of the University of Sarajevo whose ambition for higher office under socialism had been torpedoed by the Bosnian League of Communists. Kecmanović declined Ćosić's offer and agreed instead to become president of the new Reformist party in Bosnia-Herzegovina. Serb nationalist leaders in Belgrade also considered university professors Mićo Carević and Milorad Ekmečić, but both declined, preferring the academic life to politics.

The Belgrade leaders at first were unimpressed with the upstart Karadžić to lead the SDS. He lacked the public profile and prestigious academic credentials of the other candidates they had approached. But Nikola Koljević, a highly-regarded professor of communications at the University of Sarajevo, recommended his friend Karadžić to Ćosić and the Belgrade Serb intellectuals. With several leading intellectuals having spurned invitations to lead the party, Karadžić thus emerged from the scrum of contenders and agreed at the last minute to lead the party. Karadžić later asserted that he himself had played a role in evaluating potential candidates. "We did not offer that position to anyone directly and concretely, but we did have talks with a number of intellectuals because I didn't want them to be devoted to politics to the extent I am now," he told an interviewer.[39]

Following Ćosić's advice, Karadžić adopted "SDS" as the initials of the Bosnian Serb nationalist party and declared that the Bosnian SDS would model its "program and strategy" after the Croatian SDS.[40] At the 1992 funeral of Jovan Rašković, the founder of Croatia's SDS, Karadžić asserted that the Bosnian SDS had adopted the "ideology, flag, and emblems" of the Croatian SDS.[41] He and other party leaders rarely acknowledged in public that Belgrade Serb intellectuals had guided the party's formation. But the party's official paper, *Javnost* (Public), acknowledged that the party had adopted the paper's

---

[38] Ibid.
[39] "Interview probably published in *Politika* on September 10, 1990," in Radovan Karadžić, *Intervjui i govori dr Radovana Karadžića* (Interviews and speeches of Dr. Radovan Karadžić) (Belgrade: International Committee for the Truth about Radovan Karadžić, 2005), vol. 5, p. 44. This is one volume in a set of six with different titles. Each volume will be cited separately with the appropriate volume number.
[40] *Oslobodjenje*, July 6, 1990, p. 3.
[41] Karadžić, "Rašković – Borac za srpstvo i demokratiju," in Bulatović, *Radovan*, p. 126.

name "especially after a conversation with the great writer Dobrica Ćosić" and that the paper was honored to "attest to Dobrica Ćosić's Godfathership."[42]

Again heeding Ćosić's counsel, Karadžić abandoned the notion of a party with both national and social wings. He later recalled that "numerous well-intentioned and experienced people, among them the most distinguished Serb writers from Bosnia," advised him against the two-wing strategy so as "not to create factions that would divide Serbs."[43] Karadžić and the SDS Main Board formally abandoned the two-wing idea on August 8, 1990, in favor of a unified party.[44] Thereafter, Karadžić never deviated from the principles that the SDS should be a single, unified organization and the sole legitimate political representative of the Serbs of Bosnia. He strove to maintain that unity against endemic regional and ideological divisions among Serbs.

BELGRADE ANOINTS, KARADŽIĆ CONSENTS

Although many of Bosnia's leading Serb intellectuals had declined to lead the party, Karadžić had one remaining rival for the post of party president, Vladimir Srebrov, another organizer of Serb political aspirations in Sarajevo. But after Ćosić intervened in favor of Karadžić, Srebrov agreed to merge his committee with the Karadžić-led group of Sarajevo Serb intellectuals. He was made vice president of the unified SDS Main Board as a reward, but he nonetheless insisted on standing for party president at the founding assembly on July 12. Karadžić's friend Miroslav Toholj believed, more on the basis of paranoia than hard evidence, that Srebrov was a stalking horse for Rašković's short-lived aspiration to extend the Croatian SDS into Bosnia. Toholj further suggested that the Bosnian secret police were backing Srebrov's candidacy with the hope of having the worst possible candidate selected to lead the SDS.[45]

Karadžić himself, however, treated Srebrov with cordiality; he sought to mollify him by giving him a role at a press conference on July 5. But Srebrov used that platform to suggest his parity with Karadžić. The SDS founding assembly would, he asserted, bring together "two initiating efforts that once conspired against one another."[46] When the assembly was underway, Rašković told Srebrov that Ćosić and Milošević wanted him to stand aside in favor of

---

[42] *Javnost*, 1 (1), (Sarajevo), October 19, 1990, p. 1. This was the first issue of *Javnost*, the official newspaper of the SDS.

[43] Ibid.

[44] Glavni odbor Srpske demokratske stranke Bosne i Hercegovine," August 8, 1990, Item 3, ICTY, PMK, Exhibit P67A, BCS 0030–6348. See also *Oslobodjenje*, August 10, 1990, p. 5.

[45] Miroslav Toholj, "O osnivanju SDS," in Bulatović, *Radovan*, p. 113.

[46] *Oslobodjenje*, July 6, 1990, p. 3.

Karadžić. Srebrov reluctantly heeded Rašković but insisted on addressing the convocation. In thus compromising with his potential rival and gently ushering him aside, Karadžić signaled that he would use negotiation and persuasion rather than violence in dealing with fellow Serbs who challenged his leadership. On August 8, 1990, the same day the board had scuttled the idea of two wings, the SDS Main Board took another step toward party unity and "suspended the activities of Vladimir Srebrov . . . and the work of 'Young Bosnia'."[47]

Having eased his sole rival aside, Karadžić abruptly ended his irresolution and accepted the post of SDS party president. From the moment he accepted the party presidency, he devoted himself zealously to the SDS and, as he saw it, to the Serb people. He reaped handsome rewards from his months of indecision. By the time he strode onto the stage at the party's founding assembly on July 12, he had received the backing of many in the Belgrade nationalist elite and most Bosnian Serb nationalist intellectuals.[48]

POLITICS AND THE MYTH OF MARTYRDOM

Upon being chosen president of the party, Karadžić began to develop a myth of himself as founder and martyr. Not surprisingly, he inserted himself into a nationalist interpretation of the Serb people's history. From the time of the party's founding, Karadžić presented himself as the embodiment of the Serb people, a leader who would share their fate.

Karadžić described the party's founding as a response to Serb popular demand. "The past six months there have been pressures from the ground up to do something in respect to organizing the Serb people," Karadžić told the founding assembly.[49] "We postponed [founding the SDS], hoping that we would find a form of political life different from the national." The party came together, he said, from spontaneous demands for group self-defense. "The Serb people by tradition are reluctant to break away from Yugoslavia's

---

[47] "Glavni odbor Srpske demokratske stranke Bosne i Hercegovine," August 8, 1990, Items 5 and 6, ICTY, PMK, Exhibit P67A, BCS 0030–6348.

[48] The SDS founding assembly is described in Suad Arnautovic, *Izbori u Bosni i Hercegovini '90. Analiza izbornog procesa* (Elections in Bosnia and Herzegovina 1990: Analysis of electoral processes) (Sarajevo: Promocult, 1996), p. 41; *Oslobodjenje*, July 13, 1990, p. 3; Radmilo Milanović, "Tudje postuj, svojim se dići: Političko organizovanje Srba u BiH," *Sedam Dana*, July 15, 1990, p. 4; "Srpska demokratska stranka BiH: Revančizma neće biti," *Naši Dani (Our days)*, July 20, 1990, p. 12. Karadžić's hopes at this time for consensus and coexistence were spelled out in an interview, "Muslimani i Hrvati nisu naši protivnici" (Muslims and Croats are not opponents), *Naši Dani*, July 20, 1990, pp. 13–15.

[49] *Oslobodjenje*, July 6, 1990, p. 3.

common institutions for fear of being labeled 'militaristic' and 'hegemonistic'," he said. "But reality showed that national parties could not be avoided. That's why the SDS was late in organizing." He declared, "We are not creating the party, the party is creating us."[50] Two months later, he gave a similar explanation while taking credit for efforts to stimulate a popular Serb movement. "We waited for the moment when the last Serb was frightened – not by our activity, but by our inactivity," he said.[51]

In casting himself as a sacrificial founder, Karadžić erased from the story his early vacillation and Ćosić's mediating role. Instead, he cast himself as answering the entreaties of the Serb people to lead them, at the cost of his career and comfortable private life in Sarajevo. As in other exculpatory narratives he constructed during his political career, Karadžić built this one around incontrovertible facts while understating the role of others and mischaracterizing their motives. In propagating the myth of his own sacrifices, he cast both himself and the Serb people as victims and martyrs who could be saved by their own hands alone. As would be true throughout his career, once he invented a narrative, he held tenaciously to it, reiterating it again in his opening statement before the ICTY in 2010.

Karadžić insisted that he never wanted a political career. In December 1991 he said, "I told those guys, here, these are the reasons why I would never be a politician if we were living in a single nation state and why I detest the politician's calling."[52] With a sense of his own exceptionalism, he created a myth of personal sacrifice in which his every deed fulfilled his solemn obligation to the Serb people. On February 28, 1992, he indelicately threatened to quit. "Sometimes I feel like tendering my resignation and saying, go fuck yourselves, you motherfuckers," he told the SDS delegates of the Bosnian Serb Assembly. "I feel like going somewhere with my language and my degree to live and work, and I could live and work anywhere on earth. But, we don't have the right to do so."[53] In a society where most males use profanity liberally, Karadžić was not unusual in swearing during conversations with friends and associates, but he rarely used it formal gatherings such as this. His coarse language in this instance indicated anger and frustration, but he never took action to leave politics. Indeed, Karadžić did not see himself as engaging in politics in the

[50] "Ciljevi Srpske demokratske stranke," July 12, 1990, in Karadžić, *Intervjui i govori*, vol. 5, p. 32.
[51] "Interview probably published in *Politika* on September 10, 1990," in Karadžić, *Intervjui i govori*, vol. 5, p. 45.
[52] Intercept, Karadžić and Krajišnik, December 11, 1991, ICTY, PSM, Exhibit P613, Tab 135, BCS 0323-3587–0323-3590.
[53] Bosnian Serb Assembly (BSA), 9th Session, February 29, 1992, Delegates' Club Transcript, BCS SA01-1399.

conventional sense. Having cast himself as a messianic figure, he reveled in leading a transformational Serb national movement. He committed himself to the Serb utopian vision of his ideologically-inclined peers and made it his life's work to find effective methods to make it a reality, whether these were conventional political practices or policies ending in mass atrocities. In denying that he was a conventional politician, he portrayed himself as staying on the job out of duty to a cause far more elevated than politics.

In reality, Karadžić relished his new life. Denials and a few expressions of regret notwithstanding, he threw himself passionately into politics and never looked back. He was genuinely committed to advancing the interests of the Serb people in Bosnia, but he also looked after his own interests and passions. He drew liberally on party funds to support himself and his family at a level well above the average Bosnian, although he never acquired great wealth. More than anything, he valued the recognition and appreciation he received from those who accepted his leadership. The most valued benefits from his work were recognition and acclaim for his service to the Serb people. Power and fame became him. As leader of a nationalist movement, he found an audience far larger than his poetry had ever reached. He enjoyed displaying his verbal dexterity and developing simple phrases and slogans that made his political ideals more appealing. His self-mythologizing helped make him a dedicated, hardworking, and highly effective leader, at times for good and at other times for the worst evil.

CAMPAIGN OF NATIONAL REVIVAL

Karadžić soon became the principal architect of the party's message to Serb voters. He appeared before the party's founding assembly to present ideological principles and arguments in support of the party's candidates in the November balloting. Karadžić proved adept at motivating Serb voters. He exploited his own understanding of group psychology and applied it to the Serb folk idiom, achieving modestly in practice the synthesis that he had not achieved in academic or literary pursuits. Miroslav Toholj, his friend who later became editor of the party's official weekly newspaper *Javnost*, recalled at first wanting "to help him articulate multiple Serb themes," but quickly realizing that Karadžić could do it himself. Karadžić became a "brilliant formulator," wrote Toholj, and developed his "own anthology of political language."[54] He observed that Karadžić "quickly mastered the skill of communicating with the

---

[54] Toholj, "O osnivanju SDS," Bulatović, *Radovan*, p. 120.

people" and had "stumbled on a sort of catharsis which the Serb people of Bosnia shared."[55]

Karadžić communicated effectively with potential Serb voters by delivering a message of Serb inclusiveness. He called upon all Serbs to unify regardless of ideology or station in life, acknowledging that members of the SDS belonged to a variety of factions and held a variety of views. Unlike some hardline Serb nationalists, Karadžić welcomed former communists into the SDS. "There will be neither revanchism nor anti-Communism," he said. "The party will be open to all democratically-minded members of the League of Communists, the socialists or other parties, who recognize the program of the Bosnian SDS as their own."[56] Most importantly, he condemned the polarization of Serbs during the World War II. "Neither Partisan, nor Chetnik, but democratic,"[57] he repeated, warning Serbs against dividing into Chetnik supporters and communists.

Under Karadžić's leadership, the SDS campaign became a social movement dedicated to a republic-wide national awakening of the Serb people. His approach rested on the premise that the Serb people should be the sole focal point for all activities of every Serb. He blamed Serbs themselves for their demoralization and disunity. "We ourselves are more dangerous to us than all our enemies," he declared to the SDS founding assembly. "By destroying our own national and cultural identity, we continued the genocide our enemies had exerted against us. For a false peace in the house, we sacrificed our greatest values, abandoned the traditions of folk culture, neglected our ruined Church and ... divided ourselves into reds and blacks, city dwellers and peasants."[58] He blamed timid Serb intellectuals for the woeful state of the people they were supposed to be leading. "Fear among underprivileged Serb intellectuals bred various ... rationalizations, which were conducive to contempt for their own nation as a source of their fear and ultimately to a full denationalization of the most educated and talented Serbs."

Following his grim portrayal of Serbs as despairing because they were disadvantaged, Karadžić called on them to rally behind the SDS to restore their national identity and regain their pride. "The first and fundamental aim of the SDS was to tell the Serbs: 'Serbs, you do exist and you can be Serbs'," he told an interviewer in September 1990. "That small, short, but magic sentence made more than one and a half million Serbs in Bosnia stand up, look at

---

[55] Ibid., p. 116.
[56] "Ciljevi Srpske demokratske stranke," in Karadžić, *Intervjui i govori*, vol. 5, p. 34.
[57] Mirko Pejanović, *Through Bosnian Eyes: The Political Memoir of a Bosnian Serb*, trans. Marina Bowder (West Lafayette, IN: Purdue University Press, 2004), p. 24.
[58] "Ciljevi Srpske demokratske stranke," in Karadžić, *Intervjui i govori*, vol. 5, p. 31.

one another, remember who they are and set realistic and healthy political demands for establishing a Serb political presence in Bosnia."[59]

While he treated civic parties as his primary adversaries, during the campaign Karadžić referred to the HDZ and SDA as "partners." He pledged to rule harmoniously with them if SDS candidates were voted into power. In an effort to avoid catastrophic post-election feuds, leaders of the three leading nationalist parties quietly concluded a series of interparty agreements during the campaign. They agreed to divide republic and municipal offices among themselves based on formulas that used the number of votes each party received.[60]

Acutely aware of the Croatian SDS's losses to the social democrats in the April 1990 elections, Karadžić attacked them for perpetrating division among Serbs. "Decades of one-party rule have profoundly disturbed the natural course of development of the Serb people," he said.[61] "In the period of [our] utmost loyalty to the regime and the system, it was those loyal Serb regions that were impoverished the most ... and experienced economic and cultural collapse and large-scale migrations."

Karadžić made a persuasive if unfounded case that the communist authorities had drawn the boundaries of Bosnia's 109 municipalities to deprive Serbs of the benefits of economic development. Unlike the Croatian SDS, the Bosnian party made no mention of territorial autonomy in its program, but Karadžić stood firmly behind the territorial principle in denouncing what he called the communists' fragmentation of Serb-inhabited areas. "The [communist] territorial organization shattered the natural Serb units in Bosnia and put the Serb people into an unfavorable economic, demographic and political position," he told the party's founding assembly.[62] "Hundreds of thousands of Serbs left Bosnia in this period and the republic was also left without their offspring."[63] A week later he pointed to the area northeast of Sarajevo around Mount Ozren, "a compact and well-defined Serb area which was divided among five municipalities, where it can be seen how Serb areas were impoverished and depleted by emigration." With this critique of Bosnia's municipal organization, Karadžić advanced a specifically Bosnian variant of Serb nationalism that two years later would be the keystone of his plan to seize power in Bosnia at the local level.

---

[59] "Interview probably published in *Politika* on September 10, 1990," in Karadžić, *Intervjui i govori*, vol. 5, p. 47.

[60] Adil Zulfikarpašić, *The Bosniak* (London: Hurst, 1996), p. 56. The interparty agreement was not reported in the press at the time, but its footprints are visible in hundreds of disputes arbitrated by party leaders from late 1990 into early 1992.

[61] "Ciljevi Srpske demokratske stranke," in Karadžić, *Intervjui i govori*, vol. 5, p. 31.

[62] Ibid.

[63] Ibid.

He heaped blame on the communists for much that ailed the Serbs, but Karadžić uttered only praise for other nations in Bosnia. He urged reconciliation with other peoples. Like other nationalist leaders, he was compelled both by electoral logic and by his party's quest for legitimacy to express respect for those of other national groups, and to pledge cooperation in the event that nationalists of all three groups prevailed in the election.

The Bosnian Parliament's constitutional amendments of July 31, 1990, provided for a seven-member collective presidency of Bosnia consisting of two Serbs, two Croats, two Bosnian Muslims, and one representative of "Others." Each Bosnian voter, regardless of his or her nationality, could cast a total of seven votes for presidency members: two for Serb candidates, two for Croats, two for Bosniaks, and one for "others." Leaders of all three nations urged their respective constituencies to vote only for candidates of their own group, or in effect to exercise only two of their seven votes, leaving it to those of other nations to select their own representatives. Since most voters complied with this request, voters were effectively divided into three separate electorates, allowing each nationalist candidate to claim to represent his or her own nation rather than the entire population of Bosnia.

While the presidents of the HDZ and SDA became candidates for the Croat and Bosniak seats, respectively, on the Bosnian presidency, Karadžić did not run for any elective office. He directed the campaign in his capacity as party president. However, he guided the party in nominating well-regarded intellectuals, primarily professors at the University of Sarajevo, as candidates for top offices. He drafted Biljana Plavšić, a professor of biology, and his friend the literature scholar Nikola Koljević, to run for the two Serb-designated posts on the presidency.[64] Karadžić reserved for his friend and former fellow prisoner Momčilo Krajišnik the post of president of the first post-communist Bosnian Parliament.

Although Karadžić occasionally hinted that some Serbs resented Croats and Bosniaks because of their affluence and influence, during the campaign he refrained from attacking Bosniaks and Croats directly. He blamed the communists for discord among the nations. The SDS would work to calm national tensions, he assured the founding assembly, "particularly to remove the damage inflicted on Serb-Muslim relations by the ruling regime."[65] He portrayed the Serb national revival as a drive to regain equality for Serbs rather than to establish supremacy over others. "Our goal is to repair relations between the nationalities," he declared, and "to establish equality, reciprocity, and civil peace."[66]

[64] Toholj, "O osnivanju SDS," in Bulatović, *Radovan*, pp. 119–120.
[65] "Ciljevi Srpske demokratske stranke," in Karadžić, *Intervjui i govori*, vol. 5, pp. 24–25.
[66] Ibid., p. 32.

Bosniak leaders reciprocated Karadžić's expressions of good will. In the long-standing Bosnian tradition of exchanging greetings on solemn occasions, Alija Izetbegović and two other founders of the SDA attended the SDS Founding Assembly. There, Izetbegović gently chided the SDS leaders for their delay in organizing a party. "We expected you earlier, for you are necessary for this Bosnia and Hercegovina," he told the SDS founders. "People have ceased believing in big words, but they will never stop believing in love, neighbor-liness and unity."[67]

During the campaign, Karadžić expressed judicious, well-informed assess-ments of the other two nations and praised their leaders. Although Serbs had suffered the most, he said, "the Serbs and Muslims do not have conflicting interests in any field whatsoever, and neither do the Croats, except for the separatists."[68] He promised that "Serbs in Bosnia will never inaugurate a policy that would frighten Muslims or Croats." He characterized as benign the inten-tions of Croat and Bosniak political leaders toward Serbs.

Karadžić denied that the Bosniaks harbored Islamic fundamentalist views. "Bosnia is not brimming with Islamic fundamentalists or Great Serb nationalists," he told an interviewer in late June. "There are Muslims who have a need for more enhanced religious practice than has been the case so far, but they are not fundamentalists."[69] He praised Izetbegović, "who once declared himself a Serb," and distinguished him from a "few Ustashoid" Bosniaks and the "small Croatophile wing" of the SDA. Only after the elections, as national differences intensified, did antipathy toward Bosniaks enter into Karadžić's public pronouncements. As in many other aspects of his political career, his views changed rapidly under the pressure of unfold-ing events.

The Serb, Croat, and Bosniak national parties each sought greater politi-cal power in the Bosnian Parliament – in fact, veto power on behalf of the nation each claimed to represent. All three parties denounced the incum-bent communists for having failed to create a "Chamber of Peoples," a third chamber of the Bosnian Parliament in which each nation could veto laws that it believed posed a threat to its national interests. Socialist-era constitu-tions had provided for such a chamber, but one had rarely been convened. With constitutional provisions enacted in 1990, the Bosnian Parliament cre-ated instead a bicameral legislature to consist of a 130-member Chamber of Citizens and a Chamber of Municipalities with a deputy from each of Bosnia's

[67] *Oslobodjenje*, July 13, 1990, p. 3.
[68] Ibid.
[69] "Interview published in the *Nedelja* magazine on July 1, 1990," Karadžić, *Intervjui i govori*, vol. 5, pp. 24–25.

109 municipalities (*opštine*) and one from the City of Sarajevo.[70] To mollify nationalist concerns, the communist-era parliament had also provided for the possibility of a third chamber, a "Council of National Equality" to consist of members drawn from the other two chambers of parliament. Expecting to win the election and deal with the veto issue later, communist legislators had left it to the soon-to-be-elected parliament to vote such a council into existence and to determine specific rules for its procedures.

Each of the three national parties made the parliament's procrastination a major target of its campaign rhetoric and used the topic to assert its own nation's interests. "No political business in Bosnia can be completed without its peoples and consequently, without the Serbs," Karadžić declared. "We therefore demand that a council of nations be established in Bosnia, with the right of veto on certain, albeit not numerous, issues."[71]

Alone among leaders of the three national parties, Karadžić went further: he unilaterally proclaimed a Serb People's Council (*Srpsko narodno vijeće*) at a large public rally in Banja Luka on October 13, 1990.[72] Like similar councils proclaimed by Serbs in Croatia only three months before, the Serb People's Council in Bosnia was intended to represent Serbs wherever they lived rather than specified Serb-majority territories. In this proclamation, Karadžić adopted a strident tone quite out of character with the theme of national conciliation he was otherwise pursuing in the campaign. He had no legal basis to announce such a body.[73] To many, his declaration smacked of desperation before an election the Serb nationalists feared losing. One of his friends later suggested that Karadžić had announced the council as a potential vehicle to oppose Bosnia's independence in the event of an SDS electoral loss. "We needed to have some mechanism of defense from that independence," wrote Miroslav Toholj, "that is, from the transformation of Serbs into a national minority."[74]

In any case, Karadžić's move drew a torrent of criticism. The other two national parties, the HDZ and SDA, immediately denounced it; on November 2, 1990, the Constitutional Court of Bosnia declared, "The Serb

---

[70] The legislation consisted of amendments 59 through 80 to the 1974 Constitution. Part of Amendment 70 provided for a third chamber, the Council for Questions of Equality of Nations and National Minorities of Bosnia and Hercegovina, to be made up of an equal number of Muslims, Serbs, and Croats, and a proportionate number of the "others" census category. Arnautović, *Izbori u Bosni i Hercegovini '90*, pp. 179–195.

[71] "Interview probably published in *Politika* on September 10, 1990," in Karadžić, *Intervjui i govori*, vol. 5, p. 51.

[72] "In the Bosnian constitutional amendments and election laws," warned Karadžić at Banja Luka, "all the conditions were created for a complete constitutional annihilation of Serbs in Bosnia and Herzegovina." *Javnost* 1 (1), (Sarajevo), October 19, 1990, p. 1.

[73] *Oslobodjenje*, November 3, 1990.

[74] Toholj, "O osnivanju SDS," in Bulatović, *Radovan*, p. 121.

People's Council, established on 13 October, is not a legal entity and its acts do not represent a part of the legal system."[75] The court, which could render only advisory decisions, referred the issue to the Bosnian Parliament for further action, but none was ever taken.

Milošević emerged as the most powerful critic of the Serb National Council.[76] In Croatia, Milošević had backed the SDS-led Serb People's Councils as a useful tool to threaten the republic's leaders, but not so in Bosnia, a republic Milošević hoped to keep in Yugoslavia rather than see it become independent. Milošević held influence over Karadžić and his followers that no Bosnian could equal. Heeding Milošević and demonstrating again his readiness to submit to the wishes of Belgrade Serb leaders, Karadžić subsequently let the Serb People's Council vanish from public discourse.[77]

After months of accusations from civic parties that the nationalists wanted to divide Bosnia, Karadžić and other nationalist leaders held joint campaign rallies just before the elections to assure voters that they harbored no such intentions.[78] The three nationalist party presidents also came together to oppose the restrictive voting policies of the incumbent government. Less than a week before the election, Karadžić held a joint press conference with SDA President Izetbegović and HDZ President Stjepan Kljuić to protest the Electoral Commission's requirement that voters must have resided in Bosnia for at least six months to be eligible to vote.[79] Karadžić, fearful of massive voting fraud, also threatened to withhold SDS participation in government if the party failed to get a substantial share of the votes. The tripartite protest of the ethnic party leaders was successful. The Electoral Commission capitulated the next day and dropped the six-month residency requirement. The nationalists' joint rallies and promises of cooperation were evidence that most Bosnians were still opposed to physical division of the republic.

Some of Karadžić's detractors later portrayed his campaign rhetoric as a ruse to win power while hiding a deeply-rooted hatred of Croats and Bosniaks. These conspiratorial views should be rejected. Karadžić did indeed turn against the political leaders of the Bosniaks and Croats after the election, but those feelings and views evolved over a period of many months. He had lived successfully for three decades of his adult life in Sarajevo, where belief in equality and respect for those of other ethnonational identities had

75 *Nedeljni Glas*, November 3 and 4, 1990, p. 3, dateline Sarajevo, November 2, Tanjug (Yugoslav press agency).
76 Toholj, "O osnivanju SDS," in Bulatović, *Radovan*, p. 121.
77 The council, much touted when first announced, was never mentioned again in the pages of the SDS official weekly publication *Javnost*.
78 Andjelic, *Bosnia-Herzegovina: The End of a Legacy*, pp. 166–170.
79 *Oslobodjenje*, November 13, 1990, p. 1.

been the norm and universal expectation. As any politician would do, he couched his views during the election campaign in language that appealed to voters, so he understandably fashioned himself and his party as champions of equality, compromise, and harmony. In the latter half of 1990, there was little support among Bosnians of any nationality for ethnic separation, let alone war.

As the election drew near and Karadžić grew more confident of victory, he encouraged Serb nationalists to be considerate of Croats and Bosniaks in victory. As paraphrased by a reporter, he recommended to the SDS of Pale Municipality, where Serbs made up 68 percent of the population, that they "graciously assume power on November 19 without being vindictive, having in mind their good relations with their Muslim and Croat neighbors with whom they have lived in harmony for centuries in these areas."[80]

KERNEL OF CONTENTION: BOSNIA'S CONSTITUTIONAL FUTURE

Despite their rhetorical commitments to co-existence and partnership, SDS leaders made clear their sharp differences with those of other nations on the question of constitutional changes. Therein lay a kernel of contention that would later turn the three nationalist parties against one another, first in rhetoric and then in violence. HDZ candidates, looking beyond the borders of Bosnia to Croatia's quest for autonomy or independence, favored a Yugoslav "confederation" in which the republics would associate only loosely. SDS leaders objected to any weakening of the republics' ties to the federation, saying they "opposed any kind of confederal arrangement."[81] They called instead for "Bosnia as an equal republic within a ... democratic Yugoslavia structured as a modern federal state." SDS leaders hinted they were prepared to issue an ultimatum if the federal state were weakened further. "In the event that confederal structure prevails in Bosnia, the party will offer a concept of organization that best fits the Serb people," warned an addendum to the SDS platform.

Karadžić declined during the campaign to commit the SDS to Bosnian sovereignty. He rejected Bosnian independence outright. "It is not acceptable [to Serbs] for Bosnia to be an independent state in a confederal community with other states," or in "any other form of state organization in which [Bosnia's Serbs] would be divided from the whole of the Serb people or relegated to the

---

[80] *Oslobodjenje*, November 15, 1990, p. 9.
[81] "Srpska demokratska stranka Bosna i Hercegovina, Glavni odbor. Prijedlog, Okvirni program SDS BiH. Sarajevo, jula 1991. godine," ICTY, Prosecutor v. Jadranko Prlić, et al., Exhibit P 09536, BCS SA00–6847.

status of a national minority,"[82] he stated. With this proclamation, he endorsed the idea of a Great Serbia without actually uttering the words.

Karadžić's position was little different from that of Milošević, who said in October 1990, "Concerning the Serbian people, they want to live in one state. Thus any kind of division into multiple states that would divide part of the Serbian people and distribute them into various sovereign states cannot, from our viewpoint, be acceptable."[83] Karadžić and Milošević each defended federal Yugoslavia, implying that they favored the status quo, while simultaneously favoring changes to strengthen federal institutions and reduce the autonomy then enjoyed by the republics and autonomous provinces. Karadžić further echoed Milošević in warning of violence if the federal state were to be weakened. "A confederal status for Bosnia cannot be achieved without civil war,"[84] Karadžić warned at an SDS rally.

The SDA, representing Bosniaks, staked out a vague middle position between the Croat and Serb nationalist parties. "We want a contemporary state," said Party President Izetbegović. "That is, not a confederal concept as proposed by Slovenia and Croatia, nor a hard federation as offered by the Presidency of the SFRY [Socialist Federal Republic of Yugoslavia]. Bosnia and Herzegovina wants something in the middle, a formula that can span the two concepts."[85] With such ambivalent language, SDA leaders signaled their hope to avoid alienating either Serbs or Croats. From the first days of the campaign, SDA leaders preserved that studied ambiguity and sought to mollify the leaders of other groups with minor concessions. Only after the elections did the SDA come under greater pressure to abandon that ambivalence and choose a coherent position, thereby allying with either the Serbs or the Croats.

A NATIONALIST VICTORY

In the months between July and November 1990, Karadžić succeeded in nationally awakening many of Bosnia's Serbs and rallying them behind the SDS. In the November balloting, the SDS won almost all of the offices its leaders had sought, and many more than they had expected. The combined votes cast for the SDA, HDZ, and SDS far exceeded those for the civic parties combined. The SDS won 72 of the 240 seats in the parliament's two chambers; the SDA won 86, and the HDZ won 44 seats.[86] Eight other parties, including

---

[82] *Glas* (Banja Luka), November 9, 1990, p. 2, dateline Sarajevo, November 8, Tanjug.

[83] Radulović, *Sudbina Krajine*, p. 28.

[84] *Glas*, November 9, 1990, p. 2, dateline Sarajevo, November 8, Tanjug.

[85] *Nedeljni Glas* (Banja Luka), November 3 and 4, 1990, p. 4.

[86] Arnautović, *Izbori u Bosni i Hercegovini '90*, p. 108.

several civic parties, shared the remaining 38 seats. SDS candidates Plavšić and Koljević handily won the two Serb seats in the Presidency. The SDA and HDZ each won the two seats reserved for members of their nations, led by their respective party presidents, Alija Izetbegović of the SDA and Stjepan Kljuić of the HDZ. SDA candidate Ejup Ganić, who had declared himself a "Yugoslav" in the most recent census of 1981, won the seventh seat on the presidency by garnering the most votes in the category of "Other," giving SDA members three of seven votes in the presidency.

As 1991 dawned, Karadžić and the SDS moved to exercise the power they had won. Karadžić, Izetbegović, and Kljuić implemented their interparty agreements at the republic level by dividing the most influential political positions at that level among those designated for those posts by the three parties. The SDA designated Izetbegović as president of the Presidency (even though SDA candidate Fikret Abdić had won more votes); the SDS selected Karadžić's friend Momčilo Krajišnik as president of the Bosnian Parliament; and Jure Pelivan was named by the HDZ to be Prime Minister. The soundly defeated Social Democrats and Reformists joined with several other parties in a coalition known as the "opposition" or the "left bloc," but the leftists were effectively shut out of power everywhere in Bosnia except in the municipality of Tuzla, where they had received a majority of votes.

Rifts among the three nationalist parties became apparent even before the end of 1990. In a harbinger of impending disputes, party leaders wrangled for weeks before agreeing on the composition of a Council of Ministers in late January 1991. The Bosnian parliament rubber-stamped the party leaders' final agreement on January 30, 1991, allowing the newly-constituted Council of Ministers to meet for the first time the next day.[87] The nationalists took control of all but a few Bosnian municipalities, and in the main the nationalist leaders honored the interparty agreements to divide executive positions in the municipalities according to each party's proportion of the vote. But even in forming municipal governments, the nationalist parties found many reasons to disagree among themselves, and the division of offices at the municipal level proceeded only haltingly after the election.[88] In some municipalities the parties were unable to agree, and in a few instances local party units rebelled against the dictates of the republic-level party leaders.[89]

---

[87] *Oslobodjenje*, January 31, 1991, p. 1.

[88] In Sarajevo, the city council selected its new leaders at a meeting on December 20, 1990, the same day that the Bosnian parliament chose republic-level officials. The council selected the SDA candidate as Sarajevo's mayor, the SDS nominee as president of the city assembly, and the HDZ designee as president of the executive council. *Oslobodjenje*, December 21, 1990, p. 10.

[89] Klub srpskih poslanika (SDS i SPO) u Skupštini SRBiH, "Pogledi i stavovi o budućoj Bosni i Hercegovini," Sarajevo, February 14, 1991; and *Oslobodjenje*, March 29, 1992, p. 2.

The November 1990 elections in Bosnia thus marked at once the demise of communism, the triumph of tripartite nationalism, and a giant step toward Bosnia's eventual division. Although war was far from inevitable at that time, democratic practices and institutions facilitated the growth of organized nationalism, the emergence of leaders with a predilection for extreme measures, and intensified rivalry among leaders of the major ethnonational communities. The revival of political nationalism in the 1980s had posed a serious challenge to federal socialist Yugoslavia, but it took democratic multiparty elections to sweep the old order aside and pave the way for subsequent interethnic conflict and mass atrocities.

3

Naïve Nationalist

Radovan Karadžić won an impressive number of votes and received wide-spread acclaim in the November 1990 election, but he had no practical experience in wielding the power he had suddenly acquired. At first he followed the lead of Slobodan Milošević, the cunning and resourceful president of the Republic of Serbia, who sought variously to influence, goad, and restrain him. Karadžić gained competence and confidence with each decision he made and each crisis he weathered. Although he remained generally subservient to Serb leaders in Belgrade, Karadžić developed his own perspective and began to pursue his own policies, driven by his own convictions and his often volatile reaction to initiatives of other political actors in Bosnia. He soon turned against the Bosniak and Croat nationalist leaders and in a matter of months he was treating them as enemies. In fits and starts during 1991, Karadžić came into his own as the chief political leader of the Bosnian Serbs.

THE NATIONALIZATION OF POLITICS IN YUGOSLAVIA'S REPUBLICS

Nationalism surged everywhere in Yugoslavia in the aftermath of the 1990 elections. Voters had elected nationalists in most places, and nationalist impulses were manifest in the policies of newly-elected office-holders. Elections in Serbia and Montenegro confirmed Milošević and his follower President Momir Bulatović to the offices they had achieved by intra-party machinations a few years before.[1] In Croatia and Slovenia, democratically selected leaders organized plebiscites on independence and crafted declarations of sovereignty. Their parliaments declared independence simultaneously on June 25, 1991.

---

[1] Susan L. Woodward, *Balkan Odyssey: Chaos and Dissolution after the Cold War* (Washington: Brookings Institution, 1995), pp. 119–125. Woodward summarizes election results and explains why nationalism surged during and after the voting.

Two days later, the clash of Yugoslavia's nations drew first blood in Slovenia. Units of the Yugoslav People's Army (*Jugoslovenska narodna armija*, JNA) moved into Slovenia with the intent of forcing that republic to remain in Yugoslavia, but they were met with surprisingly effective resistance from Slovene territorial forces. Before either side prevailed, the European Community (EC) dispatched a trio of negotiators, known as the Troika, to pursue a ceasefire.[2] In short order, Slovenia and the JNA (acting on behalf of Yugoslavia) agreed on a ceasefire and acquiesced to the "Brioni Accord" on July 7.[3]

The accord embroiled the EC in the rapidly-shifting issues and relationships among federal Yugoslavia and its six republics. It stated that any resolution of those issues should respect "human rights, including the right of peoples to self-determination in conformity with the Charter of the United Nations and the relevant norms of international law," a provision that lifted the spirits of Slovene and Croat independence-seekers. At the same time, Milošević and Karadžić saw an opening to demand recognition of the Serb nation, since the Brioni Accord had specified that the issue of self-determination of peoples would guide future EC involvement. From that point forward, Serb nationalists and the Serbian government put the right of self-determination at the center of their arguments for recognizing the aspirations of Serbs west of the Drina.

The ceasefire took effect within days and the various parties fulfilled their specific commitments under the accord. JNA troops withdrew from Slovenia; the Republics of Serbia and Montenegro confirmed the Croat Stipe Mesić as president of the Yugoslav Federal Presidency; and Slovenia and Croatia agreed to a 90-day moratorium on the effective dates of their independence declarations. The results of the first war of Yugoslav succession had produced jubilation among Slovenes and Croats, disappointment among Serbs and the JNA, and a false sense of confidence that the EC could easily dampen the passions of war and negotiate an end to hostilities. However, warfare in Croatia and Bosnia would soon prove less amenable to a negotiated conclusion.

Bosnia was spared open warfare in the immediate aftermath of the elections, but the voting results poisoned relations among leaders of the three nationalist parties and permitted politics of national fear-mongering to prevail in the republic. Overnight, the election reduced to irrelevance the common

---

[2] James Gow, *Triumph of the Lack of Will: International Diplomacy and the Yugoslav War* (London: Hurst, 1997), pp. 50–52.

[3] "Joint Declaration of the EC Troika and the parties directly concerned with the Yugoslav crisis, the so-called 'Brioni Accord'," Brioni, July 7, 1991, in Snežana Trifunovska, ed., *Former Yugoslavia Through Documents: From its Creation to its Dissolution* (Dordrecht, Boston: Martinus Nijhoff, 1994), pp. 311–315.

opponent against which the nationalist parties could unite, communism and its democratic-era descendant, the civic option. The last vestiges of the Bosnian LC model – monolithic and a-national – vanished with the electoral defeat of the Social Democrats, laying bare the sharp differences in the interests and fears of the three nations.

Rather than turning their energies to forming coalitions and governing, leaders of all three parties at all levels continued to act as proponents of national awakenings. That meant identifying and trumpeting their constituents' fears of being conquered, subordinated, or slaughtered by rival groups. Some of those fears were well-grounded and genuine, but they were magnified many times by the fear-mongering their leaders used to mobilize their peoples. The leaders of each emphasized their own group's victimhood and complained of past and present oppression by rival ethnonational communities.

As they became more nationally conscious, Serbs feared being demographically marginalized by the faster-growing population of Bosniaks. They drew upon the high-volume propaganda being disseminated in neighboring lands, where Serb nationalist popularizers and journalists sensationalized a few interethnic incidents in Kosovo to portray that land as filled with dangers for Serbs. In Bosnia, Serbs noted with alarm the rapid growth of the Bosniak population compared to stagnation in their own (and Croat) numbers. They falsely attributed Bosniak demographic growth to a high birth rate, although Karadžić and a few other leaders recognized that emigration and Bosniak immigration were in fact the primary cause. But the demographic trends were unmistakable. If projected forward for another decade, Bosniaks might well command an absolute majority in Bosnia. More alarming still to nationally conscious Serbs, Bosniaks in a few key individual municipalities such as Prijedor were on the cusp of commanding an absolute majority. The demographic factor intensified Serb fears of being outvoted, and incited their demands for constitutional protections against what they viewed as the tyranny of majority rule. The continuing Bosniak growth further contributed to the urgency of their hopes for a "Great Serbia," a combination of all the Serb-inhabited regions into a single large Serb state.

Croats, the least populous group in Bosnia, feared being marginalized in a system of majority rule. They feared any constitutional arrangements that gave them less than a full third of representation. This fear, too, had a genuine cause: first proposals to reform the presidency gave one vote to a Croat, two votes to Serbs, and three votes to Bosniaks. However, they were revised by those who perceived that Croats would feel their influence severely diminished in such an arrangement. Bosniaks, for their part, feared that Bosnia, the republic they saw as their sole homeland, would be partitioned among Croats and Serbs – as it had been from 1939 to 1941 – with the backing of key leaders and armed forces from neighboring republics.

Bosniaks, Croats, and even some Serbs had come to fear Milošević's ambitions and the corrupted version of Yugoslavia he had created during the anti-bureaucratic revolution. That fear helped spur the Slovene and Croat drives for independence, and it led Bosnia's Croats and Bosniaks to recoil at the prospect of a Milošević-dominated Yugoslavia. Milošević did indeed insinuate himself into Bosnian affairs in several ways, most significantly through his favored acolyte, Radovan Karadžić.

MENTOR AND COLLEAGUE

Karadžić had first met Slobodan Milošević in person in September 1990. Milošević perceived the Bosnian Serb psychiatrist as a promising political novice and soon assumed the role of his political mentor and boss. Karadžić, for his part, became a loyal lieutenant to Milošević but nevertheless looked out for his own interests and those of his fellow Bosnian Serb nationalists. During 1991, the two men grew close, less as friends than as mentor and follower in powerful positions with parallel goals. Karadžić had more in common with Milošević, a man of blunt-force political skills and Machiavellian schemes, than with the avuncular Ćosić, who preferred to persuade with logic and to exercise moral authority rather than to issue direct orders.

Karadžić strove to avoid appearing subservient to the Serbian president. Looking back in 1995 to their first meeting, Karadžić claimed, "We are not inferior in relation to President Milošević, and never have been.... The first time I visited him [was] just when I understood that we had great power; that was at the end of September 1990."[4] But Karadžić was never Milošević's peer, nor treated by him as such. Milošević customarily addressed Karadžić with the informal "ti" (you), typically used between friends and equals in BCS, while Karadžić addressed Milošević with the more respectful and formal "Vi." Milošević called his Bosnian acolyte "Radovan" or, occasionally, "Doctor," with a hint of feigned deference, while Karadžić generally addressed Milošević as "President."[5] Milošević frequently summoned Karadžić to Belgrade, and Karadžić invariably cancelled or rearranged other plans to make the short trip to meet in Milošević's private office. Milošević only occasionally gave Karadžić direct orders, but when he did, Karadžić obeyed them.

[4]   BSA, 55th Session, October 22–23, 1995, Karadžić, BCS 0215–4665.
[5]   Testimony of Milan Babić, ICTY, PSM, November 20, 2002, p. 13,093. Babić, Karadžić's counterpart as leader of Croatia's Serbs, reported the same asymmetrical relationship with Milošević, calling him "Mr. President" while being called "Milan."

Transcripts of Bosnian police telephone intercepts show that by spring 1991, Karadžić and Milošević were speaking frequently by phone. One or the other often initiated a call from his home. Their conversations reflected a combination of collegiality and competition. Each strove to induce adulation from the other; both were narcissistically self-obsessed and spare with praise for one another. Each periodically bragged to the other of having rhetorically slain adversaries in debates and diplomatic encounters. Milošević's vanity was particularly evident, but the conversations reveal both men to have been confident, proud, and disinclined to self-criticism or second-guessing. While both spoke English well, Milošević was particularly vain about his English and sometimes recited drafts of his statements in that language to Karadžić.

Contrary to the widespread view of his detractors, Milošević never cultivated Karadžić's support for a political Great Serbia. Indeed, he reproved his followers for publicly endorsing the notion of combining Serb-inhabited regions into a single large Serb state. Milošević yearned to expand his personal power and become a regional strongman, but he understood Western reservations toward an expansive Serb state and the broader international antipathy to altering borders. Milošević often used Serb nationalist appeals to foment discontent when it furthered his goals, but his strong suit was clever disruptive tactics rather than long-term strategic plans or ideology. He drew Karadžić into a world of personal antagonism and shrewd machinations, thus injecting his cynicism into the mainstream of the Bosnian Serb politics.

THE DEMISE OF THE CULTURAL AUTONOMY OPTION IN CROATIA

Milošević achieved through democracy what he had failed to do by manipulating crowds. After his unsuccessful efforts in 1988 and 1989 to extend the anti-bureaucratic revolution into Croatia, Bosnia, and Slovenia, Milošević found new opportunities to mobilize Serbs for the multiparty elections of 1990 held in each Yugoslav republic. He influenced the selection of local Serb candidates to lead the SDS parties of Bosnia and of Croatia, and he supported them in their campaigns. He disavowed goals of a single, trans-republic Serb political party or a single Great Serb state. But whether his chosen party lost (as in Croatia) or won (as in Bosnia), he encouraged their leaders to pursue Serb territorial separatist projects to weaken rival republics and their leaders.

Although he acted under Milošević's influence, Karadžić was responsible for determining how to realize Bosnian Serb utopian aspirations. He was influenced by the precedents set by Serb nationalists in Croatia. He structured the Bosnian SDS electoral campaign to avoid a repeat of the SDS's losses in Croatia, and once he achieved power he continued to draw valuable lessons from both the successes and failures of the Croatian SDS. First among these issues was the appropriate post-electoral regional organization of Serbs within Bosnia, a question about which the Croatian precedent offered many insights.

Croatia's Serb nationalists had embraced regionalization in the SDS party program they published in February 1990. "The [present] regional division of Croatia ... is not at all in the historic interests of the Serb people,"[6] they asserted. They promised to "strive for an administrative division of Croatia into regions and municipalities which would reflect more appropriately the national structure in territories where we live."

Although they failed in the April 1990 elections to win key offices, SDS leaders succeeded in acquiring power in municipalities with Serb majorities. Goaded and aided by Milošević and his associates, they convinced Serb members of social democratic parties to support the SDS in demanding Serb autonomy within Croatia. Milan Babić, a dentist elected mayor of Knin in the April balloting, seized the lead. On June 6, 1990, he won the support of the Knin Municipal Assembly to form an association of Serb-majority municipalities in the hinterlands of Croatia's Dalmatian coast.[7] Following this, Serb-dominated municipal assemblies there and elsewhere in Croatia proclaimed the "Community of Municipalities of Northern Dalmatia and Lika" on June 27, 1990.[8] A week later, Babić moved from declaration to action in the streets. A crowd of Serbs gathered outside the Croatian Ministry of the Interior police station in Knin on July 5 and refused to let the Croatian police commander leave the building. The commander capitulated and gave up his post, leaving the security organs of Knin in the hands of Serb nationalists.[9]

Babić's precipitous moves alarmed Jovan Rašković, then head of Croatia's SDS. Rašković argued that Croatia's Serbs could realize their national interests through cultural autonomy rather than through territorial separatism. He publicly proclaimed his opposition to territorial separation before an estimated 100,000 Serbs gathered in Srb, Croatia, for the "First Serb Convention" on July 25, 1990. "We won't create another Serb state on Croatian territory," Rašković told the gathering. "We want only autonomy of a free and sovereign Serb existence."[10] At a rally two weeks later, he reiterated his position,

---

6   "Programski ciljevi Srpske demokratske stranke," Paragraph 16, February 17, 1990, ICTY, PSM, Exhibit P351.1, BCS 0214–1810.
7   "Zaključak o pokretanju inicijative za osnivanje Zajednice općina Sjeverne Dalmacije i Like," June 6, 1990, ICTY, PSM, Exhibit P351.5, BCS 0217–2140.
8   "Odluka o osnivanju i konstituisanju Zajednice općina Sjeverne Dalmacije i Like," June 27, 1990, ICTY, PSM, Exhibit P351.8, BCS 0217–2142–0217–2143.
9   Radulović, *Sudbina Krajine*, p. 17.
10 Ibid., p. 19.

telling the crowd, "We don't want autonomy that means creating a Serb state in Croatia; we want cultural autonomy."[11]

In advocating cultural autonomy, Rašković pitted himself against Milošević, who wanted Croatia's Serbs to control the territories where they lived. On June 28, 1990, Milošević proposed to agree to Croatia's separation from Yugoslavia on the condition that the self-proclaimed Serb areas of Croatia would "remain with our side."[12] By backing Serb territorial separatism, Milošević doomed Rašković's more modest and achievable goal of winning Serb cultural autonomy.

Milošević quietly pivoted to supporting pro-territorial Serbs in Croatia and eased Rašković out of leadership of Croatia's SDS. Babić and Knin police chief Milan Martić, both supporters of the territorial option, visited Belgrade on August 13, 1990, and met with Milošević. "We were not given any specific promise, but I was left with no doubt that we would receive support from Belgrade," Babić later testified at the ICTY. Milošević's closest advisor, Federal Presidency member Borisav Jović, promised the visiting Croatian Serbs that they "would be protected by the JNA."[13] A few days later, on the afternoon of August 17, 1990, the JNA began distributing weapons to Serb civilians in Knin,[14] allowing them to mount armed challenges to the police of the Republic of Croatia.

Only days after receiving Milošević's encouragement, the newly-formed Serb National Council in Croatia sponsored a plebiscite of Croatia's Serbs on the question of territorial autonomy from Croatia, giving voters from August 19 to September 2 to cast their ballots. Of 756,780 voters, all but 232 favored autonomy,[15] an outcome that Croatia's SDS leaders took as legitimizing further steps toward Serb separatism. On December 21, 1990, Croatia's Serbs came together to form the Serb Autonomous Region Krajina (*Srpska autonomna regija Krajina*, SAO Krajina), made up of some but not all Serb-inhabited municipalities in Croatia. A year later, on December 19, 1991, the SAO Krajina was renamed the Republic of Serb Krajina (*Republika Srpske Krajina*, RSK), and on February 26, 1992, two more Serb autonomous regions joined the RSK to make it the sole entity encompassing all Serb-controlled territories in Croatia.[16] In each of its iterations, the RSK served as the political instrument to advance Serb territorial separatism.

11 Ibid., p. 22.
12 Borisav Jović, *Poslednji dani SFRJ*, 2nd ed. (Kragujevac: Prizma, 1996), June 28, 1990, p. 161.
13 Testimony of Milan Babić, ICTY, PSM, November 18, 2002, p. 12,914.
14 Ibid., p. 12,912.
15 Radulović, *Sudbina Krajine*, p. 22.
16 Srdja Trifković, *The Krajina Chronicle: A History of Serbs in Croatia, Slavonia, and Dalmatia* (Chicago: The Lord Byron Foundation for Balkan Studies, 2010), pp. 214–216.

Although the Republic of Serb Krajina represented a triumph of Milošević's policies west of the Drina, he firmly opposed its annexation to Serbia. His opposition to such a Great Serb program emerged starkly in April 1990, when Babić proposed another plebiscite asking voters, "Are you for the unification of SAO Krajina with the Republic of Serbia?"[17] Milošević, knowing that European and North American countries would never countenance such a merger, intervened to demand a change in the wording of the referendum question. He was in fact staking out a middle ground: he favored separate Serb territories west of the Drina, but he opposed Serbia's annexation of those territories and wanted each of them to have their own identity and leaders. The assembly of SAO Krajina responded on April 30 by approving an extension that amended the referendum language. The new proposition read (added language in italics), "Are you in favor of unification of the SAO Krajina with the Republic of Serbia *and therefore to remain in Yugoslavia with Serbia, Montenegro, and others who desire to preserve Yugoslavia?*" Babić endorsed the expanded wording of the proposition, and Serb voters in Croatia overwhelmingly passed it, bringing the SAO Krajina's program back into accord with Milošević's policies. In quashing the Great Serb impulse west of the Drina, Milošević showed that those who accused him of Great Serbia ambitions – including this writer – did so in error.

REGIONALIZATION IN BOSNIAN KRAJINA

Karadžić was rightfully wary of offending Milošević and adeptly pursued policies favored by the Serbian president. He kept the Bosnian SDS free of the virus of cultural autonomy that had alienated Rašković from Milošević in Croatia, and he worked to create distinct Serb territories in Bosnia. Karadžić, on his own, had come to favor Serb territorial separatism in Bosnia, so on that policy he was aligned with Milošević even before the two men ever met. In August 1990, the Bosnian Serb social democrat, Mirko Pejanović, found Karadžić "obsessed with the idea of forming Serb municipalities,"[18] and warned him that territorial separatism could lead to violence in Bosnia (as it already had in Croatia). But Karadžić ignored that advice. He later confirmed that his vision of a separate Serb state in Bosnia dated to summer 1990. "We planned – and it came about quite similarly – what will happen in Sarajevo," Karadžić stated in spring 1992. The plan was "to link Sarajevo and Banja Luka," a northwestern Bosnian city of 123,937 with a 42 percent Serb plurality, he said. "That's a

---

[17] Radulović, *Sudbina Krajine*, pp. 29–30.
[18] Pejanović, *Through Bosnian Eyes*, p. 23.

state, that's a well-integrated nation; that was our plan long before the war."[19] Karadžić and other Bosnian Serb nationalists looked admiringly at the SAO Krajina as a precedent to be replicated in Bosnia.

In January 1991, Bosnia's SDS leaders began to implement regionalization, the term used at the time and here to mean bringing together whole existing municipalities with Serb inhabitants into associations or autonomous regions. (Not until December 1991 did SDS leaders shift to the strategy of creating separate institutions *within* each Serb-inhabited municipality.) On January 21, 1991, only two months after the elections in Bosnia, the mayors of 22 SDS-dominated municipalities in northwestern Bosnia met and laid plans for a regional institution. First labeled the "Community of Municipalities of Bosnian Krajina" (*Zajednica opština Bosanske Krajine*) in April 1991, it was renamed the "Autonomous Region of Krajina" (*Autonomna regija Krajina*, ARK) in September 1991; both are referred to here as the "ARK."[20] The mayors' action was designed to address Karadžić's complaint that "Serb areas, geographically unified areas populated by Serbs, were split up by deliberately dividing them among municipalities ... in a manner that weakened the Serb presence here."[21] (See Map 3.1.)

The SDS leaders also proposed to exploit the expansive powers granted to Bosnia's 109 municipalities under the 1974 constitution. That document designated the municipality as a "self-administering and fundamental social-political community," indicating it had inherent powers of self-government.[22] It also provided that local authorities could form communities of municipalities and pool resources for purposes specified in their charters.[23] Acting under those provisions, communist-era officials had formed the Banja Luka Regional Community of Municipalities in 1977, for administrative convenience rather than any ethnonational group's advancement (its constituent municipalities were mixed in composition).[24] The communist-era associations

---

[19] BSA, 39th Session, March 24–25, 1994, Karadžić, BCS 0215–2322.

[20] The ARK was distinct from the SAO Krajina, the association of Serb-led municipalities in Croatia established on December 21, 1990.

[21] Interview in *NIN* (Belgrade), July 20, 1990, reprinted in Bulatović, *Radovan*, pp. 151–152. Following common practice in English language works, I use the term "mayor" (BCS "gradonačelnik") rather than the technically correct but more cumbersome title, "President of the Municipal Assembly."

[22] Socijalistička Republika Bosne i Hercegovine (SRBiH), *Ustav Socijalističke Republike Bosne i Hercegovine* (Constitution of the Socialist Republic of Bosnia and Herzegovina) (Sarajevo: Službeni glasnik, 1974), Article 262, p. 148; and SRBiH, *Službeni list*, 4/74.

[23] *Ustav Socijalističke Republike Bosne i Hercegovine*, Articles 274–280, pp. 150–151.

[24] "Statut samoupravne regionalne zajednice opština Banja Luka," December 27, 1977, *Službeni glasnik Bosne i Hercegovine*, no. 11, pp. 23–28, ICTY, PMK, Exhibit P64, BCS 0040–3474–0040–3479.

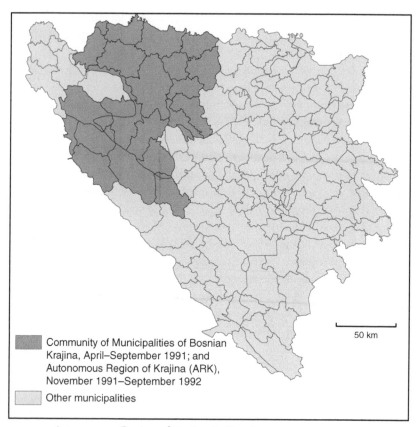

MAP 3.1. Autonomous Region of Krajina in Bosnia, 1991–1992.
Map by Nancy Thorwaldson.

had no relation to ethnic composition; they were created to pool the resources of sparsely-populated municipalities so as to reduce the cost of municipal services. But Karadžić and other Bosnian Serb nationalists insisted that they had been created with the purpose of depriving the Serb people of economic benefits and to favor Croats and Bosniaks.

Karadžić, although an enthusiastic supporter of regionalization in the abstract, only halfheartedly supported the ARK, rightfully fearing that the movement's leaders aimed to weaken the central control that he and other Sarajevo SDS leaders exercised over the party in that region. ARK leaders were the most zealous implementers of Karadžić's vision of territorial separatism, but they proved an unruly bunch, prone to challenging party discipline, undermining Karadžić's leadership, and plotting to achieve territorial autonomy for their own region.

On April 7, 1991, SDS leaders in Bosnian Krajina lifted the veil of secrecy on their project and authorized formation of the ARK at a regional meeting.[25] ARK leaders claimed that the ARK would serve only economic, cultural, and informational ends, while denying that the ARK was politically inspired by the SDS.[26] Karadžić backed them up in a statement issued in Sarajevo. "Regional organization up to this time has been centralized," he said. "Everything is decided in Sarajevo, all money flows into this city, and at the same time individual regions are held back in development."[27] He argued that the movement was ignited solely by economic grievances. "The economists here have decided, correctly, to put an end to this [centralization], something our party supports without reservation," he stated. "All political connotations in this case are attributed by others," he claimed.

SDS leaders in other parts of Bosnia failed to replicate the ARK's achievements. In May the party newspaper *Javnost* publicized SDS decisions to create additional communities of municipalities of "Eastern and Old Herzegovina" and "Romanija,"[28] but neither community sprang to life as the ARK had done. Only in Pale, one of Sarajevo's ten constituent municipalities, did local SDS leaders act in the spirit of regionalization, proclaiming unilaterally on April 29, 1991, their municipality's separation from the Sarajevo city government. Pale's SDS leaders cited the city's neglect of Pale's economic development as the cause of their need for separation.[29] However, such accusations, borrowed wholesale from ARK leaders, were meritless. Far from being neglected, Pale had become a thriving ski resort on the basis of republic-sponsored investments, including financing for major development projects to accommodate the 1984 Winter Olympic Games. Its posh resort hotel accommodations pleased Karadžić sufficiently to make the town his family's home and later his wartime headquarters.

In promoting regionalization as the central element of territorially-based national claims, Karadžić had taken a small but treacherous step toward violence against non-Serbs. Though he was still a year from sliding down the moral slope to committing mass atrocities, Karadžić knew that Serb regionalization in Croatia had led to violent clashes with Croatian security forces,

---

[25] *Nedeljnji Glas*, April 13 and 14, 1991, p. 3. An SDS spokesman announced this decision at a press conference on April 12, 1991.

[26] Examples of such public declarations are found in *Glas*, April 12, p. 7; April 18, p. 4; May 3, p. 5; and May 10, p. 8, all in 1991.

[27] *Glas*, April 17, 1991, p. 5.

[28] *Javnost*, May 11, 1991, p. 3, reported the formation of the Community of Municipalities of Romanija. *Javnost*, June 1, 1991, p. 4, noted formation of the Community of Municipalities of Eastern and Old Hercegovina.

[29] *Javnost*, May 4, 1991, p. 2. See also sources cited in Donia, *Sarajevo*, p. 265.

and Pejanović had warned him that proclaiming Serb municipalities might lead to war.

After a quiet summer, in September 1991 SDS leaders revived their regionalization campaign by renaming the Community of Municipalities of Bosnian Krajina the Autonomous Region of Krajina (*Autonomna regija Krajina*, ARK) and proclaiming four new Serb Autonomous Regions (SAOs): Romanija-Birač, Herzegovina, Semberija, and Northern Bosnia.[30] SAO Romanija-Birač was to be a Bosnian Serb counterpart to the city government of Sarajevo. On September 25, 1991, the Sarajevo City Board of the SDS appointed one representative from each of the city's ten municipalities to a committee charged with implementing the regionalization policy.[31] The regional SAOs created in autumn 1991 assumed greater importance than those perfunctorily declared earlier in the spring, and in 1992 would be integral to the mobilization of Serbs for takeover and war.

Although non-Serb political leaders viewed the Serb Autonomous Regions as ominous precursors of a Serb power grab, Karadžić later defended them as dormant entities to be held in reserve and activated only if necessary. "The Serbian autonomous areas were proclaimed but nothing was going on," he claimed at his trial in 2010. "They were there just in case something happened."[32] These characterizations of regionalization were false, as Karadžić and other Serb leaders later acknowledged.

Milošević, in a private conversation with Bosniak leader Adil Zulfikarpašić in June 1991, admitted that regionalization was intended to intimidate the Bosnian government. If confronted with hostile policies, Milošević told Zulfikarpašić, "we will take as much of Bosnia under our control as possible using regions."[33] But if the Bosnian government capitulated to his demands, Milošević assured Zulfikarpašić, "there will be no further talk of regions." In a closed wartime assembly session, Karadžić and Vojo Kuprešanin, the ARK president, both acknowledged that regionalization was a power grab aimed at crippling the Bosnian government. The regional organizations had been created out of "fear of becoming overpowered or dominated by the Izetbegović government," Karadžić said.[34] Kuprešanin was more explicit. "The task of the Region of

---

[30]   The Bosnian Serb Assembly ratified these announcements on November 21, 1991: "Odluku o verifikaciji proglašenih srpskih autonomnih oblasti u Bosni i Hercegovini," BSA, 2nd Session, November 21, 1991, BCS SA01–2030–SA01–2031. The decision was published shortly thereafter in *Javnost*, December 7, 1991, p. 10.

[31]   SDS BiH, Gradski odbor Sarajevo, "Odluku o imenovanju štaba za regionalizaciju," September 25, 1991, ICTY, PRK, Exhibit P977, BCS SA02–1150.

[32]   Karadžić Opening Statement, ICTY, PRK, March 1, 2010, p. 906.

[33]   "Sudbina Bošnjaka: Svedočenje Adila Zulfikarpašića," *NIN*, July 25, 1997.

[34]   BSA, 17th Session, July 24–26, 1992, Karadžić, BCS 0214–9509.

Krajina was to destroy Alija's state," he said in September 1992. "I think that other regions followed suit and we were successful in that respect."[35]

MILOŠEVIĆ INTERVENES AGAIN, RUDELY

Unlike Karadžić, Serb nationalists in Croatia seemed intent on defying Milošević. Rebuffed in their quest to create a Great Serbia by merging their polity with the Republic of Serbia, Croatia's Serb nationalists turned to seeking regional unification with the ARK in Bosnia. A group of SAO Krajina Serbs launched a drive to unify the two Krajinas on June 8, 1991. On that date, SAO Krajina Interior Minister Milan Martić provocatively led a paramilitary unit across the border into Bosnia. The unit held "maneuvers" in the predominantly Serb town of Titov Drvar in Bosnian Krajina, and Martić announced that their incursion had "dissolved the border" between Bosnia and Croatia,[36] symbolically implying that Serb-inhabited land on both sides of the border should be united. Like Babić before him, Martić drew loud and widespread denunciations. Political leaders from all major parties in Bosnia, including the SDS, condemned the incursion. Yugoslavia's Deputy Secretary of Defense denounced it as a provocation,[37] echoing Milošević's displeasure with efforts to promote a Great Serbia through border changes.

Karadžić likewise denounced Martić's incursion in private phone conversations with Ćosić. He ridiculed his own subordinates in the Bosnian SDS as reckless adventurers.[38] "I let them do stupid things," he told Ćosić. "They would like to do things off-hand, totally unmotivated and with no reason and no common sense." He qualified his denunciation with faint praise: "They do some really good things, but there are some hasty, quick-tempered people among them who don't know when enough is enough." Referring to the paramilitary incursion, Karadžić said, "This Milan [Martić] guy has just made a stupid mistake, and then my guys." Karadžić promised to suppress the Bosnian Serbs who were flirting with unification of the two Krajinas. "I have to calm the fools down," he assured Milošević. "They can't carry this one out now and in that way."[39]

Karadžić did not honor his promise. Deceived into believing that Milošević had changed his mind, Karadžić gave ARK leaders his approval to commit verbally to a union with SAO Krajina. On the morning of June 24, Andjelko

---

[35] BSA, 20th Session, September 14–15, 1992, Vojo Kuprešanin, BCS 0422–6268.

[36] *Glas*, June 10, 1992, p. 3; *Oslobodjenje*, June 9, 1991, p. 1.

[37] AP, Belgrade, June 9, 1991, RFE Press Archive, Munich (now in Budapest).

[38] Intercept, Karadžić and Ćosić, June 8, 1991, ICTY, PSM, Exhibit P613, Tab 6, BCS 0322–0142–0322–0154.

[39] Intercept, Karadžić and "Braco" (probably Mihalj Kertes), June 24, 1991, ICTY, PSM, Exhibit P613, Tab 10, BCS 0212–8441–0212–8447.

Grahovac, president of the ARK Executive Committee, told Karadžić by phone that Babić had received Milošević's endorsement to sign a formal agreement "on the integration of the cultural, informational, economic, political, etc., system."[40] Karadžić reacted skeptically but tried to straddle the fence. "You should pursue integration, but not sign any contract on it," he told Grahovac, making the naïve mistake of assuming that a verbal agreement would remain secret. "It is important that you are developing the gist of the cooperation," he said, "But in no way make a document, because it will become known to the world." Karadžić cautioned Grahovac against raising in public the specter of Great Serbia. "In event [of a signed agreement to unify the Krajinas], he [Izetbegović] can alarm the international public by saying, 'There – Serbs are creating Great Serbia'," he warned.

Then, compounding his error, Karadžić changed his mind and admitted to vacillating. He explained to another ARK leader that others had convinced him to go ahead. "I talked to Andjelko [Grahovac] this morning and told them not to do it, but I changed my mind while consulting with the people here, to prepare [a written agreement]," he said, "but that must not be publicized, nor made effective, but this one will.... After much discussion we decided here that they [may] prepare that, but must not publicize it."[41]

Karadžić did not wait long to see his decision play out to his embarrassment. Representatives of the two Krajinas, led by Grahovac from the ARK and Babić from SAO Krajina, met in Banja Luka a few hours after receiving Karadžić's approval on June 24 and hastened to conclude a written agreement of cooperation.[42] Rumors swirled among reporters that a "Krajina state" had been created, but Grahovac characterized the agreement as Karadžić had requested. "We are a region and have the right to cooperate, but as to a Krajina state, for now, there is nothing," he told the waiting press.[43] However, others soon betrayed Grahovac's secret and revealed his true intentions. Other SAO Krajina and ARK leaders convened a joint session of their two assemblies to proclaim the union of the two Krajinas. As if to stress their loyalty to Great Serb ideals, they met on June 27 in the Bosnian Krajina town of Bosansko Grahovo in the hall named after its native son, Gavrilo Princip, who assassinated the Habsburg Archduke Francis Ferdinand in 1914.[44]

---

[40] Intercept, Karadžić and Andjelko Grahovac, June 24, 1991, ICTY, PSM, Exhibit P613, Tab 12, BCS 0322-3497-0322-3500.

[41] Intercept, Karadžić and Radoslav Vukić, June 24, 1991, ICTY, PMS, Exhibit P613, Tab 14, BCS 0322-3513-0322-3515.

[42] "Ugovor o saradnji," June 24, 1991, ICTY, PSM, Exhibit 352, Tab 46, BCS 0216-2239-0216-2240.

[43] *Glas*, June 25, 1991, p. 7.

[44] *Glas*, June 28, 1991, p. 7; *Oslobodjenje*, June 28, 1991, last (unnumbered) page.

Even though the Krajina unifiers had defied his order, Karadžić publicly gave them his unreserved support. He proffered a narrative in which Serbs had acted in self-defense to save themselves from aggression. In an effort to obscure his own ill-advised hesitation, he told the Bosnian parliament that the declaration expressly provided that the two Krajinas would not unify unless the Yugoslav constitutional system ceased to exist. "That condition is in Point 5 of the Declaration," he stated to the Bosnian parliament. Point 5, he claimed, "decidedly states that it goes into effect and becomes valid in case the present constitutional system collapses."[45] This was untrue; Article 5 said no such thing, but instead expressly required the new polity to pursue a Great Serb agenda. "The United Krajina shall act as one," it read, "and direct its political activity to its own integration and the integration of the Serb people as a whole, all with the aim of creating a united state in which all the Serbs in the Balkans will live."

As he vacillated, backtracked, and outright lied in seeking to appease his own followers, Karadžić lost control of the SDS in Bosnian Krajina. Within days, Milošević intervened to rescue him. Milošević summoned Karadžić to Belgrade and deputized him to berate Babić for defying directives from the boss. In testimony during Milošević's trial at the ICTY in 2002, Babić described the meeting. "I got an invitation from Mr. Milošević to come, for Mr. Karadžić to tell me personally in his presence why we must not unite SAO Krajina with ARK at that time, because this was after assembly meetings of both Krajinas held on the 27th of June 1991."[46]

As Babić told it, Karadžić then boasted of his recent achievements and made the startling declaration that he would remove Bosniaks from Serb land when time and conditions permitted. "Karadžić said ... that he held Alija Izetbegović in his little pocket, that he could settle accounts with him at any time," Babić testified, "but the time was not ripe for it. So that the Serbs should not be blamed for things, it would be better to wait for Izetbegović to first make the wrong political move and that is when accounts would be settled, and the Muslims would be expelled or crammed into the river valleys and that he would link up all Serb territories in Bosnia."

According to Babić, Karadžić agreed at the meeting to act as Milošević's emissary to undo the unification of the two Krajinas. Milošević told Babić to "go with Radovan to appear [in Bosnia].... So that people in Bosnian Krajina should not stand in the way of Karadžić, and that I [Babić] shouldn't stand in his way either, so that Karadžić should show me to these people, letting them

---

[45] *Oslobodjenje*, June 28, 1991, p. 6.
[46] Testimony of Milan Babić, November 19, 2002, ICTY, PSM, p. 13,055.

know that this option was no longer valid at this point."[47] This humiliation-and-apology tour of Bosnia may have taken place, but if so, the public media took no note of it.

In the days following the Bosansko Grahovo proclamations, SDS leaders quietly allowed the union of the two Krajinas to perish from neglect. *Javnost*, the official SDS newspaper, never mentioned the Bosansko Grahovo meeting or the unification declaration. Karadžić, speaking at a press conference in early July, implicitly denied the merger by repeating the SDS's opposition to border changes.[48] ARK leaders soon got the message. Srdjo Srdić, president of the Prijedor municipality, speaking a few days later, noted with understatement that the unification "was not welcomed by the Presidency of the Bosnian SDS."[49]

Karadžić's career took a decisive turn for the better after the Belgrade meeting with Milošević and Babić. Anointed by Milošević as his primary lieutenant, Karadžić began to follow the Serbian president's advice to wait for others to provoke before acting. And he refrained from public endorsement of Great Serb ideals. Thanks to Milošević, Karadžić was again in control of the Bosnian Serb nationalist movement. Although still under Milošević's tutelage, he emerged in summer 1991 as the most powerful Serb west of the Drina.

---

[47] Ibid., p. 13,058.
[48] *Javnost*, July 13, 1991, p. 3.
[49] "Zapisnik sa sastanka predsjednika OO SDS," June 29, 1991, ICTY, PMK, Exhibit P67A, BCS 0102–1541.

4

Milošević's Willing Disciple

After deputizing Karadžić to thwart the union of the two Krajinas, Milošević increasingly relied on him as a confidant and facilitator of his ambitions in western Yugoslavia. But Karadžić became less Milošević's abject puppet than his helpful ally in Bosnia. Karadžić willingly – and at times obsequiously – obeyed his mentor's wishes, but rarely without expressing his own views to the Serbian president. He retained his Bosnian perspective on all matters, sought to advance the interests of the Bosnian Serbs, and extracted numerous concessions in exchange for implementing Milošević's schemes.

COURTING THE BOSNIAKS

Throughout 1991, Karadžić collaborated with Milošević in a campaign to persuade key Bosniak leaders to keep Bosnia within Yugoslavia. He did so without enthusiasm, and in time he grew frustrated with what he knew to be a futile endeavor. Both Karadžić and Milošević had reasons to favor the "Belgrade Initiative," the name given to the talks between Serbs and Bosniaks to keep Bosnia in Yugoslavia, but their differing interests tested the relationship between the two men and engendered distrust that foreshadowed more serious disputes to come. Milošević believed that the Bosniaks would support a federated Yugoslavia, and he was prepared to make compromises to retain their allegiance. Karadžić, more familiar with the Bosnian political scene, believed that most Bosniaks had already given up on Yugoslavia and shifted to favoring an independent, unified Bosnia outside of Yugoslavia.

Karadžić and Milošević argued about the views of Bosniak leaders during a phone conversation on May 29, 1991. Karadžić excitedly told Milošević that Izetbegović had abandoned, at least temporarily, his insistence on a unified Bosnia. "Izetbegović talked clearly and openly about the division of Bosnia; he's never been more explicit! I – we were shocked. We hadn't even considered that."[1] Karadžić had, in fact, thought a great deal about dividing Bosnia and was busily promoting separate Serb structures in Bosnian Krajina when this conversation took place. But he had not seriously considered that full separation might be achieved in a broad settlement with the Bosniak nationalists. Karadžić reported regretfully that Izetbegović had then quickly backtracked, returning to demands for a unitary Bosnia. "They went back to their earlier position," he told Milošević. "They want to give all sorts of guarantees to Serbs if they stay in a sovereign Bosnia; we said that we are offering them, as a people and as a republic, all the guarantees of citizens, nations, and republics, built into the federal constitution."

Karadžić encountered only scorn from Milošević, who demanded that Karadžić cease flirting with the idea of partitioning Bosnia. "Your position should be that you are against secession and that you want Bosnia to stay in Yugoslavia," Milošević said. "If a referendum is held on that issue, you will have a good number of Muslims supporting that position." Consistent with his opposition to annexing other Serb lands to Serbia, Milošević dismissed the idea of partitioning Bosnia: "Don't waste time on that," he said. "Nothing will come of it!" Milošević believed that most Bosniaks would choose to remain in Yugoslavia, even if their leaders did not. "Not all Muslims will do what Alija Izetbegović is doing, I am sure!" Milošević said. He dismissed the notion that Izetbegović was either a fundamentalist or a communist, viewing him instead as a secular Bosniak nationalist inclined to ethnic separatism. "Communists ... are not into national division," he told Karadžić.

Karadžić disagreed. He had changed his mind since July 1990, when he had benignly noted, "Bosnia is not brimming with Islamic fundamentalists."[2] By May 1991, Karadžić regularly labeled Izetbegović an Islamic fundamentalist and described him as a crafty politician quietly playing the Islamic card to gain support from the Arab world.[3] "I think, because he is very cunning, he doesn't articulate ... those hidden motives," he told Milošević. In Karadžić's eyes, Izetbegović was intent on discrediting Serbs by portraying them as aggressors. Izetbegović's "biggest concern," Karadžić said, "is to accuse us, and we do not give them a single reason." Izetbegović was not, in fact, a closet fundamentalist, but Karadžić was correct in discerning that Izetbegović and other SDA leaders were deeply suspicious of Serb intentions. The SDA leaders were

---

[1] Intercept, Karadžić and Milošević, May 29, 1991, ICTY, PSM, Exhibit P613, Tab 1, BCS 0212–8392–0212–8396.
[2] "Interview published in the *Nedelja* magazine on July 1, 1990," Karadžić, *Intervjui i govori*, vol. 5, pp. 24–25.
[3] Intercept, Milošević and Karadžić, May 29, 1991, ICTY, PSM, Exhibit P613, Tab 1, BCS 0212–8392–0212–8396.

not opposed in principle to staying in Yugoslavia, but they objected to the prospect of living in Milošević's degraded version of Yugoslavia, which had become a corrupt Serb-nationalist state.

Unconvinced by Karadžić's pessimism about Bosniak loyalties, Milošević was intent on demonstrating that most Bosniaks supported Yugoslavia. Speaking with Karadžić on July 9, 1991, Milošević referred to a "rally in Sarajevo for Yugoslavia" scheduled for July 11.[4] "It would be good if Serbs went to this rally in numbers," he told Karadžić. "It must be seen by the international community that there is a great disposition in favor of Yugoslavia, and that at the very center of Yugoslavia." Karadžić gave assurances that he was working to pack the rally with Serbs loyal to Milošević. "I've already given instructions for all neighboring municipalities to turn up in the greatest possible numbers," he declared.

As he had promised, Karadžić delivered several thousand demonstrators on July 11.[5] The rally featured slogans, songs, and speeches in support of Milošević and his policies. The organizers sent to the podium a disabled miner as a symbolic Bosnian "Everyman" who claimed to have been betrayed by those bent on dismembering Yugoslavia. "They promised us Sweden but gave us Lebanon!" he told the crowd. The demonstrators approved by acclamation a resolution stating, "Yugoslavia is the greatest state we have ever had.... Our proud Bosnia is only greater and greatest within it." The rally was reminiscent of the crowds that Milošević's allies had turned out elsewhere in Yugoslavia during the anti-bureaucratic revolution of 1988–89, but it lacked the fervor of the earlier rallies and its sentiments failed to spread to other areas of the republic.

Milošević nonetheless persisted in believing that the Bosniaks would rally to Yugoslavia. In mid-July 1991, Adilbeg Zulfikarpašić, leader of the Muslim Bosniak Organization (*Muslimanska bošnjačka organizacija*) in Bosnia, launched talks with Milošević that gave the Serbian president reason to believe he might succeed. The talks between Zulfikarpašić and Milošević became known as the "Belgrade Initiative," though by the end of summer the meaning of that label had broadened to encompass all hopes and efforts for a Serb-Bosniak rapprochement.

Zulfikarpašić first met with Karadžić, Krajišnik, and Koljević in the SDS party office to explore a deal.[6] At their meeting in late July of 1991, Zulfikarpašić worried aloud about potential violence between Serbs and Bosniaks. Karadžić

---

[4] Intercept, Milošević and Karadžić, July 9, 1991, ICTY, PSM, Exhibit P613, Tab 4, BCS 0206–6204–0206–6207.

[5] *Oslobodjenje*, July 11, 1991, p. 11.

[6] "Sudbina Bošnjaka: Svedočenje Adila Zulfikarpašić," *NIN* (Special supplement), July 25, 1997, pp. 40–44.

acknowledged that risk, but he complained that everything proposed by the Bosniaks "is against us." Zulfikarpašić then proposed principles for an agreement: no division of Bosnia into regions; Bosnia to have no status lesser than other Yugoslav republics, notably Croatia and Serbia; and Bosnia to share "common life and a common country with Serbia, Montenegro, Croatia and other republics."

The three Bosnian Serbs greeted this initiative coolly. Krajišnik acknowledged the proposal but said that regionalization was too advanced to be undone; at this, Zulfikarpašić threatened to end their discussions then and there. When reminded that Serbs in Croatia had already set up their own regions, Zulfikarpašić issued a veiled threat to retaliate for Serb separatist movements by inciting the Bosniaks living in the Sandžak, an area that straddled the border between the republics of Montenegro and Serbia. By merely mentioning the tens of thousands of Bosniaks living in the Sandžak, Zulfikarpašić was subtly suggesting that Bosniak leaders might undermine the governments of Serbia and Montenegro, just as the Bosnian Serbs were employing regionalization to undermine the Bosnian government.

Zulfikarpašić asked Karadžić what Milošević thought about these matters. Karadžić, skeptical that the Belgrade Initiative would succeed, leapt at the opportunity to pass the buck to his boss. He walked into the next room and placed a call to Milošević, impressing Zulfikarpašić with his ready access to the Serbian president. "Milošević is expecting you," Karadžić told Zulfikarpašić upon returning to the room. "You can go whenever you choose, tomorrow if you wish."

Seizing the moment, Zulfikarpašić traveled to Belgrade the next day and met with Milošević in his office. Describing this meeting in an article, Zulfikarpašić wrote that he was "immediately convinced that Milošević was one of the creators of policy in Bosnia, the authority who directly arranges how that policy is pursued."[7] As related by Zulfikarpašić, Milošević offered many concessions to the Bosniaks, including some that he lacked the formal authority to give. He further agreed to halt the Serb regionalization campaign in Bosnia if an agreement were reached. He offered to make a Bosniak nominated by Zulfikarpašić the next president of Yugoslavia for a term of five years. In response to complaints that Bosniaks were underrepresented in the military command structure, Milošević promised more than Zulfikarpašić had asked. "Give me a list of generals that you want," he said. "I'm prepared to arrange this immediately with the General Staff, namely that Muslim commanders will be appointed" for the four major JNA Corps in Bosnia.

---

[7] Ibid.

After further discussion, Milošević ended the meeting by urging Zulfikarpašić to return to Sarajevo and meet with Karadžić to finalize an agreement. Zulfikarpašić did so, and Karadžić sought at Milošević's behest to finalize a deal despite his skepticism of Bosniak intentions. The talks ended unexpectedly when President Izetbegović returned from a visit to the United States and learned that a deal was in the works. His abrupt intervention doomed the Belgrade Initiative.

For years thereafter, Zulfikarpašić contended that the Belgrade Initiative had been the last hope to avoid war between the Bosniaks and Serbs. He pointedly blamed Izetbegović for rejecting the incipient pact. Izetbegović did indeed preemptively end a promising set of negotiations that might have yielded an accord. But Izetbegović had good reasons to be deeply suspicious of Milošević's intentions. At the meeting with Zulfikarpašić, Milošević had rejected the possibility of an international monitor or guarantor of the pact, and he had offered no other method to assure he would carry out the lavish promises he had made. Izetbegović may have acted precipitously, but he was fundamentally justified in suspecting the Serbian president's motives. He would soon receive reinforcement for his belief in Milošević's duplicity at international talks to end the war in Croatia.

TALKING PEACE, SEEKING ADVANTAGE

Leaders of the EC, euphoric with their success in July 1991 in mediating the brief war in Slovenia, held high hopes that they could similarly negotiate an end to the conflict in Croatia. On September 2, EC diplomats mediated a ceasefire between the JNA and Croat security forces. The next day, the EC announced that British diplomat Peter Lord Carrington would lead intensive negotiations on September 7 in Geneva for a broader agreement to end and prevent conflict in the region.[8] Since the SDS was not a party to the conflict, Karadžić did not personally participate in these negotiations, but Milošević kept him informed about them by phone. Milošević and Karadžić believed that the Serbs held the upper hand as the talks began, but they worried that they would lose the moral high ground if Serbs appeared to be the aggressors by being the first to violate the ceasefire. The Croats "are desperate, they are losing," Karadžić explained to a subordinate. "And now they are looking for any way to fuck up the conference, so it will be said that the Serbs do not want peace."[9]

---

[8] Gow, *Triumph of the Lack of Will*, p. 53.
[9] Intercept, Karadžić and Brdjanin, September 6, 1991, ICTY, PSM, Exhibit P613, Tab 40, BCS 0206–6375–0206–6377.

Milošević had come up with a subterfuge to try to convince international negotiators that most Bosnians wanted to remain in Yugoslavia and that the Bosnian government had agreed to do so. He invited Serb leaders from several republics to attend a meeting in Belgrade before the peace talks began. Milošević issued an insincere invitation to Izetbegović, expecting him to decline to attend a meeting in Belgrade without the presence and implicit protection of EC negotiators who were then leading the talks in The Hague. At the same time, Milošević made sure that the Belgrade meeting would be attended by the presidents of the parliaments of Serbia and Montenegro, both of whom were Milošević loyalists. At the meeting, Milošević unveiled his plan to introduce Momčilo Krajišnik, the Bosnian Serb president of the Bosnian Parliament, as a legitimate representative of Bosnia, equal in stature to the president of the Bosnian Presidency, Izetbegović. "I will sketch a letter now and send it to Momir [Bulatović, president of Montenegro], Alija [Izetbegović], Krajišnik and the Parliament," he told Karadžić, "and suggest a meeting to talk about the formulation of the main question that solves and proposes a solution for the future of Yugoslavia, and let Alija not be there."[10] Milošević explained to Karadžić the disinformation campaign he had in mind to discredit Izetbegović. "Tomorrow we could put out that no reply has arrived from Alija but that the meeting will be held in any case," he said. "Then if he [Izetbegović] does refrain from coming, he is a fool."

Milošević convened the Belgrade meeting on August 12; the five participants – all Serbs and Milošević loyalists – pretended in their final declaration to have resolved the Yugoslav crisis. They cited a Bosniak-Serb agreement that had never been reached, since no Bosniak was present at the meeting where it was supposedly concluded. "The participants of the Belgrade meeting unanimously hailed the historic agreement between the Bosniaks and Serbs in Bosnia," said the signatories' communiqué, "emphasizing that the agreement was a big step toward a peaceful solution to the crisis and affirmation of the equality of the Yugoslav peoples."[11] They declared that the absence of Bosnia's pronouncements on independence meant that Bosnians wanted to stay in Yugoslavia. "Based on the fact that no decisions on secession and independence from Yugoslavia have been made or proclaimed in Bosnia, Montenegro and Serbia," the communiqué stated, participants at the Belgrade meeting agreed "to preserve Yugoslavia as a joint state of equal peoples and republics."

[10] Intercept, Karadžić and Milošević, August 6, 1991, ICTY, PSM, Exhibit P613, Tab 26, BCS 0212–8569–0212–8574.
[11] "Jugoslavija – zajednička država ravnopravnih naroda i republika," Belgrade, August 12, 1991, ICTY, PMK, Exhibit P67A, BCS SA01–9879–SA01–9881.

The Belgrade all-Serb meeting of August 12 was simply a public relations exercise. Milošević, however, believed he had outsmarted Izetbegović with this ham-fisted move and was further convinced that he could fool the international diplomats into thinking that Krajišnik spoke for all Bosnians. He was wrong. At the opening session of the EC-sponsored peace talks on September 6, Milošević claimed, based on the bogus Belgrade "agreement" of August 12, that Serbia, Montenegro, and Bosnia had already agreed to be part of a tripartite Yugoslav Federation. Izetbegović spoke up and contradicted him, pointing out that only two republics, Serbia and Montenegro, had been involved in the agreement. "I raised my hand again," Milošević related proudly to Karadžić a few days later, "and said that I had been very precise when stating that representatives of these three republics had launched this initiative, and I said [in English], 'I consider the President of the Bosnian Parliament, who attended that meeting, to be a top representative.'"[12]

With his crass subterfuge, Milošević not only failed to impress the Europeans, he also highlighted his own manipulative strategies and reinforced Bosniak suspicions of his intentions. Even after this episode, however, Milošević held to his naïve belief that many Bosniaks wanted to remain in Yugoslavia. In a phone conversation in November 1991, Milošević told Karadžić, "Some Muslims are nonetheless oriented to Yugoslavia."[13] Karadžić pointedly contradicted him. "But there are none, President! Not even 10 percent," he said. Karadžić beseeched Milošević to threaten the Bosniak leaders with unspecified consequences if they moved toward declaring independence. "They're destroying us; we must respond. We can't just mobilize the people for nothing," he said to the Serbian president. "Tell him [Izetbegović] that the Serbs are moving on" toward taking Serb-inhabited areas of Bosnia.

KARADŽIĆ, MILOŠEVIĆ, AND THE JNA

In addition to orchestrating political and diplomatic maneuvers, Milošević in 1991 presided over a massive movement of men and arms from east to west within Yugoslavia in support of Serbs west of the Drina. Karadžić actively facilitated Milošević's undertaking. Milošević primarily wanted to support the JNA and separatist Serbs in Croatia, but he was willing to make the Bosnian Serbs secondary beneficiaries of the arms and personnel transfers. Karadžić made

12 Intercept, Karadžić and Milošević, September 9, 1991, ICTY, PSM, Exhibit P613, Tab 48, BCS 0206–6173–0206–6176.
13 Intercept, Karadžić and Milošević, October 24, 1991, ICTY, PSM, Exhibit P613, Tab 100, BCS 0211–6674–0211–6679.

the most of his pivotal position to enhance his own prestige and gain advantages for Bosnian Serbs against their domestic rivals, the Croats and Bosniaks.[14] As they cooperated in moving arms and mobilizing men, Milošević guided Karadžić's development as a military leader.

The Yugoslav People's Army (*Jugoslovenska narodna armija*, JNA) had venerable origins and enjoyed bedrock public support throughout the communist period. The JNA was thoroughly intertwined with the country it had created and the society it served. Most Yugoslav males had spent at least 18 months in its ranks, and many of its installations were located in the country's large cities. Most Yugoslavs carried in their hearts an abiding appreciation for the JNA's role in liberating the country from occupation by German, Italian, and collaborating local forces at the end of the Second World War. The JNA largely retained its image as the embodiment of Partisan values, and it remained an effective multiethnic force longer than any other Yugoslav institution. But by 1990, the JNA was experiencing a crisis similar to that besetting the country as a whole. Yugoslavs and outside observers alike worried that the JNA would side with Serb nationalists should national tensions end in armed clashes.

The JNA, however, was not the only armed force in Yugoslavia. Alarmed by the 1968 Soviet invasion of Czechoslovakia, Tito had formed a second-tier, localized military organization known as Territorial Defense (*Teritorijalna odbrana*) based on the Yugoslav doctrine of people's defense. In the event of an invasion, Territorial Defense units were expected to resist invaders until the JNA could arrive in force. Such units were based in every factory, office, enterprise, institute, and government agency in the land, and each unit was given small arms to be secured but readily available for exercises or an actual invasion.[15] Ensnared in the complex web of shared and decentralized defense responsibilities, each municipality in Bosnia had a People's Defense Council – in effect, a Ministry of Defense at the municipal level – charged with keeping records of young men subject to military call-up and delivering reservists summoned by the JNA.

In Yugoslavia's twilight years, JNA senior officers came to fear that Territorial Defense forces, with their weapons and ordnance, might become embryonic armies of those republics seeking autonomy or independence. JNA generals redoubled their concern after the nationalists' electoral victories in Slovenia and Croatia in spring 1990, when they learned that some republic-level leaders were acquiring arms from abroad. On May 14, 1990, the JNA ordered

---

[14] "Izjava Svjedoka Miroslava Deronjića," November 25, 2003 (hereafter "Witness statement of Miroslav Deronjić"), Paragraph 8, ICTY, PSM, Exhibit P600, BCS 0344-7916–0344-7917.

[15] James Gow, *Legitimacy and the Military: The Yugoslav Crisis* (London: Pinter, 1992), pp. 46–47.

Territorial Defense weapons and ammunition transferred to the JNA's own armories to be secured under lock and key.[16] While the JNA seizure of weapons temporarily reduced the military capabilities of Croatia and Slovenia, it further breached the fragile trust among leaders in the three western republics and the JNA. In Bosnia, most Territorial Defense units complied readily with the JNA order. But after the elections of November 1990, the Territorial Defense units and police forces came under the control of the nationalist political leaders who governed in each particular municipality. Sometime before 1991, Milošević had decided to support a unified JNA and to oppose formation of separate Serb forces. Not all Serb nationalists agreed. Believing the JNA to be too communist-dominated, too indecisive, and too weak to defend Serb interests, many Serb nationalists west of the Drina aspired to form a separate Serb army to defend their interests and even take on the JNA if necessary. Milošević, on the other hand, was convinced that the JNA was the key to gaining the upper hand in the struggle for Yugoslavia. Rather than endorsing a separate Serb force or dividing the JNA among Yugoslavia's successor republics, he sought to bend the JNA to his will.

Once he decided to support the JNA, Milošević carried out his policy with great tenacity. In the early months of 1991, Milošević launched a concerted effort to redefine the JNA's mission, repopulate it with Serb draftees and volunteers, and let soldiers of other ethnicities desert without consequences. He enlisted Karadžić as the principal promoter of this campaign in Bosnia and arranged to recruit Bosnian Serbs into the JNA as it ramped up its fight against Croatian security forces. Milošević himself sought to win the favor of senior JNA generals and to convince them to back the nationalist Serbs of Croatia and Bosnia with weapons and, if necessary, support in combat.

Some JNA generals had already come to view Croatia's nationalist leaders as fascist traitors seeking to destroy Yugoslavia and refused to deal with them. In March 1991, Milošević, Federal Presidency member Borisav Jović, and Secretary of People's Defense Veljko Kadijević (in that office from May 15, 1988 to January 8, 1992) withdrew with their respective spouses for a weekend of relaxation and discussions at the resort of Kupari. Stjepan Mesić, Croatia's representative on the Federal Presidency, was not invited, nor did he otherwise enjoy ready access to top military commanders. By virtue of rotation among the republics and autonomous provinces, Mesić was then in line for a one-year term as president of the Federal Presidency beginning in May 1991. However,

---

[16] Marko Hoare, *How Bosnia Armed* (London: Saqi, 2004), p. 21; Bennett, *Yugoslavia's Bloody Collapse*, pp. 119 and 243; and Davor Marijan, "The Yugoslav National Army Role in the Aggression against the Republic of Croatia from 1990 to 1992," pp. 147–148, hrcak.srce.hr/file/28808, viewed January 10, 2014.

the four Milošević loyalists on the presidency voted against him, resulting in a 4–4 tie. Even after Mesić assumed the highest office in the land in accord with an EC-mediated agreement in July 1991, he had no contact with senior JNA officers. "Not a single general, either from the General Staff or from the Ministry of Defense, came to see me," he later recalled.[17] General Kadijević confirmed later that he and other senior officers had kept Mesić isolated. "We treated him as if he didn't exist,"[18] Kadijević later wrote.

As Milošević worked to win over senior JNA generals, lower-ranking JNA officers began supplying weapons to Serb separatists in Croatia. By September 1990, those officers were distributing arms to SDS members, emboldening them to challenge Croatian police and security forces.[19] On April 9, 1991, Bosnian police stopped and searched a truck passing through Bosnia and discovered over a thousand automatic rifles. The Bosnian police ostentatiously displayed these weapons before television cameras and journalists.[20] The arms were destined for Croatia's Serbs, according to rumors at the time, but after the discovery, the truck's drivers delivered their cargo to JNA barracks in Bosnia. Karadžić denounced the Bosnian police action as a set-up by Bosniaks and Croats to embarrass the Serbs.

Weapons transfers to SDS members and sympathizers appear to have accelerated in May 1991. That month, two SDS officials from the eastern Bosnian municipality of Bratunac met with Mihalj Kertes, a senior Milošević aide, during a visit to Belgrade. Together they toured a large warehouse containing arms destined for delivery to Serbs in Croatia and Bosnia. On May 29, vehicles dispatched from that warehouse in Serbia made the first of many arms deliveries to SDS members in Bratunac.[21] Milošević and Karadžić were determined to move weapons into SDS hands and to keep those movements from public view.

SUBDUING THE DRIVE FOR A SERB ARMY

In summer 1991, outspoken Serb nationalists in the Bosnian Krajina issued repeated calls for a separate Serb army. Many delegates in the ARK Assembly blamed the JNA for losing the 1991 war in Slovenia; some accused the army's

[17] Stjepan Mesić, "Rasprava," in Branka Magaš and Ivo Žanić, eds., *Rat u Hrvatskoj i Bosni i Hercegovini, 1991–1995* (London: Bosanski Institut, 1999), p. 130.
[18] Veljko Kadijević, *Moje Vidjenje Raspada: Vojska bez države* (Beograd: Politika, 1993), p. 38.
[19] Testimony of Milan Babić, ICTY, PSM, November 18, 2002, pp. 12,912, et seq.
[20] *Oslobodjenje*, June 8, 1991, p. 1; Radio Free Europe, July 5, 1991, p. 34.
[21] Witness statement of Miroslav Deronjić, Paragraph 23, ICTY, PSM, Exhibit P600, BCS 0344–7921.

top officers of treason. One delegate asked, "Why have the Federal Executive Council and the JNA done nothing against treason in Croatia and Slovenia?"[22] The SDS Board of Prijedor Municipality declared in a resolution, "The General Staff betrayed the country."[23] A member of the ARK Assembly advocated organizing locally. "If there is a legal organization at the municipal level, it should take up the defense," he argued. "If there is not, then the Serbs must organize the defense of their own people."[24] In early July 1991, ARK Vice President Radoslav Brdjanin, Karadžić's most loyal lieutenant in the Bosnian Krajina, told his boss in a phone call, "We, from here, personally support the creation of a Serb army."[25] He was concerned that the JNA mobilization would leave Serbs in the Bosnian Krajina defenseless. "All the Serb reservists have gone into the army now, so the Serb villages are again left with the women and children who could be slaughtered overnight," he complained to Karadžić.

Having heard many calls for a separate Serb army, Karadžić directed Brdjanin, his most loyal lieutenant in the ARK, to quell the clamor. "Look, Brdjo," he warned, "creating a Serb army would result in the collapse of this army [the JNA], and everyone would demand some of the equipment for themselves. Creating a Serb army would provide a pretext for European forces to come." Karadžić pointed out that the JNA was already becoming a Serb force as non-Serbs refused to answer the call-ups of reservists. "Yugoslavia is again being defended by the Serb people, while the rest are either actively fighting against it or are passive in its defense, not responding to the call-up." Karadžić pleaded with Brdjanin to "please, please establish these commands in the municipalities in a single day."

JNA officers seemed pleased that most Serbs responded to their call-ups while most Croats and Bosniaks stayed home. Karadžić was right. The JNA was using the differential response to call-ups to transform the JNA into an all-Serb force in both Croatia and Bosnia. With guarded bureaucratic language, General Kadijević explained in his memoirs the JNA's strategic shift in summer 1991.[26] "When the JNA failed in its efforts to orient the Muslim part of Bosnia's leadership toward a new Yugoslav state made of those Yugoslav nations who still wanted it," he wrote, "we had to orient ourselves toward concrete cooperation with the representatives of the Serb nation and with the

---

[22] *Glas*, June 28, 1991, p. 7.

[23] "Sveska zapisnika sa sastanaka Opštinskog odbora SDS Prijedor, Arhivska knjiga br. 7," June 29, 1991, ICTY, Prosecutor v. Milomir Stakić, Exhibit 12b, BCS 0102–1541–0102–1548.

[24] Ibid.

[25] Intercept, Karadžić and Radoslav Brdjanin, July 2 or 3, 1991, ICTY, PSM, Exhibit 613, Tab 16, BCS 0206–6372.

[26] Kadijević, *Moje Viđenje Raspada*, p. 147.

Serb people as a whole." Reorienting to the Serbs meant bringing more of them into the JNA, he wrote. "Thus during the war in Croatia we executed maneuvers and movements of JNA forces through Bosnia.... That made it possible for the call-ups in Serb parts of Bosnia to be very successful."

Karadžić dutifully encouraged local SDS leaders to be sure Serbs responded to the call-ups, but he also insisted that some JNA arms be funneled to the SDS in Bosnia. He asked Milošević and the JNA generals to leave some armed Serbs at home to defend the villages of Bosnian Krajina. Karadžić agreed that Bosnian Serbs should acquire weapons at home and fight in Croatia, just as Brdjanin and the Bosnian Krajina Serbs wished, but he conceded that they would do so under JNA command.

Milošević called Karadžić again on July 8 to prod him to send additional recruits to the town of Kupres in western Bosnia, where a battle was developing between Croat security forces and the JNA. Milošević referred in the conversation to "RAM," a word meaning "frame" in Serbian that also served as the code word for redeploying the JNA to encircle and defend Serb lands rather than all of Yugoslavia. Reinforcing Kupres, Milošević said, was "of strategic importance for the future RAM, you know what RAM is?" Karadžić seemed offended that Milošević had to ask. "Yes, I know, I know everything," he replied testily.

The next day, July 9, Milošević called again to stress the urgency of mobilizing Bosnia's Serbs. "All of our men must answer the call and go,"[27] he said. But even as Karadžić told Milošević what he wanted to hear, he stressed that some must stay at home to defend their villages. "I just ask that they [the JNA] train them and leave about at least a hundred here locally to make the people feel secure," Karadžić said. "We support the army and all its actions for the preservation of Yugoslavia," he reassured Milošević, "including the draft, mobilization and separation of parties in the conflict."

Milošević also arranged for General Nikola Uzelac, commander of the JNA's Fifth Corps based in Banja Luka, to call Karadžić later on July 9 and ask for his political support.[28] The resulting conversation was a landmark in forging a three-way alliance between Karadžić, Milošević, and senior JNA generals. "We haven't had a chance to meet personally, but I know you well," Uzelac tactfully told Karadžić. "You know what I'd like to ask you for?" the general asked. "Just political action.... Liven up everyone. Denounce all calls for acts of treason." Uzelac then curtly informed Karadžić that he wanted no

---

[27] Intercept, Karadžić and Milošević, July 9, 1991, ICTY, PSM, Exhibit P613, Tab 4, BCS 0206–6204–0206–6207.

[28] Intercept, Karadžić and General Uzelac, July 9, 1991, ICTY, PSM, Exhibit P613, Tab 19, BCS 0206–6224–0206–6227.

further civilian involvement in military matters. "To that effect, you should make political preparations," the general told him. Karadžić wisely promised not to meddle in military matters and gave assurance that political support was forthcoming. "We've issued instructions to mobilize everyone and to subordinate everyone to the command of the JNA," he said. He then recited the terms of their deal. "We'll put everyone under your command and no one under ours," he said. "All we ask is that you leave a number of volunteers, the older ones, in the areas, with your lieutenant and your commander."

Having reached agreement with Uzelac, Karadžić called his subordinates in Bosnian Krajina and instructed them to honor the deal. "Listen," he said. "I have agreed with them [JNA officers] that we will help reinforce the army. Therefore, put everything under JNA command and they will arm the command and leave members of their Territorial Defense on your territory and move the operative part of the units.... So the army should provide arms for all."[29]

Karadžić had reason to be pleased with the outcome of these conversations. He had mollified both Milošević and General Uzelac, while dissuading the restive ARK Serbs from derailing Milošević's plan to strengthen the JNA. Most importantly, he had crafted an agreement that satisfied the interests of all major actors, including Milošević, the senior JNA generals, the stubborn ARK Serbs, and the Sarajevo-based SDS leaders. This informal agreement had significant long-term consequences. As interethnic tensions escalated in early 1992, the JNA's backing gave the SDS its greatest advantage over the rival nationalist parties of the Croats and Bosniaks. Support from the JNA emboldened SDS leaders to hold firm and expand their demands, confident that the army could quickly vanquish the Serbs' foes if it came to war. The powerful combination of JNA arms and SDS organization made it both possible and more likely that the SDS would go to war to achieve its aims. Although cooperation was at first limited, Karadžić's informal pact with the JNA of July 1991 was a large further step toward war and mass atrocities against non-Serbs.

The war in Croatia dragged on throughout the fall of 1991, but it began to wind down toward the end of the year. On January 2, 1992, the JNA and the Croatian government signed the Vance Plan in Sarajevo. The JNA agreed to withdraw from Croatia; the UN created four adjacent United Nations Protected Areas under Serb civilian control; and the United Nations Protection Force (UNPROFOR) was deployed along the boundary between Serb- and Croat-controlled territories in Croatia. (See Map 4.1.)

---

[29] Intercept, Karadžić and Duvnjak, July 9, 1991, ICTY, PSM, Exhibit P613, Tab 20, BCS 0206–6221–0206–6223.

MAP 4.1. Croatia and Bosnia and Herzegovina, 1991.
Original Source: Library of Congress, DI Cartography Center, 753548AI
(R00389) 8–01.

The JNA began in early January 1992 to withdraw from Croatia in accord
with the Vance Plan. But the thousands of troops, almost all of them Serbs,
withdrew together with their heavy weapons not into the Yugoslav republics of
Serbia and Montenegro, but to the ill-fated Republic of Bosnia. SDS leaders
had every reason to believe that some of those same young men would willingly go to war for the Serb national cause in Bosnia. While the Croatian conflict had given Bosnians a temporary reprieve from violence, it had afforded
Bosnia's nationalists additional time to militarize their respective movements
and had given the SDS the means to prevail militarily over their rivals.

5

The Autumn of Radovan's Rage

"We have entered a phase of inebriation with the nation. That's why we are far removed from civilization, reason, and prosperity."

Mustafa Šehović, Social Democrat delegate in the
Bosnian Parliament, October 14, 1991[1]

Sometime before September 1991, Karadžić underwent a personal and political metamorphosis. Evidence of this transformation emerged in his speech, imaginings, and actions during September as he became enraged by confrontations with rivals. As he grew increasingly frustrated by his inability to dictate the course of events, he adopted distorted interpretations of events and became deeply cynical of his rivals' intentions. He indulged in fantasies of Bosniaks disappearing en masse, revealing a callous indifference toward the lives of non-Serbs. His dark, cynical imaginings would have profound implications for Bosnia's future, particularly for the Bosniaks.

SARAJEVO ENIGMA

Sarajevo, Karadžić's adopted home, is a city of seasonal rhythms. In a ritual that seems as ancient as the hills around the city, many of Sarajevo's residents return each September from languorous Adriatic Coast vacations to restore the city's throbbing energy. As adults resume their workaday routines and children return to school, cool continental breezes drive the oppressive Mediterranean summer heat from the valley. Autumnal rains transform Sarajevo's Miljacka River from a placid trickle into a roaring brown torrent, carrying mud and debris from thousands of upland peasant plots. Sarajevans, among the world's most vocal hypochondriacs even in the best of times, turn from lamenting

[1] *Oslobodjenje*, October 15, 1991, p. 3.

summer heat to complaining of "changes in pressure" and "unstable weather." They move their conversations indoors to cramped, smoke-filled cafés and reminisce about their idyllic days of leisure in the summer sun. When one of the few clear, sun-filled autumn days falls on a weekend, they trek by the tens of thousands through the surrounding hills, pausing at outdoor cafes to enjoy a cup of coffee or a robust shot of plum brandy.

Typically, returning Sarajevans find their city in autumn much the same as they left it in summer. But in the fall of 1991, they returned to a city awash with ominous rumors and rising political tensions. Unease was in the air, and fear had begun to afflict the politically savvy. The economy was in free-fall. Security was deteriorating. Gangsters emerged from the shadows to commit bolder and more conspicuous criminal acts. The three nationalist political parties were quarreling furiously over Bosnia's constitutional relationship to Yugoslavia. Political parties were securing arms for newly-formed paramilitary organizations. Forebodingly, Serbs and Croats had begun to spill each other's blood as war spread in Croatia. Sarajevo media reported on battles that left dozens dead in crossroad towns near the Bosnian border. More alarming still, incidents were increasingly intruding into Bosnian territories adjacent to Croatia.

Many long-term Sarajevo residents saw themselves as Sarajevans, Bosnians, Yugoslavs, or urbanites (in no particular order) far more than they identified as Serbs, Croats, or Bosniaks. Many Sarajevans feared that increasingly fierce feuds among nationalist groups might destroy their comfortable urban life-style. Perhaps most fearful were Sarajevo's Serbs, whose long-subdued national identity was becoming suddenly and uncomfortably salient in the city's public life. Some Serbs backed Milošević, Karadžić, and the SDS nationalists, but other Serbs worried that aggressive Serb nationalism would lead those of other nations to consider them pariahs, suspecting them, rightly or wrongly, of sepa-ratism or even treason.

With all the uncertainty and fear, no informed Sarajevan failed to speculate about Serb nationalist leader Radovan Karadžić, the rising enigma of Bosnian politics. Some had heard of him as a poet in his student days, and others knew him as a psychiatrist, but few recognized him in his new identity as a belli-cose, flamboyant Serb nationalist. By the end of summer 1991, Karadžić was no longer the affable professional family man that many Sarajevans thought they knew. He worked hard and eschewed vacations. Deep in Milošević's thrall, he frequently flew by private plane to meetings in Belgrade, spoke with the Serbian president regularly by phone, and dutifully followed the guid-ance he received from the Belgrade-based Serb leaders. He spent long hours at SDS headquarters in the Parliament building and held extensive phone conversations deep into the night from his family flat in a near west side Sarajevo housing complex.

At the same time, Karadžić led a hectic and visible public life as a person of interest to the world beyond Sarajevo. Journalists found him to be charismatic, accessible, and well-spoken. His rugged, photogenic visage fit the stereotype of an atavistic Balkan mountain man. Karadžić crowded his schedule with press interviews with foreign reporters, conferences with European diplomats, discussions with leaders of other political parties, and meetings with Serbs seeking jobs and favors.[2] He was in all respects the biggest, newest, and most unconventional power player in Sarajevo's multifaceted political landscape. With a mixture of hope and anxiety, Sarajevans wondered how far Karadžić would go in imposing his Serb nationalist zeal on his followers and their republic.

CRISIS IN KRAVICA

In September 1991, EC diplomats began an intensive effort to negotiate an end to the war in Croatia. By agreeing to an EC-mediated ceasefire on September 2, the JNA and Croat security forces had paved the way for EC-sponsored peace talks in The Hague, Netherlands. Milošević and Tudjman each hastened to warn the European negotiators that the other side was staging provocations. At the same time, each sought to keep his own forces in check. Once the talks formally began on September 7, Milošević redoubled his efforts to prevent armed Serbs – whether the JNA, local paramilitaries, or police – from opening fire. Tudjman likewise sought to restrain his forces, while secretly working to provoke Serb retaliation.

The first of four autumn crises began in the eastern Bosnia municipality of Bratunac on September 3, the first day of the Croatian ceasefire. Local armed Serbs ambushed a car containing four Bosniak men on a well-traveled road between the village of Glogova, with an almost exclusively Bosniak population (1,901 of 1,913 inhabitants) and nearby Kravica, a village inhabited almost exclusively by Serbs (357 of 363 inhabitants).[3] (See Map 4.1) The Serb attackers killed two of the Bosniaks and wounded the two others. The Sarajevo newspaper *Oslobodjenje* characterized the two who died as the first casualties of interethnic strife in Bosnia since the Second World War.[4]

---

[2] "Poslovni dnevnik," ICTY, PMK, Exhibit P67A, BCS SA04–3843–SA04–4014.
[3] Gelo, comp., *Stanovništvo Bosne i Hercegovine*, pp. 74–75.
[4] *Oslobodjenje*, September 5, 1991, p. 5; September 6, 1991, p. 5; September 7, 1991, p. 5; and September 8, 1991, p. 4.

The ambush was but the first in a string of complex and contested events in the area. Local-level SDS officials briefed Koljević and Krajišnik on that history by phone, and much of their account is corroborated by press reports.[5] Some days before the ambush, JNA officials had seized from municipal officials the lists of reservists subject to call-up for service in the JNA. Bosniaks had responded by organizing a protest during which, Serbs charged, Bosniaks had fired shots at two Serb officials, although neither was hit. Local SDS officials alleged that SDA supporters then launched an "invasion" of the Serb-dominated village of Kravica, although press reports do not mention this event. By all accounts, armed Serbs then ambushed the four Bosniaks as their vehicle approached Serb-dominated Kravica from the direction of Bosniak-majority Glogova.

The killings in Kravica escalated fears that Bosnia was on the verge of war. Following a common practice, the Bosnian presidency dispatched members from the contending nations to calm local tensions. Telephone intercepts show that Krajišnik asked Karadžić's assent on September 4 to make such a trip at the invitation of SDA leader Muhamed Čengić, vice president (deputy prime minister) of Bosnia.[6] Karadžić concurred that Krajišnik and Čengić should go to Kravica together, but he also proposed that Krajišnik exploit the peacemaking mission to issue a carefully-rehearsed verbal warning to Čengić that the Bosniaks were in danger of "disappearing" because of their provocative behavior. He told Krajišnik to tell Čengić, "You see, that's where it leads, where your policies lead!' and 'Do you realize that you will disappear in all this?" Karadžić told Krajišnik to warn them, "Man, you will disappear. Many of us will also disappear, but you will be annihilated!"

His proposed warning to Čengić indicates the source of Karadžić's wrath. His anger centered not on who the Bosniaks were, nor on any of their physical or cultural traits as a people, but rather on what they *refused* to do. They did not acknowledge that the Serb national cause was just; they did not capitulate to the demands of Karadžić and the SDS; they did not concede that Serbs killed only when they were provoked by Bosniak politicians. Karadžić was enraged at Bosniaks because they stood in the way of achieving the Serb utopian dream. His anger was directed mostly against Bosniak political leaders and elites. Other Bosniaks might die in a final apocalyptic revenge, but their deaths would be collateral damage, an inevitable consequence of their

---

[5] Intercept, Krajišnik and Trifko Komad, September 4, 1991, ICTY, PSM, Exhibit P613, Tab 35, BCS 0212–8639–0212–8640; Intercept, Koljević, Krajišnik, and Trifko Komad, September 4, 1991, Tab 36, BCS 0212–8541–0121–8645.

[6] Intercept, Krajišnik and Karadžić, September 4, 1991, ICTY, PMK, Exhibit 67A, Tab 11.1, BCS 0207–9140–0207–9142.

leaders' stubbornness. He raged as someone who felt entitled to dominate those who resisted his dictates. In autumn 1991, Karadžić appeared less a bigot than a thug and aspiring tyrant: he was mad as hell at anyone with the temerity to be in his way.

Karadžić's proposed tough talk did not sit well with Krajišnik, who recognized the danger in his leader's ominous prediction that the Bosniaks would disappear (the "disappearance discourse," as I refer to it here). Krajišnik suggested a more balanced and less threatening version of the warning. "But no, we should say that we will all disappear, both, you know," Krajišnik said. "That should be said deliberately. That's what should be done.... We should soften up, not toughen up." Since Čengić and Krajišnik never made the proposed trip to Kravica, Karadžić's intemperate language was not conveyed to the SDA vice president at that time, but Karadžić failed to heed his friend's temperate advice in the ensuing weeks.

Rather than Krajišnik and Čengić, Bosnian presidency members Ejup Ganić of the SDA and Koljević of the SDS traveled to Kravica by helicopter on September 4 with the mission of calming things down.[7] This was not what Karadžić had envisioned, and back in Sarajevo he criticized the multiethnic Bosnian police force that was part of the Bosnian Ministry of Internal Affairs (*Ministarstvo unutrašnjih poslova*, MUP).[8] Although acknowledging that "things are not completely clear," Karadžić charged that "everything began around opposition to military organs that took military records in accord with federal law." While he did not explicitly approve of the ambush on the road to Kravica, his description of the victims suggested he was not inclined to regret their deaths. In a private conversation with Milošević, he blamed Bosniaks for provoking the incident. "They shot at some of our people, wounded them, then ours killed two of theirs, of their bullies,"[9] he said. This was not completely true, but neither curiosity nor fairness drove him to seek out more information. He was more interested in blaming Bosniaks than in uncovering the facts of the case.

Following the incident, local SDS officials in Kravica appealed to the JNA's Tuzla Corps to intervene on the Serbs' behalf.[10] But the JNA generals were unwilling to fan the flames of a localized conflict on the eve of peace negotiations in The Hague, and their forces remained in Tuzla. Thanks to the

[7] Testimony of Džemal Bećirović, May 9, 2003, ICTY, PSM, pp. 20,507–20,509.

[8] *Oslobodjenje*, September 6, 1991, p. 5.

[9] Intercept, Karadžić and Milošević, September 4, 1991, ICTY, PSM, Exhibit P613, Tab 34, BCS 0212–8646–0212–8650.

[10] Intercept, Koljević, Krajišnik, and Trifko Komad, September 4, 1991, ICTY, PSM, Exhibit P613, Tab 36, BCS 0212–8541–0212–8645.

Presidency's mediation and cooler heads, tensions eased in Kravica and the crisis passed.

Although Karadžić weathered the Kravica crisis, he had not mastered it: he had only inflamed interethnic antagonism. As local political leaders and police of all ethnicities sought to mediate the crisis and calm tensions, he poured fuel on the flames by verbally attacking MUP leaders and inciting Serb fears of the unified multiethnic Bosnian police force. He engaged in ominous and threatening disappearance discourse, even if only in private conversation with a trusted associate. With such language, he crossed a threshold in imagining the previously unthinkable: the disappearance of an entire people. However, he had left unidentified the would-be agents of such disappearance.

PROVOCATION AT OKUČANI

Just as tensions in Kravica were subsiding, Karadžić received reports that Croatian forces were slaughtering Serbs near the crossroads town of Okučani in Croatia. (See Map 4.1) Koljević, with panic in his normally calm voice, called Karadžić from Banja Luka on September 6. He reported rumors among local Serbs that the JNA had withdrawn from Okučani, leaving local Serb villagers vulnerable to Croat armed attacks. "These [Serbs] in Banja Luka are furious with the army [JNA]," Koljević reported. "The [JNA] airplanes that will not take off are there, the units that withdrew are there."[11] Koljević explained that Serb militants in the ARK were clamoring to march on Okučani to rescue its allegedly endangered Serb civilians. He sketched out a scenario of Serb-initiated violence that Milošević desperately hoped to prevent. Peace talks were scheduled to begin the next day, and the Serb negotiators could ill afford an armed incident initiated by Serbs.

In their phone conversation, Karadžić assured Koljević that the JNA had not really withdrawn from Okučani but had only repositioned its forces for tactical reasons. Although he was concerned about the Okučani Serbs, Karadžić was also displeased with the possibility that well-armed Bosnian Krajina Serbs, who had pushed him to form a separate Serb army, might march into Croatia and restart the war. He also tried to convince the JNA to intervene on behalf of Okučani's Serbs. Saying he hoped to mollify the restive Bosnian Krajina Serbs by persuading the JNA to attack, Karadžić called Milošević on September 6 and implored him to order the JNA to rescue Okučani's Serbs.

---

[11] Intercept, Karadžić and Koljević, September 6, 1991, ICTY, PSM, Exhibit P613, Tab 38, BCS 0212–8659–0212–8661.

Milošević in turn phoned the JNA's two most senior generals, but he found them disinclined to order the JNA into action. "I've talked twice with Kadijević [Federal Secretary of Defense] and three times with Blagoje Adžić [Chief of the General Staff of the JNA]," Milošević reported back to Karadžić. "He [probably Adžić] claims that there has been no slaughter anywhere, and that they didn't withdraw any troops except for one unit which was deployed where it shouldn't have been, and which has been relocated."[12] Unpersuaded, Karadžić continued to urge Milošević to act to save Okučani's Serbs. "No, here I have information . . . [that] between Okučani and Gradiška the army has weakened, that it has withdrawn and is exposed," he told Milošević.

Having failed to alleviate Karadžić's concerns, Milošević told him to take his case directly to the generals. "Please, call Adžić personally," he said to Karadžić. "I've already told him. . . . It would be good if you listen to him, because he keeps getting information from Bosnia that actually nothing is going on there [in Okučani]."

Karadžić thereupon called the highest-ranking general in the JNA, with whom he had apparently never before spoken, and expressed his concerns with appropriate deference. "President Milošević tells me that the civilian assessment of this varies from yours about this situation in, near Okučani,"[13] he said to Adžić. The general responded that both Serbs and Croats in that area were becoming agitated. Karadžić persisted: "According to some information I received from these civilians of mine, they say the checkpoint, in fact, the highway, has been abandoned [by the JNA], Okučani is surrounded and they are afraid they will be massacred."

Adžić rebuffed Karadžić coolly but politely. "Fears are one thing, but reality is something else, you know?" he said. Adžić then changed the subject and told Karadžić of his greatest concern, namely that Serb volunteers from Bosnia might make an ill-advised foray across the border and attack Croatian forces around Okučani. Adžić had already heard from Vojislav Kuprešanin, president of the ARK, that Bosnian Krajina Serbs would march in a matter of hours if the JNA did not act. The general worried aloud that an armed Bosnian Serb incursion might torpedo the peace talks in The Hague. He asked Karadžić to get involved. "Well, now, I wanted to ask you," he said to Karadžić, "We have not had a chance to meet and see each other; this is probably, in a way, our first contact, and they sent me what amounts to an ultimatum from the Bosnian Krajina." Adžić pleaded with Karadžić to keep the Bosnian Krajina Serbs

[12] Intercept, Karadžić and Milošević, n.d. but probably September 6, 1991, ICTY, PSM, Exhibit P613, Tab 37, BCS 0206–6246–0206–6249.

[13] Intercept, Karadžić, Lieutenant Colonel Bojović, and Colonel General Blagoje Adžić, September 6, 1991, ICTY, PSM, Exhibit P613, Tab 39, BCS 0206–6299–0206–6304.

home. "If we decide to provoke [the Croats] and do that now," he explained, "it will suit them well, since they can hardly wait to say, 'See, the Serbs do not want a ceasefire, the army [JNA] does not want a ceasefire.'"

Adžić then told Karadžić that Croat commanders had been ordered to provoke the JNA into attacking the crossroads at Okučani, and he had hard evidence that Karadžić's information was a Croat-inspired trap. "See, today we published an order we intercepted which [the Croats had] issued, commanding that this crossroads in Okučani has to fall [to the JNA] at any cost.... And that is exactly what they want, to challenge the army to launch an attack ... then they can say, 'You see, the army does not want a ceasefire'." Calmly, without making a direct accusation, Adžić suggested that Karadžić had fallen for the Croat ruse.

Karadžić was displeased that Adžić refused to act, but he promised to restrain the Bosnian Krajina Serbs. "I will work in that direction," he assured the general. Adžić expressing himself more firmly, sought to make sure that Karadžić understood. "I think it would be a good idea to call [ARK Assembly President] Kuprešanin after all," he told Karadžić, and for the Bosnian Krajina Serbs "not to make problems about it, not to start mobilizing or something like that." Karadžić agreed, but instead of calling the volatile Kuprešanin, Karadžić rang Radoslav Brdjanin, his most trusted lieutenant in Bosnian Krajina, and told him to calm the agitated Serbs.[14] Brdjanin reluctantly agreed and soon thereafter suspended the ill-advised mobilization of volunteers. To the relief of their senior political leaders, the hotheaded Serbs of Bosnian Krajina stayed home.

Karadžić spoke to General Adžić the next morning to report that he had managed to restrain the Bosnian Krajina Serbs.[15] As in his first conversation with Adžić, Karadžić failed to get what he wanted, but he accepted what he was told. He promised to make the best of the situation: "Very well. I will not be able to comfort them much but I'll tell them I was in contact with you and that they should hold back as much as they can." Even though he failed to get the military intervention he sought, Karadžić had boosted his reputation for loyalty to the JNA's senior commanders.

INCIDENTS AT BOSANSKA KRUPA AND OTOKA

New trouble arose in the municipality of Bosanska Krupa on September 8, the second day of EC-sponsored talks in The Hague. On that morning, Bosnian

---

[14] Intercept, Karadžić and Radoslav Brdjanin, September 6, 1991, ICTY, PSM, Exhibit P613, Tab 40, BCS 0206–6375–0206–6377.

[15] Intercept, Karadžić and Adžić, September 7, 1991, ICTY, PSM, Exhibit P613, Tab 42, BCS 0206–6305–0206–6310.

police stopped a vehicle on the road between the town of Bosanska Krupa (largest in the municipality with which it shared a name) and the village of Otoka, both close to the Una River, the border between Bosnia and Serb-controlled territory in Croatia. (See Map 4.1) The car was transporting four men, one of whom fled when the occupants were asked to produce identification. Police detained the other three upon determining that they were clad in SAO Krajina army camouflage uniforms and carrying black ski masks. The three were taken to the police station in Bosanska Krupa, but shortly thereafter another ten or so SAO Krajina soldiers wearing masks appeared at the police station to demand the release of their three fellow soldiers. Police agreeably turned the three soldiers over to the newly-arrived troops, and the SAO Krajina force promptly and peacefully left Bosnian territory using the bridge into Serb-held areas in Croatia.[16]

Concerned by the ease with which SAO Krajina soldiers could enter and exit their municipality, Bosniaks of the local SDA branch mobilized reserve policemen and set up patrols on the bridges across the Una River to intercept possible Serb armed incursions from Croatia. There was nothing particularly unusual about this step. At that time, police officials and local leaders from all political groups occasionally established checkpoints around villages and on roads and bridges. Locals grew accustomed to groups of military-aged men with hunting rifles hanging around checkpoints, typically chain-smoking, drinking, and bored. Such local patrols generally conducted only perfunctory inquiries and allowed vehicles to proceed.

The evening of September 8 was different. A few hours after the three RSK troops were freed in Bosanska Krupa, a car bearing JNA license plates and transporting Milan Martić, then SAO Krajina's Minister of the Interior, approached the bridge across the Una. Within minutes, Serbia's Minister of Interior Jovića Stanišić called Karadžić from Belgrade to relay information, as yet unconfirmed, that a JNA car transporting Martić had been detained while crossing the bridge. Stanišić reported that Martić was being held in the police station in the village of Otoka on the Bosnian side of the border with Croatia.[17] Thus began the Otoka incident.

When told by Stanišić of Martić's detention, Karadžić first assumed that this report referred to the earlier incident involving three low-ranking RSK soldiers. Scoffing at the idea that Martić was involved, Karadžić said to Stanišić, "No, no, Martić wasn't there." He then leapt to the conclusion that the story

[16] *Oslobodjenje*, September 10, 1991, p. 3.
[17] Intercept, Karadžić and Jovića Stanišić, September 8, 1991, ICTY, PSM, Exhibit P613, Tab 44, BCS 0206–6190–0206–6192.

of Martić's arrest, like the exaggerated reports of Serbs being slaughtered at Okučani, was a Croat provocation designed to elicit a heavy-handed Serb response. Nonetheless he blamed the Bosniaks without knowing much of what happened. "They need a crisis and I think they staged it all," he told Stanišić. As with the episode of the killings in Kravica several days earlier, Karadžić showed little curiosity about the underlying facts and rushed to conclude that Bosniaks or Croats had incited the incident.

Still apparently referring to the Bosanska Krupa incident with the three soldiers, Karadžić told Stanišić that Milan Babić had already investigated the matter. "It is all staged, because Babić has no information about it; he investigated whether any groups went anywhere, and there is nothing about this," he told Stanišić. He further insisted that Serbs from Croatia need not interfere in Bosnia, as Bosnian Serbs required no assistance from their fellow Serbs in Croatia. "They should be told not to go anywhere in Bosnia because in our municipalities we keep things in hand, no need for anyone to come anywhere," he said. "They have no need to come at all; those [soldiers] are not Martić men for sure but they need a crisis and drama and so on."

Karadžić further told Stanišić that he discerned a Croat plot in rumors of murdered Serbs in Okučani, conveniently omitting that he was only repeating Adzić's report. "They were looking for an opportunity for someone to make a move so they can fuck up the conference in The Hague," he told Stanišić. Like his mental restructuring of the SDS founding a year before, Karadžić in this conversation positioned himself as the architect of events that had, in fact, been shaped by others. He boasted to a senior official of Serbia that he held Bosnian affairs firmly in his grasp and needed no assistance from Serbs in Croatia.

Karadžić was flat wrong in dismissing Stanišić's information. Martić was indeed in Bosnian police custody, and reports to that effect were no invention. A group of local Bosniak reserve policemen had stopped Martić's car as it crossed the bridge, recognized Martić, and escorted the four occupants to the local police station in Otoka at about 10:00 p.m. on September 8.[18] A crowd of Bosniaks gathered and surrounded the building to prevent Martić and his party from departing. As word spread, the crowd grew through the night to number several thousand, leaving Martić and his three companions

---

[18] Three newspaper accounts, the titles of their articles translated here to indicate their viewpoints, provide details of the Otoka episode: "Rastjerani suzavcem" (Dispersed with tear gas), *Oslobodjenje*, September 10, 1991, p. 3, is from the Yugoslav news agency Tanjug; "Pod kišom kamenja i metaka" (Under a hail of stones and bullets), *Oslobodjenje*, September 10, 1991, p. 3, was written by two *Oslobodjenje* journalists dispatched to the scene; and "Izbjegnut linč" (Lynching avoided), *Glas* (Banja Luka), September 10, 1991, p. 5. Both papers carried statements from various political leaders and government agencies.

under siege by the Bosniak mob. Some in the crowd carried makeshift signs saying "Turn him over to Tudjman" and "Death to Martić."[19] It fell to the Bosnian police – under Bosniak leaders – to prevent the crowd from carrying out either step.

Soon after hearing from Stanišić, Karadžić received a phone call from JNA Lieutenant Colonel Kostić confirming Stanišić's report that Martić had been detained. However, Kostić seemed unaware that local Bosniaks in Bosanska Krupa had earlier mobilized police reservists and established patrols on the bridge across the Una in response to the liberation of the RSK soldiers.[20] Kostić fed Karadžić's paranoia by telling him it was improbable that such a crowd would gather at that hour unless the SDA had planned in advance to ambush Martić. With this erroneous information, Karadžić finally understood that Martić's detention by the SDA-inspired bridge patrol was a separate incident from the earlier arrest of three RSK soldiers. But he still did not know that the two incidents were linked by the SDA's "mobilization" of police reservists; he assumed – wrongly – that the crowd besieging Martić had assembled on orders of SDA leaders from Sarajevo.

Karadžić went into a towering rage upon learning that the Bosniak crowd had surrounded the police station where Martić was being held. He called Milošević at 2:00 a.m., four hours after the Bosniaks had begun to gather, to ask his help in demanding that the JNA intervene to force Martić's release.[21] Milošević, surprisingly alert for that hour of the morning, did as Karadžić asked. He called General Adžić for the second time in as many days and underlined the gravity of the situation. Milošević then called Karadžić back. "[Adžić] didn't know anything; he was sleeping.... I presented it to him as being very serious," Milošević said.[22] "[Adžić] said he would immediately take measures. Banja Luka is the nearest place where there are substantial forces to deal with it immediately. It is night time and helicopters can't fly immediately, but we'll see how to deal with it as soon as it dawns. Jovića [Stanišić] tells me that some helicopter has left to get this person [Martić]."

Karadžić was not satisfied. Dawn was too late, in his view. "Nothing has left and that's the problem," he told Milošević. "I'm afraid that MUP, the Bosniak part of MUP, will hand him over to the Croatian MUP, someone

[19] *Oslobodjenje*, September 10, 1991, p. 3.
[20] Intercept, Karadžić and Lieutenant Colonel Kostić, n.d., probably early morning hours of September 9, 1991, ICTY, PSM, Exhibit P613, Tab 47, BCS 0206–6186–0206–6189.
[21] Intercept, Karadžić and Milošević, 2:00 a.m. on September 9, 1991, incorrectly dated December 20, 1991, ICTY, PSM, Exhibit P613, Tab 52, BCS 0206–6168–0206–6169.
[22] ICTY, PSM, Exhibit P613, Tab 48, Intercept, Karadžić and Milošević, n.d., probably September 9, 1991, BCS 0206–6173–0206–6176.

might arrange this, and then it will be war in Bosnia; then no one will be able to stop it."

Karadžić asked Milošević if he should call General Kadijević, the Federal secretary of defense. Sensing another opportunity to promote dialogue between Karadžić and the senior JNA generals, Milošević assented. "Better for me to call him [Kadijević], but you can call him too," Milošević replied. "One call does not preclude the other." However the Serbian president, hopeful that the Bosniaks would prove conciliatory, urged Karadžić to seek a political agreement with the SDA before calling in the JNA. Karadžić seemed reluctant to call Izetbegović, but he agreed. "I'll phone Alija now to tell him that, because I am in contact with his Vice President, and they [Bosniak leaders] are supposedly making an effort [to disperse the crowd]," Karadžić said, "but I don't believe them." He explained to Milošević that Martić's release was being blocked by the crowd of Bosniaks, not by the police. Karadžić, growing more belligerent, insisted that the Otoka demonstration justified drastic Serb retaliation against Bosniaks. "The people around there have gathered.... There are 3,000 or 4,000 people there.... It's a full demonstration of enmity towards the Serbs and we won't let them forget it; it will have far-reaching consequences for our discussions, there's no question about it."

As he sought to rally a JNA response, Karadžić received a tantalizing suggestion. Sometime after dawn on September 9, Bosnian Serb nationalist Malko Koroman, the police chief of Pale municipality in the region of Romanija east of Sarajevo, called Karadžić to propose a siege of Sarajevo as a response to Otoka events. Koroman said he had learned of Martić's detention from Serbs in the Bosnian Krajina and he promised Karadžić that his men around Sarajevo were ready to act: "You are to tell this to [SDA vice president] Čengić freely, that if Mr. Martić isn't released, he [Čengić] is going to have the entire Romanija region in action above Sarajevo tonight. I spoke with our Romanija people and our attitude is that we're not going to let things end this way." Koroman promised that the Romanija volunteers would join the fray only if Karadžić approved. "Could I be in touch with you, to know what is at hand, so that we do not arouse the people if there is no need," Koroman said, then promised that if authorized he would "stand them up completely."[23] With that, the SDS Serbs of Romanija joined the ARK Serbs in eagerly awaiting a green light from Karadžić to make war.

Surprised but intrigued by Koroman's proposal to cut off Sarajevo, Karadžić immediately sensed the possibility of laying siege to the republic's largest city.

---

[23] Intercept, Karadžić and Malko Koroman (incorrectly identified as General), September 9, 1991, ICTY, PSM, Exhibit P613, Tab 53, BCS 0323–2953–0323–2955.

He praised Koroman for his efforts and promised to take action. "Yes, yes. You have it prepared, you have to have the people prepared if they [the Bosniaks] fuck around, but I will, I will finish it now," he told Koroman. "You have the people prepared and not only you, but all of Krajina will, and we will send them all to fucking hell because of this."

Prompted by Koroman's proposal, Karadžić shared the threat with other Serb leaders, seemingly eager to exploit the Otoka episode to trigger armed Serb action. He subsequently spoke to Koljević and conveyed with relish his intended rhetoric. "They'll cut off Sarajevo!" he said. "Nobody will be able to leave Sarajevo in any direction. Nobody in any direction! ... We'll put an end to all this."[24] Karadžić warned Koljević, as he had Milošević, that the crowd's gathering in Otoka was an ominous SDA threat to Serbs.[25] In a separate call, Karadžić told Milošević that the Otoka events presented a welcome occasion for Serbs to initiate a takeover of Bosnia. "We'll take advantage of this politically," he told Milošević. "They are simply heading into a division of Bosnia, and we will ... establish our police where we are in power, because what they have done is intolerable."[26] Karadžić saw the threat of Romanija mobilization as an opportune occasion to threaten Bosniak leaders: "It's the spreading of the conflict into Bosnia and Herzegovina. Romanija has informed me that they are getting ready to seal off Sarajevo," he said. "No one will be able to leave Sarajevo, it will be a disaster. Now I will phone Izetbegović and tell him this also."

Karadžić insisted that SDA leaders had instigated the Otoka demonstration. "We don't believe their claim that this was a spontaneous gathering" he said. "The SDA has both influence and power there and everything goes there as they wish, but if the army doesn't send a helicopter and get the man out, or an armored personnel carrier as soon as possible, the danger will be great.... It would be a disaster if that happened." In truth, Karadžić did not know what role, if any, the SDA had played in abducting Martić. Nor did he care; the actual situation on the ground at Otoka became irrelevant. "I don't care at all how they end this," he told Koljević.[27] "They had no legal grounds to detain him, and they reportedly didn't even detain him, but people flooded the place when they found out he was there. We don't care either," he said.

---

[24] Intercept, Karadžić and Koljević, September 9, 1991, ICTY, PSM, Exhibit P613, Tab 50, BCS 0211–6618–0211–6621.

[25] Intercept, Karadžić and Koljević, September 9, 1991, ICTY, PSM, Exhibit P613, Tab 49, BCS 0212–8664–0212–8668.

[26] Intercept, Karadžić and Milošević, n.d., probably September 9, 1991, ICTY, PSM, Exhibit P613, Tab 48, BCS 0206–6173–0206–6176.

[27] Intercept, Karadžić and Koljević, September 9, 1991, ICTY, PSM, Exhibit P613, Tab 49, BCS 0212–8664–0212–8668.

"We absolutely don't care." Karadžić said he intended to threaten Izetbegović: "Today at three o'clock we'll inform him that the state is finished if something like this happens even one more time, and if they don't confront their local apes."

Karadžić was determined to free Martić as quickly as possible. Having been rebuffed by the JNA, Karadžić turned to the nearest available Serb forces to liberate Martić by armed intervention. He called RSK leader Milan Babić and asked him to send a unit of armed Serbs from Croatia into Bosnia to liberate Martić. He presumed the authority to order Babić to invade Bosnia: "I give you full authority – as far as the Bosnian side is concerned, and particularly these Serb municipalities, to prepare everything."[28] Karadžić saw this as a definitive reckoning with his enemies: "Milošević will inform Kadijević and the army will get fully involved. We'll bring this stupidity with our 'partners' to an end, and they'll never forget it; what they did tonight will cost them a state."

With Karadžić in a rage and Babić's RSK troops advancing on the Bosnian border, war in Bosnia seemed imminent. But contrary to Karadžić's cynical expectations, Izetbegović and the Bosnian police not only made an effort to free Martić, they acted decisively and impartially in rescuing him and bringing the crisis to an end. Izetbegović summoned the deputy chief of the Bosnian police, the Bosniak Avdo Humo, to his office in Sarajevo and ordered him to resolve the crisis in any way he saw fit. After receiving those instructions, Humo, a veteran police commander, acted like a professional cop rather than a Bosniak nationalist. Together with a senior Serb officer of the unified Bosnian MUP, he flew by helicopter to Otoka on the morning of September 9 and took personal command of the beleaguered police force there. He addressed the assembled Bosniak demonstrators with a bull horn and demanded that they disperse. When they shouted him down with catcalls and pelted him with stones, he authorized the police to use tear gas. The police then escorted Martić and the other hostages from the station in police vehicles as tear gas clouded their exit route.

Martić and his party were brought out of Otoka through a hail of insults and rocks from the Bosniak crowd. Reporters at the scene heard shots fired, but they reported that no one was injured. The Bosnian police took Martić and his three companions to a JNA installation; from there, a JNA helicopter picked them up and flew them to safety in Knin, the capital of the SAO Krajina.

The unified Bosnian MUP, under the joint leadership of senior Bosniak and Serb officers, had saved the four Serb hostages from the crowd. Martić

---

[28] Intercept, Karadžić and Babić, undated, probably September 9, 1991, ICTY, PSM, Exhibit P613, Tab 46, BCS 0219–4704–0219–4707.

gratefully acknowledged the police rescue and told Radio Belgrade in an interview that the "police in Otoka were very correct."[29] The Banja Luka newspaper *Glas* likewise praised the Bosnian MUP for preventing a "lynching" of the four hostages and called the decisive police action a "successful test of the state organs of Bosnia and Herzegovina."[30] The public did not learn that the RSK force had been poised to attack. The police had acted just in time. Babić's troops stood down, and an incendiary engagement with Bosnian security forces on Bosnian soil was barely averted.

Karadžić was unmoved by the Bosnian MUP's courageous rescue. He issued a public statement filled with harsh criticism and vehement hostility.[31] Calling the episode a "demonstration of hatred against the Serb people," he told the Yugoslav news agency Tanjug that the incident revealed to everyone "the kind of Bosnia in which Serbs would live if they were separated from Yugoslavia or if their constitutional legal situation were to change." Wrongly suggesting that Bosnian policemen had initiated the incident, he demanded suspension and punishment for the police patrol that detained Martić the night before. The incident resulted in "grave political damage, first and foremost to the Bosniak people," he stated. Crediting himself and his party with restraining Romanija's Serbs, he asserted that the SDS had, "with exceptional effort, prevented the people from moving, from blocking off everything that could be blocked off" in several parts of the country.

Karadžić had something else in mind. Rather than use the resolution of the crisis to calm tensions, he misrepresented the outcome to justify creating a separate Serb police force in the municipality. After the Otoka crisis, residents of Bosanska Krupa feared further ethnic violence. One journalist wrote, "Both Serbs and Muslims slept last night with their eyes open."[32] Taking advantage of the tension, Karadžić supported local SDS leaders in withdrawing Serbs from the unified MUP on September 10 to form their own police force in a separate town, leaving the residual force predominantly Bosniak in composition.[33] Karadžić and Krajišnik falsely claimed that Bosniaks had initiated the separation by "distributing the police station's weapons solely to Muslims," and that this may have delivered a "final blow to peace in Bosanska Krupa." By misrepresenting the nature of police and Bosniak behavior during the Otoka crisis, Karadžić succeeded in making

[29] Belgrade (Tanjug, the Belgrade-based wire service serving all media in Yugoslavia), *Oslobodjenje*, September 10, 1991, p. 3.

[30] *Glas*, September 11, 1991, p. 2.

[31] *Oslobodjenje*, September 10, 1991, p. 3; *Glas*, September 10, 1991, p. 5.

[32] *Glas*, September 11, 1991, p. 11.

[33] *Òslobodjenje*, September 11, 1991, p. 4.

Bosanska Krupa the first municipality with its police divided between Serb and largely Bosniak forces.

Despite his volcanic rage throughout the Otoka crisis, Karadžić exercised surprising restraint when it came to authorizing his Serb followers to commit violence. Karadžić either persuaded himself or was persuaded by others to halt the advance of RSK troops into Bosnia. He also refrained from authorizing Koroman and the Romanija volunteers to seal off Sarajevo, and he chose not to order Serb-commanded police in nearby municipalities to rescue Martić and the other three hostages. At most times during the four sequential crises of early September, Karadžić had suspended his normally acute rational judgment, abandoned his pursuit of the facts, and vented his rage at the affronts, both real and imagined, inflicted by SDA leaders. But he wisely and quietly denied his combat-eager fellow Serbs the order to advance into Bosnia.

Events in Otoka proved seminal in the lead-up to the Bosnian war. For the first time, Karadžić on his own initiative had convinced the JNA to intervene in Bosnia on Serbs' behalf. And despite his restraint, the changes in Karadžić wrought by the Otoka affair were profound and enduring. He had previously disparaged Alija Izetbegović and the SDA, but after the Otoka affair he repeatedly evidenced a deep desire to punish physically the Bosniak leaders and their followers. In a profanity-laced diatribe during a phone conversation with Milan Babić, Karadžić insisted that his new-found antipathy toward Bosniak activists would endure permanently. "In that part of Krupa they will never again be able to do that," he said to Babić as the crisis was coming to an end. "Tonight ... they have changed some things within me. They will not do that again, they will not; that will cost them, and they will remember what they have done here."[34]

Karadžić's metamorphosis in autumn 1991 was not so much ideological as passionate and personal. By August 1991 he had been a convinced nationalist for over a year, and the measured, dispassionate views of his first days in politics had given way to beliefs typical of contemporary Serb nationalists. Under pressure of the four crises in early September 1991, his anger forged within him a steely resolve to impose the will of the Serb people on Bosnia at any cost. Furthermore, his previously private anger finally broke out in public after the four crises of September. As his rage rose in response to behavior by Bosniaks and Croats that he viewed as provocative, he would spew forth the toxic words of the disappearance dialogue at the podium of the Bosnian Parliament.

---

[34] Intercept, Karadžić and Milan Babić, September 8, 1991, ICTY, PSM, Exhibit P613, Tab 46, BCS 0219-4704–0219-4707.

HEART OF DARKNESS: THE DISAPPEARANCE
DISCOURSE EMERGES IN PUBLIC

After a lengthy summer break, the Bosnian Parliament reconvened in late September 1991 to debate Bosnia's future constitutional relationship with Yugoslavia. SDA and HDZ delegates proposed that the parliament "draw attention" to declarations of Bosnia's sovereignty contained in constitutional amendment 60 of July 1990 (discussed in the Introduction), which everyone understood to be a major step toward Bosnia's independence. The HDZ and SDA joined in submitting two documents: a "Memorandum: Letter of Intent," called here simply the "memorandum," and a "Platform on the Position of Bosnia and Herzegovina and the Future Organization of the Yugoslav Community," referred to here as the "platform."[35] Both documents contained carefully-formulated constitutional arguments and temperate language that seemed calculated to avoid offending their opponents.

Karadžić, however, was outraged. With jut-jawed belligerence, Karadžić denounced the HDZ and SDA in Parliament for initiating Bosnia's secession from Yugoslavia. His bitter determination and wrathful vengeance inflamed the SDS delegates well before the parliamentary vote on the memorandum and platform. He would "never accept a document that took Serbs out of Yugoslavia," he vowed on October 14. "Secession could ignite the flame of civil war in Bosnia,"[36] he warned. He seemed at times receptive to compromise. After a flurry of behind-the-scenes negotiations on the same day, he fleetingly reached an agreement with Izetbegović to renounce the use of force and to submit the two proposals to a referendum. Such tentative agreements among party leaders were commonplace in Parliament, but they were not always ratified by rank-and-file delegates of each party. After further belligerent language from Karadžić, Croat leaders and some Bosniak delegates swept the verbal accord aside.[37] Nevertheless, Karadžić found in the short-lived agreement a basis to claim for the rest of his life that his adversaries had broken their word and again betrayed the Serbs.

Airing his disappearance discourse, Karadžić named the "Serb people" – if he identified anyone at all – as the probable initiator of the Bosniaks' extermination, while acknowledging that Serbs, too, might experience many casualties. Karadžić always avoided implicating himself as a protagonist in

---

[35] Socialist Republic of Bosnia and Herzegovina, *Službeni list*, no. 32, October 16, 1991, items 356 and 357. The published official version differs little from the drafts submitted by SDA and HDZ leaders.
[36] *Oslobodjenje*, October 15, 1991, p. 3.
[37] *Oslobodjenje*, October 16, 1991, p. 3.

the final Serb reckoning: the words "I" and "we" were markedly absent from
the ominous prognoses he recited in many phone conversations. He claimed,
then and later, to be unable to prevent Serbs from wreaking bloody revenge
on non-Serbs. This was the curious logic whereby Karadžić, the undisputed
leader of the Bosnian Serb nationalists, denied his own culpability for whatever harm might come to his adversaries. In private, and increasingly in public, Karadžić revived some of the fatalistic sensibility and images that had
marked his youthful poetry: brooding, unpredictable, powerful forces were
about to unleash themselves from the subterranean world of nature to wreak
havoc on the world.

On October 12, 1991, two days before the scheduled parliamentary vote on
the platform and memorandum, Karadžić spoke at length by phone with his
friend and fellow writer Gojko Djogo, who was then in Belgrade. Karadžić
predicted that Izetbegović would begin a conflict. "They are preparing for
war," Karadžić told Gjogo. "I think they should be beaten if they start a war. . . .
They will disappear, that people will disappear from the face of the earth if
they insist now."[38] Serbs had, he said, already been too generous in the negotiations: "Their only chance was to accept what we offered them. . . . We offered
them too much. . . . They do not understand . . . how Serbs seethe, how Serbs
ignite with anger slowly but burn long once they are aroused; they have no
idea."

Karadžić said, "I cannot make these Muslims – our 'partners' – I cannot
make them understand; shall I say, 'screw you, don't you know that the Serbs
will fight to the last Serb for their state?'" He accused Bosniak leaders of
endangering their own people by refusing Serb demands, "I have told them in
private a hundred times," he said to Djogo, "Don't live in denial, there is no
chance that we would sign anything for you; in two hours the whole of Bosnia
would rise and burn!"

The consequences of Bosnia's secession would, he warned, be horrific: "They do not understand that there would be rivers of blood ['blood
to the knees'] and that the Muslim people would disappear," he exclaimed.
"Impoverished Muslims would disappear, those who don't know where they
are headed or where he [Izetbegović] is leading them, to what he is leading
them." Karadžić singled out the Bosniaks of Sarajevo as destined for disappearance: "They must know, man, that there are 20,000 armed Serbs around
Sarajevo. That is not normal! They will disappear. Sarajevo will be a melting
pot in which 300,000 Muslims will die; they are not normal." He believed the

---

[38] Intercept, Karadžić and Gojko Djogo, October 12, 1991, ICTY, PSM, Exhibit P613, Tab 88,
BCS 0212–8922–0212–8935.

Muslim leaders failed to understand how vulnerable their people were. "I'll now have to tell them openly, people, don't push your fucking luck – there are three, four hundred thousand armed Serbs in Bosnia."

As he continued speaking to Djogo, Karadžić began to specify who should be killed and who should be spared. His threats were directed not against pro-Yugoslav Bosniaks, but against Bosniak nationalist leaders and those who were armed. "As far as the leadership is concerned, there should be no, no hesitation; they must know that if they want to secede, they will have to, to start a war against us and to hit and beat us, and then they will get their answer back and, and that is clear." After these ruminations on the mass extermination of the Bosniaks, Karadžić ended the conversation with pleasantries. "Say hello to Vera and the kids," he told Djogo.

The day after speaking with Djogo, Karadžić repeated some of his apocalyptic vision to Krajišnik.[39] Referring to himself in the third person, Karadžić spoke as if he were an impersonal observer of the bloody outcome. "That has nothing to do with the decision of Karadžić or the decision of anyone else," he said. Then he returned to the disappearance discourse, this time concentrating on Sarajevo, where he foresaw that many Bosniaks, and even some Serbs, would perish. "After two or three days Sarajevo will disappear and there will be 500,000 dead; after a month Muslims will disappear in Bosnia, the number of Serbs will be diminished; the Croats will surely profit the most, because they will keep their municipalities, " he stated.

Until mid-October 1991, Karadžić had shared these threats and foreboding fantasies with only a few associates and friends in private conversations. But in the waning hours of the Bosnian Parliament's 8th session, he vented those feeling for the first time in public, irrevocably alienating most non-Serbs and publicly threatening Bosniaks with mass extermination.

Parliament began deliberating at 10:00 a.m. on October 14, and the debates went well past midnight into October 15. Just before a vote was to be taken, Karadžić took the podium to denounce the proposed SDA-HDZ referendum and platform. Repeatedly wagging his finger at the delegates and throwing his mane of hair back from his forehead, he alternately implored and threatened delegates of the other two nationalist parties. "I am trying, in the calmest way possible to ... tell you that the Serb people know what you want," he declared. "You want to achieve [it] in [negotiations at] The Hague, to show that you are the third or the fourth [republic] that doesn't want to live in Yugoslavia anymore, but you can't do that, because we want to live in Yugoslavia."

---

[39] Intercept, Karadžić and Krajišnik, October 13, 1991, ICTY, PSM, Exhibit P613, Tab 89, BCS 0321–9651–0321–9654.

Increasingly consumed by his anger, Karadžić gradually slipped into the disappearance discourse. "After the constitutional violence, all other violence will come, we won't be consulted regarding the situation anymore," he declared, "knowing that in Bosnia and Herzegovina, that hell would be one thousand times worse and there would be no way to stop it." He returned briefly to persuasion and pleading: "I am asking you one more time, I am not threatening, but asking, to take seriously the interpretation of the political will of the Serb people."

Then, using the passive voice, he reverted to his former dark visions of Bosniak disappearance. "It is not good what you are doing. This is the road that you want Bosnia and Herzegovina to take, the same highway of hell and suffering that Slovenia and Croatia went through." Stabbing at the lectern with his finger, he uttered a convoluted threat of disappearance in just the formulation that Krajišnik had warned him against six weeks before. "Don't think that you won't lead Bosnia and Herzegovina into hell and possibly the Muslim nation to disappear, for the Muslim people will not be able to defend itself if it comes to war here!"[40]

Karadžić's agitated pronouncement roiled the hall. Bosniak and Croat delegates shouted denunciations before Krajišnik gaveled them back to order. After Karadžić took his seat, Izetbegović went to the podium to respond. Calm and composed, Izetbegović chose his words carefully. "Karadžić's presentation, his manner and his message, all explain just why we may not remain in Yugoslavia,"[41] Izetbegović said.

Krajišnik then invoked his prerogative as parliament president and adjourned the session before a vote could be taken on the memorandum or platform.[42] But the HDZ and SDA delegates were determined to act. As Karadžić and the SDS delegates gathered their papers and briefcases and slowly filtered out of the hall, Parliament Vice President Mariofil Ljubić, an HDZ member, reconvened the session as chair. When he called for votes on the proposed platform and draft memorandum, the remaining delegates voted 136 in favor of the platform and 133 in favor of the memorandum, with a few abstentions for each. Then, as a final blow to SDS hopes for keeping Bosnia in Yugoslavia, the delegates rejected a social democratic counterproposal by a vote of 124 to 0 with 12 abstentions. Before Ljubić closed the session, delegates also voted

[40] Videotape, Republic of Bosnia and Herzegovina, Parliament, Karadžić, October 15, 1991, ICTY, PMK, Exhibit P69, ERN V000–0270.

[41] *Oslobodjenje*, October 15, 1991, p. 1.

[42] "Zapisnik 8. zajedničke sjednice vijeća Skupštine Socijalističke Republike Bosna i Hercegovina, ordžane 10, 11. i 14. oktobra 1991. godine," ICTY, PMK, Exhibit 67A, BCS 0218–9560–0218–9564.

down an alternative draft memorandum submitted earlier by members of the left opposition.

Karadžić was furious. Later in the day of October 15, in a conversation with his brother Luka, he went on a verbal rampage.[43] "This is an illegal continuation of the Parliament, because the president [Krajišnik] adjourned the session.... It is not only a rump, it's illegal." He predicted that Bosnia's Serbs would go eagerly to war: "This is a huge battle, you know, but none of the Serbs, not even a half a percent of them, is against what we're doing, no way." He repeated the threats he had uttered a few hours before. "That would mean war to their extinction," he declared. This time, he specified both the perpetrators and victims: "The Serbs would never forgive them [the Bosniaks] such a thing, it would destroy them completely. First, none of their leaders would survive. They'd all be killed in three to four hours. They'd stand no chance of surviving whatsoever." The sentiments he voiced in private were more specific, but his venomous intent was equally clear in public and private pronouncements.

The Bosnian Parliament's stormy session of October 14–15 marked several milestones. The votes taken in the absence of SDS delegates ended any hope of interparty consensus in the Bosnian Parliament. In the last few hours of the Parliament's Eighth Session, Bosniaks of the SDA and Croats of the HDZ had routed Karadžić and the SDS, nullified the veto power that Serb leaders had counted upon, and ended the last real prospect that Bosnia would remain in Yugoslavia. And for the first time in public, Karadžić predicted the physical annihilation of the Bosniak people if their leaders did not yield to his demands.

Karadžić had spent all of September and half of October 1991 reacting to events that he perceived as affronts to Serbs. His rage led him to state explicitly that Bosniaks faced the danger of perishing. Perhaps with the counsel of cooler heads, he curtailed his use of the disappearance discourse after October 15. But having imbibed the vitriolic language of hyperbolic Serb nationalism, he was compelled by its imperatives to act. His rage arose from his disdain for Bosniak political leaders who refused to capitulate to Serb demands and from his own inability to foresee or control events. But rage gave Karadžić no mechanism to control the situation and move his agenda forward. To gain the initiative and control events, Karadžić needed something more. He needed a plan.

---

[43] Intercept, Radovan Karadžić, Miodrag Davidović, and Luka Karadžić (Radovan's brother), October 15, 1991, ICTY, PSM, Exhibit P613, Tab 93, BCS 0211–6649–0211–6660.

6

Visionary Planner

"Every Serb has a pistol and a map."

Momčilo Krajišnik
February 28, 1992[1]

Karadžić's period of rage came to an abrupt end following the conclusion of the Bosnian Parliament's Eighth Session. With no apparent hesitation or introspection, he introduced a new strategy only hours after the session closed. In one of the most dramatic transformations of his life, Karadžić the enraged firebrand became Karadžić the visionary architect and systematic planner. His new path led him, with still more twists and turns, to the war and mass atrocities that would make him infamous.

A NEW COURSE

Karadžić implemented a new strategy for the Bosnian Serb nationalists consisting of two tracks: publicly creating the infrastructure of a separate Bosnian Serb state, and privately implementing a municipal strategy for a Serb nationalist armed takeover. Each component depended on the success of the other. The new institutions of state were to authorize, oversee, and legitimize the municipal strategy, while municipal-level authorities were to seize control of territories to be governed by the new institutions. Until mid-December 1991, the two tracks were intertwined. Then, on December 19, Karadžić issued a set of detailed instructions to municipal SDS leaders to seize power locally and thereby pursue separately the municipal strategy and public activities of statemaking.

[1] BSA, 8th Session, February 28, 1992, SDS Delegates' Club, BCS SA01–1349–SA01–1415.

Karadžić's new strategy accounted more than any other factor for the success of the Serb nationalist project in Bosnia. Only the party's close alliance with the JNA rivalled it in importance. He and his fellow SDS members planned more systematically and thoroughly than the SDA, the HDZ, or the social democrats of the left opposition. Many published accounts of the war, written without access to SDS documents in the ICTY archives, fail to note the SDS strategic shift of mid-October and therefore understate the importance of SDS municipal-level planning. But the Serb-generated documents in the ICTY archives show that Karadžić and his associates meticulously premeditated the Serb seizure of power and planned for war should diplomacy fail.

As they pivoted from the goal of remaining in Yugoslavia to building a new state, Bosnian Serb nationalists were most concerned with establishing the political legitimacy of their new polity. They initiated two key steps also taken by several other nationalist movements in Yugoslavia at the time: they formed a single-nation legislative body and held a plebiscite to ratify their movement's popular legitimacy. In doing so, they elaborated romantic nationalist themes to mobilize the Bosnian Serbs and cited the Yugoslav and Bosnian constitutions to construct an intellectual justification for their separatist project.

Within hours of the end of the Bosnian Parliament's Eighth Session on October 15, Karadžić acted to channel his outrage against the SDA and HDZ. Late in the day, he convened a meeting of the SDS Party Council, an advisory body with considerable influence but no apparent formal decision-making role in the party. At the meeting, the party's senior intellectuals joined top political operatives in offering advice for subsequent action to achieve the Bosnian Serb utopia. They generally agreed to use populist democratic practices to form Serb-dominated institutions much like those that Croatia's Serbs had created. Their deliberations show that Karadžić shared the views of the attendees in favoring a turn toward a separate state and was largely "leading from behind" in implementing the new strategy.[2]

Most participants in the SDS meeting agreed that the SDA and HDZ should be given an ultimatum and a deadline to rescind their votes in favor of the memorandum and platform. Although the leaders of those parties were unlikely to comply, the SDS leaders favored giving them a week to reconsider. Aleksandar Buha, later named the first Foreign Minister of Republika Srpska, advocated organizing a separate Serb legislative body only if their adversaries refused to retract their votes. "We must request the [Bosniak-Croat] coalition

---

[2] "Srpska demokratska stranka Bosne i Hercegovine. Savjet stranke, Zabilješke," October 15, 1991, ICTY, PMK, Exhibit P67A, BCS 0055–1718–0055–1722. All quotations and information from the meeting are taken from these typewritten notes.

to revoke the adopted decision and, if not, we shall establish a Serbian Assembly," he said. Koljević favored organizing a plebiscite before convening such a body. "We should ... hold the plebiscite for Yugoslavia as a federal state with Serbia and Montenegro as soon as possible," he urged. Milorad Ekmečić agreed. "The plebiscite will not only confirm that the Serbs do not wish to leave Yugoslavia, but also that the Croats and the Muslims wish to do so," he said. "Therefore we need to continue contacts with the leaders of the HDZ and SDA, with the aim of finding a political solution."

Several participants in the meeting expressed concern with the Bosnian Serbs' growing alienation from Europe, but they did not favor altering their position or strategy. The minutes record that Slavko Leovac, the aged academic who had sympathized with Karadžić during the student revolt of 1968, favored strict attention to legality. "We have acted and must continue to act in accordance with the law," he said. "But the actual state of affairs is such that the world does not want accurate information about us.... No one can proclaim us a minority because we are a constituent nation." Milivoje Tutnjević predicted that European powers would reluctantly acknowledge the Serb quest for independence: "All the means of partnership [with Bosniaks and Croats] have been exhausted. Europe is not our ally, because they will accept the adopted assembly decision as a fact, so do not delude yourselves that this decision has no legal effect."

Pleased that leading Serb intellectuals found consensus on steps that he himself was contemplating, Karadžić underlined their grievances in summarizing the deliberations. "The constitutional and legal orders collapsed yesterday in Yugoslavia and Bosnia and Herzegovina and the Serbian people were deprived of their political role," he told the council. "We must provide for the Serb people and their sovereignty. Our people must follow us in all the organs." The Party Council meeting proved decisive in giving Karadžić a mandate to initiate creation of a separate Serb state.

Three days later he convened a meeting of key Bosnian government officeholders who were Serbs, including SDS delegates in the Bosnian Parliament, Serb ministers in the Bosnian Council of Ministers, and the two Serb members of the Bosnian Presidency.[3] Attendees at the meeting approved and moved to implement the Party Council recommendations. Resolving the only issue on which members of the Party Council had not fully agreed, the party officials resolved first to form a separate Serb assembly and then have the assembly authorize a plebiscite. They determined that Serb delegates in the Bosnian

---

[3]   On this meeting and its outcomes, see *Oslobodjenje*, October 19, 1991, p. 20; October 20, 1991, p. 3; and several articles in *Glas*, October 21, 1991, p. 5.

Parliament would gather as a "club of delegates" and declare themselves a separate Serb assembly. They then ratified the Party Council's proposal to issue an ultimatum to the other two nationalist parties to rescind their votes for the sovereignty declaration and platform by 5:00 p.m. on October 24, 1991. Karadžić, not seriously expecting his rivals to change their minds, made plans to convene a Bosnian Serb Assembly at 6:00 p.m. on the same day, just one hour after the ultimatum expired.

With this attention to constitutional and legal niceties, Karadžić and his SDS associates laid the foundation for several governing bodies, each one authorized by its predecessor. Although the technique was of dubious constitutionality, it followed precedents the Communist Party had set in forming the Yugoslav socialist state in the 1940s. Behind each step stood the SDS, the unacknowledged but all-powerful source of all decisions. The SDS replicated the role played during socialism by the Communist Party (in 1953 renamed the League of Communists). In paying meticulous attention to legal and constitutional procedures, Karadžić was playing to three audiences: other Serbs, the non-Serbs of Bosnia, and most significantly, the international community. All three would have a say in whether the new Serb polity achieved recognition as a sovereign state.

Although Karadžić had thus far proceeded in apparent unanimity with other SDS leaders, he waited until the last minute to inform Milošević of his plans for a separate assembly. A few hours before the 5:00 p.m. deadline on October 24, he called the Serbian president and at first told him only that Izetbegović was not responding to the Bosnian Serb ultimatum.[4] "They don't intend to abolish" the resolutions, he told Milošević. "They think they're acting legally, but we will respond with all means possible." Using the "Yugoslav" terminology favored by the Serbian president, Karadžić expressed his intent to "establish Yugoslavia in all the areas where we live."

Milošević was surprised and dismayed. Karadžić, showing that his strategic planning was well advanced, argued forcefully for challenging his adversaries with a separate assembly, insisting that Serbs could no longer co-exist with others. "No, they [HDZ and SDA] want The Hague, that is, Europe, to give them a state in which we would be locked within these borders by international agreements," Karadžić declared. "We have prepared everything to create a tactical situation ... on which they will break their teeth.... Under no circumstances will we live in a country with them. Under no circumstances; that's it."

---

4 Intercept, Karadžić and Milošević, October 24, 1991, ICTY, PSM, Exhibit P613, Tab 100, BCS 0211-6674-0211-6679.

Milošević offered a simple suggestion. "Why, why don't you, I mean, have a talk with Alija and tell him exactly that," he proposed. Karadžić, who had spent the last several weeks threatening SDA leaders using just such language, made short work of Milošević's suggestion. "President, Alija is intent on his goal with the conviction of a religious fanatic and there's no talking with him," he told Milošević. He let loose a brief rant: "I guarantee you that after Friday 500,000 Serbs must rise again," he said. "This is destroying, exhausting, crippling, and dragging us into the winter and we will all be ruined."

Karadžić then sprang the news that he was planning to convene a separate Bosnian Serb assembly in a matter of hours. Milošević, taken aback and displeased with his erstwhile acolyte, asked, "Is that wise, responding to one illegitimate act with another, or to question the legitimacy of the whole thing?" Increasingly agitated, Karadžić tried to point out that the SDS was in a position of strength to act decisively. "President, we hold power in 37 municipalities and we have a majority in, in about ten more municipalities, and we will refuse to implement any of their decisions," he asserted. "It's just that I would hold back a little on that, you know, assembly," Milošević replied, "because it will be just as illegal as their session."

Karadžić cut him off. "But we have to proclaim it!" he retorted. "This is an obligation of the Serb people and the representatives of the Serb people in their executive authority, because [otherwise] they will start arresting us, they'll start pacifying municipalities by force, installing special forces, we will not allow that.... The HDZ and SDA, they are the worst Ustasha."

Milošević tried to calm him. "But I am saying that now everything should be considered without getting excited," he urged. But Karadžić was not only agitated; he was in denial. He reiterated that his plans were already in the works. "No, we're not excited at all. Those are calculated steps, and we have to establish authority and control over all our territories, so that he [Izetbegović] cannot get a sovereign Bosnia. Croatia doesn't control 30 percent of its territory [then controlled by Serbs], and [Izetbegović's] Bosnia will not control 60 percent of its territory!"

Karadžić finally relented when Milošević changed the topic, but the two remained at odds over the wisdom of convening the assembly. Karadžić was emerging as an increasingly confident and belligerent leader. Milošević, although clearly displeased, did not insist that Karadžić cancel the imminent founding of the Bosnian Serb Assembly. Over the next three years he repeated this pattern many times, reproaching the Bosnian Serbs but then giving them tacit approval and even the material support to proceed as they chose.

STEPS TOWARD SEPARATION

Karadžić and his fellow Bosnian Serb nationalists founded their separate Serb assembly on the evening of October 24. As planned, the delegates first met as the Club of Serb Delegates in the Bosnian Parliament, then unanimously voted to rename their club the "Assembly of the Serb People of Bosnia and Herzegovina" (hereafter referred to as the "Bosnian Serb Assembly" or simply "assembly," abbreviated in citations as "BSA").[5] The SDS delegates' club did not disappear, however: it met prior to most assembly sessions to prepare delegates for the formal assembly session that followed. By including only those Serbs elected to the Bosnian Parliament in the 1990 elections, when national votes were mostly cast only for national candidates, Karadžić could argue that the delegates were democratically chosen representatives of the Serb people in Bosnia. The Serb delegates selected Momčilo Krajišnik as assembly president, the same position he held in the Bosnian Parliament, and they retained their seats in the Bosnian Parliament even as they worked as a[rival,] parallel Serb body.

From its first session, the assembly was both the supreme decision-making body of the incipient Bosnian Serb state and a broadcaster of that state's ideology. Faithful to his populist values, Karadžić sought the assembly's approval for every major initiative he proposed over the next four years. Most assembly delegates proved pliant in endorsing Karadžić's proposals, and even delegates who spoke against them in debate usually ended up voting in favor. The institution survived the Dayton Peace Agreement intact to become the single-chamber legislative body of post-war Republika Srpska and continued to consist of the same number of delegates (83) as when it first met in October 1991.

As its first order of business after opening speeches, the Bosnian Serb Assembly delegates approved by acclamation a declaration of Serbs' wish to remain in Yugoslavia. The delegates then voted unanimously to hold a plebiscite on November 9 and 10, 1991, less than three weeks away. The drafters carefully specified that Serbs would remain in Yugoslavia rather than seceding from Bosnia, using language designed to avoid Milošević's wrath:

> Do you agree with the decision of the Assembly of the Serb People in Bosnia and Herzegovina, dated October 24, 1991, that the Serb people remain in the joint state of Yugoslavia, with Serbia, Montenegro, SAO Krajina ... and others who declare themselves in favor?[6]

[5] Bosnian Serb Assembly (BSA), First (Constituting) Session, October 24, 1991, "Odluku o osnivanju skupštine srpskog naroda u Bosni i Hercegovini," BCS SA01-2068-SA01-2070.

[6] "Odluka o raspisivanju i provodjenju plebiscite srpskog naroda u Bosni i Hercegovini," Republika Srpska, *Službeni Glasnik Srpskog naroda u Bosni i Hercegovini*, Broj 1, strana 2, October 24, 1991, Sarajevo.

Notwithstanding the resolution's reference to remaining in Yugoslavia, Karadžić was already looking beyond that chimerical goal. In a far-ranging speech at a closed meeting of SDS leaders sometime between the first assembly session on October 24 and the first day of voting on November 9, Karadžić outlined the strategy he intended to pursue after the plebiscite.[7] He planned to exploit the plebiscite vote to justify several actions well beyond the resolution's parameters.

In his speech, Karadžić portrayed the plebiscite as the basis to claim territory everywhere Serbs had voted, regardless of the voting outcome or the percentage of Serbs in the municipality. He advocated separation, not total conquest. "We have to save our state for ourselves," he declared, "and make it possible for them to have their state." Serbs first had to delineate their own state, he said. "If we don't manage to – the ladies will excuse the expression – mark our territory like dogs, then nothing will come of it." Although the plebiscite question said nothing about separation or delineation, Karadžić pledged to use the results to draw boundaries to claim Serb land. "It is important for us to establish how each place voted so that we can say that, out of the number of adults and the number of inhabitants, such and such a place, for example Pozarnica, or the place next to the first traffic lights in Tuzla, voted for Yugoslavia," he said, and then proceed to claim that territory for Serbs. "Then nobody will drag that area into a sovereign Bosnia.... Whatever is ours, we will record as ours."

Karadžić asked those attending the closed meeting to seize land for Serbs to compensate for anti-Serb political and demographic engineering, again denouncing allegedly discriminatory municipal boundaries. "Municipalities are not God-given. They were established to the disadvantage of the Serb people, in such a way that all Serb units in Bosnia were split and Serbs became a minority instead of having their own municipality in which they were a majority," he declared. "Let them [Bosniaks and Croats] also have a majority in their own municipalities."

At the plebiscite on November 9 and 10, most Bosniaks and Croats heeded their nationalist leaders and stayed home; only a few joined the vast majority of Serbs flocking to the SDS-run polling places. As if to highlight the SDS's insistence on national separation, Serb votes were tabulated separately from those of "others."[8] The plebiscite results attest to the near-total influence

---

7   "Govor Radovana Karadžića na 'Plebiscitu srpskog naroda' dana novembar 1991. u Sarajevu," ICTY, PMK, Exhibit P67A, BCS 0027–0628–0027–0639. This is often referred to as Karadžić's "Plebiscite speech." Quotations in the next several paragraphs are from this transcript of the speech.

8   BSA, 2nd Session, November 21, 1991, Petko Čančar, BCS SA01–2012–SA01–2016.

that Karadžić and the SDS exercised over the vast majority of Serbs, although it should be noted that most Serbs were unaware of Karadžić's plans to extend the plebiscite's mandate to justify separatism and even violence. Serb residents of Bosnia voted 1,161,146 to 398 in favor of the resolution.[9] "Others" – non-Serbs identifiable by their yellow ballots – voted 48,895 to 397 to support the resolution. Additionally, some 348,204 "citizens of Serb nationality temporarily living outside Bosnia" approved the resolution; only two voted "no." The results echoed those of earlier referendums in Croatia and Slovenia showing nearly unanimous ethnonational solidarity among voters.

Karadžić was jubilant. He called Milošević to gloat. "Where have you been?" he rhetorically asked the Serbian president. "Even my enemies have been phoning to congratulate me, but nothing from you," he chided Milošević. "This is great, brilliant, what has taken place."[10] Karadžić claimed the voting results would prevent Bosnia's independence. "We have more than a third [of all Bosnians], and we have two reasons that Bosnia cannot separate," he told Milošević. "First, ... one of the nations does not give its consent, and second, they [the SDA and HDZ] don't even have two-thirds among all citizens."

At the second assembly session on November 21, 1991, delegates began to implement Karadžić's proposal to cite plebiscite results in asserting territorial claims. By resolution, they formalized Karadžić's argument that Serbs could claim land anywhere that plebiscite voting took place, regardless of the outcome or percent of Serbs in the population. The resolution asserted that the "territories of municipalities, local communities and inhabited areas where the plebiscite of November 9 and 10 was held" were part of the "core of the common state of Yugoslavia."[11] The Bosnian Serb nationalists had already contorted the vote for remaining in Yugoslavia into an expression of near-universal Serb opposition to Bosnia's independence.

In their next decision, assembly delegates voted to confirm the establishment of five Serb Autonomous Regions (SAOs) and to rename the Community of Municipalities of Bosnian Krajina as the Autonomous Region of Krajina (ARK), the equivalent of a sixth SAO. Further stretching their interpretation of the plebiscite results, the delegates ratified the SAOs' own declarations of their existence "based on the results of the plebiscite of the Serb people held on November 9 and 10." They also cited the Yugoslav Constitution and the assembly's rules of procedure. Although the regional bodies proved to be

---

[9] "Izvještaj o rezultatima plebiscita srpskog naroda u Bosni i Hercegovini, provedenog 9. i 10. novembra 1991. godine," ICTY, PMK, Exhibit 65A, BCS SA02–0831–SA02–0834.

[10] Intercept, Karadžić and Milošević, November 1991, probably November 11 or 12, 1991, ICTY, PSM, Exhibit 613, Tab 115, BCS 0206–6164–0206–6166.

[11] BSA, 2nd Session, November 21, 1991, Milovan Milanović, BCS SA01–2026.

largely empty vessels – with the marked exception of the ARK and partial exception of Romanija – their existence posed a direct challenge to Bosnian state sovereignty and roiled Croats and Bosniaks who saw them as precursors of Serb state separation.

In overseeing these moves, Karadžić showed that he had learned some lessons from Milošević. By moving deliberately, Karadžić had made premeditated Serb actions appear to be reactions to SDA-HDZ provocations. In 1993 he explained that he had awaited provocative steps by his rivals. "Each of our moves was caused by some move by Izetbegović," he told the assembly. "By doing so, we have been justified through all this time in the eyes of the international public and in the eyes of Muslims throughout Bosnia. They do something, we do something."[12] In 1994 Karadžić recalled with satisfaction his strategy of making pre-planned steps appear to be defensive reactions. "You remember before the war, all the SAOs and all those measures followed Alija's mistakes," he told the assembly. "We had 9–10 steps that we conceived together, but we didn't immediately initiate all 9 steps; with some we initiated when Alija made a mistake.... Then the Muslims cursed their mothers and not us."[13]

By sublimating and restraining his anger, Karadžić gained confidence in his ability to control his own destiny. "Now we have the initiative,"[14] he told Dobrica Ćosić in November. "If they commit even the smallest stupidity, we have a very realistic response." He next turned to shaping a specific plan to seize power and create a separate Bosnian Serb state.

THE MUNICIPAL STRATEGY

Armed with his intimate familiarity with Bosnian territory, Karadžić oversaw development of a plan to claim much of it for a Bosnian Serb state. He and Krajišnik first gave specific substance to the plan in early December 1991 at the assembly's third session. Rather than insisting on redrawing municipal boundaries, a measure that Karadžić had long championed, the two men proposed to create parallel Serb institutions within Serb-inhabited municipalities.

The significance of this nuanced change seemed to evade all but a few assembly members, but Karadžić's new proposal had profound implications for future SDS actions. Redrawing municipal boundaries – Karadžić's old demand – might potentially be accomplished peacefully through negotiations

[12] BSA, 34th Session, August 27–October 1, 1993, Karadžić, BCS 0215–0895–0215–0896.
[13] BSA, 38th Session, January 17, 1994, Karadžić, BCS 0215–2234.
[14] Intercept, Karadžić and Ćosić, November 1991, ICTY, PSM, Exhibit 613, Tab 113, BCS 0206–6253–0206–6261.

with Croats and Bosniaks, but they would be sure to see his new proposal as a prescription for the violent division of Bosnia they had long feared. The new proposal would turn each cohabited Bosnian municipality into a micro-combat zone, fracturing the republic into dozens of individualized struggles that would offer the stronger force an opportunity to eliminate unwanted peoples from its area of control.

Karadžić had Krajišnik submit the proposal at the third assembly session on December 11. As presiding officer, Krajišnik asked delegates to authorize local party officials to "form municipal assemblies of the Serb people in existing municipalities where the SDS does not have a majority of seats."[15] In structure and nomenclature, the proposed Serb municipal assemblies were to be local replicas of the republic-level Bosnian Serb Assembly. Just as the existence of the Bosnian Serb Assembly contested the authority of the Bosnian parliament, SDS-proclaimed assemblies would challenge the right of elected municipal assemblies to govern Serb-inhabited parts of their municipalities. The resolution specified that Serb municipal assembly delegates, while meeting as a Serb-only assembly, were also to "continue work in the [existing] municipal assemblies and their working bodies, unless that contravenes the requirements for preserving the equality and interests of the Serb people." That provision, too, paralleled the position of the republic-level assembly.

The idea of creating parallel Serb municipal assemblies was hardly new. Krajišnik and Karadžić were merely singling out one approach and giving it priority over others, without necessarily discarding other options. Neither man gave the assembly much of a rationale for their recommendation, but Karadžić mentioned that he had just received a strong dose of political realism from his talks with the chief UN negotiator, former U.S. Secretary of State Cyrus Vance. Karadžić concluded that international negotiators were more likely to accept municipal-level separation than to endorse redrawing Bosnia's administrative map. He myopically speculated that Bosniak and Croat leaders might even accept the concept endorsed in the proposed recommendation. "Even the smallest community can have three municipalities, if we all agree on that," he noted.

Krajišnik immediately called upon the assembly to vote, giving the delegates no time to consider or muster opposition to the idea. The recommendation passed overwhelmingly, but a single delegate, Momčilo Golijanin from Sarajevo, voted "No." Evidently hoping to achieve unanimity, Krajišnik asked Golijanin to explain his opposition. To Karadžić's surprise and dismay,

---

[15] BSA, 3rd Session, December 11, 1991, "Preporuka o osnivanju skupština opština srpskog naroda u Bosni i Hercegovini," BCS SA02–4945–SA02–4946.

Golijanin, followed by other speakers, expressed confusion, frustration, and anger with the proposal. Golijanin began by pointing out the legal and logical contradiction inherent in the SDS position. Since the party was advocating remaining in Yugoslavia – that is, the status quo – Golijanin wondered why it was necessary to form any new bodies. "If the SDS upheld Yugoslavia, and the position of all the municipalities with respect to the JNA is known, why should we make recommendations for establishing municipalities while emphasizing that we are called Yugoslavia?" he asked with impeccable logic.

Other delegates indicated that they were uncomfortable with the idea of abruptly separating peoples as Karadžić proposed. Some were concerned that proclaiming Serb assemblies would rupture relations with Bosniaks and Croats, particularly in those municipalities where interparty agreements were being honored and good relations among local party branches allowed the assemblies to govern effectively. "We might impose self-isolation on ourselves in places where it is premature to do this, such as in municipalities where we can have a large majority, especially those with a mixed population," Golijanin noted. Another delegate warned, "In this way we are only making an unproductive ghetto for ourselves, believe me." He bemoaned the economic "position ... we are inflicting on ourselves."

Others were concerned that Serb municipal assemblies might spur Muslims and Croats to declare their own separate institutions in Serb-dominated municipalities. Serbs could hardly oppose such steps, argued Golijanin. "If we are demanding our rights in municipalities where we are in the minority," he asserted, "it is only natural likewise to expect that we give them rights in municipalities where we are in the majority." Another delegate feared that a chain reaction might be set off: "That is now the beginning, but where will it end and what will it be like? I think that, to put it mildly, chaos will prevail." Krajišnik interrupted these objections by asking delegates "not to discuss what the Muslims will do.... They will, like us, do what they are going to do. They won't ask our approval, and it's none of our business." Yet he saw that the recommended formation of Serb municipalities involved an inherent inconsistency. "We are imposing our will on them [Muslims and Croats] too, I can't say we aren't, but municipal delegates of the Serb people are in question here," he admitted.

Vojo Kuprešanin, president of the ARK, ignored Krajišnik's appeal. He expressed hope that redrawing municipal boundaries would isolate Bosniaks in tiny enclaves and render them economically dependent on Serbs. (In retrospect he appears to have been prescient in describing how Bosnia would look after the war began.) "Why are we doing this?" he asked. "I personally think that our living space and the territory where we live and work is threatened, and we must avert that danger. In fact we must prevent Muslims from moving into our territories and space." He cited a Bosniak-majority pocket in northwestern Bosnia. "In Cazin Krajina there are about 250,000 to 300,000 Muslims, and they are in a very small space," he noted. "We can simply lock them in that ring, ... it does not suit us at all for them to join us." He could hardly wait to get started. "I am for continuing to organize Serb municipalities, Serb territories, to do that faster and more efficiently, and to set a deadline by which we must carry this out," he declared.

Faced with such reservations and outright criticism, Krajišnik conceded that forming Serb assemblies should be made voluntary. "The cover letter would specify that this is recommended where necessary, and should in no case be across the board, because the latter would be unnecessary," he said. After accepting these amendments and caveats, the delegates unanimously passed the recommendation. As they would do many times in the ensuing years, they first freely criticized their leaders' policies in debate, then approved the leaders' proposals in unanimous votes.

After the third session ended at 11:00 p.m. and Karadžić and Krajišnik returned to their homes, they reviewed the session in a phone call. They were forced to concede that the assembly was no longer a harmonious gathering of enthusiastic and obedient followers. They spewed expletives, deriding in the harshest language those who had criticized them.[16] "To hell with them, both Krajina and Herzegovina," Krajišnik said. Speaking of Vojo Kuprešanin, the loose-lipped president of the ARK, Krajišnik said, "That idiot Vojo, fuck his family.... I have to coddle him all the time." Karadžić piled on: "He is always the first, the first to start discussion and he's forever spitting on and blackening something," Karadžić said. He likened Kuprešanin to members of the more radical Serb Renewal Party, who were "pure madmen whose eyes dance on the top of their heads ... and whose beards sprout."

The two men agreed to tighten the reins on future assembly sessions. "Do you know what has to be done in the future?" Karadžić asked. "They should behave, prepare experts, there is not enough room for every fool to debate, for every idiocy.... I think we coddled them too much." Accordingly, both men thereafter strove to plan the assembly sessions and control the discourse during them. But in the next few days, Karadžić went a further step. He removed the municipal strategy's planning process from the assembly and pursued it instead in private communications and closed meetings under his personal control. It was one of the few occasions when he abandoned his populist instincts and moved forward without the assembly's sanction.

---

[16] Intercept, Karadžić and Krajišnik, December 11, 1991, ICTY, PSM, Exhibit P613, Tab 135, BCS 0323–3587–0323–3590.

A SECRET PLAN

Karadžić needed a plan to seize power swiftly and certainly; merely defining territory, or attaching territories to dysfunctional political entities, was not enough. On December 19, just eight days after the stormy third assembly session, Karadžić intervened personally to impose a single, comprehensive plan to seize authority in mixed municipalities. He convened a meeting of assembly delegates and SDS municipal board presidents in Sarajevo and distributed to them an eight-page set of instructions.[17] Entitled "Instructions for the Organization and Activity of Organs of the Serb People in Bosnia and Hercegovina in Extraordinary Circumstances," Karadžić's directive was tactical rather than strategic in nature.[18] It prescribed instruments and methods of change, rather than the nature of the political and demographic changes that Karadžić and the SDS sought. Its drafters assumed that SDS municipal officials shared a commitment to seize power on behalf of the Serb people and to exclude non-Serbs from power. Nowhere do the instructions speak of "regionalization" (the joining of intact municipalities in larger region bodies) or suggest redrawing municipal boundaries. The instructions represented the new variant of the municipal strategy, one centered on creating separate Serb institutions within existing municipalities and preparing them for armed takeover. The document was leaked to the Sarajevo news magazine *Slobodna Bosna* and published in its entirety in March 1992, revealing the entire scheme to the Bosnian public just before war began.[19]

In addition to requiring subordinates to create an "Assembly of the Serb people" in each municipality (as the assembly resolution of December 11 had only recommended), Karadžić's instructions directed officials to "immediately form a Crisis Staff of the Serb people." In "A" municipalities, defined in the document as those in which Serbs were a majority, the crisis staff was to be headed by the president of the assembly or president of the executive board. In "B" municipalities, defined as those where Serbs did not command a majority, the Serb crisis staff was to be headed by the president of the SDS Municipal Board. The crisis staff was designed to reach decisions expeditiously and function with only a few participants, making it a smaller, streamlined version of a Serb municipal assembly.

---

[17] Witness statement of Miroslav Deronjić, ICTY, PSM, Exhibit P600, BCS 0344–7928.

[18] Srpska demokratska stranka, Glavni odbor, "Uputstvo o organizovanju i djelovanju organa srpskog naroda u Bosni i Hercegovini u vanrednim okolnostima" (hereafter "Instructions"), December 19, 1991, ICTY, Prosecutor v. Radoslav Brdjanin (hereafter PRB), Exhibit P25b, BCS 0025–2738–0025–2747. Quotations and summary information in the next several paragraphs are taken from this document.

[19] *Slobodna Bosna* (Sarajevo), March 12, 1992, p. 3.

The instructions were filled with directives to coordinate civilian and military undertakings for a Serb takeover. The instructions assigned a military title to a top SDS civilian official in each municipality, referring to the crisis staff head as a "commander." In both "A" and "B" municipalities, the newly-created municipal bodies were to "carry out preparations" to take over the security services and assume power in their respective municipalities. In the first, preparatory phase, SDS municipal leaders were to "make preparations to take over the staff, facilities and equipment of the Security Services Centers and prepare their integration into the newly-established internal affairs body in the center's headquarters." In the second phase, implementation, they were to "mobilize all police forces from the ranks of the Serb people and in cooperation with the command posts and headquarters of the JNA, ensure their gradual subordination." To care for Serb settlements in "B" municipalities, where Serbs were not in the majority and did not control the administration, SDS officials were told "to establish secret warehouses and depots for storing food and other scarce materials and manufacturing components, which should be removed through secret channels from commodity reserves warehouses at all levels." If implemented, these steps would assure that SDS leaders acquired military superiority, controlled the police, and could commandeer essential provisions from non-Serbs in order to feed Serb civilians.

Although the instructions went into detail about preparing to seize power, they never overtly mentioned killing or eliminating non-Serbs. Still, it is difficult to imagine that the A-B instructions could be carried out without substantial numbers of non-Serbs being intimidated, seized, expelled, or killed in the rush to consolidate Serb land and resources in mixed municipalities. Later events showed that eliminating non-Serbs, often glossed as "separation" of Serbs from others, was an indispensable part of the republic-wide Serb seizure of power.

With the A-B instructions, Karadžić standardized and centralized SDS plans to seize power in much of Bosnia by calling upon local SDS leaders to carry out the takeover. SDS operatives were instructed to create new municipal-level institutions, galvanize the party for takeover, and prepare for armed conflict. If implemented, the instructions would unleash massive political transformations and create a new municipal order wherever Serbs lived. SDS Serbs would either enjoy a monopoly on the use of force or acquire resources to become a second armed security force that would sustain and protect only Serbs. Many local SDS committees already possessed ample weaponry to overwhelm local Bosniaks and Croats, and some had enough to wage a wider war. The instructions were a critical step in Karadžić's transformation from a frustrated and enraged ideologue into the chief architect and planner of a Serb seizure of power.

Thus Karadžić took another transformative step in his personal moral descent. By sheer dint of rational planning, Karadžić seized control of himself, his followers, and his situation. He bestowed on SDS municipal officials the organizations, tactics, and authority to seize power from their non-Serb competitors. With the lethal combination of arms and a plan, Karadžić gained the confidence to face the Bosniaks boldly and decisively. "They want a war, and they're preparing for it," Karadžić told a woman in Milošević's office on January 5, 1992, "but we too are ready, so let them do it."[20] As the assembly debate on December 11 showed, however, Karadžić had yet to persuade many wary SDS municipal officials to implement the instructions he had issued.

[20] Intercept, Karadžić, Milošević, and unidentified female (probably Milošević's secretary), January 5, 1992, ICTY, PSM, Exhibit P613, Tab 153, BCS 0212–9250.

7

Euroskeptic

As he moved forward with plans to create a Bosnian Serb state in late 1991, Karadžić was acutely aware that the new polity could not be established permanently unless it won European and U.S. recognition. He and Milošević had hoped that the Europeans would apply the international legal principle of self-determination to recognize the national aspirations of Serbs in Croatia and Bosnia. They were disappointed to learn that, while EC diplomats were prepared to grant self-determination to any of the six republics, they were loath to do the same for groups within a republic or across two or more republics. The Serb leaders seemed unaware that Europe was in the grip of its own euphoria at having established and maintained the kind of multicultural society that the Serbs were intent on dismantling. But Karadžić proved to be a Euroskeptic: he had no interest in the values of individual rights and majority rule, and he took offense when EC diplomats emphasized those values in dealing with the Yugoslav crisis. This chapter relates his encounters with European officials and examines how the Europeans' viewpoints typically diverged from those of Karadžić and other Serb nationalists.

THE EC QUEST FOR PEACE

Having successfully mediated an end to the brief war in Slovenia, EC negotiators were confident they could secure peace in Croatia as well. On August 28, 1991, as Serb-Croat violence was spreading in Croatia, the EC created two institutions to promote peace: the EC Conference on Yugoslavia, chaired by the former NATO Secretary General and British diplomat Lord Carrington; and an Arbitration Commission headed by French jurist Robert Badinter. The EC charged its Conference on Yugoslavia with ending hostilities through negotiations and its Arbitration Commission with establishing guidelines for EC recognition of new states emerging from Yugoslavia and the Soviet

Union.[1] The commission was to apply principles of international law as fairly and quickly as possible to establish and maintain peace in the region. Its opinions suggest that the commission's greatest concern was avoiding further war and imposing conditions on those states seeking independence.[2] The EC was already complicit in Slovene and Croat declarations of independence, having in July 1991 persuaded those two republics to accept a ninety-day moratorium on the effective dates of their declarations of independence.[3]

Milošević and Karadžić believed that the principle of self-determination would compel the Arbitration Commission to recognize the aspirations of the Serb people. Noting that the EC-negotiated Brioni Agreement of July 1991 invoked that principle, the two men planned to cite that acknowledgment and argue that it should be applied to the Serb people as well as to Slovenes and Croats in their requests for independence.[4] They had reasons at first to be optimistic. The United States and several European countries – Austria, Belgium, Germany, and Switzerland – were structured as federal states, and dozens of other countries around the world had adopted some form of consociational democracy to preserve the rights of groups within their boundaries.

In the end, however, they were disappointed and angered by the commission's process and by its individual opinions. Commission members took as their starting point the deteriorating situation in Yugoslavia and searched for a consistent approach to minimize the likelihood of further war. "The Socialist Federal Republic of Yugoslavia is in the process of dissolution," the commission declared on November 29, 1991, in its Opinion Number One, citing referendums in Slovenia, Croatia, and Macedonia in which most voters had opted for independence.[5] In this and other opinions, the commission limited its application of self-determination to republics, ignoring sub-units such as

---

[1] The Badinter Commission's work, well studied by political scientists, historians, and legal scholars, remains controversial. See, for example, Josip Glaurdić, *The Hour of Europe: Western Powers and the Breakup of Yugoslavia* (New Haven: Yale University Press, 2011), which locates the Badinter Commission's role in the broader context of the western role in Yugoslavia's demise; Steve Terrett, *The Dissolution of Yugoslavia and the Badinter Arbitration Commission: A Contextual Study of Peace-making Efforts in the Post–Cold War World* (Burlington, VT: Ashgate/Dartmouth, 2000), p. 149; and *Yugoslav Survey*, XXXII, no. 4 (1991), pp. 17–19, specifically p. 19. Our focus is Karadžić's views and reactions to these decisions, a topic little noted in existing studies of the commission.

[2] B.G. Ramcharan, ed., *The International Conference on the Former Yugoslavia: Official Papers*, Vol. 1 (The Hague: Kluwer Law International, 1997), pp. 1259–1281.

[3] Bennett, *Yugoslavia's Bloody Collapse*, p. 160.

[4] Intercept, Karadžić and Budimir Kosutić, February 7, 1992, ICTY, PSM, Exhibit P613, Tab 171, BCS 0211–6595–0211–6602.

[5] Ramcharan, *The International Conference on the Former Yugoslavia*, Opinion No. 1, (3), pp. 1259–61.

the Albanian-majority region of Kosovo (constitutionally a part of Serbia) and peoples, most significantly the Serb people. The commission recognized the existence of peoples living in one or more republics, but it transferred responsibility for respecting such groups' rights to the republics. Specifically, each applying republic had to guarantee in its constitution "regard for human rights and the rights of peoples and minorities" and pledge to respect a number of international conventions.[6] The commission declared, "The Serbian population in Bosnia-Herzegovina and Croatia must therefore be afforded every right accorded to minorities under international convention."[7]

The term "minorities" in this opinion was a red flag for Serb nationalists; it was used in reference to Serbs in other opinions as well. Seen through European eyes, protecting minority rights was laudable for any state, but to Serb nationalists, it confirmed fears of being demoted from a "constituent nation," the highest rank in Yugoslavia's constitutional hierarchy of groups, to a "minority," the lowest rank.

As EC ministers debated Yugoslavia's fate on the evening of December 16 in Brussels, Karadžić was returning by car from four days of meetings in Belgrade. He learned of the EC declarations the next morning. Milošević called him that day with a gloomy assessment of the EC actions.[8] "That is a complete ... termination of Yugoslavia," the Serbian president told him, "if they let anyone apply who wishes to be recognized.... I think we cannot expect anything from The Hague conference or from the twelve [EC members]." He told Karadžić that the decision was grim news for the Serbs of Bosnia. "You know what will be the biggest problem for you and for all of us?" he asked rhetorically. "The fact that Alija Izetbegović will ask for recognition in the name of Bosnia."

The prospect of European recognition of Bosnia's independence angered Karadžić. "Bosnia has no right to apply," he told Milošević. "Then that is war." Milošević encouraged him to convey the threat to Izetbegović: "You should explain to Alija what it means if he sends the request." Karadžić continued: "Then that is war, then it cannot ... there is nothing ... nobody can prevent that."

As Milošević had predicted, Bosnia's top Bosniak and Croat officials felt that they had little alternative but to apply. Few actually favored abruptly declaring independence, but they saw the EC invitation as a one-time opportunity to free Bosnia, with Europe's support, from Milošević's clutches. To avoid a repeat of the raucous assembly meeting at which the memorandum and platform had

[6]   Ibid., Opinion No. 1, (3), p. 1261.
[7]   Ibid., Opinion No. 2, (1), p. 1262.
[8]   Intercept, Karadžić and Milošević, December 17, 1991, ICTY, PSM, Exhibit P613, Tab 140, BCS 0212–9217–0212–9220.

been adopted, they circumvented the Bosnian Parliament altogether. They turned instead to the seven-person Bosnian Presidency and the Council of Ministers, neither of which had procedural rules providing for a single nation to veto. On December 20, the five Bosniak and Croat members of the Bosnian Presidency voted in favor of asking the EC to recognize Bosnia as an independent state. SDS members Koljević and Plavšić dissented, calling the vote a violation of the SFRY constitution.[9] The Bosnian Council of Ministers voted 12–8 to apply for EC recognition; all eight dissenting votes came from Serbs. Bosnia thereupon applied to the EC for recognition.

On December 21, Karadžić and his fellow SDS leaders issued a defiant retort to Bosniak and Croat leaders at the 4th session of the Bosnian Serb Assembly. The assembly approved a letter to Lord Carrington, Chairman of the Conference on Yugoslavia, warning that the Bosnian Presidency's application for recognition "can only lead to the deepening of the crisis and its culmination in unimaginable and tragic consequences." The assembly adopted a decision to "commence preparations for the establishment of the republic of Serb Bosnia and Herzegovina as a federal unit within Yugoslavia," thereby declaring its intent to establish a separate Serb polity within Bosnia.

The commission's response to Bosnia's application, contained in Opinion 4, was likewise unfavorable to Serb nationalists, even though the commission's opinions acknowledged that many Serbs opposed Bosnia's independence. The commission began by noting that Bosnia had applied for recognition and expressed its desire for independence with parliament's passage of the memorandum of sovereignty on October 15. But it also cited three Serb steps taken to oppose independence: the SDS-sponsored plebiscite of November 9 and 10; the Bosnian Serb Assembly's resolution of December 21 to prepare for a Serb state; and the assembly's definitive proclamation of the Republika Srpska on January 9, 1992.[10] In view of the dispute between Serbs and the Bosnian government, the commission concluded, "the will of the peoples of Bosnia and Herzegovina to constitute ... a sovereign and independent State cannot be held to have been fully established." Serb nationalists were less upset with that wording than with the commission's recommendation to resolve the conflicting claims through "a referendum of all the citizens of [Bosnia] without

---

9   *Oslobodjenje*, December 21, 1991, p. 3.
10 Ramcharan, *The International Conference on the Former Yugoslavia*, Opinion No. 4, (3), pp. 1267–68. The commission's opinion stated, erroneously, that the assembly had "proclaimed the independence" of the Serb state on January 9. The assembly had in fact only proclaimed the existence of the state, but did not declare it independent until April 6, a nuance of little significance except to the law-conscious Bosnian Serb nationalists.

distinction, carried out under international supervision."[11] The phrase "without distinction" implied that the Bosnian government should count all votes together rather than divide votes into three ethnonational categories. Counting all votes together meant that no ethnonational community, even if all its members voted alike, could veto the will of the majority.

Other Serb-controlled entities hastened to denounce the commission's opinion. They accused the Europeans of interfering in Yugoslav's domestic affairs, ignoring the constitution of the SFRY, inciting republics to secede, and contributing to the armed conflicts in Slovenia and Croatia. "The right to self-determination and secession is the right of nations and not the right of republics,"[12] stated the SFRY Presidency in support of the Serb position.

EUROPE REJECTS THE SERB NATIONALISTS

Karadžić's blunt talk and implicit threats failed to slow the Europeans' rush to recognition. Even before the commission recommended recognizing the new states, the German Chancellor on December 17, 1991, announced Germany's intention to recognize Croatia and Slovenia on January 15, provided those two states met the EC's criteria. The commission recommendations, although formally dated January 15, were announced on January 11, 1992.

Karadžić and his associates learned of the imminent recommendations well before January 11 and prepared preemptive action. Delegates to the assembly proclaimed the "Republic of the Serb People of Bosnia" (in August 1992 renamed *Republika Srpska*, abbreviated here RS) on January 9 in a well-publicized spectacle. The session featured bellicose speeches and cries of betrayal. The assembly's resolution included the provision that its decision might be rescinded if the Bosniak and Croat leaders abandoned their quest for an independent Bosnia, but that unlikely outcome grew more improbable with a referendum on Bosnia's independence in the offing. By the time the Badinter Commission announced its opinions on January 15, Karadžić and the SDS were actively forming Serb municipalities in many parts of Bosnia.

In the end, the commission served the EC's political aims more than it followed its mandate to apply international law to the recognition of new states.[13] The commission ignored, and thereby implicitly dismissed, the Serb

---

11 Ibid., Opinion No. 4, (4), p. 1268.
12 "SFRY Presidency Views Regarding the Opinion of the Arbitration Committee," *Yugoslav Survey*, XXXII, no. 4 (1991), p. 20.
13 Brad R. Roth, "Secessions, Coups and the International Rule of Law: Assessing the Decline of the Effective Control Doctrine," *Melbourne Journal of International Law*, vol. 11 (2010), pp. 409–415.

nationalists' argument that, as a "constituent nation," SDS Serbs held an absolute right of veto over decisions of vital interest to their nation. It took no note of Serb claims that the Bosnian parliament's passage of the memorandum had been unconstitutional and illegal. The Badinter Commission's analysis of Bosnia's constitution was thus distinctly Western and literal in attributing no special significance to those ethnonational groups designated as "constituent nations" in the Bosnian and Yugoslav constitutions. The decision is evidence of profound dissonance between the EC's professed liberal democratic values and the interpretation given to the constitution by Karadžić and the Bosnian Serb nationalists. The Badinter Commission opinions rejected Serb claims, whether tendered by the Serbian government or by the Bosnian Serbs.

The Bosnian Serb nationalists, in turn, rejected Europe. Although they had anticipated unfavorable rulings from the Badinter Commission for some time, SDS leaders were crestfallen when the decision was announced publicly. Karadžić's hopes had been dashed, Koljević told Dobrica Ćosić on the day the Badinter opinion was announced.[14] "What our leader thought was going in our direction, now that same picture looks upside down, as in a mirror; it's going against us," Koljević reported. "You recognize them [various republics] one by one and, at the end, you're left with Serbia only" for Serbs. He dismissed as merely palliative the commission's insistence on democratic values: "Of course, you know, calming us down, guarantees, democratic reconstruction of our Republic and things like that, you know, are all like compresses ... so you feel a little better."

Ćosić replied with avuncular empathy. "Oh, Nikola, Nikola....What can I say?" he asked. "I'm thinking the same thing, I'm thinking the same thing you are." But like Karadžić, Koljević remained undeterred in insisting on a separate Serb state. "We cannot give up, listen, that would be a disaster ... a disaster for the entire people." With the same fatalism that permeated his novels, Ćosić said the Serbs would have to go it alone. "There's nothing else we can do, there's nowhere else we can go, we have to ... we have to persist, no matter what happens."

Encouraged by Milošević and the Belgrade leadership, Karadžić and his close associates denounced EC policies and criticized Europe's selective application of the principle of self-determination in the waning days of 1991. In so doing, they extended the narrative of Serb victimhood by lumping the Europeans together with the Serbs' domestic enemies, painting both as perpetual collaborators intent on destroying the Serb people. But even while

---

[14] Intercept, Koljević and Dobrica Ćosić, January 15, 1992, ICTY, PSM, Exhibit P613, Tab 164, BCS 0212–9303–0212–9307.

rejecting Europe, Karadžić was aware that international recognition would make or break the nascent Bosnian Serb state. Like Milošević, but unlike his fellow Bosnian Serb nationalists, he understood the EC's power to decide who would be admitted to the international community of states. Angered by Europe's failure to accept the moral and legal arguments offered for Serb self-determination, he moved to present Europe with a *fait accompli*, to be achieved by force if necessary.

CAUTIOUS CROAT COLLABORATOR

Although Karadžić rejected many premises of liberal Western democratic thought, he found some compatibility with Croatian nationalists even though it did not come easily. Karadžić had come to associate Tudjman and the HDZ with the Ustasha, the Serbs' archenemy from World War II. But he cooperated guardedly with them when their interests coincided. He and his associates (principally Koljević) pursued agreement with erstwhile Croat rivals while deeply distrusting their intentions.

Serb and Croat nationalists held territorial ambitions that overlapped in Bosnia, making it at times a battleground of contested Serb and Croat aims and at other times a buffer between them. Serb and Croat political leaders found it easy to compromise if each backed the other's claims to Bosnian territory; thus good Serb-Croat relations frequently came at the expense of Bosnia and the Bosniaks. Serb and Croat interest in dividing Bosnia again became apparent in March 1991, when Presidents Milošević of Serbia and Tudjman of Croatia met privately in Karadjordjevo, a former royal hunting lodge near Belgrade, to discuss their respective approaches to Bosnia. Both Milošević and Tudjman remained silent in public about their discussions, as journalists and other political leaders engaged in rampant speculation.[15] Although the talks did not end with a definitive agreement to divide Bosnia, the two presidents found sufficient common ground to meet again a few weeks later. They were unable to agree on a map, but they concurred on creating a joint commission to draft plans for dividing Bosnia. The commission met only a few times and failed to agree on a proposal but its neighbors' hostile intentions became known in Bosnia and alarmed its leaders.

After meeting with Milošević, Tudjman showed a new urgency to acquire Croat-inhabited parts of Bosnia for Croatia. Twice in June 1991 he summoned

---

[15] The Karadjordjevo meeting has been the topic of many interpretations and much speculation. These are summarized in Miloš Milić, *Dogovori u Karadjordjevo o podeli Bosne i Hercegovine* (Sarajevo: Rabic, 1998).

a select group of Bosnian Croat leaders to his office to discuss a common approach to advancing Croat interests in Bosnia. Mate Boban, a Croat from western Herzegovina, emerged as a Tudjman favorite. Boban subsequently became president of the HDZ in Bosnia and used his position to carry out Tudjman's wishes. "The only things beyond doubt are the national interest and what President Tudjman says," he once told an interviewer. Summing up Boban's career as leader of Bosnian Croat nationalists, the interviewer concluded that "Boban's loyalty and obedience were limitless."[16]

Tudjman drew on the willing services of Mate Boban and other Bosnian Croat separatists to increase his influence in Bosnia. In the second week of November 1991, a group of pro-separatist Bosnian Croats proclaimed the "Croat Community of Herceg-Bosna" (Hrvatska zajednice – Herceg-Bosna), an association of thirty municipalities in western Herzegovina and central Bosnia, and the "Croat Community of the Bosnian Posavina" (Hrvatska zajednica Bosanska Posavina), consisting of eight municipalities in northern Bosnia.[17] They eventually merged these and another association into a single entity named "Herzeg-Bosna," turning a neutral term referring to Bosnia and Herzegovina into one with Croat nationalist connotations.

The two associations bore a striking resemblance to the Serb Autonomous Regions (SAOs) that had been proclaimed in the preceding weeks. Taking the first letter from the BCS term for Croat (*Hrvat*), pundits took to calling them HAOs. The municipalities proclaimed as members of the HAOs corresponded neither to areas with an absolute majority of Croat inhabitants nor to areas where the Bosnian HDZ had won the most seats in the 1990 elections. Like the SAOs, the newly-proclaimed Croat communities included many ethnically mixed municipalities.

KARADŽIĆ RESPONDS CAUTIOUSLY

Karadžić was slow to capitalize on the extraordinary opportunities that Tudjman's moves in Bosnia presented to the SDS. He had grown accustomed to portraying the HDZ-SDA coalition within Bosnia as a reincarnation of Ustasha rule and the archenemy of Serbs. Warming to the Croats would force Karadžić to abandon or soften his attacks on a favored propaganda target, and in any case he was deeply suspicious of Croats in both Bosnia and Croatia. Despite his distrust of Croat leaders, Karadžić

---

[16] Miljenko Jergovic, "Mate Boban 1940–1997: Karadžić's 'brother in Christ'," *Bosnian Report*, www.barnsdle.demon.co.uk/bosnia/boban.html, viewed January 2014.

[17] *Oslobodjenje*, November 20, 1991, p. 3.

authorized Koljević to explore common ground with them. Koljević saw an opening in Tudjman's conciliatory statements toward Serbs following the signing of the Vance peace agreement that ended war in Croatia on January 2, 1992. Koljević conferred with Franjo Boras, the Croat member of the Bosnian Presidency who was known to be closer to Tudjman than the independent-minded Kljuić. With Boras spearheading the initiative, the two men travelled to Zagreb and met with Tudjman and several of his advisors on January 8. At their meeting, Koljević confirmed to Tudjman's advisors that the Bosnian Serbs were planning to declare their own republic the next day, and he expressed the hope that Bosnia's Croat nationalists would follow a similar path.[18] Koljević theatrically opened the January 8 meeting with an obsequious apology to all Croats, hoping to clear the way for a candid exchange of views. "I want to express my condolences for the great suffering of the Croatian people and Croatia at the hands of the people of whom I am a part and the misfortune that befell us," he declared. He went on to speak of impending reconciliation in terms he knew would appeal to his Croat counterparts. "Pacification can be accomplished through separation," he said. "If you wish to keep people from fighting, or create confidence among them, you first must divide them." He reported that Karadžić endorsed his foray into Zagreb. "I spoke with Radovan Karadžić about this last night," Koljević said. "We both think that this could be the beginning of an overall settlement of Serbo-Croatian relations."

Koljević next explained the Bosnian Serb nationalists' proposal for a partition of Bosnia among its three major peoples, arguing that such a confederal state would fulfill Croat as well as Serb aspirations. "Let there be a sovereign Muslim Bosnia and a sovereign Serb Bosnia and a sovereign Croat Bosnia," he declared. "We essentially proposed a tripartite community," he said, in order "to live next to each other. Not on top of one another." Achieving ethnically separate sovereign territories would "first require a reconstitution of Bosnian municipalities that were constructed to the detriment of Croat and Serb peoples," he said. "But the possibilities of transfers would exist, the possibility of exchanges."

Perhaps in disbelief, Tudjman's adviser Josip Manolić sought a clarification. "The goal of that [municipal] reorganization would in fact be the homogeneity of certain areas?" he asked. "Yes, homogenization of certain areas," Koljević replied. "We noticed that people are already simply moving, they are

---

[18] "Zapisnik sa sastanka predsjednika Republike Hrvatske, dr Franje Tudjmana i suradnicima sa članovima Predsjedništva Bosne i Hercegovine, gospodinom prof. Nikolom Koljevićem i gospodinom Franjom Borasom, održanog 8. siječnja 1992. godine u Zagrebu," ICTY, Prosecutor v. Mladen Naletilić and Vinko Martinović, Exhibit PT-3, BCS 0150–9173–0150–9240.

exchanging flats on their own, ... [so] it would be a good thing to establish an agency for the regulation of property exchange." He asserted that putting spontaneous population movements under government supervision would "raise this to a civilized level." Thus, he concluded, "It is not so impossible to divide Bosnia." The Serb and Croat participants agreed that Bosniaks should not live in areas that either of them controlled. He urged Tudjman and his advisors to join the SDS in committing to use government's coercive powers to carry out population transfers in Bosnia. Tudjman, although he arrived late to the meeting, seemed receptive to Koljević's proposals. "Whatever imagined national problems emerged, as they did with us, ... that was resolved, from the First and Second World Wars, that was concluded by exchanges," he stated. Tudjman warmed to Koljević's ideas as he listened and soon turned to practical questions of reaching their common goals. He said he was ready to move forward in the coming weeks. "When the process of Croatia's recognition is finished around 15 January, then one can proceed to defining these [matters], yes," he said.

During the meeting, both Serb and Croat participants aired their shared perception that the Bosniaks constituted the primary obstacle to Bosnia's division. They found common cause in deriding the Bosniaks for their civic political philosophy and allegedly high birth rates. "Because of what is going on at present, the birth rate and the emigration [of non-Muslims], the Muslims hold the majority," Koljević said. Boras envisioned that governments of the proposed Serb and Croat statelets should collaborate to prevent the Bosniaks from returning to their former homes. "We had the idea that if we were to delimit this territorially and administratively, then there would be no possibility of [Muslims] spreading to Serb and Croat territories," he proposed, "because building permits would be under the jurisdiction of those [administrative] parts, and [so would] moving in."

Koljević jubilantly concurred, and before adjourning for dinner, both sides expressed satisfaction with their progress. They had agreed on the need for ethnically pure territories and on using governmental authority to achieve and perpetuate the separation of peoples. Neither Serb nor Croat participants had proposed using armed force to drive people from their homes, but they did agree that population exchanges might be necessary and desirable. Europe's political leaders of the 1990s abhorred such an idea, but seventy years earlier, European and American diplomats had mandated massive forced population exchanges between Greece and Turkey in the Lausanne Agreement of 1923. Europeans of the 1990s viewed such forced migrations as inhumane aberrations of an earlier time.

KARADŽIĆ MEETS THE CROATS

Despite reservations, Karadžić personally took the next step in the search for a bilateral agreement with the Croats. On February 26, he and Koljević traveled to Graz, Austria, for a secret meeting with Croat leaders to negotiate a bilateral territorial division of Bosnia. He made the one-day trip without notifying the EC negotiators, who were desperately seeking an agreement on Bosnia's internal reorganization into ethnonational units before the independence referendum scheduled for February 29 and March 1. The EC negotiators quickly became worried by Karadžić's unexplained absence from the talks. They searched in vain for him all day on February 26, and that evening they issued a public appeal for Karadžić to contact them.[19] But Karadžić remained elusive. Although some word of the meeting leaked out, "The [Graz] talks were held behind tightly closed doors with the utmost secrecy, and neither the Serbian security service nor the provincial police would confirm that the Graz meeting actually took place,"[20] reported the Yugoslav news agency Tanjug.

At Graz, Karadžić and Boban explored, with mutual sympathy, the prospect of separating peoples, but they failed to reach a formal agreement in February. "We talked about the need to sort out the relations between Serbs and Croats in general, not only in Bosnia but everywhere,"[21] Karadžić related to the Serb Delegates' Club two days later. Of more immediate importance to Serb nationalists, Tudjman replaced several members of the Bosnian Croat delegation to the peace talks with pro-separatist negotiators. Karadžić was delighted: "Lasić has been eliminated, and a delegation has arrived which fully shares our views of how Bosnia should be set up,"[22] he told the assembly. The change left the Bosnian government delegation the sole opponent of internal partition. EC negotiators soon proposed dividing Bosnia into three ethnonational components and pressured Izetbegović to concur.

More than two months later, on May 6, 1992, Karadžić and Boban met again in Graz and agreed formally on a territorial division of Bosnia.[23] By then, armed hostilities were underway and Serb forces had seized control of much of the republic. In the agreement, Karadžić and Boban expressed support for territorial separatism and invoking the principles of the EC talks. Each

---

[19] *Oslobodjenje*, February 26, 1992, p. 1.

[20] Foreign Broadcast Information Service (FBIS), EEU-92–039, February 27, 1992, citing Tanjug in English, Vienna, February 26, 1992.

[21] BSA, 9th Session, February 28, 1992, Karadžić, BCS SA01–1356.

[22] BSA, 9th Session, February 28, 1992, Karadžić, BCS SA01–1357.

[23] *Oslobodjenje*, May 8, 1992, p. 3, citing Tanjug, May 7, 1992.

committed his side to "respect the agreed standards for defining the national territories in all disputed points, with the arbitration of the EC." The two leaders agreed that "compactness of areas and communications" should be taken into account in defining the boundaries between their respective units.[24] This signaled that the Serb quest for strategically viable territorial arrangements had superseded territorial claims based on residence.

To lure the EC into embracing their agreement, Karadžić and Boban invited the EC to arbitrate between them regarding territory along the Neretva River south of Mostar in Herzegovina. Apart from this strip of territory, the signatories professed complete unity on a territorial division and called for a "general and permanent truce," since "no more reasons obtain for an armed conflict between the Croats and Serbs in the entire territory of Bosnia-Herzegovina."[25] Major newspapers throughout the world reported with approval and relief that the conflict between Serbs and Croats was over and that war with the Bosnian government was likely to end shortly. But the Graz Agreement mentioned neither the Republic of Bosnia nor the Bosniaks. Karadžić's public relations firm in fact trumpeted the agreement's ominous import for those excluded from the talks. "The agreement overturns the mandate of the Bosnian independence referendum for self-determination for a Bosnian state," the firm's press release claimed. "Instead the mandate will be reversed. Bosnia will be divided and in its place three separate states will be formed."[26] The agreement also displeased Croat moderates who favored keeping Bosnia intact.[27]

EC negotiators were dismayed with the bilateral agreement and offended that they had not been informed in advance of the discussions. When the news broke on May 7, Portuguese Foreign Minister Jose Cutileiro, who was leading the negotiations for the EC, wrote to his fellow negotiator Colm Doyle in Sarajevo, "Could you, in your Conference capacity, try to elucidate with the principals the exact terms and meaning of their alleged agreement? And Muslim views on the matter?"[28] After learning that Bosniak representatives had not even been a party to the Graz talks, Cutileiro publicly denounced the agreement, emphasizing that the EC "completely and unreservedly rejects

---

[24] "Razgraničenje do 15. maja," *Oslobodjenje*, May 8, 1992, p. 3, citing Tanjug, May 7, 1992.

[25] Ibid.

[26] Lan Greer Associates Limited, Public Affairs Consultants, "Serb and Croat Leaders Sign Peace Deal," May 7, 1992. The press release concludes, "Mr. Karadžić is available for interviews in Belgrade." ENG 0033–2081.

[27] Ivo Komšić, *Preživljena zemlja: Tko je, kada i gdje dilelio BiH* (Zagreb: Promotej, 2006), p. 81.

[28] Robert Donia, "Bosnian Krajina in the History of Bosnia and Herzegovina," submitted January 24, 2002, including citation to José Cutileiro to Colm Doyle, London, May 7, 1992, ICTY, PRB, Exhibit P5, ENG 0033–2077.

any form of territorial division and agreement that does not enjoy the support of all three sides in the negotiations."[29] The EC negotiators subsequently disregarded the bilateral agreement, treating it as a subterfuge to draw them into isolating the Bosnian government.

Tudjman ousted Mate Boban in 1995 from his post as HDZ president at the insistence of Western peace negotiators. Boban died in 1997, remembered as a fiercely loyal Tudjman lieutenant, an ally of Serb nationalists, and an implacable adversary of the Bosniaks. One obituary writer recalled him saying, "We are bound to the Serbs by brotherhood in Christ, but nothing at all binds us to the Muslims except the fact that for five centuries they violated our mothers and sisters."[30] Karadžić could not have invented a Croat negotiating partner more favorably disposed to the Bosnian Serb nationalists than Mate Boban. Between them, they promoted separation and division at the expense of Bosniaks and dampened, although without completely extinguishing, clashes between Serbs and Croats in Bosnia.

---

[29] *Oslobodjenje*, May 9, 1992, p. 6. The EC also refused to conduct the arbitration requested by the Croatian and Serbian representatives.
[30] Jergovic, "Mate Boban 1940–1997: Karadžić's 'brother in Christ.'"

8

Imperious Serb Unifier

"What do we want? We want to realize our sovereign right, our state-forming right, here where we are. And whether we will one day create ties with Serbia, when and to what extent, that's not their business. It is important for us to bake our little state here, to stir it and bake it and to keep it together in one piece."

Radovan Karadžić
February 28, 1992[1]

In late December 1991, Karadžić led the SDS and the Bosnian Serb Assembly in laying the foundations of a separate Bosnian Serb state. Guided by senior party officials, the assembly established a Council of Ministers on December 2, proclaimed the Republika Srpska (RS) on January 9, 1992, debated and promulgated a constitution on February 28, and – in a seemingly redundant gesture – declared the state to be independent on April 7. The assembly sessions in this period served as ceremonial public performances, replete with self-congratulatory speeches, pledges of loyalty, and rallying cries to mobilize Serb support for the new state. Despite demonstrably celebrating their many common goals, however, the Bosnian Serb nationalists were a diverse and fractious bunch who resisted the unity that Karadžić sought to impose on them. During 1992, as this chapter recounts, the willful Serbs of the Bosnian Krajina again raised the spectre of regional separatism, complicating the task of forming the new state and posing a threat to Karadžić's leadership.

MUTINY IN THE ARK

As Karadžić moved to form a Serb state in Bosnia, SDS Serbs in the ARK raised a cry that the newly-proclaimed Bosnian Serb state would, like the

---

[1]   BSA, February 28, 1991, Delegates' Club, Karadžić, BCS SA01–1404.

Bosnian republic government, seek to dominate them from Sarajevo. Their objections were familiar. Shortly after the assembly voted on December 21 to "commence preparations for the establishment of the Republic of Serb Bosnia and Herzegovina as a federal unit within Yugoslavia,"[2] Serb leaders in the Bosnian Krajina demanded autonomy within the Bosnian Serb state or equal status with it. The ARK Assembly, meeting in Banja Luka on January 8, approved a proposal entitled, "The Bosnian Krajina as a Constituent Part of the New Yugoslav Federation."[3] Delegates underlined their intent to circumvent Karadžić and his yet-to-be-proclaimed Serb polity by approving a five-member commission to "have talks with Slobodan Milošević in Belgrade about the position of the Serb people outside Serbia."

Karadžić and Krajišnik were alarmed by the rumblings in the ARK, but for the time being they wisely ignored the sideshow in Banja Luka. On January 9, 1992, they proceeded as planned and led the assembly in publicly proclaiming the new Republika Srpska. Karadžić and his associates arranged a high-profile public performance to justify and promote their new polity. Speaker after speaker valorized Serbs' sacrifices and excoriated their Bosniak and Croat counterparts. The ARK autonomists in the assembly felt compelled to join other delegates in wallowing in Serb suffering, and they were unwilling to dampen the euphoria by challenging Karadžić on his home turf. Although they were reluctant to admit it, Karadžić intimidated them. Brdjanin, once Karadžić's trusted and obedient lieutenant in the Bosnian Krajina but now overtly an autonomist, addressed the assembly at some length without even mentioning the ARK Assembly's defiant resolution of the previous day. Radoslav Vukić, the mayor of Banja Luka, waited until the last sentence of his speech to suggest obliquely "that we create not individual principalities but strong autonomous regions that will defend our Serb Bosnia militarily and economically."

The same supporters of Bosnian Krajina autonomy, although silent in the assembly in Sarajevo, became outspoken on their home turf in Banja Luka. During February they intensified their campaign by forming an ad-hoc body with an ungainly name, the "Political and Economic Councils of the Banja Luka SDS and the Executive Committee of the Club of Intellectuals Expanded by Numerous Members of the Club," to serve as their forum to debate and organize protests. On February 23, that organization held a mass meeting to demand for the ARK the same level of autonomy that Karadžić was seeking for

---

[2] BSA, 4th Session, December 21, 1991, BCS 0089–8153.
[3] "Izvod iz zapisnika sa XI sjednice Skupštine autonomne regije Krajina održane 8.01.1992. godine" (hereafter "ARK Assembly" with session number and date), ICTY, PRB, Exhibits P31a and P31b, BCS 0040–3873–0040–3876.

a separate Serb entity within Bosnia.[4] They declared their resolve to proclaim a republic of their own if the assembly failed to provide for Bosnian Krajina autonomy in a draft constitution then under consideration.

Brdjanin demanded that Banja Luka be named the capital of the RS, a proposal that became central to the autonomists' agenda. "It was impossible that Sarajevo would be the capital city of the Serb people," he told the ARK Assembly, "for there would be no way to prevent the same old situation." He promised to fight for ARK autonomy in the assembly session scheduled for the next day in Sarajevo. "In Sarajevo tomorrow we must embrace the view that the cantons should be on the highest level of autonomy,"[5] he declared. In several "conclusions," the entire ARK Assembly endorsed Brdjanin's proposals.

Major Bosnian media outlets reported discontent in the ARK Assembly, raising the visibility of the incendiary Serb mutiny as a threat to Karadžić's plans for approving a constitution. The Bosnian Krajina delegates travelled to Sarajevo for the assembly meeting of February 25 with the intent of dividing Karadžić's state-building project in two. Little did they expect that their movement would collide with the EC quest for a negotiated agreement to avert war in Bosnia.

AN EC-SPONSORED PLAN TO PARTITION BOSNIA

To Karadžić's delight, the EC-led negotiations unexpectedly turned favorable to him in early 1992. When Portugal assumed the six-month rotating EC Presidency from the Netherlands in January 1992, Foreign Minister Jose Cutileiro took over as chief negotiator and brought a new approach to the talks. Cutileiro was sympathetic to an internal ethnonational partition of Bosnia and vigorously promoted such a resolution. Combined with the Tudjman-ordered changes in the Bosnian Croat delegation, the European push for partition left Izetbegović and his delegation isolated as the only opponents of partition. Already known for vacillating in the negotiations, Izetbegović came under immense pressure to agree to a carve-up. But on the home front, many Bosniaks and some Croats vehemently opposed trisecting Bosnia into ethnonational units.

In early February 1992, Cutileiro summoned representatives of the three parties to Lisbon in hopes of securing an agreement to divide Bosnia into three "constituent units." He faced a daunting task, owing to factors not of his

---

[4]   ARK Assembly, 13th Session, February 24, 1992, ICTY, PRB, Exhibit 32b, BCS 0040–3902–0040–3907.

[5]   Ibid.

making. By insisting that Bosnia hold a referendum as a condition of recognizing its independence, EC leaders had put its own negotiators under pressure
to conclude an agreement quickly. The independence referendum, scheduled for February 29 and March 1, enjoyed widespread Bosniak and Croat
support. If it passed – and it was all but certain to do so – the EC would
be compelled to recognize Bosnia's independence and thereby remove any
incentive for the Bosniaks and pro-Bosnian Croats to agree to partition. With
the date of the referendum looming as a *de facto* deadline, Cutileiro pushed
hard for an agreement before the end of February.

Cutileiro achieved a breakthrough in Lisbon on February 23 by winning
the assent of all three nationalist party leaders to a "Statement of Principles for
New Constitutional Arrangements for Bosnia and Herzegovina."[6] (The Lisbon
statement of February 23 is not to be confused with a similar EC-negotiated
agreement in principle reached on March 15 in Sarajevo, which is also known
as the Cutileiro Plan or the Lisbon Agreement.) The participants agreed to
continue the talks in Sarajevo to finalize the agreement. Izetbegović hoped to
defer the Sarajevo session until after the referendum, but in deference to Serb
demands, Cutileiro scheduled resumption of the talks for February 27, two
days before the independence balloting began.

Unfortunately for Cutileiro, the agreement in principle was reached on the
same day that the Bosnian Krajina autonomists aired their grievances in the
ARK Assembly. Karadžić returned triumphantly from Lisbon to Sarajevo on
February 24 and publicly gloated to his Serb followers that he had achieved
a partition of Bosnia. But he was immediately given the sour news that the
Bosnian Krajina Serbs were in the midst of a noisy mutiny against the draft constitution. Quite inadvertently, the ARK leaders, in publicly airing their challenge to Karadžić, gave Izetbegović a pretext to delay further EC-sponsored
talks – enough, he hoped, to delay the talks until after Bosnians had voted for
independence on February 29 and March 1. In a letter to chief EC negotiator
Cutileiro, Izetbegović wrote, "A meeting of the illegal Serb assembly [mean-
ing the Bosnian Serb Assembly] is scheduled for tomorrow in Banja Luka to
consider the constitution of the so-called Serb Republic of Bosnia ... in complete contravention of the Constitution of Bosnia."[7] Izetbegović had learned
of Karadžić's intentions from the press coverage of the ARK Assembly session.
He pleaded with the Portuguese minister to use his influence with Karadžić
to dissuade the Serbs from enacting a constitution. Unless Karadžić could be

---

[6] David Campbell, *National Deconstruction: Violence, Identity and Justice in Bosnia*
(Minneapolis: University of Minnesota Press, 1998), pp. 128–129; *Oslobodjenje*, February 24,
1992, pp. 1 and 3.
[7] *Oslobodjenje*, February 25, 1992, p. 1.

stopped, he wrote, "The meeting you have scheduled for Thursday [February 27] in Sarajevo would serve no purpose."

At first, Karadžić appeared oblivious to Izetbegović's troubling letter to Cutileiro. On February 25, at the assembly's 8th Session in Sarajevo, he and Krajišnik blithely moved to proclaim the RS constitution.[8] As the session began, even Bosnian Krajina representatives joined other delegates in approving an agenda that included a "discussion of the draft and adoption of the proposed constitution" of the fledging Serb state. Karadžić, as usual the session's lead speaker, triumphantly declared that the final communiqué in Lisbon had incorporated many points of the Serb proposal to divide Bosnia. "The principle was affirmed that Bosnia is not unitary," he noted with approval. "We never for a moment allowed it to be called a state."

Karadžić's jubilation was short-lived. An aide approached him on the podium and interrupted him in mid-sentence to say that Cutileiro was waiting to speak to him by phone. Karadžić immediately excused himself, asked Koljević to take the floor, and strode off to take the phone call. As Koljević gave a meandering report on the Lisbon talks, Cutileiro filled Karadžić's ear with concern about Izetbegović's threat to withdraw from the talks. Realizing how desperately the Serbs wanted an agreement before the referendum, Cutileiro suggested to Karadžić that the EC delegation might not appear for the talks unless Karadžić halted preparations to approve the constitution. With that threat, Cutileiro convinced Karadžić that the EC would retract the Serbs' hard-won negotiating triumph if the assembly defied the EC by voting to approve the constitution.

When Karadžić finished the call and returned to the assembly podium, his ebullience had vanished. "First, let me tell you that Cutileiro has asked for clarification because Alija Izetbegović sent a letter after the [ARK] assembly session, a letter saying that any meeting [of negotiators] would be pointless," Karadžić told the delegates. He explained that Cutileiro wanted to reach an agreement before the referendum, while Izetbegović wanted the referendum to take place before the talks resumed. But Karadžić knew that getting an EC-sponsored deal before the referendum was more important than formally approving a constitution. Cutileiro had further assured Karadžić that a final agreement was within sight if all parties showed up for the talks in Sarajevo, meaning that he would pressure Izetbegović to accept the deal. Karadžić wisely counseled the delegates to heed Cutileiro's request and put off proclaiming the constitution. "It would not be a good idea to adopt the Constitution today," Karadžić explained, "as that would be reason for Cutileiro not to attend."

---

[8] BSA, 8th Session, February 25, 1992, BCS SA01–1416–SA01–1504.

Karadžić quickly discovered that Cutileiro's telephone interruption gave him a powerful weapon to wield against the Bosnian Krajina autonomists. Karadžić redirected his displeasure against them – not so much for their autonomist impulses as for endangering his hard-won negotiating gains in Lisbon. Their well-publicized deliberations had, after all, alerted Izetbegović to the SDS plan to proclaim the constitution. But before displaying anger, he calmly made an intellectual case for unity by explaining the need for all Bosnian Serbs to preserve gains at the negotiating table. "We must make the most of what we have today and create opportunities to our advantage," he argued. Then, having first appealed to reason, he let his emotions take over, this time to great effect, unlike his futile ranting the previous September and October. He accused the ARK mutineers of obstructing creation of a Serb state. "Some of our people, whether consciously or not, make the job much more difficult," he charged. He reminded the ARK delegates of the damage they had done to the Serb cause in hosting Milan Martić's "border-dissolving" incursion into the town of Titov Drvar on June 8, 1991, and in proclaiming the unity of the two Krajinas on June 27. The ARK Assembly's separatist demands were only the latest, he said, in a series of steps that threatened to derail the Bosnian Serb statemaking campaign.

After Karadžić finished speaking, Krajišnik returned the assembly's attention to the agenda. "I propose that we discuss both the Constitution and the laws [today] and that we finish on Thursday the meeting that we intend to hold," he said. "Then we will adopt the Constitution and the laws." The delegates concurred. After debating the constitution at some length, they adjourned for the day without voting on it.

Karadžić, however, was not done with the ARK autonomists. After discussion of the constitution had ended, he took to the podium again to deride and marginalize the autonomists and to praise the "loyal" Serbs who differed with them. He verbally reduced the dissidents to a misguided few. "We cannot allow five people with personal ambitions to destroy our chances," Karadžić said. "We are very close to achieving our strategic objectives." He then singled out his one-time protégé Radoslav Brdjanin and challenged him directly. "Neither Brdjo [Brdjanin] nor anyone else can act out of step with this assembly," he said. "Once we reach a decision, no one has the right to sabotage it." Karadžić's attack had become personal, but by identifying only a few isolated individuals as the culprits, he exempted the vast majority of delegates from his stinging attack. "Maybe 99 percent of our delegates from the [Bosnian] Krajina are loyal to this assembly," he said. Karadžić found, with this encounter and others, that a strategy of restraint and generosity toward opponents was highly effective in re-establishing unity in the party.

Vojo Kuprešanin, the voluble but weak-willed ARK president, was the first to capitulate to Karadžić's withering attack. He had been an unequivocal advocate of ARK autonomy while in Banja Luka, but he completely reversed his position in addressing the assembly in Sarajevo. He rose to assure the delegates that he was firmly committed to the basic principles of the Bosnian Serb nationalist project. "I am against any kind of joint institutions with the Muslims and Croats of Bosnia," he said. "I personally consider them to be our natural enemies.... We can never again live together." He then lavishly praised Karadžić as the supreme leader of the Bosnian Serbs. "I know that Karadžić, as President of the SDS, is truly the leading figure among the Serb people," he proclaimed, "and five of his sentences are enough to change the entire course of the session."

At the same time, Kuprešanin had a duty to discharge in his capacity as ARK president. It fell to him to read to the assembly verbatim the harsh, pro-autonomist declaration that the ARK Assembly had passed only days before. No sooner had he read the declaration aloud than he hastened to renounce the very words he had just spoken. "I think we know what will happen if the Republic of Krajina is proclaimed," Kuprešanin said. "We cannot wage war for even five days because we will find ourselves without fuel. This means that our war, our Republic, our state is a mere fiction and nonsense." In distancing himself from the ARK Assembly's declaration, Kuprešanin handed Karadžić a victory over the group he was supposed to be leading.

Riding the crest of victory over the autonomists, Krajišnik offered a suggestion: "If the people of Krajina cannot secure what they want, let us all go to Banja Luka and say everything we have to say," he urged. The delegates assented, giving Karadžić and Krajišnik another triumph at the session on February 25. The assembly thereupon adjourned without enacting the draft constitution, in accord with Cutileiro's request and Karadžić's recommendation. The assembly also handed back to Cutileiro the task of persuading Izetbegović to attend the negotiating session scheduled for February 27. Izetbegović, his conditions met and his bluff called, showed up on that date as Cutileiro demanded. Karadžić appeared to have a negotiated partition of Bosnia within his grasp.

HARDENING THE SERB NEGOTIATING STANCE

After successfully routing the autonomists in the assembly, Karadžić and his fellow Bosnian Serb negotiators botched an opportunity for an agreement at the EC-sponsored negotiating session on February 27. At that meeting, Cutileiro was eager to formalize the unwritten partition agreement of February 23 but equally insistent that the Bosnian Serb nationalists acknowledge Bosnia's imminent independence. "We thought we would be discussing the competencies [of the constituent units], the division of power," Karadžić told the assembly. "We assessed that they [EC negotiators] needed the word ["independence"] just after the referendum as something that even the Serbs had accepted," he speculated. "We deem that the people in Europe can't decide on everything until they have obtained the Serbs' agreement." Karadžić described how he had hardened his stance. "We ... did not want to allow the power in constituent units to devolve from the power of the Republic," he argued, "but vice versa, that the power should derive solely from the original sovereign right, which fundamentally belongs to a citizen and a people and is realized primarily in constituent units." On this relatively minor nuance, Karadžić stood firm and sabotaged the agreement that had seemed secure only two days before. The negotiating session ended in acrimony without the agreement Cutileiro had sought.

Pushing the Serb case even further, Krajišnik told the negotiators that the assembly was preparing to fulfill deferred plans by proclaiming a constitution the next day, after having halted the earlier planned proclamation at Cutileiro's request. This was a bold assertion that the Bosnian Serb nationalists privileged their self-proclaimed institutions over a European-sponsored negotiated settlement. "That shocked them," Krajišnik reported to the assembly. "We spoke at length and said if this were not proclaimed, the Serb people would not be protected against the referendum." Claiming that the Serb people were demanding action from their leaders, Krajišnik said, "Gentlemen, we will have to pass the Constitution and the legislation to calm down our people about the referendum.... Any stalling would cause unrest among our people." Subsequently, Krajišnik warned the assembly ruefully that the Serbs should be prepared for Europe's ire. "The Constitution and legislation will be a problem [for the Europeans]," he noted. "We are sabotaging [negotiations] and can easily be blamed." He was correct on both counts, but the snub did not deter Cutileiro from trying to appease the Serbs again after Bosnians voted in overwhelming numbers for independence.

OVERPOWERING THE AUTONOMISTS

While largely quiescent in the Bosnian Serb Assembly, leading ARK dissidents unrepentantly resumed their crusade in their own assembly and in public. Radislav Vukić, president of the ARK Regional Board of the SDS, told a press conference, "The Bosnian Krajina wants to form cantons, for its goal is to retain control over the flow of funds."[9] Furthermore, he claimed, Bosnian

---

[9] *Glas*, February 28, 1992, p. 3.

Krajina delegates bore "the moral right and duty to protect tens of thousands of its soldiers who must return from the front [in Croatia] as heroes, not as war criminals, and to that end the Bosnian Krajina must have a special status and autonomy." He also confirmed that the ARK Assembly would meet in Banja Luka on February 29 at a session to be attended by "all delegates of the Bosnian Serb Assembly" in addition to its own delegates. The ARK needed greater autonomy he said, in a swipe at Karadžić. "No one has the right in the name of the Serb people to decide things in private offices."[10] The stage was set for an open clash between Karadžić and the autonomists in Banja Luka.

But before heading to Banja Luka for the confrontation, Karadžić shored up his support in Sarajevo. On February 28, he addressed the SDS Delegates' Club.[11] After reporting on the failed talks with Cutileiro the previous day, Karadžić showed his wrath, accusing the ARK autonomists of sabotaging his cause. "We are on the threshold of realizing our goal," he said. "We have taken the safe road, we have made the required moves, we have prepared them in advance, and now we have, every now and again, idiots barging in like bandits and causing problems." Separation of peoples was particularly important for the Bosnian Krajina, he argued. "Muslims cannot live with others. We must be clear on that. They couldn't live with the Hindus, who are peaceful as sheep," he asserted. "Yet they set up the Bosnian Krajina there and in two years' time you have problems again, to separate every village there, because with their birth rate and their gimmicks, they will overwhelm you. We cannot allow that to happen."

His wrath rekindled, he spared neither SDS leaders nor their intellectual allies from increasingly personal attacks. "Now we've let fifteen idiots screw the entire Serb people," he raged. The Bosnian Krajina dissidents "will have to roll over, especially after we achieve progress on the constitution," he insisted. Karadžić bitterly denounced the autonomists' ringleader. "They want everything: honor, power, money – they want it all," he said. "When Brdjo appears somewhere, he's like a bomb, he blows up everything."

In the formal assembly session following the Delegates' Club meeting on February 28, Karadžić and Krajišnik followed through on their threat to proclaim the same constitution they had held up at Cutileiro's behest only three days before. They incorporated two concessions to the Bosnian Krajina separatists. Article Two read, "The territory of the Republic consists of autonomous regions, municipalities, and other Serb ethnic areas, including areas on which the crime of genocide was committed against the Serb people in the Second World War." The constitution thus identified the autonomous regions as an

[10] *Glas*, February 28, 1992, p. 3.
[11] BSA, 9th Session, February 28, 1992, Delegates' Club, Karadžić, BCS SA01–1349–SA01–1415.

integral part of the RS territory, though without specifying what powers the ARK would retain in the newly-formed RS. And in identifying "areas in which the crime of genocide was committed," the constitution gave the ARK autonomists an elastic definition of Serb land that they could use to justify expansive territorial claims. Karadžić and Krajišnik had again shown great aptitude for restoring unity to their movement. They overwhelmed the dissidents politically and then graciously granted them most of what they had sought.

STORMING BANJA LUKA

With the assembly's promulgation of the constitution on February 28, Karadžić held a trump card to subdue the ARK dissidents. Even so, he realized that the ARK Assembly remained a hornet's nest of opposition to a unified RS, one which he hoped to subdue. But he evidently decided against moving the entire Bosnian Serb Assembly to Banja Luka to overwhelm the autonomists. Instead, on the morning of February 29, he and a few trusted associates traveled to Banja Luka to confront the dissidents in person on their home turf.

This historic confrontation took place in a setting replete with symbolic significance as a center of bygone Serb grandeur and of Serb suffering in the Second World War. In the city's central square was an empty field where a large Serbian Orthodox Church stood until the Ustasha destroyed it in 1941. On one side of the square was the Ban's Palace, the regional headquarters during the period of Royal Yugoslavia (1918–41). Nearby stood the Cultural Center, a socialist-era building with a Great Hall where well-orchestrated political gatherings had been held under Tito's rule.

Karadžić arrived in Banja Luka on February 29 with an autocratic air and an entourage befitting a head of state. Rather than transporting all delegates of the Bosnian Serb Assembly and the SDS Main Board to Banja Luka, as he had promised the previous day, Karadžić brought along only Koljević (a Banja Luka native), Krajišnik, and RS Information Minister Vojislav Maksimović. They were accompanied by a contingent of armed bodyguards, one of whom confiscated two rolls of film from a photojournalist suspected of taking pictures in a closed assembly session. But most intimidating was Karadžić himself, fresh from his triumphs with the Croats in Graz and EC negotiators in Sarajevo.

The timing, although probably coincidental, added further gravitas to the occasion. February 29 was the first of two days of voting in Bosnia's independence referendum. As Croats and Bosniaks streamed in large numbers to polls across the republic, President Kuprešanin gaveled the ARK Assembly to order at 11:00 a.m. in the Cultural Center's Great Hall to hear what Karadžić had to say. As had become commonplace in deliberative bodies at the time, the elected delegates were joined by many other influential and interested persons in attending the session, so the hall was crowded and noisy.

Jovan Čizmović, a Karadžić loyalist, first argued that the RS constitution had already made substantial concessions to the Krajina autonomists. "With approval of the Serb constitution, the cantons [SAOs] received maximum autonomy, but not statehood," he said. "If a Republic of Krajina were declared, all Serbs outside its territory would suffer the consequences."[12]

Karadžić then took the floor to do the heavy lifting. For three and a half hours he persuaded, cajoled, bullied, intimidated, and threatened the ARK Assembly delegates. Answering questions and deflecting challenges, he sought to dominate his challengers and force them to abandon the folly of Krajina separatism. "This is a national movement," he declared.[13] "[Our] program has both strategic objectives and tactical resources." For the first time, he said, Serbs "control their own destiny, such that the Serb people are a great Balkan and European power."[14] Krajina autonomists threatened those achievements, he warned. "Such actions as yours here must not be allowed to undermine all that we in the SDS are doing for Bosnia," he said.[15] "The Banja Luka SDS must harmonize its activities with the [party] program or create a new program, change its name, and repeat elections."

After several hours of testy exchanges, ARK President Kuprešanin resumed control of the meeting and instructed the unauthorized hangers-on to depart, leaving only delegates of the ARK and Karadžić, Koljević, and Maksimović. As the debate resumed with only authorized delegates present, Karadžić redoubled his attacks on the dissenters and painted with vivid images the dangers they posed. "It would be a crime against the Krajina to declare it a Republic," he said. "Those who advocate such childish ideas are exposing the Serb people to trouble."[16] To allay the long-standing fears of some ARK delegates that their lands and people would be left militarily vulnerable, Karadžić assured them of the JNA's protection. "If [the JNA] withdraws," he declared, "the remaining army will simply change uniforms, since it is already overwhelmingly Serb!"[17] After more hours of Karadžić's intimidating rhetoric, Brdjanin, Vukić, and a few other die-hard autonomists walked out, leaving Karadžić to dominate the room and shape the outcome of the voting.[18]

---

[12] ARK Assembly, 14th Session, February 29, 1992, ICTY, PRB, Exhibit P35b, BCS 0040–3935.

[13] *Oslobodjenje*, March 2, 1992, p. 2.

[14] *Glas*, March 1, 1992, p. 3.

[15] *Oslobodjenje*, March 2, 1992, p. 2.

[16] ARK Assembly, 14th Session, February 29, 1992, ICTY, PRB, Exhibits P35a and P35b, BCS 0040–3934–0040–3936.

[17] *Glas*, March 1, 1992, pp. 2 and 3.

[18] *Glas*, March 1, 1992, p. 3.

Late in the afternoon of February 29, ARK Assembly delegates capitulated to Karadžić. They voted 148 to 0 with 3 abstentions to accept the Constitution of the RS, conceding that "the status of the ARK will be incorporated into the Constitution of the RS in accordance with its practical needs in order to achieve its free economic development." As a reporter wrote, "Thanks only to Karadžić's authority, things settled down and the assembly session peacefully ended – with wholehearted support for Karadžić."[19]

But the day was far from over. Emerging from his triumph in the Great Hall, Karadžić encountered a hostile crowd of several hundred Serbs who had gathered in anticipation that the ARK Assembly would proclaim a Krajina Serb state. Using a megaphone, Karadžić gave them a dose of the hyperbolic language he had used to crush the opposition inside the hall.[20] "Yesterday a state was born in Sarajevo and has begun to walk," he declared, "and subsequently its constitution was proclaimed, which we likewise approved here." He trumpeted the historical significance of the RS constitution. "All the demands of Krajina delegates, those which could be incorporated, are already incorporated in the constitution, and now, my dear friends, the Serb people in Bosnia for the first time in history have only their own authority over their heads." Karadžić addressed a press conference to report, with great satisfaction, the resolutions that the ARK Assembly had passed.

He still was not done for the day. Some leading autonomists, after being driven from the ARK Assembly session by Karadžić's domineering rhetoric, reassembled as the expanded "Political and Economic Councils of the Banja Luka SDS." As one of their number was denouncing the evils of Sarajevo centralization, Karadžić and his entourage ostentatiously entered, creating a "terrible disturbance in the uncomfortably packed council hall."[21] Amid loud discussion and cursing, Karadžić strode to the front of the hall and took over the meeting. Eventually he succeeded in driving the leading autonomists out of their own forum. The dissidents made plans for another meeting two days hence, on March 2, but they had been thoroughly and publicly intimidated by Karadžić's booming rhetoric.

With his rough-and-tumble populist politics, Karadžić cemented his stature as the undisputed strongman of the Bosnian Serb nationalists. Throughout many contention-filled hours, he had deftly wielded the populist's twin tools of persuasion and intimidation. He had co-opted, isolated, demeaned, rhetorically overpowered, and stilled his challengers, then demonstrated great

[19] *Glas*, March 2, 1992, p. 2.
[20] *Glas*, March 1, 1992, p. 2; and *Oslobodjenje*, March 2, 1992, p. 2. Both accounts quote Karadžić and provide strikingly similar, if not identical, reports of his words.
[21] *Glas*, March 2, 1992, p. 2.

political skill in allowing his defeated opponents to concede without undue public humiliation or personal danger. From the low point of his abject dependence upon Milošević in summer 1991, Karadžić had become by March 1992 a powerful unifier of the Bosnian Serbs and a tough negotiator on their behalf. He had only begun to reveal a tendency to overplay his hand in negotiations; he had yet to pay a price for his arrogance.

Standing at the zenith of his political career, as February gave way to March in 1992, Karadžić might have taken a few days to revel in his victory and bask in his followers' accolades. Instead, after dominating the autonomists on February 29 in Banja Luka, Karadžić did what he had often done during major crises in Bosnia.

He went to Belgrade.

9

Triumphant Conspirator

Brimming with confidence from subduing the Krajina separatists, Karadžić went to Belgrade on March 1, the second of two days of voting in the referendum for Bosnia's independence. That evening and the next day, March 2, he orchestrated from afar an SDS paramilitary campaign to erect barricades in Sarajevo. While SDS operatives in Sarajevo were carrying out his instructions, he also advanced the Bosnian Serb cause politically in the Yugoslav Expanded Presidency, a body made up of eight presidency members and specially invited guests. Even though Karadžić seemed arrogant and ineffective at that session, he walked away with assurances of Belgrade's military and diplomatic support for the Bosnian Serb nationalist cause. Significant victories both in a Belgrade conference room and on the streets of Sarajevo reassured Karadžić that he could challenge Bosnia's imminent independence with Serb arms and men.

DISPUTED BARRICADES

As Karadžić was berating the ARK separatists in Banja Luka throughout the day on February 29, Bosnian citizens were casting their ballots on the first day of voting in the Bosnian independence referendum. In that balloting, voters of all three nations largely complied with the instructions of their nationalist leaders. Bosniaks and Croats turned out in overwhelming numbers on February 29 and March 1 to vote "Yes" on independence, while most Serbs boycotted the vote as the SDS had requested. The balloting proceeded without organized interference from any nationalist party, and European monitors subsequently affirmed the basic fairness of the procedures and vote count. The voting returns provided further evidence that most of the Serb population was firmly under the sway of the SDS and supported Karadžić's campaign.

A seemingly unrelated incident of violence in Sarajevo marred the otherwise calm final day of referendum voting. Serbs had worshipped peacefully for centuries at the Old Serbian Orthodox Church that stood in the heart of Sarajevo's old town amid a cluster of mosques, Islamic institutions of learning, a Jewish synagogue, and the bustling Main Market (Baščaršija). In the latter part of the twentieth century, it was one of several Sarajevo landmarks frequented by tourists. But on March 1, the quiet church became the central site of events that contributed to the outbreak of war in Bosnia.

A Serb wedding was held in the church in the afternoon of March 1. Such an event was unremarkable, but after the wedding, members of the wedding party unfurled a Serb flag in the Bosniak-majority city center and paraded through the Main Market in a provocative celebration. As they held the Serbian flag aloft, a burst of gunfire killed the bridegroom's father, Nikola Gardović, and wounded the Serbian Orthodox priest who conducted the ceremony. Viktor Meier, a correspondent of the German newspaper *Frankfurter Allgemeine Zeitung*, heard the gunshots and witnessed the ensuing chaos.[1]

Other witnesses identified the perpetrator as Ramiz Delalić, a small-time Bosniak gangster known as Ćelo, who had become an increasingly brazen criminal after communism's collapse. Earlier he had been implicated in a shooting and a rape. Local reporters learned that he had been treated by psychiatrists (evidently not by Karadžić) at a Sarajevo hospital.[2] On March 3, Sarajevo police issued an arrest warrant for Delalić and one other suspected assailant in the killing. Despite the warrant, Sarajevo police made little effort to find the suspects, and both remained at large.[3]

SDS leaders in Sarajevo publicly denounced the killing.[4] In Belgrade, Karadžić told a TV interviewer that the shootings proved that all Serbs in Bosnia lived in grave danger.[5] Other SDS spokesmen charged that the police failure to arrest Delalić was due to SDA or government complicity in the shooting, just as the independence referendum showed the government's intent to violate the rights of Serbs in Bosnia. Fate could not have presented SDS leaders with a] more unsavory perpetrator to pillory, and ever since they have periodically reminded the global public of his misdeeds. Bosnian police chronicled Delalić's many criminal acts, and he himself later admitted in

---

[1]   Viktor Meier, *Yugoslavia: A History of its Demise* (trans. Sabrina Ramet) (London: Routledge, 1999), p. 211.
[2]   *Oslobodjenje*, March 6, 1992, p. 8.
[3]   *Oslobodjenje*, March 4, 1992, p. 20.
[4]   *Oslobodjenje*, March 3, 1992, p. 12.
[5]   *Oslobodjenje*, March 4, 1992, p. 4.

testimony at the ICTY that he had been charged and acquitted numerous times for various offenses both before and after killing Gardović.[6]

Although they were correct that Gardović's killer was a Bosniak, SDS leaders had no evidence implicating the SDA in the shootings. Delalić did later serve the government of Bosnia by aiding in Sarajevo's defense throughout the siege. His role in defending the city earned him a certain informal immunity from prosecution that kept him out of jail even though he beat, shot at, and terrorized a number of civilians during and after the war. Not until 2007 was he brought to trial for shooting Gardović in March 1992. On the trial's first day, confident prosecutors showed the jury a dramatic videotape of the shooting that confirmed Delalić's earlier confession that he had fired the fatal shots.[7] Free on bail after the first day of court proceedings, he was assassinated on June 27, 2007, by rival gangsters who pumped six bullets into Delalić and wounded one of his companions as they left a local café. Delalić died as he had lived, a violent man and combatant in the vicious wars of the Sarajevo underworld. He took with him to the grave any knowledge he may have had of co-perpetrators or others who might have commissioned or sanctioned the 1992 shootings.[8]

SDS leaders cared little about Delalić personally, but they seized upon the Main Market killing as a pretext to launch an armed action in Sarajevo's streets, the first since World War II. Karadžić personally authorized the action on the evening of March 1 in a phone conversation with Rajko Dukić, president of the SDS Executive Committee and a trusted colleague. In that call, Dukić first told Karadžić that several local party leaders were incensed about the shooting and the desecration of the Serb flag.[9] "I'd do anything, Radovan, but [Dragan] Kalinić just called," Dukić reported. "He's completely shocked and he said, 'what the fuck have we come to, if they're shooting at our flag' .... Momo Pejić called me ... and said, 'come on, let's get the people to rise up tomorrow'."

Karadžić had been presented with a similar opportunity in September 1991 when Pale Police Chief Malko Koroman offered to unleash his followers in Romanija to cut off Sarajevo (described in Chapter 6). On that occasion, Karadžić declined to authorize a Serb armed attack. But in March 1992, with

---

[6] Testimony of Ramiz Delalić, ICTY, Prosecutor v. Sefer Halilović, May 17, 2005, pp. 9–11.

[7] *Nezavisne novine* (Banja Luka), May 18, 2007, w.nezavisne.com/novosti/hronika/Emitovan-videozapis-u-slucaju-Gardovic-9716.html, viewed March 23, 2014.

[8] *Nezavisna novine*, June 28, 2007, www.nezavisne.com/novosti/bih/Federalni-MUP-na-tragu-ubicama-Ramiza-Delalica-Cele-11295.html, viewed March 23, 2014.

[9] Intercept, Karadžić and Rajko Dukić, March 1, 1992, ICTY, PSM, Exhibit P613, Tab 178, BCS 0324-5643–0324-5644.

the referendum completed and Europe's recognition of Bosnian independence imminent, Karadžić leaped at the opportunity to wreak havoc in his adopted home town. He authorized Dukić to mobilize SDS members for a barricade campaign to strangle traffic on major thoroughfares and intersections. "Get them to rise up, and have things prepared," he told Dukić. "They should close everything tonight ... all the exits.... Have it all closed down. It's better if it ends like that, than if the people get on the move themselves.... It should be fast and ... we all go out."

Dukić spread word of Karadžić's assent. In the late evening of March 1, SDS members and their supporters took up arms, donned masks, and erected over twenty barricades at key transit points throughout the city. Responding swiftly and in kind, SDA members put up their own makeshift barricades, most of them directly opposite the SDS-controlled roadblocks, creating what became known locally as "sandwich barricades." Unsurprisingly, the proximity of the adversaries' barricades led to violence. Serb militants shot several demonstrators who were attempting to dismantle a barricade. One of them died.

The barricade campaign had been orchestrated to bring the city to a halt. Jovan Tintor, president of the SDS in the western Sarajevo municipality of Vogošća, looked back two years later with pride on the success and efficiency of the operation:

> When the barricades began, I was in Sarajevo. But only once I successfully made it into town ..., because I was in the headquarters and involved in the organization, at the top of the organization for the barricades.... I was responsible for that part in Vogošća and Ilijaš, I had regular contacts with everybody. I believe that it was a brilliantly performed action ... for which all organizers, military organizers could envy us.[10]

Concerned that the Bosnian government might use force against those who ordered and manned the barricades, Dukić moved SDS party headquarters from the Bosnian Parliament Building across the street to the Holiday Inn, a hotel owned by a Serb sympathetic to the SDS. "I think it's better, safer, more secure, and ... we operate better from here," Dukić told Karadžić by phone the next day.[11] The SDS quickly turned the entire hotel into a stronghold for Bosnian Serb leaders and a billet for the growing contingent of Karadžić's bodyguards. Florence Hartman, then a correspondent for a French newspaper and later press spokesperson at the ICTY, reported a few days later that the

---

[10] "Opis video-dokumentacije, 'Moj gost – njegova istina,' Jovan Tintor," Serbia Radio Television, July and August 1994," ICTY, PRK, BCS 0025–5236–0025–5237.

[11] Intercept, Karadžić and Rajko Dukić, March 2, 1992, ICTY, PSM, Exhibit P613, Tab 179, BCS 0324–5654–0324–5655.

restaurant in the hotel basement, an elegant and expensive eatery in the pre-war city, had become the SDS mess hall. Karadžić's bodyguards and SDS offi-cials came, ate, and left without paying, while the restaurant's other patrons were served separately and paid full fare.[12]

Dukić reported to Karadžić by phone that one Serb had been killed in an exchange of fire near one of the barricades in Sarajevo's western suburbs, but that otherwise the barricade campaign was on track.[13] (His report of a Serb death was never independently confirmed and was likely in error.) Karadžić asked if barricades had been erected in the city center as well as the western thorough-fares. "It's all been cut off, we're holding everything," Dukić responded. "Until now it's mainly been all right. There are enough men. [Those in] the field are completely informed and have instructions.... The people are calling in.... Everything here is under control," he said. "Biljana [Plavšić] was here as well. She's gone to the Presidency. We had contact with the army and such."

Karadžić was pleased. "Good, excellent," he replied. "We just need to hold on to that firmly and get things out into the clear." He need not worry, Dukić told him. "Sarajevo is under a complete blockade," he reported without exag-geration. Indeed, the city was immobilized. Commerce came to a halt; shops closed; public transportation stopped running; and private vehicular traffic ceased. SDS militants commandeered buses and trams to use as makeshift barricades, inflicting considerable damage on the city's public transportation fleet. SDS operatives erected barricades on thoroughfares that entered the city and at major intersections within it. The barricade campaign ignored the murdered father of the Serb bridegroom and the injured priest. No barricades were set up near the site of the shootings, and no one made a makeshift memo-rial such as often appears spontaneously at the site of a martyr's death.

SDS militants erected about twenty-two barricades on March 1 and 2. Their locations and functions foreshadowed the Serb siege established two months later. Karadžić exploited the Main Market killing and the barricade campaign to demonstrate the Bosnian government's vulnerability and the SDS willing-ness to use force in the city center. In publicly linking the shootings and the referendum, Karadžić underlined the Serbs' determination to resist Bosnia's independence. And the world took notice. EC election observers, caught in the tumult, were unable to travel from their hotel to the airport and were forced to stay another day. Journalists saw a city grind to a halt, its citizens cowed by gun-toting Serbs. Karadžić was proving adept at scripting public performances to dramatize his grim determination to achieve his goals.

---

[12] *Oslobodjenje*, March 5, 1992, p. 3.
[13] Intercept, Karadžić and Rajko Dukić, March 2, 1992, ICTY, PSM, Exhibit P613, Tab 179, BCS 0324-5654–0324-5655.

PERSUADING THE PRESIDENTS

Meanwhile, in Belgrade, Karadžić approached the impending meeting of the Yugoslav Expanded Presidency on March 2 with confidence and high expectations.[14] He realized that his hopes to divide Bosnia, whether by negotiated settlement or military conquest, depended greatly upon the men and arms of the JNA. With Milošević's encouragement, he had been courting senior generals for nearly a year, but he was impatient with their failure to act more aggressively on behalf of the Bosnian Serbs. In the fall of 1991, Karadžić later related, he had appealed to the federal presidency to transform the JNA into a Serb army and to "pronounce unification, secure the borders, declare war. We'll defend ourselves, we have the resources, we have the equipment; we have everything."[15] But the federal presidency had rebuffed his appeal. For the next three months he remained uncertain but optimistic that the presidency and the generals would commit the JNA to the Bosnian Serb nationalist cause.

By March 1992, Karadžić had reason to expect that the JNA would support him, but the majority vote for Bosnia's independence had raised new doubts. He wanted binding assurances from the federal presidency that it would keep the JNA in Bosnia. He hoped to secure from the presidency a public promise that he could use to boost morale among his constituents and wave it in front of international negotiators. The Serbs of the Croatian Krajina, who feared that the recently-arrived United Nations Protection Force (UNPROFOR) would be unable to protect them against Croat forces, had already received such a guarantee. Karadžić was prepared to point to his party's barricading of Sarajevo to play upon presidency members' fears of wider conflict if Bosnian Serb requests were ignored.

Although Karadžić knew what he wanted from the Expanded Presidency, its key members, Branko Kostić and Borisav Jović, had convened the meeting for another purpose. They planned to relay the news that the two Serb polities west of the Drina, the Republic of Serb Krajina (RSK) and Republika Srpska (RS), would be excluded from Yugoslavia's constitutional restructuring. Well before the meeting, Milošević and his lieutenants had decided to reduce Yugoslavia to just two republics: Montenegro and Serbia (the latter including

---

[14] "Stenografske beleške sa proširene sednice Predsedništva Socijalističke Federativne Republike Jugoslavije održane 2. marta 1992. godine," ICTY, PMK, Exhibit P67A, BCS 0294–2750–0294–2904. Unless otherwise noted, quotations in the following account are taken from this 54-page verbatim transcript of the March 2 meeting.

[15] Bosnian Serb Assembly, 54th Session, October 15–16, 1995, Karadžić, BCS 0215–4552. He repeated the claim in the 55th Session, October 22–23, 1995, BCS 0215–4666.

its two autonomous provinces, Vojvodina and Kosovo). They planned to exclude all of Macedonia, Slovenia, Croatia, and Bosnia, thereby leaving out the RSK and RS as well. They foresaw that their decision would create widespread consternation among Serbs west of the Drina. To compensate for demolishing the Great Serb hopes of their fellow Serbs, Milošević and his lieutenants were prepared to ramp up their military and administrative support for the RSK and RS.[16]

Presidency members from Serbia and Montenegro, as well as Milošević, had good reason to favor the two-republic formula. Milošević understood that leading major international actors, particularly the European Community and the United States, would not tolerate border changes among the republics. Milošević had come under UN pressure to require the RSK to declare its permanent separation from the Republic of Serbia before the peacekeeping forces deployed. Additionally, the EC's imminent recognition of Bosnia's independence served as a warning to Serbia and Montenegro to stay out of Bosnian affairs. The moment Bosnia became recognized as an independent state, the JNA would become an occupying army in a foreign land, and calls for its immediate withdrawal were sure to follow. In planning for this scenario, the presidency faced a dilemma. JNA senior commanders had long ago ruled out one option, similar to the option adopted as the Soviet Union collapsed, in which the JNA would divide into several parts, each assigned to one of the republics. That left two possibilities. Should the JNA withdraw from both Croatia and Bosnia to the two republics of Serbia and Montenegro, leaving Serbs west of the Drina to fend for themselves? Or should the JNA remain in place, perhaps rebadged as an armed force of the Republic of Bosnia or the RS?

General Blagoje Adžic, Chief of the General Staff of the JNA, opened the meeting of the Expanded Presidency with a briefing on the security situation. Sarajevo was at a standstill, he reported. Rather than attribute the barricades to Karadžić and the SDS members who had ordered them installed, he portrayed the barricades as spontaneous Bosniak and Serb responses to rising ethnonational tensions in the aftermath of the independence referendum. "The roadblocks were put up by all sides – each side in accord with its nationality and the territory it controls," General Adžić told the presidency. "The successful referendum was being celebrated [by Muslims and Croats] and then, there were probably some provocative responses to the gunfire." Adžić was most alarmed about the symbolic manifestation of anti-Serb sentiment. "As you know, one Serb [Gardović] was killed yesterday and another wounded," he

---

[16] Mladić diaries, February 21, 1992, ENG 0668–2993–0668–3195-ET, p. 43.

reported. "*Even more seriously,* symbols were attacked – the flag of the Serbian Orthodox Church, which was supposed to be destroyed, which means the humiliation of the Serb people." (Emphasis added.) The situation was grave, he warned, and "any minute could escalate into a serious conflict."

Jović suggested that the presidency "hear from the comrades from Bosnia." Kostić called on Karadžić, who was identified in the minutes as the "representative of the Serb people of Bosnia tasked with cooperation with the Presidency of the Socialist Federal Republic of Yugoslavia." Karadžić could have found no better time to make his case. His party's barricades were proclaiming violent outrage in Sarajevo, his personal bodyguards and coarse rhetoric had silenced the separatists in Banja Luka the previous day, and he, together with Krajišnik, had just brazenly defied European diplomats by declaring a constitution for the RS. Karadžić dispensed with charm and began boasting of his successes in the European negotiations. He began with an outright lie: "We initiated the Conference on Bosnia and Herzegovina," he claimed. "We named it 'The conference of the three national communities in Bosnia and Herzegovina,' the essence of which is that the three national communities in Bosnia [must] reach some consensus regarding a solution to the political crisis, regardless of whether Bosnia leaves Yugoslavia. " The conference had not, in fact, been launched by Karadžić but rather was established by the European Community Conference on Yugoslavia as one of its subcommittees.

Continuing his pompous monologue, Karadžić claimed he had intimidated the Europeans and Americans by stoking their fears of uncontrollable violence in Bosnia. When those diplomats berated him for demanding the partition of Bosnia, Karadžić told the presidency, he had chosen a more palatable term to describe the separation. "This does not concern partition, but internal transformation," he said he had told the international diplomats, "and they swallowed that." He further claimed to have convinced the diplomats that separation of Bosnia's peoples was imminent. "We pointed out that this concerns three peoples, three faiths, three cultures, we can say two or two and a half languages," he said, "in any case three very different entities, that unfortunately can live together only under occupation or dictatorship." Drawing parallels with Lebanon, Cyprus, and India, Karadžić said he had "warned the Europeans and Americans that the mere mention of independence for Bosnia may trigger an uncontrolled process which no one will be able to pacify and will result in war."

Karadžić next turned to stoking presidency members' fears by warning of volatile, uncontrollable Serbs west of the Drina. He set forth a paradoxical narrative, claiming both that he was helpless to control the Bosnian Serbs and that only he could restrain them. Serbs were already raging out of his control, requiring adept leadership to calm them down, he asserted. "We cannot predict how things down there will turn out," he said. "We will work for calm, but in fact if we work tactlessly and with unclear goals, we might lose the confidence of the people and cause them to turn to other leaders . . . and disperse politically." The presidency members had to trust him to control the hotheads, he suggested, pausing to regale them with his triumph in Banja Luka. "We barely reconciled one such process in the Bosnian Krajina which might have grievously harmed the [EC] Conference and [held] many other implications if the Bosnian Krajina had been proclaimed a republic," he said. He, Koljević, and Krajišnik had been indispensable to containing the impulsive Bosnian Serbs, he asserted, referring to his performance in Banja Luka two days before. "We three were there. . . . We pledged our authority and invested much effort to resolve the thing."

He hinted at dire consequences if the presidency ordered the JNA out of Bosnia. "I cannot guarantee that we can go before the Serbs in Bosnia and say, 'Never mind that Bosnia will be sovereign and independent, don't worry that it will be Alija's, and it's all right if the JNA withdraws.' We don't have the power to do that." He cautioned the presidency against appearing too conciliatory in its public communiqué after the meeting. "I am agreed that we issue an announcement, and of course it's understandable that it will appeal for reason and peace, but an announcement shouldn't thrust the Serb people there [in Bosnia] into despair [by suggesting] that this state and this body and its institutions cannot protect them." Perhaps sensing that he had gone too far in suggesting that he would defy Yugoslavia's leaders, he held out the lure of Yugoslav police patrolling much of Bosnia. "The federal police can operate in around 40 municipalities, on 60 percent of Bosnian territory," he claimed, "and we will obey orders of the Federal Secretariat for National Defense and every decision of the presidency."

PRESIDENTIAL PLEDGES

Despite Karadžić's belated pledge to submit to federal authority, the meeting's conveners could not have been pleased with either Karadžić's message or its tone. Jović, presiding over the meeting, urged a calmer approach. "It's very important here not to dramatize things with negative presuppositions about those events," he cautioned. With developments moving quickly and uncertainly, he argued, it was premature to decide definitively the question of the JNA's future role. But Karadžić was undeterred. He asked the presidency to promise that the JNA would not withdraw from Bosnia. "We created the constitutional presuppositions that we have our guard, that we have our army," he related. He pointed out that the pivotal event – Europe's recognition of Bosnia – was only two or three weeks away. "We as a state [Yugoslavia] must take a specific stand on whether the JNA in Bosnia ceases to be Yugoslav," he insisted. Jović, refusing to take that step, would only agree to note that the presidency and JNA had pledged to defend the RSK if it were attacked and that the same should go for Bosnia.

Karadžić next turned to Koljević and Krajišnik to reinforce his message. As on other occasions, the two men magnified Karadžić's impact by putting his concerns into sharper focus and using more dispassionate logic, and this time they also buffered his bombast with more palatable proposals for compromise. For the remainder of the meeting, both men tempered Karadžić's mercurial monologues with appeals to constitutional principles, the Bosnian Serb popular will, and workable compromises.

Karadžić, however, become even more incendiary. "Is Bosnia in Yugoslavia?" he asked rhetorically. Jović responded calmly that he was prepared only to state publicly that the presidency would respect every decision reached through consensus; that formulation, he claimed, implied the presidency would adopt a similar approach in regard to the JNA. But Karadžić hectored Jović for an answer, asking "The question remains, until such time as we reach a consensus, is Bosnia in Yugoslavia?" he asked. Jović was perplexed and angry. "Then where is it? That means it's not in the sky and is nowhere on earth. It cannot be in any other place [than in Yugoslavia]!" But Karadžić had set a logical trap, and he confidently tripped it. "If [Bosnia is] in Yugoslavia in the state-political sense, then this presidency and the complete federal apparatus must hold to the position that Bosnia cannot leave Yugoslavia without the agreement among all three nations. That solves everything: The army doesn't withdraw." Suppressing his anger, Jović held firmly to the wording he had earlier proposed. "The solution which we articulated covers everything," he insisted.

To Karadžić's delight, Branko Kostić, the president of the Presidency, spurned Jović's proposal to defer a decision and expressed firm support for the Bosnian Serbs. "I've pledged that the JNA will not withdraw from Bosnia while I am in this position," Kostić declared, "except with the agreement of all three constituent nations" of Bosnia.

General Adžić, a Bosnian-born Yugoslav loyalist who had witnessed Ustasha troops massacre his family during the Second World War, identified personally with the Bosnian Serb nationalist cause. He not only agreed with Kostić that the JNA should not leave Bosnia, he goaded the Bosnian Serbs to make war. "I think the Serbs in Bosnia are on the right path," he said. "The Serb people must say as one to the whole world, 'You will honor our minimum demands for existence in these parts, and not drive us out, divide us, or annihilate us.

Otherwise we will take the course of self-annihilation, and we are prepared to annihilate just as many others.'" Adžić urged the presidency to keep the JNA in Bosnia but not to publicize the decision. He urged the Bosnian Serbs to remain firm. "Now the Serbs, particularly the Serbs in Bosnia, must be extremely decisive," he said. "They have the arms, they have the power, and they have the will."

By predicting imminent war and urging the Bosnian Serbs to prepare for it, Adžić had spoken the words Karadžić wanted to hear. But Karadžić said nothing. As the discussion turned next to the JNA's plans to support UNPROFOR in Croatia, he quietly slipped from the room. When he returned some time later, he was jubilant and eager to speak. After apologizing for his brief absence, Karadžić declared, "I have good news!" Referring to the impact the barricade campaign in Sarajevo was having on global opinion, he reported, "The world is astonished. In London it is considered 100 percent probable that no one can recognize Bosnia, that the conference on Bosnia must be expedited, and that no solution will be achieved without consensus." Other meeting participants evidently responded with less delight than Karadžić had hoped. "In a sea of bad news, this would be good," he was forced to explain to them.

Good news or not, Karadžić's information was wrong. The EC had not abandoned its intent to recognize Bosnia in early April. But the erroneous report re-ignited Karadžić's braggadocio. Based on the rumor from London, he leaped to the conclusion that the Sarajevo barricade campaign had accomplished its goals. He appealed for quick action: "I think we must move as quick as lightning to create new facts; we have legality, we have continuity," he said. "We have a state organization, the Serbs in Bosnia, we have land we control, we have laws in harmony with the Yugoslav constitution and laws, and we respect the priority of the Federal Constitution."

Jović, frustrated again by Karadžić's erratic musings and incessant demands, warned against precipitous acts. "Shall we, with one such step, wipe out everything like an elephant in a glass factory," he cautioned, "or do we dare await a common solution, and work this in parallel? That is very delicate and we must seriously think that over." Krajišnik then took the floor, ending the increasingly unproductive disagreement between Karadžić and Jović by proposing a compromise.

Aside from the formal decisions, which in any case were foregone conclusions, key participants in the meeting gave Karadžić what he sought. They pledged support for ordering the JNA to stand by the Bosnian Serbs, though they did not specify whether or not that force might be rebadged as the armed forces of the Republika Srpska. These decisions emboldened Karadžić to press the demands of the Bosnian Serbs in international negotiations and in arming for war. With legal, historical, and practical arguments and a bombastic succession of nationalist clichés, Karadžić felt he could not and would not be ignored in calculations about Yugoslavia's future. He had increased his own stature as leader of the powerful movement for a Bosnian Serb state and had moved the Bosnian Serbs one step closer to war.

THE BARRICADES COME DOWN

While Karadžić was bragging at the presidency meeting in Belgrade on March 2, other SDS leaders in Sarajevo undertook to extract maximum advantage from the barricade campaign. At a press conference in the Holiday Inn, Dukić and RS Minister of Information Velibor Ostojić pressed their propaganda advantage by attributing the barricades to Serbs' spontaneous outrage at the Main Market killing and the "illegal" independence referendum.[17] Dukić publicly announced extravagant Serb demands in exchange for taking down the barricades. He asked that the "presidency, assembly, and government of Bosnia cease all activities for the international recognition of Bosnia until the [EC] Conference on Bosnia is concluded." He further insisted that the Bosnian police be ethnically divided and that the SDA disband its paramilitary force. Addressing the press as president of the "Crisis Staff of the Serb People in Bosnia," which he himself had formed just hours before, Dukić denounced another crisis staff, that of the Bosnian Presidency, as an "unconstitutional organ," and demanded its dissolution. This contradictory demand drew a sharp question from a reporter who wanted to know by what authority he had formed his own crisis staff.

Karadžić had relied on Dukić to orchestrate the campaign to erect the barricades, and he turned to him again to negotiate to take them down. He authorized Dukić to speak for the SDS, even though presidency member Biljana Plavšić was the ranking Serb nationalist still in Sarajevo. Dukić presented the SDS demands to a meeting of the Bosnian presidency convened by JNA General Milutin Kukanjac, commander of the Sarajevo-based Second Military District. Kukanjac persuaded the Bosniak and Serb nationalist leaders to urge their followers to dismantle the barricades, but neither side budged for hours after the proclamation. Karadžić phoned Ejup Ganić, Izetbegović's most trusted associate and the third Bosniak member of the Bosnian Presidency, and said (according to Ganić), "the problem of the barricades can be resolved with representatives of the SDS who are in Sarajevo."[18] In opting out of a personal role in

---

[17]   *Oslobodjenje*, March 3, 1992, p. 12.
[18]   *Oslobodjenje*, March 3, 1992, p. 1.

the negotiations, Karadžić implicitly acknowledged that he trusted Dukić and was prepared to delegate important responsibilities to trusted associates. Ganić, however, saw an opportunity for a minor public relations victory. Referring to his talk with Karadžić, he announced, "Representatives of the SDS have confirmed that they can remove the barricades, which in other words confirms that the SDS organized the barricades." But Ganić's minor triumph in the blame game did not change the Bosnian government's obvious impotence and humiliation in the face of a grave challenge to public order in its capital city.

The people of Sarajevo also became engaged in the barricade dispute by launching a movement for peace. Two large crowds gathered late in the day on March 2, one in the city center and the other in one of Sarajevo's western suburbs.[19] The two groups marched from opposite directions toward the Bosnian parliament building to demand that the barricades be dismantled and to protest the provocative behavior of the various nationalist parties. The demonstrations intensified pressure on the nationalist leaders and on General Kukanjac to end the impasse. With the barricades still intact and neither Serbs nor Bosniaks moving to dismantle them, the Bosnian presidency assembled again at 5:00 p.m. at Dukić's behest to negotiate a removal of the barricades.

Prior to that presidency meeting, Karadžić decided that he had accomplished his goals. Having secured the assurances he sought from the federal presidency, he was ready to abandon the barricade campaign. He called Dukić and said, "There is no more need for barricades; they have done what they needed to do.... I have the assurance of President Kostić that it is agreed and that is already public. Take down those barricades."[20] Dukić, who was running the entire operation from SDS headquarters, returned to the Bosnian presidency to wring whatever concessions he could before ordering SDS operatives to take down the barricades. Within the hour, he sat down to dictate SDS terms to Izetbegović and others government officials who were desperate to restore Sarajevo to normality.[21]

At the meeting of the Bosnian presidency, Dukić proved a tough and able negotiator. He tenaciously stuck to the fiction that the Serb people had spontaneously erected the barricades in outrage over the Main Market killing. He then invented a tale of popular Serb demand for the party to erect the barricades: "At 6:00 [in the evening of March 1] they called me to party headquarters, and there I found three clerics who told me what happened" in the

---

[19] See Donia, *Sarajevo*, pp. 278–279, and the sources there cited.

[20] Sinan Alić, report on interview with Rajko Dukić, March 21, 2000, Milići, Bosnia; typescript in author's possession, pp. 3–4.

[21] The demands were contained in a document entitled "Obavještenje kriznog štaba srpskog naroda BiH," copy provided by Dukić to Alić during the March 21, 2000, interview.

Main Market.[22] "After that a group of citizens arrived with certain demands; the phones rang, and so it went." He denied that he had spoken with Karadžić before authorizing the barricade campaign and lied about the timing of their conversations. "Concretely, I did not succeed in contacting Mr. Karadžić. . . . Only this morning [March 2] did I speak with him. That excludes all possibilities for any coordination, manipulation, and so on."

At the time they met, the presidency members could not have cared less about Dukić's cover-up of Karadžić's role. Frightened for the city and their republic, they hastened to reach an agreement with him to end the city's paralysis. They accepted most of his demands in a public statement, but they never enacted the promised measures. Dukić reveled in the SDS public relations victory in demonstrating the Bosnian government's weakness and its inability to keep order in its capital. In Belgrade, Karadžić reiterated Dukić's tale that the barricade campaign was a spontaneous Serb retaliation for the Main Market shootings and the independence referendum.

These false accounts of the barricade campaign comported with the grand Bosnian Serb narrative of repression, victimhood, and justifiable revenge. Although many questions remain unanswered about who did what in the troubled two days following the end of referendum balloting, events themselves exposed the implausible narrative. Those who ostensibly mourned Gardović did not do what mourners might be expected to do. They neither spontaneously erected a monument nor held a protest rally. Similar to those federal presidency members who were more concerned about the Serb flag than the death of an actual Serb, SDS leaders were more concerned with demonstrating military clout than with Serb victims. They succeeded for a full day in closing down the city's major transportation systems and blocking the busiest intersections and thoroughfares. Their swift response reinforced the already widespread view among Bosnians that the barricade crusade had been premeditated. Indeed, Karadžić and other SDS leaders later confirmed in conversations and retrospective accounts that they had planned the operation.

The Sarajevo barricade campaign, along with declarations of the expanded federal presidency in Belgrade, constituted major steps toward realizing the Serb nationalist political project. The two events also inaugurated a month of intensive planning, preparations, and maneuvering under Karadžić's leadership. With a month remaining until the Europeans and Americans recognized Bosnia's independence, the pace of events accelerated. The prospect of armed conflict loomed ever larger.

22 "Magnotofonski snimak 56. sjednice Predsjedništva SRBiH, održane 2. marta 1992 godine," typescript, p. 26. Dukić provided a copy of this document, the official transcript of the Bosnian Presidency meeting on March 2, to Alić during the March 21, 2000, interview.

10

Strategic Multitasker

Karadžić returned to Sarajevo in early March 1992 in the strongest position he had yet enjoyed, owing to his successes in Banja Luka, Belgrade, and Sarajevo. By directing the building and dismantling of the barricades in Sarajevo, he had demonstrated the Bosnian government's vulnerability and his willingness to use force to achieve his aims. In ending the ARK separatist threat in Banja Luka, he had strengthened his control over the SDS. And in securing promises of support from the federal presidency in Belgrade, he knew the JNA stood ready to support his actions to contest Bosnia's independence. Even in his strengthened position, however, Karadžić faced major challenges with the approach of April 6, the scheduled date for Europe's recognition of Bosnia's independence. To meet those challenges, Karadžić became a strategic multitasker. In this chapter we trace his simultaneous quests for a negotiated agreement to partition Bosnia and for Bosnian Serb readiness for armed takeover, as violent incidents proliferated and popular apprehension surged during March.

THE QUEST FOR NEGOTIATED PARTITION

Facing the *de facto* deadline of April 6, EC negotiator Jose Cutileiro made another attempt to secure a negotiated partition of the soon-to-be-independent state. In late February, Cutileiro's efforts to reach an EC-sponsored agreement had foundered on the rock of Bosnian Serb intransigence (described in Chapter 9). As he convened the fifth round of talks in the historic Konak building in Sarajevo on March 16,[1] he was aware that April 6 would end his best chance to avert war. If the EC recognition were to become effective on April 6 without an agreement, Izetbegović and the Bosnian government would

---

[1] *Oslobodjenje*, March 17, 1992, p. 1.

have little incentive to grant concessions to EC negotiators, let alone agree to partition their newly-recognized state. But Karadžić and the SDS, backed by the JNA and the Serbian government, had threatened war if Bosnia were to become independent without a tripartite partition agreement in place.

Although he was genuinely committed to a peaceful resolution, Cutileiro had effectively tied his own hands in early February by announcing the principles to guide the negotiations.[2] The principles included the continued existence of Bosnia and a commitment to respect the interests of all three "peoples," which in practice meant he would not proceed without the approval of all three nationalist leaders.

According to Cutilheiro's Principle One, Bosnia was to be "composed of three constituent units, based on national principles and taking into account economic, geographic and other criteria." By insisting on respecting the interests of all three peoples, Cutileiro effectively gave each nationalist party a veto over any final agreement, while completely ignoring other political formations in Bosnia, most significantly the left opposition. He had opted to side with the separatists, but he lacked either diplomatic or military leverage to compel any party to accept and honor an agreement. Nonetheless, on March 18 Cutileiro secured an agreement-in-principle among the three nationalist leaders. The agreement, however, was specifically styled as a basis for further negotiations rather than as a final accord. A map showing approximate boundaries of three proposed territorial units accompanied the agreement.

Karadžić later claimed that the agreement was definitive and that it obligated the EC to grant Serbs a separate territory within Bosnia. In the months after these talks, he crafted a legend of March 18 that blamed other parties while absolving himself and the Bosnian Serb nationalists of any culpability for subsequent violence. He rhetorically magnified and elevated the agreement in principle (often called the Cutileiro Plan or the Lisbon Agreement, although it was reached in Sarajevo) to the level of an irrevocable, binding accord that committed the parties to honor it for all time. He endeavored to make March 18 a landmark date, with connotations of perfidy by the Europeans, Croats, and Bosniaks. He set forth his view of events during his opening statement at trial in 2010. "On the 18th of March, we agreed that there would be three Bosnias within one," he stated. "That is the most painful compromise that the Serbs had to make. At that point, all three parties accepted this, and we expressed our great pleasure."[3]

---

2   Gow, *Triumph of the Lack of Will*, pp. 80–81. Text of the principles is found in Campbell, *National Deconstruction*, p. 128.
3   Opening Statement of Radovan Karadžić, ICTY, PRK, March 1, 2010, pp. 820–821.

Other participants and observers told a different story in the hours after the talks ended. Carefully noting the distinction between an agreement in principal and a final accord, the newspaper *Oslobodjenje* carried the headline, "Agreed – but not signed!"[4] Alija Izetbegović, the Bosniak representative, reported that he had assented conditionally only after being threatened that the Europeans would otherwise withhold recognition.[5] "In the event of our negative stand, the international legal recognition of Bosnia came into question, which is surely at the moment our greatest interest and which, by patient work here and abroad, will soon be at hand," he said. Asked what it meant to agree "conditionally," Izetbegović explained, "That means that nothing is definitively decided and that the people must express their wishes on the EC proposal at a referendum."

However adamantly he later insisted that the agreement was conclusive and binding, Karadžić repeatedly attested to its provisional character on the day of the agreement in principle. His presentation to the assembly on March 18, only a few hours after he left the talks, reveals that he himself denied its finality and related that the parties had agreed on the principle of geographic separation rather than specifically how that was to take place.[6] "The essence of the matter is this: The principle that Bosnia is indivisible using ethnic criteria is not correct," he said. "Bosnia is divisible along ethnic lines and it can be divided in three. All else is a technical matter." In speaking to the assembly, Karadžić emphasized the provisional character of the map, but he expressed approval that the talks had come to maps of division rather than debates about whether or not partition was desirable. "For the first time, maps are in circulation, and they have indeed become an integral part of the document," he said. "They are also subject to further agreements, but the fact is that we have finally come to maps, and that maps are an integral part of our work." He was pleased that he had not signed the accord. "The document has been accepted as a basis, as a foundation for further negotiations," said Karadžić. "The document has not been signed. We would never sign anything that we did not agree upon." For emphasis, he read verbatim the key passages of the accord. "On the back [of the document] is printed in block letters, 'This paper is a basis for further negotiations,'" he read.

This was not the only time that Karadžić misrepresented a statement of principle for a binding commitment. In cross-examining me at trial in June

---

4   *Oslobodjenje*, March 19, 1992, p. 1.
5   *Oslobodjenje*, March 25, 1992, p. 1.
6   BSA, 11th Session, March 18, 1992, Karadžić, BCS SA01–1174.

2010, Karadžić similarly argued that proclamations by others constituted eternally binding promises to Serbs. He introduced into evidence a copy of U.S. President Woodrow Wilson's Fourteen Points of 1918 and had me read Point 11, which included the provision, "Serbia [should be] accorded free and secure access to the sea." Then he asked, "Do you see, Mr. Donia, that your country owes us access to the sea?" I replied, "No, I don't.... This document is not a promise for all time and eternity; it's a set of guidelines."[7] Undeterred, he went back even further in history to justify the claim, reminding the court "that coast had belonged to the Serbian Emperor Dušan," who had ruled for a decade in the fourteenth century. Karadžić was unabashed by resorting to the long reach in justifying Serb territorial claims.

Elated though he was in March 1992 with the principles he believed had been established, Karadžić expressed the hope of acquiring additional specific concessions in subsequent talks. He recited the point made by Izetbegović that any definitive agreement would depend on voter approval in a popular referendum, and he added that it required approval of the Bosnian Parliament. "A bill of constitutional law ... will be prepared and submitted to the parliament as soon as possible," he said. "It will need to be confirmed at the referendum of the people, under international control." He expected the proposal to be defeated by popular vote. "I think that the SDA accepted the three constituent units, hoping that it would all fall through at referendum," he said. (In the event, war mooted such a vote, and no referendum on the proposal was ever held.)

Even though he repeatedly underlined the provisional character of the agreement, Karadžić urged the delegates to take advantage of the agreement and tentative map by seizing power unilaterally in areas awarded to Serbs on the tentative map. "We have to be quick in consolidating our state unit and bringing it into function, keeping the question of border territories completely open because they require adjustments and because the will of the people should be respected," he said. Krajišnik backed Karadžić's suggestion. "It would be good if we could do one thing for strategic reasons: if we could start implementing what we have agreed upon, ethnic division on the ground," Krajišnik said. He expected the Serb side to be blamed. "I cannot say whether this will be politically honorable; there is not much honor in politics after all, and yes, if it does not turn out to be honorable, the Serb people will be blamed," he admitted. "But we cannot accept the state imagined in the minds of the SDA people."

7　Karadžić Cross-examination of Donia, ICTY, PRK, June 1, 2010, pp. 3,172–73.

IMPLEMENTING THE MUNICIPAL STRATEGY

As he negotiated for a division of Bosnia by diplomatic accord, Karadžić also worked to implement the municipal strategy in preparation for an armed takeover. He directed his formidable powers of persuasion principally to SDS local leaders, since in his instructions of December 19, 1991, he had tasked them with forming assemblies and crisis staffs critical to the municipal strategy. Despite his best efforts, many SDS municipal officials implemented the instructions only half-heartedly or not at all. Karadžić turned to his trusted senior SDS colleagues to push and prod recalcitrant local officials to implement the "A-B" instructions of December 19, 1991, in which he had ordered them to form those local bodies. He and other senior SDS officials became increasingly insistent in late March, but many local leaders carried out the strategy in their respective municipalities only after the assembly issued a deadline and gave an ultimatum for full compliance.

Later in the war, Karadžić reflected on the prewar era, idealizing it as a time of Serb harmony and successes. In 1995, he waxed nostalgic about the ease with which municipal leaders took up a military role. "You will remember the A and B variants," he said, speaking of his instructions of December 1991. "In the B variant [municipalities], where we were in the minority – 20 percent, 15 percent," he said, "we established our authority and set up a brigade, a unit no matter what size, but there was a detachment with a commander."[8] In these retrospective ruminations, he rightly noted that many civilian municipal leaders had become soldiers in 1992, but he romanticized and exaggerated the readiness of many SDS officials to implement the municipal strategy. It was in fact a tough slog, and Karadžić got what he wanted in the end only through tenacity and the application of relentless pressure on his subordinates in the party.

On February 17, Karadžić sounded a note of urgency that would also characterize his subsequent appeals. He was paraphrased as stating that it was "necessary to activate the second step of the position of the Main Board of the Bosnian SDS,"[9] that is, to move the municipal strategy from preparation to active implementation. In the instructions of December 1991, Karadžić had directed, "The order to carry out the specified tasks, measures and other activities in these Instructions is given exclusively by the Bosnian SDS president using a secret, pre-established procedure." Because officials in different

---

[8] BSA, 50th Session, April 15–16, 1995, Karadžić, BCS 0084–6058.
[9] "Sveska zapisnika sa sastanaka Opštinskog odbora SDS Prijedor, Arhivska knjiga br. 7," February 17, 1992, ICTY, Prosecutor v. Milomir Stakić, Exhibit 12b, BCS 0102–1678.

municipalities were implementing the instructions at different paces, the distinction between the two phases soon became blurred. Still, he urged immediate action. "Each should secure his own area," he reportedly directed.

Rajko Dukić, president of the SDS Executive Committee, was the first to set a firm deadline for action. In a memo of mid-March 1992, he wrote to local officials, "In accord with the position adopted, you are required to assess the possibility of establishing a Serb municipality in your area."[10] He asked each committee to "inform us of your stand, and the area to be included in a Serb municipality, by letter or fax, by Tuesday, March 17, at the latest." The response should include "a list of local communities and populated areas, or parts of populated areas, that would fall within the Serb municipality," he directed. Although it has not been possible to track the responses to this memo, Karadžić and other SDS officials continued to act as though compliance was partial, slow, and reluctant.

Karadžić further ramped up pressure on March 23 in a letter addressed to "all presidents of municipalities" in which he linked municipal activities closely with preparations for war.[11] "Protection of the Serb people in the current situation requires rapid and timely transfer of data and information relevant to defense and security," he wrote. "The municipalities now face an urgent obligation to link their own information centers with the regional centers and provide for the personnel and other requirements in order to monitor the situation in the field." His message suggested that operations were about to begin: "Keeping in mind the current situation in the Republic," he wrote them, "it is necessary to cooperate with the Public Security Service by providing centers with a duty shift and ability to convey and receive information, 24 hours a day, non-stop, including Saturdays and Sundays."

The day after he had admonished local committees to prepare for armed conflict, Karadžić again told assembly delegates that it was time to implement the plan in full. "Newly established municipalities must establish their organs as soon as possible, have their [official] stamps made and start to work," he instructed. "The police, that is, our organs, must be positioned at the border.... Freedom of movement would, of course, be granted, but they [Bosnian government police] must not enter the area with armed forces or anything else that would threaten our territory, our municipality."[12]

[10] "Svim opštinskim odborima Srpske demokratske stranke," signed by Rajko Dukić, President of the Executive Committee of the SDS, ICTY, PMK, Exhibit 67A, BCS 0018–4291.

[11] "Svim predsjednicima opština," signed by Radovan Karadžić with stamp of SDS Presidency and designated "Strictly confidential, destroy after reading" (Strogo povjerljivo, nakon čitanja obavezno uništiti), March 23, 1992, ICTY, PMK, Exhibit 67A, ENG 0044–3795 (BCS ERN not available).

[12] BSA, 12th Session, March 24, 1992, Karadžić, BCS 0089–6886.

In conveying rising urgency, Karadžić hinted at, but never expressly mentioned, mass atrocities against non-Serbs. In directing that Serb municipality leaders take over the police, territorial defense, and special units,[13] he referred cryptically to the specific measures he was preparing to order. "Then, at a given moment, in another three or four days, there will be a single method used and you will be able to apply it in the municipalities you represent, and how and what to do," he said, then elaborated, "how to take resources that belong to the Serb people, how to take command," he elaborated. "The police force there must be under the command of civilian authority."

Even after earnest pleas from their leaders to meet deadlines, some municipal leaders refrained from establishing separate local Serb institutions. Perhaps as many as half of all local SDS committees had not formed separate bodies when the war began in early April. The uneven pace of institutional formation helps explain why the Serb attacks in local municipalities were spread over April, May, and June of 1992. Although the A-B instructions were implemented incompletely and erratically, they probably would not have been followed at all without Karadžić's persistent exhortations. He had made the creation of separate local Serb institutions the keystone of his municipal strategy. In a matter of weeks, those institutions vindicated the importance he ascribed to them.

DIVIDING THE JNA

Karadžić assigned high priority to securing the weapons, ordnance, and Serb manpower of the JNA for the Bosnian Serb cause. He simultaneously engaged in negotiations, implemented the municipal strategy, and oversaw the military preparations of the Bosnian Serbs. Throughout March, he sought to coordinate the maneuvers of the JNA and the political work of the SDS, as he later affirmed. "Distribution of arms was carried out thanks to the JNA," he told the assembly. "What could be withdrawn was withdrawn and distributed to the people in Serb areas, but it was the SDS which organized the people and created the army." Karadžić, who never served a day in uniform, gradually acquired control of a mighty fighting force and oversaw its transformation into an agent of warfare and mass atrocities.

JNA General Milutin Kukanjac directed the JNA's coordination with the Bosnian Serbs. On January 1, 1992, he had been appointed commander of the Second Army District, with headquarters in Sarajevo and responsibility for almost all of Bosnia.[14] In his several months as commander in Sarajevo, he

---

[13] BSA, 12th Session, March 24, 1992, Karadžić, BCS 0089–6894.
[14] *Oslobodjenje*, January 5, 1992, p. 4.

worked to defuse tensions. He facilitated negotiations among nationalist party leaders, promoted political solutions, and no doubt delayed the outbreak of war. But notwithstanding his conciliatory actions, Kukanjac harbored a deep disdain for Croats and Bosniaks, whom he labelled "Ustasha hordes" in official reports. He later claimed to have promoted joint police-army patrols in Sarajevo to give the Bosnian Serbs more time to prepare for conflict. "The patrols postponed some events, and that was in the interest of the Serbs," Kukanjac stated in a television interview in 1994.[15] Kukanjac retained command of the JNA's Bosnian half until he was dismissed on May 8, 1992, and he proved to be a willful commander who often disregarded Karadžić's wishes. But he must be credited with preparing the army's Bosnia-based units to serve the demands of Karadžić and the SDS.

As described by the historian Marko Hoare, senior commanders were "compelled to divide the JNA into formally separate" Yugoslav and Bosnian Serb armies (named the VJ – *Vojska Jugoslavija* – and VRS – *Vojska Republika Srpska* – respectively) in April and May 1992.[16] (See Chapter 11). Three factors facilitated the task of conversion. First, tens of thousands of Bosnian Serb recruits and volunteers had fought in Croatia and were already more or less in step with the new, Serb nationalist role of the JNA. Second, Milošević had ordered the transfer of Bosnian-born recruits from JNA units elsewhere in Yugoslavia back to Bosnia, and he had also directed that natives of other republics be transferred out of Bosnia to their home republics. And most important, SDS local committees everywhere were already in close touch with JNA units, having secured weapons from them in many cases and extended them welcome support against occasional anti-army demonstrations and actions. Karadžić had persuaded most SDS leaders that the JNA was their best friend.

As joint police-army patrols kept the peace in Sarajevo's streets in early March, General Kukanjac oversaw a large-scale redeployment of JNA assets to municipalities with Serb majorities and into the hands of local SDS committees. In an article published in 2000, he described his actions of 1992 on behalf of the Bosnian Serbs: "At the right time, we began the redeployment of the entire movable property owned by the JNA.... With extraordinary organization we withdrew, saved, and preserved everything.... Not a single airplane, helicopter, tank, armored personnel carrier, cannon, mortar, or motorized vehicle fell into the hands of the Muslim-Croat hordes."[17] In his report of

---

15   Milutin Kukanjac, "My Guest – My Truth" (television show), Pale, July 12, 1994.
16   Hoare, *How Bosnia Armed*, p. 39.
17   "General Milutin Kukanjac. Moja istina," *NIN*, January 6, 2000, p. 57.

March 19, 1992, General Kukanjac informed his superiors that a total of 69,198 men from 75 of Bosnia's 109 municipalities were ready for combat.[18]

Karadžić was emboldened by the JNA's presence, and he daily increased his influence over it. He was right in his 1995 pronouncement: although the JNA did not seize Bosnia for the SDS, it was indispensable to the party's takeover. The A-B instructions had tasked local SDS leaders to form military organizations and to "assure their complete subordination" to the JNA. So it was in the hectic days of March, but as operations began, roles were reversed. The SDS gradually subordinated the Bosnian half of the JNA to its own purposes.

Karadžić also oversaw the establishment of a separate Serb police force. On March 31, SDS member Momčilo Mandić, then the Deputy Commander of the unified MUP of Bosnia, declared in a telex to all police stations that a separate Serb MUP would begin operating throughout Bosnia the next day.[19] His order of April 1 led to the completion of a process that was already underway in most municipalities where Serbs served as policemen.

BUTTRESSING JUSTIFICATION

While he was finalizing institutional and military preparations for action, Karadžić and the SDS convened two gatherings to publicize the Serb nationalist cause. He addressed a special "ceremonial" session of the assembly called to promulgate a constitution for the RS, and he convened a one-day "Congress of Serb Intellectuals" to give a public platform for leading Serb academicians to bemoan the suffering of the Serb people. The two events capped months of meetings and propaganda efforts to persuade skeptical Bosnian and global publics that Bosnian Serbs would be justified when they took rage-fueled revenge against domestic enemies.

Promulgating the constitution was multiply redundant. The assembly had already authorized preparation of a draft in February 1991, discussed it but deferred voting on it (to mollify Cutileiro) on February 25, and "approved" it on February 28. Karadžić and Krajišnik arranged the repetitive "promulgation" in order to command the public square once more to underline their blustery claim that perpetual Serb suffering warranted Serb retribution.[20] As

[18] Kukanjac outlined in some detail the progress in relocating JNA assets in "Zaključci iz procene stanja na prostoru BiH u zoni odgovornosti 2. VO. Mart, 1992. godine," ICTY, PMK, Exhibit P67A, BCS 0060-9218–0060-9229. This document was also published in Hasan Efendić, *Ko je branio Bosnu* (Sarajevo: Oko, 1998), pp. 45–54.

[19] "MUP SRBiH UZSK, broj 02-2482, Pomoćnik ministra za unutrašnje poslove Momčilo Mandić," March 31, 1992, ICTY, PMK, Exhibit P67A, BCS 0049–0125.

[20] BSA, 14th Session, March 27, 1992, ENG 0092-6762–0092-6786, BCS 0090-8340-0090-8381.

the assembly transcript reported, "the anthem was sung ... followed by long and tumultuous applause." Drinks were then served "on a modest scale, felicitations were exchanged, and the deputies had their photographs taken with Dr. Radovan Karadžić [and] Momčilo Krajišnik ... their faces glowing with enthusiasm and joy."

Karadžić invoked God, history, and the Serb people to justify the creation of a Serb state. "The objective was inscribed deeply within us," he said "It is holy in the sense that it derives from God and was not placed there by human hand.... It derives from the most profound being of the Serb people, the most profound core of every Serb." he said. "Not a single Serb rejected the ultimate strategic goal of the Serb people to live in one state, in one united state." He contended that the need for separation of peoples was intrinsically part of the human and natural order. Even "in the middle of Europe there exist national communities that cannot live together," he said. "In the plant world, there are plants which cannot grow [if they are close] together. They have to be separate to flourish."

He further defended the steps he had taken and the strategies he had employed. "Our people have occasionally criticized us for taking steps with undue haste and of being coerced to do so," he acknowledged. "But we are clean before God, because we have not made a single move which was not provoked. Maybe there is God's will in all this." Separation – a sacrosanct principle in Bosnian Serb nationalist ideology – was initiated by others, he claimed; Serbs adopted it reluctantly in reaction to the destructive urges of other peoples. "We wanted no divisions. We did not want the destruction of the things we had in common," he claimed. "For 73 years we lived in a joint state, denying ourselves our plans, disregarding our development, diminishing our size and strength, all so we could preserve our joint state. Even in these times [1990s], we were the last to found a political party to represent our people. We sacrificed everything so that the powers of unity would prevail over the powers of destruction."

The next day, March 28, Karadžić resumed building the intellectual case for Serb action, this time with the help of his most influential intellectual sympathizers. Some 500 attendees, including 40 from Serbia, packed the conference hall of the Holiday Inn at a gathering called the "Congress of Serb Intellectuals."[21] The SDS and the Serb cultural society *Prosvjeta* (Enlightenment) sponsored the congress and the party paid for the gathering.[22] The SDS carefully vetted the invitees for their nationalist

---

[21]   *Oslobodjenje*, March 29, 1992, p. 2; and March 30, 1992, p. 3.
[22]   BSA, 11th Session, March 18, 1992, BCS SA01–1237.

views. Among those not invited was Boris Nilević, director of the Institute for History in Sarajevo and scholar of the Serbian Orthodox Church, who was also an outspoken critic of Karadžić and the SDS's Serb nationalism. Professor Slavko Leovac, president of the SDS Political Council, presided over the congress's one-day session. Karadžić opened the congress by welcoming the participants in the name of the SDS, but he let the leading Serb nationalist intellectuals hold forth at length on the past and present suffering of the Serb people.

Throughout the day, most of them spoke extensively about genocide, a term they used in the congress to characterize the killings of Serbs in the Second World War but would never accept in reference to Serb actions. The speakers' inordinate emphasis on genocide comported with the SDS claim that Bosniaks and Croats in the 1990s were resurrecting Ustasha policies. In straining to portray genocide as the central historical Bosnian Serb experience of the twentieth century, the speakers intended to persuade a skeptical public that Serbs were justified in using armed force to ward off the alleged imminent threat to the Serb people. The speakers also pressed the notion that wartime genocide warranted Serb seizures of much of Bosnia.

Milorad Ekmečić, Professor of Modern History at the University of Sarajevo and a member of the SDS Political Council, used statistics to dramatic effect in characterizing Serb suffering in the twentieth century. He told the 500 participants that the Serbs' disproportionate losses in both world wars had destroyed their former demographic advantage in Bosnia. Of 1.9 million victims in the First World War, he asserted, 65 percent were Serbs, and their losses were proportionately even greater among the 3.2 million victims of World War II. "In the history of the world only the Jews have paid more than the Serbs for their freedom,"[23] claimed Ekmečić. He blamed wartime deaths for the Serb population's fall from first to second place among the peoples of Bosnia and said that the demographic inversion forced Serbs to fight for their very survival. Serbs "bear the invisible brand of the battle for biological existence,"[24] he contended, a classic Serb-nationalist statement of perpetual victimhood.

Although Ekmečić's formulations drew the attention of the press and public, his numbers were at odds with several highly-regarded demographic studies. Two independent studies, one published by a Serb and another by a Croat, showed that Bosniaks and Serbs perished in approximately equal numbers in Bosnia during the Second World War, and that wartime deaths had totaled

[23] *Oslobodjenje*, March 29, 1992, p. 2.
[24] Ibid.

just a little over 1 million, rather than the 1.9 million claimed by Ekmečić.[25] Furthermore, Serb deaths were only slightly higher as a percentage of their group (6.9 percent according to Kočović) than those of Bosniaks (6.8 percent) in the war. Since these surprisingly similar findings were published, they have been widely cited by scholars to refute the politically-motivated estimates of both Croat and Serb nationalists.[26]

Speakers at the Congress of Serb Intellectuals placed a final public exclamation mark on the fallacy-filled Serb nationalist justifications for driving non-Serbs from the new Serb state. On April 1, paramilitary units crossed the Drina and entered Bijeljina, a city in northeastern Bosnia with a population of 36,414 that was 52 percent Bosniak, 29 percent Serb, 9 percent Yugoslav, and 1 percent Croat. There, Serb paramilitary forces initiated the first mass atrocities in a Bosnian city with a combination of killings, beatings, torture, and expulsions.[27] Further atrocities were to follow in the next several weeks in many other Bosnian municipalities. The Serb effort to build a purely Serb state had already been launched, and the battle for Bosnia was about to begin.

---

[25] Bogoljub Kočović, *Žrtve Drugog svjetskog rata u Jugoslaviji* (London: Naše Delo, 1985); and Vladimir Žerjavić, *Gubici stanovništva Jugoslavije u drugom svjetskom ratu* (Zagreb: Jugoslavensko viktimološko društvo, 1989).

[26] See, for example, Aleksa Djilas, *The Contested Country: Yugoslav Unity and Communist Revolution, 1919–1953* (Cambridge: Harvard University Press, 1991), pp. 125–127.

[27] For the account of a prominent Bosniak community leader in Bijeljina who was both a victim and a witness in the first days of these events, see Jusuf Trbić, *Gluho doba: Kolumne reminiscencije, analize i rasprave* (Tuzla: Kujundžić, 2006), pp. 130–140.

11

Callous Perpetrator

"The birth of a state and the creation of borders do not occur without war."

Radovan Karadžić[1]

April 6, the anniversary of the Partisans' liberation of Sarajevo in 1945 from German and Ustasha occupiers, had been a special holiday in Bosnia ever since then. But in 1992, that date acquired an additional and different association as the beginning of the longest, bloodiest war in Europe since the Second World War. In the first weeks after April 6, SDS local officials and their allies implemented the municipal strategy largely as they had planned by launching temporally and geographically staggered attacks and carrying out mass atrocities against non-Serbs. Karadžić fled Sarajevo in the first days of fighting; by the end of May he was directing the campaign from Pale, seventeen kilometers east of the city center. This chapter describes his harrowing flight and examines his transformation from a planner and political leader to the head of an armed takeover, and it discusses how he established state territories purged of non-Serb inhabitants.

FLIGHT

For the first six days of April, Karadžić remained in Sarajevo. Although large-scale conflict had yet to begin, there was nothing tranquil about the city in those days. SDS leaders were forming a separate Serb police force in each jurisdiction, touching off struggles with non-Serb officers for control of police stations and neighborhoods.[2] Residents formed committees by block, street, or

---

[1] Mladić diaries, May 27, 1992, p. 99.
[2] On the preparation and implementation of the Sarajevo siege from 1992–1995, see Robert J. Donia, "Bosnian Serb Leadership and the Siege of Sarajevo," ICTY, PRK, Exhibit P977, admitted into evidence on June 1, 2010, pp. 3,151–3,152.

neighborhood to secure their homes against uncertain threats, turning parts of the city into warrens of checkpoints and barbed wire barriers. Criminal gangs, many of them Bosniak in leadership and composition, controlled whole sections of the city while also defending those areas against Serb paramilitary and police units.

Alarmed by the rising violence, thousands of peace demonstrators from all ethnonational groups rallied on the spacious square in front of the Bosnian Parliament Building on Sarajevo's near west side. They protested the belligerence of the three nationalist parties (SDA, SDS, and HDZ) and pleaded for them to avert a war. Many of the same demonstrators had first taken to the streets to protest and dismantle the barricades erected by the SDS and SDA on March 1–2, and they had returned to the streets several times in March to protest bellicose nationalism. Their rally on April 5 was the beginning of a two-day effort to call down blame and shame on all three nationalist parties.

The demonstrators gathered only a few hundred meters from a major assault by Serb forces on the Bosnian police academy at Vraca, a hill just south of the Bosnian Parliament Building. That attack was intended to cripple the republic's police force, which had become largely Bosniak in composition after Serb officers withdrew from the common force on the last day of March. The Serb troops attacked the academy with tanks, artillery, and infantry, readily overpowering the few hundred police cadets and staff who were trapped in the building. By the end of the day of April 5, the building's occupants surrendered and were taken prisoner by Serb forces, but while the battle was still raging, Serb troops also opened fire on some nearby demonstrators. Gunmen shot and killed Suada Dilberović, a Bosniak medical student born in Dubrovnik, as she stood on the Vrbanje Bridge between the Bosnian Parliament building and the Grbavica neighborhood of high-rise apartment buildings at the foot of the Vraca hill. She and a young Croat woman named Olga Sučić are remembered as the first fatalities of the war in Sarajevo; elsewhere in Bosnia, dozens of deaths had preceded theirs.

Despite these killings, the peace demonstrators were undeterred. Thousands of them entered the Bosnian Parliament building in the evening of April 5 (unopposed by security forces) and took over the parliament hall. After hours of speeches, they selected an ephemeral "Government of National Salvation" made up of leading non-partisan academics who favored the civic option and opposed national division. This government never controlled anything outside of the parliament hall, and that only for the night of April 5–6, but it is remembered as a testament to the thousands of Sarajevans who abjured nationalism and stood unarmed in opposition to the nationalist parties.

While Sarajevo was being territorially divided by various armed formations and the demonstrations were growing, Karadžić had a hotel, a security zone, and an armed security force all to himself. After Rajko Dukić moved SDS headquarters from the assembly building across the street to the Holiday Inn on March 2, the hotel and surrounding area had come under Karadžić's control. From party headquarters on the upper floors of the hotel, Karadžić and his armed entourage could look across the street at the Bosnian parliament building and the square in front of it. They had a front row seat from which to view a large gathering of antiwar protestors on April 5 and 6. But on April 6, their headquarters, and the Holiday Inn where it was housed, attracted unwanted attention from the demonstrators. The largely leaderless protesters remained in the square in front of the parliament building during the morning, but many drifted across the street to the area around the Holiday Inn where they believed senior SDS officials to be. As they gathered near the hotel, gunmen opened fire from the upper floors on the unarmed civilians below, killing six protesters and injuring many more.

Serb propagandists were quick to claim that the shots came from the roof of a government-controlled military hospital a block away, but few doubted that the shooters were Serbs or that Karadžić or other senior SDS officials had authorized the attack. After the shootings, a special police detachment loyal to the Bosnian government entered the hotel and arrested several gunmen on the upper floors. One of Karadžić's bodyguards was among those arrested, but Karadžić and his other bodyguards were nowhere to be found. Telephone intercepts show that by the time of the shooting, Karadžić was on the move in search of a safe route out of the city. Sometime in the afternoon of April 6, he placed a call to a subordinate, who called Karadžić "boss" (*šefe*) and who may have been at SDS headquarters in the Holiday Inn.[3] Although he spoke in terse sentences that left much of the call unintelligible, Karadžić clearly was about to depart Sarajevo's contested near west side for areas under Serb control, either in Pale to the east or to the suburb of Ilidža six kilometers west of the city center.

Karadžić seized upon evidence that appeared to reinforce his belief that the peace demonstrators were hostile to Serbs. The unidentified telephone caller proposed to Karadžić that SDS spokesmen should warn government officials that "aggression will not be tolerated."[4] The statement ignited Karadžić's rage. "They will all be killed," he said twice, reminiscent of the disappearance discourse he had used in fall 1991. "They shouldn't try to enter Serb [territory]."

[3] Intercept, Karadžić and unidentified male subordinate, April 6, 1992, ICTY, PSM, Exhibit P613, Tab 183, BCS 0324–5726–0324–5730.
[4] Ibid.

Karadžić's interlocutor then reiterated the view that the demonstrators were Bosniak provocateurs. "Yes, and they [SDA leaders] have thrown their people in there [amongst the demonstrators]," the unknown speaker said to Karadžić. "We have information, that half the people in this gathering are armed.... By God there will be corpses all around because ... they are killing our people, just like that."

The intercept of Karadžić's phone call suggest that he ordered his followers to impose the siege on Sarajevo as vengeance against the demonstrators, the government, and the SDA. On that pivotal day when Bosnia was recognized as independent and its streets and squares turned violent, he saw the peace demonstrations as yet another manifestation of Bosniak perfidy and proof of a massive Bosniak plot orchestrated by Izetbegović against Serbs.

He could not have been more wrong. The Bosniak nationalists of the SDA thoroughly detested the protests and denounced the demonstrators for weakening the will of Sarajevans to resist Serb attacks. The demonstrations were directed against the SDA as well as the SDS and HDZ, something Karadžić stubbornly refused to acknowledge. Mischaracterizing the origins of the protest, Karadžić remained consistent with his earlier inclination to attribute the worst of intentions to his political rivals. He directed that much of Sarajevo be surrounded and cut off from surrounding towns in retaliation for Izetbegović's alleged organizing of the demonstrations. "Second of all, please call around ... the city should be 100 percent closed. No buses can arrive anymore," he said to his unidentified interlocutor. "Alija came up with all [the demonstrations]. Nothing must get through either from Semizovac [to the northwest] or from Ilijaš [to the west].... I've told that to [JNA General] Kukanjac as well," he said.

Karadžić eventually reached Ilidža in the far western part of the city and re-established his base of operations in the Hotel Serbia, which had served Habsburg officials as a resort and spa in the early twentieth century. Although it proved a temporary haven, he was welcomed by local SDS officials there. One of them reported, "When he visited us in Ilidža and encouraged us, Serbs in Sarajevo from those areas retained control and even extended their territory in certain parts, driving the Muslims out of the territories where they actually had a majority."[5]

A few weeks later Karadžić relocated to Pale. Ski resort hotels in Pale were commandeered for meetings of RS executive bodies, offices, and assembly sessions. Nearly invulnerable to invasion from below, the village had ample accommodations for officials and their guests. Although far from the sort of

---

5   BSA, 17th Session, July 24–26, 1992, Nedeljko Prstojević, BCS 0214–9561.

major city that is usually conjured by the word "capital," Karadžić owned a home there, and it was compatible with the Serb nationalist glorification of nature and the rural lifestyle.

MAKING WAR AND DIRECTING ATROCITIES

Once in Pale, Karadžić worked to implement plans for a separate Serb state. As president of the RS, he worked to strengthen the security and political authority of the new state, and as commander in chief, he oversaw armed conquests and mass atrocities by Bosnian Serbs against their adversaries. As the president of the three-member Presidency of the RS (the other members were Koljević and Plavšić), he began convening periodic meetings around the time of the 16th assembly session on May 12, 1992. Prime Minister Branko Djerić also attended most meetings; General Ratko Mladić, Commander of the General Staff of VRS, attended only infrequently, usually when a specific purpose required his presence. The minutes of those meetings, most of which came into the possession of the ICTY, are sketchy and mostly uninformative for reasons explained in the minutes of the 21st presidency session, held on August 2, 1992: "Due to security considerations and the detailed nature of the information, the conclusions and alternatives were adopted [but] were not put on the record."[6]

During their meetings, presidency members discussed the military situation, monitored the progress of mass atrocities, and praised those who committed them. Among the evidence of this is the account of a visit by Miroslav Deronjić, president of the Municipal SDS Board in Bratunac in eastern Bosnia. He testified in a written witness statement at the ICTY that he visited Pale on May 10 or 11, 1991, to find Karadžić, Mladić, and several SDS local leaders gathered around a table in a large conference room.[7] Maps on the wall showed the ethnic composition of various areas by color. Sixty-five Muslims, he told them, had been killed "in the course of fulfilling the operational plan to displace permanently Bosnian Muslims from the Bratunac Municipality." Deronjić reported that the town of Glogova had been partly destroyed and its Bosniak inhabitants forcibly removed. The assembled leaders in Pale "greeted my report with applause," he stated, "and Velibor Ostojic commented, 'now we can color Bratunac blue'," to indicate Serb domination (Bosniak settlements were colored green). Deronjić's account suggests that Karadžić and Mladić oversaw the commission of mass atrocities with attention to detail and

---

[6] "Zapisnik sa 21. sjednice Predsjedništva Srpske Republike Bosne i Hercegovine," August 2, 1992, ICTY, PMK, Exhibit P67A, BCS 0076-7993 – 0076-7795.

[7] Witness statement of Miroslav Deronjić, Paragraph 106, ICTY, PSM, Exhibit P600, BCS 0344-7921.

a reporting system, complete with a ritual coloring of a map and recognition of the local official's achievements, as if he were a salesman being recognized for selling the most products.

The presidency also made sure that statemaking proceeded even where local SDS officials were unwilling or unable to act. The presidency appointed assembly delegates to serve as "trustees" in their home areas. Trustees were tasked with establishing Serb municipalities where none yet existed and coordinating military and civilian activities with the aim of getting everyone to work together to purge non-Serbs from the land. "Sometime around the end of May or beginning of June, by decision of our war presidency, war trusteeships were formed for individual areas and, in the main, assembly delegates who reported for that duty were named," delegate Vojislav Maksimović explained to the assembly in November 1992.[8] Their task was to "establish our Serb state on the ground," he said. Trustees also served as couriers, conveying information in person between the RS presidency and individual municipalities, thereby avoiding the use of vulnerable electronic communications. These activities indicate that some local Serb leaders continued passively resisting statemaking plans and mass atrocities well into wartime; they also suggest that Karadžić was determined to avoid leaving written evidence of the nature and scope of Bosnian Serb activities and his own role in directing them.

SARAJEVO

Even as he was exploring his options to leave the central city, Karadžić was seeking to isolate Sarajevo for strategic reasons. He had threatened to do so, then backed down, on two previous occasions (September 1991 and March 2, 1992). In April 1992, however, Karadžić directed the complete cutoff of Sarajevo as retaliation for what he perceived as Bosniak nationalist instigation of the peace demonstrators. As fighting spread and bombardments became more frequent, he proved incurious about events but relentless in employing violence as revenge for supposed indignities suffered by Serbs.

The Serb attack on the police academy on April 5 inaugurated months of fighting among Bosniak, Serb, and Croat armed units for control of the western suburbs and of the vital routes into the city from the west and north. Serbs needed to control only the flat, open access from the west to achieve Karadžić's stated aim of cutting off the town. In moving to establish that control militarily, Serb forces encountered fierce resistance from a combination of units loyal to the government, including several well-armed criminal gangs.

[8] BSA, 22nd Session, November 23–24, 1992, Vojislav Maksimović, BCS 0214-9732–0214-9733.

Those forces mounted a stout defense and launched offensives of their own, making Sarajevo one of the few areas of Bosnia where government loyalists were able to mount significant resistance to Serb conquest. Sarajevo's western approaches became a bitter battleground for many different military and paramilitary forces, many of them acting independently but loyal to one of the three nationalist parties. Some Croat and Bosniak units committed crimes against Serbs during these battles; as a result many Serbs who had at first stayed in their homes began to flee the central city for its Serb-controlled suburbs. However, Serb forces were more comprehensive and systematic in conducting atrocities than their Croat and Bosniak counterparts.

As elsewhere, Serbs undertook to remove non-Serbs who might become armed opponents, and they sought to secure a compact, contiguous Serb territorial unit to fulfill the Serb utopian dream. In an intercepted phone conversation in 1992, SDS activist Jovan Tintor stated, "We know what is ours! ... We will attach and join [territories] together in order to make a whole, which is normal! We have [land] from Sarajevo to ... when I stand in the morning in front of my house, I can drive to Niš [in southern Serbia] and stop nowhere except on Serb land!"[9]

In the Serb quest to control Sarajevo's western approach to cut off the city, the JNA's contribution proved decisive. The hills around the city bristled with hundreds of tanks, heavy artillery, and mortars, poised to pound the city from close range. JNA units in barracks in Sarajevo, however, were vulnerable to Bosnian government pressure. JNA troops and their families were scattered in 22 different facilities within Sarajevo. The largest and best known was the Marshal Tito Barracks just west of the Holiday Inn. Starting on May 2, Bosnian government forces besieged the JNA installations throughout Sarajevo, turning potential Serb aggressors into hostages. For the next six weeks, Bosnian government negotiators refused to let the besieged troops leave unless they agreed to leave their weapons behind. The talks eventually led to agreements in June 1992, but fighting broke out as some units tried to take their weapons with them. Once out of Sarajevo, the JNA soldiers joined their Serb co-nationals in Serb controlled territories around Sarajevo; few of them actually redeployed to Serbia or Montenegro.

The combined Serb forces carried out the isolation and bombardment of Sarajevo in full view of international officials and a host of war correspondents. Karadžić struggled to provide them with an explanation consistent with his narrative of non-Serb provocations and Serb suffering. At a press conference at the

9   Intercept, Jovan Tintor and interlocutor identified as "Žika," March 7, 1992, ICTY, PMK, BCS 0328–8666.

Hotel Serbia on April 18, he gave an astonishing answer when a reporter questioned him about shelling civilians in the inner city. "We only know that some
families of these people are arrested in Old Town," he said.[10] The family members of arrested Serbs "shelled the headquarters of Green Berets [a Bosniak
paramilitary organization], but they were poor shots. Those are unusual people, they shot without sense. What has happened in Sarajevo is regrettable, but
the sole explanation is that they don't know how to shoot." Asked if he intended
to continue targeting the inner city, Karadžić equivocated. "We hope that we
won't, but the terror directed at Sarajevo must stop," he said. "I cannot say to
every Serb, don't shoot, when he hears that his uncle was beaten."

Although Karadžić's explanation seemed ludicrous, his claim of sloppy
marksmanship had some basis in fact. A 1993 internal RS analysis of combat
readiness and activities skewered artillery units for expending ordnance recklessly in bombardments during 1992.[11] "There was shooting in all directions,
even just for boosting morale,"[12] the analysis concluded. It blamed excessive
fire on ill-trained soldiers who were manning the heavy weapons around town.
"An enormous quantity of ordnance was given to people who either were dealing with such systems for the first time or who knew a little about other, older
systems."[13] From the perspective of 1993, it hailed as a "positive solution" that
"cities and inhabited places are no longer shelled and destroyed,"[14] confirming
that such places had been shelled earlier.

In subsequent weeks, Karadžić developed a different response to inquiring
reporters and diplomats. The siege did not exist at all, he claimed. Bosniaks
were launching deadly attacks against Serb villages in the hills surrounding
the city, he explained, and Serb forces were merely defending their own people against attacks by Islamic fundamentalists. That interpretation was contradicted daily by reporters who witnessed the artillery attacks on the city, by UN
officials who counted the number of shells that hit each day, and by the Serb
assembly delegates who, in closed sessions, described the city as in the tight
grip of Serb forces.[15] But Karadžić continued his public denials that Serbs were
besieging Sarajevo until very late in the war.

---

[10] *Oslobodjenje*, April 19, 1992, p. 4. Karadžić's responses were also reported, but not directly
quoted, in *Duga*, no. 474, April 25–May 8, 1992, p. 19.

[11] Republika Srpska, Glavni štab Vojske Republike Srpske, "Analiza borbene gotovosti i
aktivnosti Vojske Republike Srpske u 1992. godini," April 1993, ICTY, PMK, Exhibit P67A,
BCS 0060–7339–0060–7480.

[12] Ibid., BCS 0060–7354.

[13] Ibid., BCS 0060–7353.

[14] Ibid., BCS 0060–7355.

[15] Robert J. Donia, ed., *From the Republika Srpska Assembly, 1991–1996: Excerpts from Delegates'
Speeches at the Republika Srpska Assembly as Evidence for the International Criminal Tribunal
at the Hague* (Sarajevo: University Press, 2012), pp. 171–177.

SPORADIC, SYSTEMATIC VIOLENCE

The Bosnian Serb nationalists seized about 70 percent of Bosnia in spring and early summer of 1992, but it is something of an exaggeration to call these one-sided skirmishes a "war." No large force invaded or launched a frontal assault on defenders; no major set-piece battles took place; in only a few areas were non-Serbs able to mount significant resistance to the armed Serb formations. Serb nationalist forces conquered Bosnia one municipality at a time, just as they had planned, with a series of blitzkriegs at various times and locations. Local SDS officials typically coordinated the raids in their municipality; they were aided by various combinations of paramilitary forces, police special units, territorial defense units, volunteers, and the JNA. The SDS and its armed Serb allies seized power and territory by executing Karadžić's plans imperfectly, irregularly, and with many local variations.

Most Serb operations shared certain features.[16] Local SDS or military leaders, who enjoyed an advantage in weaponry in almost every municipality, made exorbitant demands of Croat and Bosniak nationalist leaders. They often held sham negotiations to discuss these demands, then issued an ultimatum with a short deadline, demanding separation of the municipality into Serb and non-Serb parts. The removal of non-Serbs rarely began until the deadline passed. Moreover, Serb nationalists rarely began their cleansing operations without a violent provocation, whether great or small, authentic or staged. They thereby followed Karadžić's policy, originally proposed by Milošević, that aggressive actions should await a provocation by the other side. Before launching an operation, Bosnian Serb perpetrators pointed to the provocation, whatever it was, to brand their non-Serb victims as terrorists, extremists, Ustasha, fundamentalists, or criminals. In both internal documents and public announcements, Serb officials used such labels to imply or state that all non-Serbs were armed enemy combatants; this offered a justification to attack all inhabitants rather than targeting only armed provocateurs.

After a provocation, Serb forces struck swiftly and with overwhelming force. They deployed thousands of armed men in municipalities where they anticipated resistance or expected to eliminate large numbers of non-Serbs, but in other municipalities, they deployed only a handful of police and armed SDS members. They typically first seized the buildings of key local institutions,

---

[16] For the common elements of Serb mass atrocities in 1992, see James Gow, *The Serbian Project and its Adversaries: A Strategy of War Crimes* (Montreal: McGill–Queens University Press, 2003), pp. 118–144; and Robert J. Donia, "Bosanski Šamac and the History of Bosnia and Herzegovina," ICTY, Prosecutor v. Blagoje Simić et al., admitted into evidence on September 10, 2001, pp. 40–42.

including the municipal hall, police station, post office, radio station, and local newspaper (if there was one). They often used local media outlets to order non-Serbs to gather in a central location, such as a central square, school, city hall, or soccer stadium, and to turn over any weapons they possessed.

After disseminating these orders, police and SDS officials typically cordoned off the town or village, conducted a house by house sweep, and forced the recalcitrant from their homes. As they went, they killed some, beat others, raped and otherwise abused women, and herded their victims into the designated central assembly point. There they escorted their victims onto buses, sometimes confiscating their possessions as they boarded. Some non-Serbs were transported directly to killing locations for immediate execution. Others were taken to camps to face possible beatings, starvation, torture, and death. The more fortunate among the victims were taken to the boundary of Serb nationalist territory and released, or were held for a time before being swapped for Serb prisoners held by other forces. Most fortunate, though still genuinely miserable, were those who fled before the roundups and killings began.

In most places, these operations left the area firmly under Serb nationalist control and largely devoid of non-Serbs. The general pattern had many local variants; we examine two of them here: Pale, and Prijedor.[17]

PALE

Karadžić may well have wished that everything went as it did in his chosen capital village of Pale, the single Serb-majority municipality among the ten that made up the city of Sarajevo. The police chief, Malko Koroman, was Karadžić's man. He had played an important role in Karadžić's development as a Serb leader in early September 1991, when he had offered to "have all Romanija region above Sarajevo tonight," as described in Chapter 5. That tantalizing suggestion ignited Karadžić's wild imaginings of mass killings of Bosniaks by Serbs. Karadžić never authorized Koroman to carry out that threat in fall 1991, but Koroman used the occasion to extend Serb territorial control over additional areas adjacent to Pale municipality. "In September 1991, we 'moved' the Pale municipality borders to Lapišnica, that is [at] Brus on [Mount] Trebević," he told an interviewer, "so as to protect all the Serb settlements and population that were on our territory."[18] Other Serb leaders employed the same

---

17   Gerard Toal and Carl T. Dahlman, *Bosnia Remade: Ethnic Cleansing and its Reversal* (Oxford University Press, 2011), pp. 112–125. This work provides an account of similar events in Zvornik, a town on the Drina River in eastern Bosnia.

18   "Odbrana spoljnih granica i unutrašnja bezbjednosti – osnovni zadaci policije" (Defense of external boundaries and internal security – the basic police tasks), *Policajac, List Ministarstva*

euphemism – securing the boundaries around the Serb population and land –
to describe operations to eliminate non-Serbs from territory they controlled.
But Koroman forcibly removed no one in fall 1991; he simply established police
control, and no one dared challenge his right to do so.

Delineating boundaries was but one measure in the step-by-step process of
consolidating SDS control in Pale. The police, under Koroman's command,
established checkpoints and routinely stopped visitors on roads into and out of
the municipality. A reporter visiting from downtown Sarajevo in late January
1992 wrote of being stopped by the police twice during the short drive to Pale
and of seeing a sign with the word "Serbia" in large red letters at the edge of
the village.[19] Also in January, representatives of several hotels and the ski center in Pale announced that they had separated Pale-based enterprises from
their headquarters in downtown Sarajevo and stopped forwarding monthly
revenues from Pale to the central office.[20]

Asserting that the Bosnian Serbs had "lost confidence in the possibility
of agreement with the Muslim nation" and had been attacked by militant
Bosniaks, a body calling itself the "Crisis Staff of SAO Romanija" declared
on March 3, 1992, that the Bosnian Serbs would "undertake all measures to
assume full control on the territory of SAO Romanija."[21] Subsequently, on
March 24, Koroman terminated all five of the non-Serb police officers in
Pale and three non-Serb officers in the nearby municipality of Sokolac. He
relieved them of their weapons and equipment, explaining that he was acting
"in accord with decisions made by the government of SAO Romanija, which
had given the order."[22] These actions, he claimed, were in retaliation for the
departure (under no apparent duress) of Bosnian Serb policemen from their
posts in Sarajevo's Old Town, but Koroman insisted that the non-Serb officers
had fled of their own accord. Several of the non-Serb police officers from Pale
contested that account and claimed that they had been forced out of their jobs
in Pale.[23] But Koroman stuck to his story throughout the years: "Muslims and
Croats fled from our police forces before the beginning of the war," Koroman
told an interviewer in 1994.[24]

---

unutrašnjih poslova Republike Srpske, November 1994, pp. 4–5. In this interview, Koroman
recounted his strategies and activities in moving boundaries, conquering territory, and forcing
non-Serbs from the Pale municipality, as reported in the following paragraphs.

[19] *Oslobodjenje*, January 29, 1992, p. 11.

[20] Ibid.

[21] *Oslobodjenje*, March 5, 1992, p. 4.

[22] *Oslobodjenje*, March 26, 1992, p. 20.

[23] "Izjava milicionara muslimanske nacionalnosti o njihovim udaljavanju iz SJB Pale i SJB
Sokolac," March 24, 1992, ICTY, PMK, BCS 0204–8150–0204–8151.

[24] "Odbrana spoljnih granica," *Policajac*.

Koroman was more than a chief of police; he was the commander of a sizeable, well-armed military force. A sympathetic interviewer described him as a warrior and an adversary feared by Bosniaks. "He was on the most difficult battlefields, from the preparations to save the Serb people from the threatening contemporary Ottoman Jihad invasion, the aim of which was a fundamentalist state without the Serb people," the reporter wrote. Koroman saw military conquest as a prerequisite for policing. "We are aware that, first and foremost, we must first defend the territory and only then have control over it," he stated; his actions suggested that the word "defend" meant clearing territory of non-Serbs. A policeman "goes to the battlefield and afterwards does the police job," he said. On March 1, 1992, in the battle of the Sarajevo barricades described in Chapter 9, he led his forces in erecting and defending barricades at Lapišnica and Brus, two communities that he had included within the boundaries of Pale in September 1991. With 300 men under his command, he was immediately treated as a war hero. "The first rally took place in the Romanija Football Stadium in Pale, where I was greeted with the slogans, 'God Helps Brave Men' and 'God Help You, Duke'." (Serb nationalists had assigned the title "Duke" to leaders of Chetnik bands throughout the twentieth century.) "Already," said Koroman proudly, "I was not a [police] chief but a Duke to them."

As Koroman described it in the interview, he and his men roamed far from Pale to aid Serb units fighting in other municipalities, particularly during the early weeks of the war. He contributed to the Serb attack on the police academy in Vraca (although in the interview he misdated that attack as May 12 rather than April 5) and "established control over our Serb regions – villages toward Renovica and Goražde," he told the interviewer. Only after those conquests did he return to attend to Pale. "Later we mainly concerned ourselves with the defense of Serb land in Pale municipality," he said, in another euphemistic reference to ridding the land of non-Serbs. "In Pale, all the institutions of authority existed. We performed all the police work, securing individuals and buildings, … and there, today, Pale is free, Serb, and a wonder for all the world." In his view, security operations involved both expanding the boundaries of Serb control and aiding Serbs elsewhere to complete their conquests in other municipalities.

In none of these descriptions did he specify the means: mass atrocities, killings, and the elimination of non-Serbs from areas where their families had lived for generations. Others of Pale's former residents have recounted in grim detail what Koroman's account omitted. Veteran Sarajevo journalist Mladen Vuksanović was one of many Pale residents who rejected ethnonational affiliation; he identified himself as a professional, non-partisan journalist without ethnic loyalties, and detested the nationalist parties for seeking to divide the country. He was the son of a Croat Catholic mother and a Serbian Orthodox Montenegrin-born father. Both were deceased by 1992, and buried in Pale cemeteries on opposite sides of the village.[25] As Koroman tightened the Serb grip on Pale in early 1992, Vuksanović heard more and more helicopters rumbling overhead, saw many Pale Serbs walking purposefully in uniform past his home, and watched his Bosniak neighbors cower in fear when they were told to leave Pale.

His description of the Serb takeover during April, May, and June 1992 is eerily consistent with Koroman's, although told from the viewpoint of a frightened victim rather than a police official. "The new Serb authorities have taken over all the hotels in Pale and Jahorina for their personal use," Vuksanović wrote. "The hotel in Koran has been turned into a military hospital, staffed by Serb doctors who left Sarajevo in advance [of the siege] and transferred to Pale." He went on to describe the manifestations of party and police control in the area. "The SDS flag flutters over the police station," he wrote. "Everywhere in Pale and on the surrounding hills, checkpoints have been set up, in order to control the movement of civilians."[26] He reported that several Bosniaks who spoke out against Serb seizures had been found murdered. When he was sheltering non-Serbs in his home, he feared that their presence would lead Serb police or gangs to target him.

On July 2 and again on July 4, Vuksanović observed long lines of empty buses idling in streets near his home, an invitation to non-Serbs to board them and leave Pale while they safely could. (Throughout Bosnia, this became a mutually understood signal that mandatory expulsions were imminent.) On July 2, according to Sarajevo diarist Dane Olbina, "A group of 400 inhabitants of Pale, of Muslim and Croat nationality, were forced to leave their hearths."[27] Soon Vuksanović was told that his home would be given to a family of Serb refugees. On July 11 he gave the new arrivals a tour of his family home and showed them how to use the appliances.[28] On 13 July, he bought two bus tickets and left Pale with his wife, never to return.[29] He was among the last of

---

[25] Mladen Vuksanović, *From Enemy Territory: Pale Diary (5 April to 15 July 1992)* (London: Saqi, 2004), p. 10. First published as Vuksanović, *Pale: dnevnik 5.4–15.7.1993* (Zagreb: Durieux, 1996), p. 15.

[26] Vuksanović, *From Enemy Territory*, entry of April 15, 1992, p. 35.

[27] Dane Olbina, *Dani i godine opsade* (Sarajevo: Istorijski arhiv Sarajevo, 2002), entry of July 2, 1992, p. 93.

[28] Vuksanović, *From Enemy Territory*, entry of July 11, 1992, p. 160.

[29] Vuksanović, *From Enemy Territory*, entry of July 13, 1992, p. 162.

the non-Serbs to depart. He died in exile in 1999 at age 57. Pale's slow-motion removal of non-Serbs had been accomplished through physical and verbal intimidation, selective killings, and an offer of free transportation to go elsewhere, with its implied threat.

Koroman and Vuksanović, in their starkly contrasting accounts, mirrored the broad divide between Serb nationalists and non-Serbs in Bosnia. Karadžić and his fellow Serb nationalists imagined the armed struggles of 1992–95 as a series of Serb security operations in defense of the Serb people and Serb land. Non-Serbs viewed it as a sustained campaign of genocide. In refusing to acknowledge having driven nearly all non-Serbs from Serb-conquered land, Serb national apologists – led by Karadžić – revealed their claim of justified self-defense to be a routine denial narrative rather than a plausible characterization of the conflict.

PRIJEDOR

In contrast to the slow-motion, low-violence removal of non-Serbs from Pale, Serb nationalists rid Prijedor of non-Serbs suddenly, violently, and thoroughly. The municipality of Prijedor, with a population of 112,543 in 1991, occupied a key demographic, strategic, and political position in Bosnia.[30] Most east-west rail and vehicular traffic in northern Bosnia ran through it to link the city of Banja Luka to the east with western Bosnia and Croatia. Prijedor was heavily industrialized. Many Prijedorans derived their livelihood from the iron mine at nearby Ljubija, and the iron extracted from the mine was strategically and economically significant for all of Bosnia. Prijedor was also historically significant: every Yugoslav schoolchild learned of the heroic Partisan resistance to German encirclement at nearby Mrakovica on Mount Kozara during 1943, and many visited the towering Partisan memorial that memorialized the battles there.

Immersed in the Partisan legacy, many Prijedor residents declared themselves "Yugoslavs," angering SDS leaders who contended that those declaring themselves Yugoslavs were simply nationally unawakened Serbs. SDS efforts to "awaken" the Yugoslavs to their Serb national consciousness assumed particular urgency because Bosniaks slightly outnumbered Serbs according to the 1991 census: the Serbs of Prijedor could claim a relative majority only by including all Yugoslavs in their numbers.

[30] Robert J. Donia, "Prijedor in the Bosnian Krajina: A Background Report," April 18, 2002, ICTY, Prosecutor v. Milomir Stakić (IT-97-24), Exhibit SK 42, pp. 1–2.

From their first days in power, Karadžić and Krajišnik paid special attention to Prijedor. Vexed by factionalism within the Prijedor SDS, they intervened directly to alter the composition of the SDS board. On September 11, 1991, Karadžić's intervention led to the election of local physician Milomir Stakić, replacing the voluble but ineffective former party president, Srdjo Srdić. In overseeing the change, Karadžić displayed his uncanny ability to identify leaders willing and able to carry out mass atrocities in their areas. Stakić quickly showed himself to be a reliable Karadžić lieutenant. In December 1991 he implemented the first phase of Karadžić's A-B instructions immediately upon receiving them, making Prijedor one of the first municipalities to do so. As head of the Prijedor SDS Crisis Staff, he led the SDS in carrying out mass atrocities in May 1992. His effective leadership earned him a trial at the ICTY; in March 2006 he was convicted and sentenced to 40 years in prison for crimes committed in Prijedor.

As in Pale, Serb nationalists in Prijedor seized power well before they began mass atrocities. The ICTY Trial Chamber described the takeover, drawn from the testimony of dozens of witnesses and hundreds of documents. As stated in the chamber's judgment, "Employees of the public security station and reserve police" gathered on the evening of April 29. "Only Serbs were present and some of them were wearing military uniforms," said the judgment. "Those who refused to participate had to hand in their ID and weapon and leave." The remaining Serb security personnel were divided into five groups of about twenty, and "each was ordered to gain control of certain buildings," the judges wrote. "One group was responsible for the Municipal Assembly building, one for the SUP [police] building, one for the courts, one for the bank and the last for the post-office." Early in the morning of April 30, "the SDS definitively took over power in Prijedor," said the judgment. "The central authorities were replaced by SDS or SDS-loyal personnel.... The residents of Prijedor ... observed that checkpoints had been established throughout the town overnight."

The Trial Chamber characterized the "takeover by the SDS as an illegal *coup d'état*, which was planned and coordinated a long time in advance with the ultimate aim of creating a pure Serb municipality." As in Pale, atrocities followed the takeover rather than being an integral part of it. In the two weeks after the takeover on April 30, SDS Serbs tightened their control over the city, mobilized its Serb citizens for military or police duty, dismissed non-Serbs from their jobs, and declared that key posts "may only be held by personnel of Serb nationality." In mid-May, SDS leaders issued several ultimatums "calling citizens to surrender weapons in order to maintain peace in the area." They set a deadline of midnight on May 14, 1992, for full compliance, but May 14 came and went without Bosniak compliance and without Serb attacks. Local SDS Serbs apparently awaited a Bosniak provocation to trigger their removal of non-Serbs.

Neither Bosniaks nor Croats had an armed force capable of challenging the well-armed, JNA-backed Serb nationalists, but they were not so naïve as to give up their few weapons to the forces arrayed against them. As Serbs tightened their grip on the city of Prijedor, Bosniaks put up roadblocks on access roads to several Bosniak-majority villages in the area, protecting them from easy Serb seizure. Around 7:00 p.m. on May 22, Bosniaks manning a checkpoint controlling access to Hambarine, one of the Bosniak-majority villages, stopped a vehicle carrying six JNA soldiers. Although witnesses at the Stakić trial disagreed on who shot first, everyone agreed that Bosniaks were responsible for wounding the car's occupants in the ensuing firefight. The Trial Chamber concluded that the Bosniaks had indeed opened fire first, but they attached little weight to that conclusion in light of what followed. "The Trial Chamber recognizes that, as a matter of principle, the soldiers in the car at the checkpoint in Hambarine and the Serb columns in Kozarac, when attacked at Jakupovići, had a right to self-defense," wrote the judges. "However, the Trial Chamber stresses that any armed response must be proportionate to the initial attack."

The injuries to the six JNA soldiers (four Serbs and two Croats), provided SDS leaders had a putative "provocation," and they hastened to exploit it, according to the ICTY judgment:

> The Serb authorities used the incidents in Hambarine and Kozarac as a pretext for initiating full-scale armed conflict in the municipality against the civilian population and non-Serb paramilitary forces. It was the trigger that allowed the Serbs to use the overwhelming military power at their disposal. They demanded that the village inhabitants hand over the shooter and surrender all weapons within a few hours. At noon on the 23rd, tanks and armored personnel carriers began shelling Hambarine, and approximately a thousand soldiers launched an attack on the village.

The Trial Chamber characterized the operation as "planned, co-ordinated, and sustained armed attacks on civilian settlements." Starting with the attack on Hambarine, Bosnian Serb nationalists killed thousands of non-Serbs in Prijedor. Stakić alone was responsible for over 1,500 deaths, according to the Trial Chamber in his case at the ICTY. The Prijedor Serb nationalists gained particular notoriety for driving thousands of their victims into camps where they beat, tortured, starved, or killed them. Separately from the Stakić case, the ICTY tried and sentenced five perpetrators to prison terms of five to

25 years for atrocities against Bosniaks and Croats in the Prijedor-area camps at Omarska, Trnopolje, and Keraterm.[31]

Trials at the ICTY highlighted the sordid brutality of mass atrocities in Prijedor, but of course SDS leaders characterized events differently. In the SDS narrative, the provocative shooting was no pretext but the first evidence of a deadly threat to the Serb people (disregarding the fact that two of the JNA passengers were Croats) posed by non-Serb military formations. The SDS ethnically cleansed the municipality out of necessity to preserve the Serb people. But in a remarkably candid admission, Srdjo Srdić (purged at Karadžić's initiative from his post as SDS president) claimed before the Bosnian Serb Assembly that local Serbs, rather than Karadžić, were responsible for atrocities in Prijedor. "We didn't ask you, or Mr. Karadžić, or Mr. Krajišnik what we should do in Prijedor. Prijedor was the only green [i.e., Bosniak] municipality in Bosnian Krajina; if we had been listening to you we would still be green today," Srdić said. "We fixed them and firmly sent them packing where they belong," he declared to delegate applause.[32] On another occasion, in 1993, Srdić chastised SDS leaders in other municipalities for vacillating in ridding their areas of non-Serbs. "They should have cleansed their municipalities, as we had done," he declared, "and they would not have had any problems."[33]

BOSNIAN SERB STRATEGIC GOALS

By early May of 1992, Bosnian Serb nationalists and the JNA supporting them controlled about 70 percent of Bosnia. In possibly their most important session of the war, assembly delegates gathered in Banja Luka on May 12 to establish their own military force and formalize the goals they were already in the process of accomplishing. They voted to form the Army of Republika Srpska (*Vojska Republika Srpska*, VRS) and to appoint General Ratko Mladić as Commander of its General Staff, a position in JNA nomenclature equivalent to a supreme commander of the army. On May 19, these decisions formally took effect when they were promulgated by the RS tripartite presidency (Karadžić, Koljević, and Plavšić), a body also formed by assembly vote on May 12.[34] Both formation of the VRS and the Mladić appointment were largely cosmetic, in that they renamed existing institutions. The JNA stationed units in Bosnia, with their commanders, men, munitions, and weaponry, were for the most

---

[31] "Judgement," February 28, 2005, ICTY, Prosecutor v. Miroslav Kvočka, et al., IT-98-30-1-T.

[32] BSA, 22nd Session, November 23–24, 1992, Srdjo Srdić, BCS 0214-9745.

[33] BSA, 34th Session, August 27–October 1, 1993, Srdić, BCS 0215-0676.

[34] BSA, 16th Session, May 12, 1992, Minutes, Item 8, BCS 0084-7713; and Hoare, *How Bosnia Armed*, pp. 40–42.

part simply rebadged as the VRS. Mladić's title was changed but his new role was nearly identical to that before: until May 19 he had been Commander and Chief of Staff of the 2nd Military District headquartered in Sarajevo, a post that gave him the powers of the supreme commander of JNA forces in Bosnia. By acquiring the JNA forces and appointing Mladić its new commander, the VRS at the moment of its creation held overwhelming military advantage over the next largest forces in Bosnia, the Army of the Republic of Bosnia and Herzegovina (*Armija Republika Bosna i Hercegovina*, ARBiH) and the Croatian Defense Council (*Hrvatska vijeće obrane*, HVO).

In addition to supporting the military decisions, Karadžić presented to the assembly the six strategic goals formulated to guide the political and military policies of the SDS and RS.[35] The goals expanded Bosnian Serb territorial ambitions in specifying a few strategic imperatives and broad swaths of territory rather than their previous, less comprehensive claims to lands where Serbs lived. Although records of the session fail to show whether the six goals were formally adopted, they were published in the Official Gazette in November 1993 as if they had been.[36] Bosnian Serb nationalist leaders regarded the goals not as aspirational but as mandatory and irrevocable codifications of their solemn duties. Assembly delegates invoked the goals many times in their speeches, nearly always treating them as sacrosanct. Not until late 1995 did any delegate dare question the validity and importance of these goals, and he earned a sharp rebuke from Krajišnik, who insisted that the goals were inviolable.[37]

At the assembly session on May 12, Karadžić identified the first goal as "separation from the other two national communities, state separation."[38] Krajišnik asserted that the first goal was the "most important one," while the other five goals were "sub-items of the first one."[39] [On May 12, and again at subsequent assembly sessions,] Karadžić and Krajišnik each emphasized their irrevocable commitment to the principle of] separation. Krajišnik was ready to trade conquered land for a pure Serb state. "Believe me, the greatest tragedy would be if the Muslims agreed to live with us now," he told the assembly. "That is the one thing I would never accept and I would rather accept a smaller percentage of territory, ... provided we remain separate from the Muslims and have

---

[35] BSA, 16th Session, May 12, 1992, Karadžić, BCS 0084–7722 – 0084–7724.

[36] "Odluku o strateškim ciljevima srpskog naroda u Bosni i Hercegovini," *Službeni glasnik Republike Srpske*, no. 22, November 26, 1993, p. 866.

[37] BSA, 56th Session, December 17, 1995, Grujo Lalović, BCS 0215–4789, and Krajišnik, BCS 0215–4843.

[38] BSA, 16th Session, May 12, 1992, Karadžić, BCS 0084–7722.

[39] BSA, 16th Session, May 12, 1992, Krajišnik, BCS 0084–7752.

our country."[40] Karadžić later acknowledged that it meant driving non-Serbs from the land. "We know for sure that we have to give up something [i.e., territory]," Karadžić told the assembly in July 1994, "if we wish to achieve our primary strategic aim ... to rid the house of our enemies, the Croats and Muslims, and not to be in the same state with them anymore."[41]

Krajišnik explained that the first goal required removing Serbs from lands controlled by others as well as ridding Serb territory of non-Serbs. "We shall, in an organized and fair manner, provide our people with a roof over their heads," he said. "Resettle them if need be; we shall not put them in a genocidal position."[42] (By "genocidal position," Krajišnik meant leaving them vulnerable to attack by armed formations of other peoples.) Indeed, during the war Bosnian Serb leaders frequently pressured international leaders to transfer Serbs (whom they characterized as "hostages") from government-held territory to the RS. With this manipulation of terminology, Serb leaders further expanded the meaning of "separation" beyond boundary-drawing to encompass massive, reciprocal, and largely involuntary uprooting of long-term residents based on national identity.

The remaining five goals spelled out the Bosnian Serb nationalists' territorial ambitions. Senior SDS and RS officials never sought the complete conquest of all Bosnia. The goal of "separation" required that some areas belong to the other two peoples, but the strategic goals adopted by the assembly implied that the land left for others, particularly the Bosniaks, would be scant and crowded.

The next two goals defined Serb territorial ambitions in northern and eastern Bosnia. The second goal was to establish a corridor across northern Bosnia, linking the eastern and western portions of the RS. The third goal demanded elimination of the Drina River as a border between Bosnia and Serbia, a goal that would have meant a de facto unification under Serb control of eastern Bosnia and the Republic of Serbia. The two corridors intersected in Bijeljina in northeastern Bosnia, where the municipality (but not the town) of that name had an absolute majority (59 percent) of Serb inhabitants. But no other Serb-majority municipalities were among those claimed for some distance to the south and west of Bijeljina. None of the first six municipalities to the west had an absolute Serb majority, and the first four municipalities south of Bijeljina each had an absolute Bosniak majority in 1991. These numbers highlight the fact that Serb territorial claims found no justification

---

[40] [BSA,] 37th Session, January 10, 1994, Krajišnik, BCS 0215–2152.
[41] BSA, 42nd Session, July 18–19, 1994, Karadžić, BCS 0215–2880–0215–2881.
[42] BSA, 16th Session, May 12, 1992, Krajišnik, BCS 0084–7752–0084–7753.

based on Serb habitation. However, except for a few pockets of land held by Croats in the north and Bosniaks in the east, areas along both the Sava and Drina rivers were conquered by the VRS by July 1995 and their non-Serbs eliminated or removed. Thus the Serb shift from residence-based ambitions to broader strategic goals involved more and larger mass atrocities than if only Serb-inhabited lands had been conquered.

The fourth goal, "establishment of borders on the Una and Neretva Rivers," demarcated large swaths of territory in western and central Bosnia to be controlled by Serbs. The fifth goal called for "division of Sarajevo into Serb and Muslim parts and establishment of effective state authority in each part." Karadžić saw the strategic value in cutting off and bombarding the city as well as dividing it. "The battle in Sarajevo and for Sarajevo, seen strategically and tactically, is of decisive importance, because it does not allow the establishment of even the illusion of a [Bosnian] state," he said in explaining the fifth goal on May 12. "The fighting around Sarajevo will decide the destiny of Bosnia and Herzegovina.... We suspected and said before that, if there were a war, it would start in Sarajevo and end in Sarajevo." He often spoke of tightening the siege to force concessions at the bargaining table. "We have to maintain the character of the Berlin kind of corridor in order to get Sarajevo definitely divided and the territories to become compact," he explained in 1994. "Then we will give them one square meter of the hill between Vogošća and Vis [in Sarajevo], and we will take away from them an entire square kilometer on the Drina."[43]

The sixth goal, "access for the RS to the sea," was the only one that proposed to expand the RS to include land beyond the borders of Bosnia. With this goal, the Bosnian Serb nationalists implicitly dismissed neighboring Montenegro's lengthy seacoast as insufficient for their needs, revealing a desire that their newly-formed state be able to stand fully on its own without any dependence on established Serb states. The sixth goal became a staple in Bosnian Serb demands during the war, but it proved the only one so overreaching that it was never realized even in part.

In adopting the six strategic goals, Karadžić and the Bosnian Serbs completed their transition to a full war footing, having already eliminated much of the Bosniak and Croat presence in Serb-conquered areas with the support and engagement of the JNA. Although they controlled most of Bosnia by the time they embraced the six goals on May 12, 1992, the SDS leaders and VRS forces continued thereafter to engage in further conquests and mass atrocities to rid the conquered land of non-Serbs. They pursued their objectives

---

[43] BSA, 40th Session, May 10–11, 1994, Karadžić, BCS 0215–2545.

piecemeal, one municipality at a time, scattered over many dates and locations. Their actions had many local variations, since Karadžić had delegated to municipal-level SDS officials much of the responsibility for carrying out their tasks. Conceived and guided from above, the removal of Bosnia's non-Serbs was carried out from below by local political leaders and the particular military and police forces available to support them.

12

Duplicitous Diplomat

"The art of statesmanship is to foresee the inevitable and expedite its occurrence."

Charles Maurice de Talleyrand

"We are a sad orphan without a friend...

"We are just a mouse in the claws of a few cats at play."

Radovan Karadžić, 17th Bosnian Serb Assembly Session, July 1992[1]

After the Serb takeover of much of Bosnia in spring 1992, Karadžić increasingly became engaged in diplomatic activities. This chapter deals with his successes and failures as a negotiator from war's beginning until the final Serb rejection of the Vance-Owen Peace Plan (VOPP) in May 1993. He relished his role as chief negotiator for the Bosnian Serbs and proved adept both at winning key concessions and at denying international negotiators grounds for taking military action. But as the war dragged on, he became more transparently duplicitous and alienated many of his interlocutors. Plain-spoken and often blunt, he practiced few diplomatic niceties. He expressed blustery confidence in himself and his cause, and he contemptuously rejected the criticism of others. But along with bravado, he evidenced vulnerability and paranoia on occasion during the negotiations. Toward the end of the war he became marginalized personally, even as international leaders reluctantly acquiesced to many demands of the Bosnian Serb nationalists.

KARADŽIĆ AND THE PEACEMAKERS: "ACQUIESCE AND IGNORE"

During the forty-four months of armed conflict, a rotating cast of international facilitators stepped up to sponsor talks and propose peace plans to the Bosnian belligerents. At one time or another, the UN, the EC, the International

[1]   BSA, 17th Session, July 25–26, 1992, Karadžić, BCS 0214–9505 and 0214–9951.

Conference on the Former Yugoslavia, the Contact Group (the United States, Russia, Germany, France, and Britain), and the United States itself assumed the lead; each held, for a time, primary responsibility for facilitating negotiations with the three adversaries. With the support of the UN, the United States, and leading European states, each facilitator sought to maintain harmony among the other international actors. In contrast to the international actors, the three Bosnian nationalist contenders were in the position of supplicants. They were constantly pressured to accept draft peace plans and were relegated to reacting to proposals presented to them. Their own initiatives were ignored or spurned by the internationals, and they rarely negotiated directly among themselves outside the framework of internationally-supervised talks.

International sponsors espoused values that contrasted in many ways with those held by each of the Bosnian parties, but especially the Bosnian Serb nationalists. European and North American diplomats, coming from a world that had vanquished fascism in the 1940s and rejoiced at the collapse of communism in 1989–91, reveled in the illusion that they were champions of democracy and reason against ideologically misguided extremists. The internationals touted the principles of non-interference of one country in the affairs of another, free markets, respect for human rights, multiculturalism, the resolution of differences through negotiation and compromises, and free and fair elections (the chief preoccupation of the Organization for Security and Cooperation in Europe, OSCE). They embraced the ideals of the many international conventions adopted after World War II, most significantly the UN Charter, the Universal Declaration of Human Rights, and the Helsinki Final Act. Even when individual countries among the internationals followed their own national interests more than their lofty ideals – and that was most of the time – they normally justified their policies as founded on high ideals.

Serb nationalists resisted those values often in the early 1990s. The internationals wrongly perceived Milošević as seeking to redraw borders and create a Great Serbia; in fact, as we have seen, he sternly reprimanded other Serb leaders for espousing Great Serb ideals. Most international negotiators rightly perceived Serb leaders as the primary instigators of mass atrocities. They were further outraged by the ease with which Serb leaders reneged on their commitments to respect widely-accepted international norms. Many internationals concluded that among the various combatants in the Yugoslav wars, Serb nationalists were the primary violators of European ideals.

In the months before war began, Karadžić became profoundly unhappy with his inferior diplomatic role. He was particularly offended by Western threats and attempts at intimidation. Because he saw the world through a prism of values that assigned supreme importance to the Serb people and Serb land, Karadžić found little merit or relevance in the Euro-Atlantic values of his interlocutors. He viewed the international hectoring about human rights as a diversion from the craven national interests that had long guided European policies and Europe's long-standing desire to crush the Serb people. He selectively embraced international legal principles that favored his cause and rejected those that did not. He found great merit in international agreements that established the right of self-determination, but he dismissed most other human rights provisions of those same accords. He pointed to Italy and Germany as embodying the hypocrisy of Western values: he felt that Italians and Germans had climbed the ladder to national unity in the nineteenth century and then pulled it up after them, denying to Serbs in the 1990s the self-determination and unification that they had achieved a century before. Those countries, he reasoned, were unlikely to accede to Serb demands unless forced to grant them by a *fait accompli* on the ground.

Karadžić's favored negotiating strategy during wartime talks was first to acquiesce to proposed agreements and then selectively ignore their provisions. Karadžić and Mladić typically negotiated long and hard before agreeing to limitations on their conduct of war, but their adherence to any such agreements was often sporadic and short-lived. The two Serb leaders often waited until another party violated some aspect of an accord before reneging on their own commitments so they could claim "provocation."

In the early weeks of the war, Karadžić developed a formulaic narrative in support of his negotiating strategy and mostly maintained it for the duration of the war. In the narrative, he denied outright most alleged misdeeds by Serbs who, Karadžić contended, only wanted peace and were fighting a purely defensive war. He parried accusations of wrongdoing with counter-charges against the Bosniaks and Croats while alleging that international officials ignored widespread atrocities against Serbs. He conceded that warfare was taking place, but he consistently maintained that Bosniaks and Croats were responsible for initiating the war and each violent incident within it. In one of the least plausible renditions of his narrative, he denied that his forces held Sarajevo under siege, arguing instead that Serbs were defending their homes in the surrounding highlands against Bosnian government attacks from below.

Karadžić and the Bosnian Serbs reaped many benefits from their duplicitous approach early in the war, but their strategy did not endure. The Bosnian Serb leaders could ignore their own commitments only so many times before the internationals demanded more than verbal acquiescence to new peace proposals. International involvement progressively deepened, and the internationals turned from debating hypothetical armed intervention to making hard-headed decisions about how most effectively to end hostilities. Their threats eventually led to action, as NATO warplanes, the heavy artillery of a Rapid Reaction Force, and Croat-Bosniak military successes turned the tide against the Bosnian Serbs in summer 1995.

BOSNIAN NARRATIVE, AMERICAN FAREWELL

Upon learning of the atrocities committed by Serbs in spring 1992, international critics and diplomats directed harsh criticism at Karadžić, Milošević, and their followers. American officials, among the most vocal of these critics, condemned Serb leaders for ordering JNA attacks on civilians, accusing them of seeking to create a Great Serbia. When public denunciations and private remonstrances produced no change in Serb behavior, the United States announced that it would withdraw its ambassador to Yugoslavia, Warren Zimmermann, effective May 16, 1992. Two days before his departure, Zimmermann met with Karadžić and Koljević at their request. The meeting bristled with mutual antagonism, and the heated exchange of May 14 became a prototype for many of Karadžić's subsequent meetings with international officials. In a cable to Washington entitled "Karadžić Unrepentant," Zimmermann reported that in their meeting, he himself had "unloaded on Bosnian Serb strongman Radovan Karadžić and his deputy Nikola Koljević."[2]

Karadžić arrived first and "appeared nervous," according to Zimmermann in his cable. He began by telling the American ambassador that a unilateral Serb-proclaimed ceasefire was then breaking down owing to a "savage attack" on Serb positions in the western Sarajevo suburb of Ilidža. Karadžić was not completely inventing this: at 5:00 a.m. that day, Bosnian government forces had begun a desperate effort to break through VRS lines then encircling non-Serbs in Ilidža.[3] But Karadžić conveniently omitted mentioning to Zimmermann that the unsuccessful government effort had been followed by a VRS infantry

---

[2] "Karadžić Unrepentant," Ambassador Warren Zimmermann to U.S. Secretary of State, May 14, 1992. The U.S. Department of State released Zimmermann's cable in 2008 in response to the author's Freedom of Information Act request. This cable is not to be confused with Zimmermann's eloquent cable entitled "Who Killed Yugoslavia?" dated May 12, 1992, and reproduced in Warren Zimmermann, *Origins of a Catastrophe: Yugoslavia and its Destroyers – America's Last Ambassador Tells What Happened and Why* (New York: Random House, 1996), pp. 245–254.

[3] United Nations Security Council, *Annexes to the Final Report of the Commission of Experts Established Pursuant to Security Council Resolution 780 (1992)*, Volume II, Annex VI, Part 1 (hereafter "Commission of Experts"), p. 183; Jonathan S. Landay, "New Fighting Rages in Sarajevo," UPI, May 14, 1992; and Zijad Rujanac, *Opsjednuti grad Sarajevo* (The besieged city of Sarajevo) (Sarajevo: Bosanski kulturni centar, 2003), pp. 254–255.

counterattack and massive Serb artillery assaults on civilian areas near Iližda. "Brushing aside the blows like a punch-drunk boxer," Zimmermann wrote, "Karadžić parried with a sharp attack on Izetbegović, charging him with scuttling cease-fire negotiations and sabotaging negotiations."[4]

Zimmermann bluntly dismissed Karadžić's myriad excuses. He reported to Washington that he had accused the two Bosnian Serb leaders of "following a two-track approach: On the one hand, claiming openness to negotiations and ceasefires, while in the meantime using force to establish the borders of the so-called Serb Republic of Bosnia." The SDS was working "hand in glove with Milošević," Zimmermann told Karadžić and Koljević. He upbraided Karadžić for breaking his pledge to remove heavy weapons. "SDS gunners are again pounding the city from the hills," Zimmermann said, despite Karadžić's "assurances that Serb artillery above the city would be removed." Emphasizing that he spoke for the American government, Zimmermann told Karadžić, "After Serb actions over the past month, the world considers you barbarians." Zimmermann demanded that the Bosnian Serbs immediately "take the big guns and tanks out of Bosnia; open the airport; end the siege [of Sarajevo]; and let the relief agencies' convoy" into Sarajevo.

Karadžić parried with denials of all wrongdoing and thrust back with the narrative that he had developed for such occasions, that the war was "imposed on us" by Croats and Bosniaks. Serbs were not drawing maps to divide Bosnia, Karadžić claimed: "[We] only want to protect ourselves." Additionally, he pleaded that he could not "control the actions of all the Serbs in Bosnia." He did not dispute that violence had taken place, but he explicitly rejected Zimmermann's charges that he was cooperating with Milošević and that irregulars from Serbia were fighting in Bosnia. He readily acknowledged that "Serb forces have occupied majority Muslim parts of the republic" but claimed that the SDS had no intention of retaining control over "non-Serb cities like Višegrad." (In fact, Višegrad remained a part of the RS throughout the war and afterward.) In a rare admission, he conceded that "the SDS has sealed off Sarajevo" but offered as feeble justifications for the siege: "Serbs own most of Bosnian land" and "Serbs' money ... built Sarajevo."

Incensed though he was with Karadžić and the Bosnian Serbs, Zimmermann had no means other than moral suasion to force them to change their behavior. He threatened "new and stronger actions" if the SDS did not change course, but other than additional UN sanctions, he could not and did not specify possible punitive actions. Beneath his bluster and acrid criticism, Zimmermann knew that the United States and the international community

---

4　Zimmermann, "Karadžić Unrepentant."

lacked the resolve to prevent or punish Serb actions. He hoped that international opprobrium would be enough to end Serb atrocities, but Karadžić remained defiant. "It was like punching a pillow," Zimmermann wrote. "The message that isolation awaits the FRY [Federal Republic of Yugoslavia] and its Bosnian Serb dependency could not have been laid out more clearly, but there was no sign that Karadžić and Koljević care." Zimmermann concluded his cable with a grim but accurate assessment. "Karadžić in particular, seeing the world in stark terms of ethnic divisions and hatreds, seems ready to march to hell if that's what it takes to get his Serbian Republic," he wrote. "Within his world view, years of purgatory may be a small price to pay."

Zimmermann's harsh remonstrances and Karadžić's retorts inaugurated a dialogue of the deaf that recurred periodically between Bosnian Serb leaders and Western diplomats over the next three years. Sovereign states and the UN Security Council denounced Serb behavior and appealed to Serb leaders to halt their violent attacks on civilians. However, those issuing the threats were unwilling or unable to back them with robust measures to punish or deter atrocities, a situation aptly labelled by James Gow "the triumph of the lack of will."[5] Karadžić claimed clean hands and heaped blame on others for initiating the violence. In confessing to cutting off Sarajevo and conquering non-Serb land, Karadžić conceded more to Zimmermann than he ever did in public, but his response to the ambassador's accusations was otherwise similar in tone and substance to his public statements. Zimmermann concluded that both Karadžić and Koljević were lying about what they knew and how much they controlled.

FAILURE TO LAND: THE SARAJEVO AIRPORT AGREEMENT

Lacking the will to back their verbal protests with meaningful actions, international diplomats tried to persuade the Bosnian Serbs to turn over the Sarajevo airport to the UN and allow it to return to full and unimpeded operations. The JNA had seized the airport when hostilities began on April 6, and Karadžić and Mladić thereafter held a stranglehold on the flow of aid and all flights into and out of Sarajevo. UN Secretary General Boutros Boutros-Ghali drew attention to the humanitarian catastrophe unfolding in Sarajevo. "For some of the parties, the infliction of hardship on civilians is actually a war aim," he reported to the Security Council in obvious reference to the Bosnian Serbs.[6]

---

[5] Gow, *Triumph of the Lack of Will.*

[6] "Report of the Secretary-General Pursuant to Security Council Resolution 752 (1992)," in Daniel Bethlehem and Marc Weller, eds., *The "Yugoslav Crisis" in International Law: General Issues* (New York: Cambridge University Press, 1997), Vol. 1, p. 16.

"Intimidation of the non-Serb population" was a key element in the "concerted effort by the Serbs of Bosnia ... to create 'ethnically pure' regions in the context of negotiations on the 'cantonization' of the Republic," he wrote.[7]

Faced with a looming disaster, international diplomats directed their efforts to opening the airport. They believed that a functioning, UN-controlled airport would both restore the flow of humanitarian aid into the city and prove a critical first step on the path to a comprehensive peace agreement. But not until late May did the Bosnian Serbs indicate a willingness to entertain the UN request to take over the airport and its operations.[8] On May 26, 1992, Karadžić announced his readiness for talks, and Mladić shortly thereafter stopped insisting that the airport issue be linked to the fate of hundreds of JNA soldiers then under siege by Bosnian government troops in Sarajevo's Marshal Tito Barracks. Steven Burg and Paul Shoup have argued convincingly that Karadžić and Mladić softened their stance at the behest of Milošević, who worried the UN might impose further international sanctions on Yugoslavia if the Bosnian Serbs continued to balk.[9] Seizing upon the Bosnian Serbs' sudden change of heart, Boutros-Ghali in early June dispatched Cedric Thornberry and Colonel John Wilson to reach an agreement with Karadžić and Mladić.[10]

From June 3 to 5, 1992, the two UN envoys held lengthy talks in Sarajevo with Karadžić, Mladić, and representatives of the Bosnian government. The UN negotiators faced a task greater than acquiring control of the airport itself. Above that airport in the mountainous terrain to the south and west, the VRS had positioned hundreds of artillery, mortars, anti-aircraft weapons, and tanks, any of which could strike the airport or an airplane at will. To assure delivery of aid, therefore, the UN needed to know that the Bosnian Serb gunmen would cease firing from the surrounding hills and allow the unimpeded flow of aid on land routes into town. Thornberry proposed to "revive the ceasefire and have it within a 30-kilometer [20 mile] circle around Sarajevo with the centre at the airport," as Mladić summarized it in his notes.[11] Thornberry added that "a corridor under UN control would have to exist for humanitarian

7 "Further Report of the Secretary-General Pursuant to Security Council Resolution 749 (1992)," in Bethlehem and Weller, *Yugoslav Crisis*, Vol. 1, p. 509.

8 "The Leadership of the SDS Announced its Readiness to Open Sarajevo Airport for Humanitarian Transports," Lisbon, May 27, 1992, signed by Dr. Radovan Karadžić, ICTY, PRK, ENG 0034–0745.

9 Steven L. Burg and Paul S. Shoup, *The War in Bosnia-Herzegovina: Ethnic Conflict and International Intervention* (Armonk, NY: M.E. Sharpe, 1999), pp. 206–208.

10 "Report of the Secretary-General Pursuant to Security Council Resolution 757 (1992)," in Bethlehem and Weller, *Yugoslav Crisis*, Vol. 1, p. 519.

11 Mladić diaries, June 3–5, 1992, ENG 0668–3197–0668–3594-ET, p. 73.

aid to be driven away."[12] He knew it would not be easy to secure either or both of these provisions along with acquiring control of the airport.

Karadžić was eager to avoid concessions that would limit Serb military operations in the Sarajevo area. Just two days before the talks began, he publicly revealed his intention to preserve his military options, although, as always, he preceded his threat of war with a proclamation of his abhorrence for it. "We do not need war, and therefore we did not begin it," he told an interviewer. "Sarajevo is our city, and we will never abandon our part of Sarajevo." He then employed the innocuous notion of a "boundary" to declare his intent to press for maximum Bosnian Serb territory. "We will be positioned on the boundary of our state, and there it will be clear to the whole world that we are not aggressors, but defenders,"[13] he said. Karadžić often used phrases such as, "be positioned on the boundary of our state" and "surround the territory of our state" to describe the conquest and delineation of a given territory and the removal of non-Serbs from it.

Just as UN negotiators were nearing agreement with Karadžić and Mladić, the Bosnian government agreed to lift the siege of the Marshal Tito Barracks and to allow the hundreds of JNA soldiers and their dependents to leave. Boutros-Ghali had intervened to secure the Bosnian government's agreement,[14] giving Karadžić and Mladić a concession that they had long sought and only recently abandoned. Izetbegović agreed to the release on condition that the JNA troops leave their weapons and ammunition behind, and for the most part they did. In a remarkably cordial procedure, Bosnian officers entered the barracks on the morning of June 5 and facilitated the peaceful withdrawal of JNA soldiers, their dependents, and their vehicles.[15] The last vehicles in a long convoy left the barracks during the afternoon of June 5, about the same time that Thornberry, Karadžić, and Mladić were finalizing the accord on turning over the airport to the UN.

In the airport agreement, Karadžić and Mladić "reaffirmed" a ceasefire of June 1 that both they and the Bosnian government had repeatedly violated. They agreed to turn over the airport to the UN and pledged "not to interfere in any way with the free movement of UNPROFOR-supervised air traffic into and out of Sarajevo airport."[16] They further pledged that "security corridors

[12] Ibid., p. 75.
[13] *Oslobodjenje*, June 1, 1992, p. 3, citing Tanjug, May 31, 1992.
[14] "Security Council Resolution 758 (1992)," in Bethlehem and Weller, *The Yugoslav Crisis*, Vol. 1, p. 12.
[15] Murat Kahrović, *Kako smo branili Sarajev: Prva sandžačka brigada* (Sarajevo: Udruženje gradjana Bošnjaka porijeklom iz Sandžaka, 2001), p. 108; and Stjepan Šiber, *Prevare, zablude, istina* (Sarajevo: Rabic, 2000), pp. 88–90.
[16] "Report of the Secretary-General Pursuant to Security Council Resolution 757 (1992) (S/24075, June 6, 1992), Annex," in Bethlehem and Weller, *Yugoslav Crisis*, Vol. 1, p. 521.

between the airport and the city will be established and will function under the control of UNPROFOR." To address Karadžić's concern that aid flights might be used to smuggle arms to Bosnian government forces, the UN promised "to ensure that no warlike materials are imported." The parties agreed that heavy weapons "within range of the airport will be concentrated in areas agreed by UNPROFOR and subject to UNPROFOR observation at the firing line." The latter provision was a disingenuous ploy by the Bosnian Serb leaders, in that it gave UN officers the right to observe heavy weapons but did not expressly forbid the Bosnian Serbs from firing them. The compromise language set the stage for Bosnian Serb gunners to pound civilian targets in Sarajevo with impunity while UN observers stood by and perfunctorily recorded every shell strike in their notebooks.

Despite dangerous ambiguities in the agreement, UN officials were elated. They proclaimed the deal as the first step toward further agreements and eventually to peace. The Secretary General praised the airport agreement as "a significant breakthrough in the tragic conflict" and immediately asked UNPROFOR Commander General Satish Nambiar "to pursue negotiations for a broader security zone encompassing the city of Sarajevo as a whole, as a second phase of negotiations."[17] The Security Council promptly authorized the dispatch of additional UNPROFOR peacekeepers in three separate resolutions passed in June and July.[18] The Secretary General tempered official UN optimism by warning that compliance with the accord was voluntary. "Given that heavy weapons will remain in the hills overlooking Sarajevo and its airport, albeit supervised by UNPROFOR, the viability of the [airport] agreement will depend on the good faith of the parties," he wrote, "and especially the Bosnian Serb party."[19]

Reflecting on these events in 1995, Karadžić defended the airport agreement as necessary to mollify the UN; the accord, he noted, had in fact cleared the way for Serbs to renew military action. It allowed for a Serb assault on the western Sarajevo high-rise housing complex of Dobrinja, a lightly defended high-rise residential settlement built as housing for athletes prior to the 1984 Winter Olympic Games. "I know when we were doing [attacking] Dobrinja, we knew what would happen, we [would] have to give up the airport," he told the Bosnian Serb Assembly, "and we gave the order to go for Dobrinja."[20]

[17] Ibid., p. 520.
[18] "Resolution 758 of June 8, Resolution 761 of June 29, 1991," and "Resolution 764 of July 13, 1992," in Bethlehem and Weller, *Yugoslav Crisis*, Vol. 1, pp. 12–15.
[19] "Report of the Secretary-General Pursuant to Security Council Resolution 757 (1992)," in Bethlehem and Weller, *Yugoslav Crisis*, Vol. 1, p. 520.
[20] BSA, 53rd Session, August 28, 1995, Karadžić, BCS 0215–4382.

Karadžić, of course, never revealed to Thornberry and Wilson his intent to resume Serb conquests upon reaching an agreement with them. He declared only that he was "very concerned about the need to protect the Serb population."[21] Together with Mladić he pressed to modify or eliminate specific provisions that would have constrained their actions after reaching an accord. Desperate for some sort of agreement, Thornberry was obsequiously conciliatory. "I would like you to understand that we respect your concerns about security," he told Karadžić.[22] He promised the Bosnian Serbs that the UN would not take advantage of concessions to weaken the Serb siege; their concessions would "have no impact on the strategic situation around Sarajevo,"[23] he said. Later he added, "We don't wish to influence anyone's military position."[24] Wilson, the UN military specialist, yielding to Serb objections, dropped the UN's insistence on a heavy weapons exclusion zone. He settled instead for a "security guarantee" and a provision that Serb artillery "be concentrated in five places ... [with UN] observers at the firing positions."[25]

Good faith was the farthest thing from Karadžić's mind in reaching an agreement on the airport. He saw in the agreement and the end of the Tito Barracks siege an opportunity to resume attacks on Sarajevo. General Mladić recorded in his diary at the time that Karadžić gathered his senior advisors at 4:00 p.m. on June 5, minutes after signing the accord, and ordered Bosnian Serb forces to step up their attacks on the city. Using the term "boundary" as a euphemism for siege lines, Karadžić directed his forces to "occupy the boundary in the city and reinforce it." He told the gathering, "Sarajevo has to be resolved politically while we act quietly, inch by inch."[26] Referring to several communities in western Sarajevo, Karadžić urged the VRS to "liberate the road through Zlatište" and to "cleanse Butmir, Hrasnica, Dobrinja and Sokolović Kolonija, and [take action] in the town of Hrasno in the direction of Mojmilo Hill."[27] In his notes, Mladić attributed to Karadžić the word "očistiti," which can mean either to "clear" or "mop up" in the military sense of completing a conquest, or to "cleanse," in the sense of ridding an area of undesired inhabitants.

The VRS wasted no time renewing its operations as Karadžić had directed. VRS artillery and tank fire raked the Marshal Tito Barracks even as the last Serbs were leaving the site, and the VRS launched an artillery assault on all

[21] Mladić diaries, June 3–5, 1992, ENG 0668–3197–0668–3594-ET, p. 77.
[22] Ibid., p. 82.
[23] Ibid., p. 84.
[24] Ibid., p. 92.
[25] Ibid., pp. 92–93.
[26] Ibid., 94–95.
[27] Ibid.

parts of the city. UN observers reported that the shelling lasted for three days with few pauses, and they described the attacks as the most intense and destructive to date.[28] Bosnian government forces mounted a counteroffensive on June 8, but their effort to break out of Sarajevo sputtered to a halt after several days.[29] On June 15, the VRS launched its planned offensive against the Dobrinja housing compound. Serb commanders positioned tanks in front of the high-rise apartment buildings and blasted away for days at the homes of Dobrinja's 40,000 inhabitants. Confronted with determined resistance from a small Bosnian government force and Bosniak volunteers, the VRS conquered only part of the complex. In violation of the agreement of June 5, the VRS kept control of the airport through the end of June and closed it to most air traffic.

As the Bosnian Serbs fired at will in violation of their ceasefire pledge, the Security Council drew attention to broken promises in several resolutions. Not until June 29, 1992, twenty-four days after the airport agreement was signed, did VRS soldiers begin to withdraw from their positions at the airport, and then only three minutes before expiration of the Security Council's ultimatum threatening to impose additional sanctions on Yugoslavia.[30] An hour later, an advance party of twenty UNPROFOR soldiers from Canada took over the seriously damaged passenger terminal.[31] The advance UN unit was reinforced by an additional 850 Canadian troops a few days later. As the transfer was taking place, the Security Council passed Resolution 761, a classic statement of unfounded optimism that praised the "considerable progress" made in turning over the airport and noted "the need to maintain this favorable momentum."[32] By starting their withdrawal just minutes before the Security Council's deadline, the Bosnian Serbs left little doubt that they had again been motivated by Milošević's fear of further sanctions, but they had retained their grip on the airport as long as possible.

The UN thereafter controlled the airport and its terminal through the end of the war. But the VRS kept heavy weapons entrenched in the hilly terrain nearby, and Karadžić and Mladić retained the capability to halt flights at will.

---

[28] United Nations Security Council, "Annexes to the Final Report of the United Nations Commission of Experts established pursuant to Security Council Resolution 780 (1992)," Annex VI, "Study of the Battle and Siege of Sarajevo" (New York: UN Security Council, 1994), vol. 2, part 1, Entries of June 6, 7, and 8, 1992, pp. 200–203.

[29] Zijad Rujanac, *Opsjednuti grad Sarajevo* (Sarajevo: Bosanski kulturni centar, 2003), pp. 265–270; Kahrović, *Kako smo branili Sarajevo*, pp. 190–191; and U.S. Central Intelligence Agency, *Balkan Battlegrounds: A Military History of the Yugoslav Conflict, 1990–1995* (Washington, DC: Central Intelligence Agency, 2002), Vol. I, pp. 153–154.

[30] *Oslobodjenje*, June 30, 1992, p. 1.

[31] Commission of Experts, p. 220; and *New York Times*, July 1, 1992.

[32] "Security Council Resolution 761 (1992)," in Bethlehem and Weller, *Yugoslav Crisis*, Vol. 1, p. 13.

For the next two years, the Bosnian Serb leaders regularly disregarded their commitments by firing on the airport and blockading roads into Sarajevo. Although various international negotiators pressed them to move their big guns out of firing range, the Bosnian Serbs held the airport hostage, frequently forcing its closure with artillery strikes to retaliate for setbacks in battle or negotiations. Even after February 1994, when they eventually withdrew their heavy artillery outside a 30-kilometer exclusion zone, the Bosnian Serbs intermittently used small arms fire to force airport closures.

Although he had achieved a notable success in negotiating the airport agreement, Karadžić touched off another round of international condemnation by renewing military operations in western Sarajevo. Many international observers and policy-makers increasingly concluded that Karadžić was unwilling or unable to keep his word. Some even suspected that he cynically made agreements expressly to highlight the impotence of his adversaries and his own readiness to act with impunity. Although it came at a high price in their international stature, Karadžić and Mladić retained a stranglehold on the flow of aid into besieged Sarajevo. Their concerted maneuvers to prevent humanitarian aid from reaching Sarajevo reinforced the views of those who saw the Bosnian crisis primarily as a human rights catastrophe rather than a military struggle.

CLASH OF VALUES: KARADŽIĆ AND THE LONDON CONFERENCES OF AUGUST 1992

With the failures of both the UN and the EC to broker a peace, international officials decided to merge the two negotiating efforts under a single organizational sponsor. When Britain assumed the rotating Presidency of the EC Council of Ministers on July 1, 1992, British Prime Minister John Major replaced Portuguese Prime Minister Cutileiro as the EC's lead negotiator for Bosnian peace talks. Major abandoned the personal mediation practiced by Cutileiro and instead created a semi-permanent negotiating institution, the International Conference on the Former Yugoslavia, under joint sponsorship of the EC and the UN. (This international body superseded, and is often confused with, the similarly-named European Community Conference on Yugoslavia, which had proven ineffective and ceased to function as of July 1992.) Major and UN Secretary General Boutros-Ghali co-chaired the new institution.[33] They, in turn, designated former British Foreign Secretary Lord

---

[33] "The London Conference, LC/C4 (Final), August 27, 1992," in Ramcharan, *The International Conference on the Former Yugoslavia*, Vol. 1, pp. 34–35.

David Owen and former U.S. Secretary of State Cyrus Vance as co-chairs of a Steering Committee to do the day-to-day work of conducting negotiations. Major launched the new initiative by hosting two conferences in London, a preliminary one in July 1992 and a more comprehensive gathering on August 26–27. Karadžić attended both as the leading representative of the Bosnian Serb nationalists.

Karadžić had no illusions about the London meetings. Before setting out for the first London meeting, he gloomily told assembly delegates that the Serbs would be isolated and impotent in the impending talks. He predicted that the major European powers would continue their anti-Serb crusade.[34] The Western powers had created and recognized Bosnia as "a rock to break further the Serb national being and statehood," he told the assembly on July 17. "We are facing the prospect of military intervention exclusively against the Serbs, under the guise of a humanitarian intervention," he warned. "There is terrible pressure on all Serbs, especially the Bosnian Serbs, because of their armed rebellion to defend their rights, rights to survival, to protect the people and the territory of Serb Bosnia and Herzegovina."

Karadžić lamented the end of the Cutileiro-led talks, which he perceived as relatively hospitable to the Serb desire for partition, and he even falsely claimed to have initiated those negotiations. "The European Conference on Bosnia and Herzegovina, which we initiated, was under way," he told the assembly. "Its decisions and results were like we wanted them to be, that is, going in the direction of creating a tripartite Bosnia." Wary that Major might give greater emphasis to human rights, Karadžić said he anticipated an international initiative based on geostrategic interests that favored one or two Bosnian nations at the expense of a third. "We don't know if Major will liquidate the conference … and accuse the Serbs," he told the assembly, "or whether he hopes to finish the business, to advance the thing so the Serbs and Croats divide Bosnia in two, … or to give some kind of autonomy to one and to the other, to liquidate the Muslim state in the Balkans."[35] In any case, he believed the Serbs were at the mercy of the EC, the United States, and the UN.

Though he reveled in his role as chief negotiator, Karadžić expressed a willingness to defer to the assembly on peacemaking matters.[36] In that spirit, he asked the delegates to choose members of the negotiating team for the London meetings. But even as the assembly prepared to select the negotiators for London, Karadžić elected "to usurp the right to choose himself," as

34 BSA, 17th Session, July 25–26, 1992, Karadžić, BCS 0214–9551.
35 Ibid.
36 BSA, 18th Session, August 11, 1992, Karadžić, BCS 0214–9608.

Krajišnik put it.[37] The assembly meekly acquiesced to Karadžić's self-appointment and further authorized him to select two other members of the delegation. To no one's surprise, Karadžić chose his two closest advisors and friends, Krajišnik and Koljević, as co-members of the negotiating team. The assembly then authorized the negotiators to "make concessions, but not at the expense of centuries-long disputable territories."

With Karadžić's approval, the assembly soon erected barriers to territorial concessions by the Bosnian Serb negotiating team. Meeting again in the interval between the first and second London conferences, assembly delegates supported a decision that the borders of the RS should be determined by plebiscite.[38] Serb voters in the RS, euphoric over wartime victories, were unlikely to vote in significant numbers to surrender conquered land, so the plebiscite provision in effect doomed any concessions the leaders might make at the negotiating table. Shortly after the second London Conference, the assembly raised the bar for compromise even higher by requiring "a three-quarter majority of the total number of registered voters" for any plebiscite resolution.[39] With these acts, the Bosnian Serb leaders further sharpened their populist swords and prepared to make the plebiscite their ultimate weapon to repel unwanted international peace proposals.

Karadžić, Koljević, and Krajišnik arrived at the second and definitive London Conference to find their wartime conduct at the center of international scrutiny. In the weeks before the conference, *Newsweek's* Roy Gutman had published shocking photos of emaciated Bosniak inmates in Bosnian Serb prison camps, and former Polish Prime Minister Tadeusz Mazowiecki had submitted his account of widespread atrocities to the UN Commission on Human Rights.[40] As Karadžić had feared, the European powers were shocked by the revelations and had come to view the Bosnian war more as an ongoing human rights catastrophe than as a military struggle for Serb autonomy. Karadžić retorted that the Bosnian Serbs had fulfilled their human rights commitments by turning the Sarajevo airport over to UNPROFOR, giving security guarantees for corridors into the city, and opening their prisons to international inspection.[41] Though he was technically correct that the Bosnian

---

[37] BSA, 17th Session, July 25–26, 1992. Krajišnik. ENG 0214-9496–0214-9600, p. 80 of 104.

[38] BSA, 18th Session, August 11, 1992, Milanović, BCS 0214-9610.

[39] *Službeni Glasnik Republike Srpske*, I, no. 15, September 29, 1992, p. 569.

[40] United Nations Commission on Human Rights, "Report on the Situation of Human Rights in the Territory of the former Yugoslavia submitted by Mr. Tadeusz Mazowiecki, Special Rapporteur of the Commission on Human Rights," August 28, 1992; and Roy Gutman, *A Witness to Genocide: The 1993 Pulitzer Prize-Winning Dispatches on the "Ethnic Cleansing" of Bosnia* (New York: Macmillan, 1993), pp. 20–76.

[41] BSA, 18th Session, August 11, 1992, Karadžić, BCS 0214-9622.

Serb party had turned over the airport and given security guarantees, he failed to mention that those guarantees were not being consistently honored. His voice went largely unheeded at the conference, largely because he so glibly disregarded the primary concerns of the conference organizers.

He was further frustrated to find that he and other representatives of the Bosnian belligerents were excluded from conference sessions where representatives of other countries drafted the principles to guide negotiations. Victor Jackovich, the principal U.S. observer at the London Conference and later the first U.S. Ambassador to Bosnia, came upon him "jacketless, the sleeves of his white shirt rolled up above the elbows, in the conference hall's downtown cafeteria," bodyguards at his side. "Accompanied by a cohort in identical attire," Jackovich reported, "Karadžić was shouting rather crudely in broken English and waving leaflets and one-page press releases at anyone who strayed near his vantage point."[42] No doubt frustrated with being excluded from the deliberations, Karadžić was revealing his need for recognition as a powerful player in determining Bosnia's future.

The London Conference abounded in lofty statements of unrealistic principles that the sponsoring states hoped would guide subsequent peace talks. The conference approved thirteen principles as "the basis for a negotiated settlement of the problems of the former Yugoslavia" and another nine principles to guide a political settlement in Bosnia.[43] Characterized by Major as a "code of conduct" and bearing signs of hasty preparation, the list of nine consisted of two genuine principles and seven additional "arrangements" demanding that Serb conquests and ethnic expulsions be undone. All parties should "cease fighting and the use of force" and agree to "non-recognition of all advantages gained by force or *fait accompli*," according to the proposed code. The conference issued a "total condemnation of forcible expulsions, illegal detentions and attempts to change the ethnic composition of populations; and [demanded] effective promotion of the closure of detention camps, and of the safe return to their homes of all persons displaced by the hostilities who wish this."[44]

The principles further called for respecting the Geneva Conventions and the various conventions on human rights adopted by the UN and the EC. In language remarkably similar to that used by the Badinter Commission in late 1991, the principles spoke of "fundamental freedoms of persons belonging

---

[42] Victor Jackovich, "Conversations with Karadžić," typescript, September 23, 2013, p. 11.

[43] Ramcharan, *The International Conference on the Former Yugoslavia*, Vol. 1, pp. 33–34 and 37–38.

[44] Bertrand de Rossanet, *Peacemaking and Peacekeeping in Yugoslavia* (The Hague: Kluwer Law International, 1996), p. 6.

to ethnic and national communities and minorities." Nowhere was Sarajevo mentioned by name, but one of the "arrangements" obliquely referred to sieges in demanding the "grouping of heavy weaponry under international control" and the "demilitarization of major towns." Not since the Badinter Commission findings of nine months earlier had Karadžić faced such an array of human rights principles, many of them at odds with Serb nationalist ambitions. He knew that if London Conference principles were ever implemented, his own achievements would be ruined and the Republika Srpska would lose all semblance of a sovereign, contiguous, ethnically-defined polity as outlined in the strategic goals.

Despite finding the conference's principles odious, Milošević and Karadžić joined in accepting the "complex regimen of principles and actions" demanded of them; but "they did so with something less than grace,"[45] in the understatement of one journalist. Even as he signed on to the plan, Karadžić realized that the principles and arrangements were rife with opportunities for creative reinterpretation and evasion. "Karadžić told journalists he encountered in a hallway that his Bosnian Serbs weren't besieging Sarajevo, so such strictures didn't apply to him," the same journalist noted. Karadžić knew the international community still lacked the will and means to enforce a peace, let alone reverse Serb conquests and ethnic cleansing. The UN Secretary General bluntly told conference conveners of the EC and UN that they had not allocated the resources necessary to force compliance with their principles. "The expectations of the international community … continue to exceed the resources and capacity of UNPROFOR," Boutros-Ghali reminded the conference.[46] "UNPROFOR has been explicitly authorized and equipped to implement only the June 5, 1992 [airport] agreement," he continued. "The UN mission with its present mandate cannot, by itself, bring this crisis to an end."

Karadžić soon cynically reinterpreted the international strictures to the benefit of Bosnian Serb nationalists. As he explained at the next assembly session on September 14, 1992, he intended to make minor concessions and wait for international negotiators to abandon their exorbitant demands. "There can be some negotiations about the borders – a village here or there, that can be decided locally – but the objective is to protect our territory and to endure long enough for all [contending] parties to agree," he declared. "Whether it will be on this side of the creek or on the other, a local commander can

[45] *New York Times*, August 28, 1992, p. A6.

[46] "Address by Secretary-General Boutros Boutros-Ghali to the International Conference on the Former Federal Republic of Yugoslavia," August 26, 1992, Ramcharan, *The International Conference on the Former Yugoslavia*, Vol. 1, pp. 60–61.

decide."[47] He saw no reason to stop shelling Sarajevo, taking advantage of the minimalist provision that the UN would monitor but not interrupt attacks on the town. "We don't care if UNPROFOR stands next to our cannons," he said. "When they [Bosnian government forces] start firing at us, we will tell them [the UN observers], sorry guys, move away; and we'll fire back [at the Bosnians]." In the event the government mounted an infantry assault, he said, "we [will] phone them [UN observers] and say that we are under attack.... We'll fire at positions there [in Sarajevo] but we won't open fire at a skyscraper which would burn to no purpose."

Karadžić further proposed respecting international law by releasing imprisoned Bosniaks and Croats and closing prison camps, with the purpose of securing a Serb propaganda victory. "Disbanding Trnopolje [the camp in Prijedor visited by Gutman] does not mean letting up, if they want to take them [released prisoners] abroad, let them," he said. "That will give us great credit among the international public, we want to cooperate, we want to deal with humanitarian issues and that helps us." He belatedly and reluctantly acknowledged the need to comply with international law, but at the same time he expressed regret that Serbs had not killed more Bosniak soldiers. "If only all the Green Berets [Muslim paramilitary troops] had been killed with a rifle in their hand," he said to the delegates, "but once they have been captured, then we must abide by the Geneva Conventions and it's all for nothing." In the next several months, he would lead the Bosnian Serbs in turning these planned evasions into reality. The VRS tightened its siege of major cities, continued mass atrocities (although at a reduced pace), and held its expanded territory against the first major military counteroffensives.

THE ASSEMBLY AWAKES: KARADŽIĆ AND THE VANCE-OWEN PEACE PLAN

Although charged at the London Conference with implementing lofty human rights principles, Vance and Owen had no means at their disposal to impose such requirements on the Bosnian belligerents. As they shuttled around Southeast Europe, Vance and Owen became quintessential pragmatists in desperate search of a map and a formula for division that could win the assent of the three recalcitrant parties. Although all participants continued to give lip service to human rights concerns, those principles were pushed aside as negotiators increasingly focused on complex issues of boundary delineation and the relationship of territorial subunits to a central Bosnian state.

---

47 BSA, 20th Session, September 14, 1992, Karadžić, BCS 0422–6252.

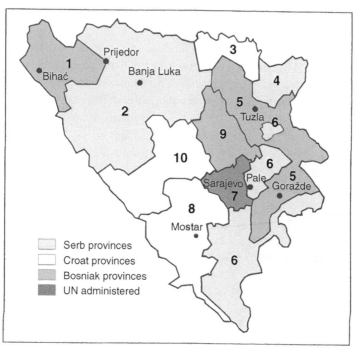

MAP 12.1. Vance-Owen Peace Plan, January 1993.
Original Source: UN Security Council S/25050 (January 6, 1993).

After talks and consultations that consumed the last four months of 1992, Vance and Owen presented their peace plan to the Balkan parties and the global public on January 2, 1993.[48] The Vance-Owen Peace Plan (VOPP) was a complex document with many appendices and annexes; only a few of its provisions recognizably embodied the lofty ideals expressed at the London Conference. At the heart of the plan were two elements: a map dividing Bosnia into ten "provinces," and constitutional provisions for a weak Bosnian central government.[49] (See Map 12.1.) The proposal aimed to give each nation a pre-eminent role in three provinces where it had commanded an absolute or relative majority of inhabitants at the time of the 1991 census, while the province of Sarajevo was to be demilitarized and administered jointly. The plan divided Serb holdings into five parts: two of the three Serb-governed provinces (numbered two and four on the map) consisted of one piece each, while the third (numbered six) was divided into three non-contiguous areas. The Serb

[48] Burg and Shoup, *The War in Bosnia-Herzegovina*, pp. 219–222.
[49] "The Vance-Owen Plan," in Ramcharan, *The International Conference on the Former Yugoslavia*, Vol. 1, No. 249–274.

provinces included many Bosniaks and Croats, and the three together contained only 52.8 percent of Bosnia's Serbs.[50]

The Bosnian Serb nationalists were angered but not surprised by the VOPP. It denied the Bosnian Serbs their first strategic goal of separation from Bosniaks and Croats and, by fragmenting Serb territory into five pieces, it shattered Karadžić's dream of a compact, contiguous, strategically viable Serb polity. Momir Tošić, assembly delegate from Romanija, succinctly summarized the Bosnian Serb opposition to the VOPP. "Eagles don't live in cages," he declared, "and the Serbs of the Republika Srpska will not live in cantons."[51]

The Bosnian Croats fared much better in the VOPP. Each of their three provinces (numbered 3, 8 and 10) shared a border with Croatia, and they received a greater part of the republic's territory than either their proportion of the population in 1991 (17 percent) or the territory then controlled by their army, the HVO. Delighted with these provisions, Bosnian Croat leader Mate Boban accepted all elements of the plan and signed it on January 4, 1993.[52] Bosniaks and the Bosnian government representatives, on the other hand, were generally disappointed by the plan, as it gave them less land than their part of the population in 1991 and divided them among three non-contiguous provinces.

When Vance and Owen called for the Bosnian parties to agree to the plan on January 4, Izetbegović accepted the plan but rejected the map as overly generous to Bosnian Serbs and Bosnian Croats. Karadžić, on behalf of the Bosnian Serbs, also objected. He, too, rejected the map, but he agreed to submit the VOPP to the assembly for a vote. He knew, of course, that the assembly would reject the VOPP, which it did on January 19 and 20.

Vance and Owen, undeterred by the Serb and Bosniak rejections, initiated a new round of talks in hopes of mollifying Karadžić and Izetbegović with minor adjustments. The negotiations dragged on for several months. Vance and Owen repeatedly summoned leaders of the three Bosnian groups to Geneva for often testy talks on alterations to the plan. The differences among the three parties remained profound, and the conference co-chairs were hampered by their lack of coercive mechanisms to coax the parties to an agreement.

The physical arrangements for conference participants emblemized their differences. The three Bosnian delegations shuttled between Bosnia and

50 Mladen Klemenčić, "Territorial Proposals for the Settlement of the War in Bosnia-Herzegovina," *Boundary and Territory Briefing*, vol. 1, no. 1 (Durham, UK: University of Durham, Department of Geography, 1994), eds. Martin Pratt and Clive Schofield, p. 10.

51 BSA, 24th Session, January 8, 1993, Momir Tošić, BCS 0214–9904.

52 Burg and Shoup, *The War in Bosnia-Herzegovina*, p. 224; and Mladić diaries, January 4, 1993, entry labeled "Plenary Session," BCS J000–0300.

Geneva in three separate aircraft and stayed in separate accommodations in the Swiss capital. Karadžić showed signs of stress and worry that were noticed by other diplomats. While in Geneva, he and the negotiating team eschewed Geneva's luxury hotels in favor of a villa, owned by a Serb supporter, located on the opposite side of Lake Geneva. The villa struck U.S. observer Victor Jackovich as "a veritable 'fortress Serbia' away from home."[53] Its bookshelves were lined with Serbian-language volumes; the villa's temporary occupants kept the television tuned to a Serbian station and listened to Radio Belgrade on a short-wave radio. The villa ensured a "cocoon-like existence, a self-imposed isolation," Jackovich observed, leaving the Bosnian Serbs "free to craft their own universe, to spin their own talks, to perpetuate their own self-assessments." Jackovich wrote that Karadžić feared being assassinated while abroad for the talks. Lord Owen similarly attested to Karadžić's fear. "His bitten-down fingernails are witness to an anxiety underneath," Owen wrote. Karadžić "lacked Milošević's boldness and self-confidence," according to Owen, evidenced by "frequently claiming that he would be killed by his own people if he agreed to some difficult compromise."[54]

As Karadžić was shuttling to and from Geneva for talks, he also met frequently with the assembly from January to April of 1993. Delegates vehemently denounced the VOPP as a plot to deny the Serb people their fundamental right to a state of their own on contiguous territory. Karadžić worried aloud in the assembly about threats of airstrikes or a NATO ground invasion. He appealed to the assembly to refrain from rejecting the VOPP outright and instead to pledge to continue negotiations. He hoped international negotiators would see Izetbegović as the principal saboteur of the plan. Karadžić also reminded delegates of their own constitutional provision (enacted in September 1992) that territorial changes required a three-quarters approval vote at a referendum. To win over global public opinion, he recommended that the assembly insist that any agreement cite the right of self-determination and reference the Helsinki Final Act, the UN Charter, the Universal Declaration of Human Rights, OSCE documents, and "international legislation that plays into our hands."[55]

As the negotiations dragged on, Milošević in March 1993 proposed a massive territorial swap that he believed would resolve the conflict. He urged Karadžić to surrender Serb holdings around Sarajevo to the Bosnian government in

[53] Jackovich, "Conversations with Karadžić," p. 11.
[54] David Owen, *Balkan Odyssey* (New York: Harcourt Brace, 1995), p. 51.
[55] Meeting of Delegates' Club prior to BSA 24th Session, January 8, 1993, Karadžić, BCS 0214–9857.

trade for government-held enclaves in eastern Bosnia.[56] The exchange of territories would leave both the Serbs and the Bosniaks in control of large, contiguous territorial blocks. It took little imagination to see that mass atrocities were almost certain to follow such a trade. French President Mitterrand first suggested the swap to Milošević, who then passed it along approvingly to the Bosnian Serbs. Karadžić had already adopted plans to move whole factories from Sarajevo's Serb-controlled suburbs to other locations in the RS, thus preparing to salvage some economic resources if he were forced to give up western Sarajevo.[57] But he rejected the swap for the time being (although in December 1994 he changed his mind and openly advocated it) and instead urged his fellow Bosnian Serbs to create a "Serb Sarajevo," an alternative urban center in the southwestern suburbs with its own mayor and government.[58] Had Karadžić endorsed a wholesale territorial exchange, he might have cleared the way for a more compact, contiguous, and ethnically homogeneous Serb territory, but his opposition to the VOPP was deeply entrenched.

In March 1993, Vance and Owen moved the talks to New York to redouble the pressure on Izetbegović and Karadžić to sign. Despite having spent a year at Columbia University as a young man, Karadžić felt uncomfortable in New York. Confined for security reasons to a ten-block area near the UN Building, he complained of being denied his right to worship in a Serbian Orthodox Church located outside the restricted zone.[59] While in New York, he ran the risk of being served a summons in a civil case filed in U.S. federal court accusing him of human rights violations. Despite these anxieties and concerted international pressure, Karadžić continued his refusal to sign the VOPP. Izetbegović, on the other hand, yielded and signed the entire plan in New York on March 25, 1993. He qualified his endorsement with a threat to withdraw his signature if the Bosnian Serbs failed to ratify the plan in short order. But Vance and Owen had what they wanted, and they subsequently directed all their energies at persuading the lone holdouts, Karadžić and the obdurate Bosnian Serbs, to sign the accord.

They failed. Karadžić encouraged opposition by the assembly in the expectation of using that body to sabotage any agreement he might be forced to make. On April 2, the assembly adopted a seven-point "Declaration on the Continuation of the Peace Process" that all parties understood to be an outright

[56] Nikola Koljević, *Stvaranje Republike Srpske; Dnevnik 1993–1995* (2 vols.) (ed. Milica Koljević) (Banja Luka: Službeni glasnik Republike Srpske, 2008), March 13, 1993, Vol. 1, p. 154.

[57] Koljević, *Republike Srpske*, February 21, 1993, Vol. 1, pp. 115–116.

[58] "Statutarnu odluku o organizaciji srpskog grada Sarajeva," signed by Trifko Radić, March 13, 1993, *Službeni glasnik Republike Srpske*, no. 11, p. 457.

[59] Owen, *Balkan Odyssey*, p. 114.

rejection,[60] albeit disguised as a qualified acceptance. Vance and Owen, striving to put more pressure on Karadžić, turned to the Bosnian Serbs' staunchest international supporters for help. Leaders of Russia, Greece, and Yugoslavia summoned Karadžić to Athens on May 1–2 and pressured him relentlessly to accept the plan. As added incentive, the negotiators offered Karadžić two major concessions. They agreed to allow Serb police to remain in areas that Serbs would turn over to Croats and Bosniaks, and they conceded that the VRS would be superseded in such areas only by UNPROFOR, rather than by Croat or Bosnian government forces. Neither concession came close to granting Karadžić's demands, but after pressing in vain to retain his basic goal, Karadžić signed the VOPP in Athens. "I was acting under a lot of pressure, totally consciously," he said in justifying his decision to the assembly. "I was convinced that I had to sign it before this assembly [session] since the threats against our people were enormous."[61]

With Karadžić having signed the VOPP, it remained for the assembly to approve or reject the accord. International diplomats mustered the Bosnian Serbs' principal supporters to urge the assembly to approve. The assembly met in Pale on May 5 and 6, 1993, in the presence of presidents Milošević of Serbia, Ćosić of Yugoslavia, Bulatović of Montenegro, and Prime Minister Constantine Mitsotakis of Greece. Despite the urgings of these regional leaders, Karadžić was the only leader in the hall with enough clout to sway the assembly vote, and he declined to do so. Instead, appearing to be mired in ambivalence, he spoke despairingly of imminent NATO air strikes and a possible ground invasion.

Chastened by months of verbal thrashings from diplomats, Karadžić seemed incapable of asking the assembly either to accept or to reject the VOPP. But with his tortured ambivalence, he revealed his disapproval of the plan without explicitly asking the delegates to reject it. He whined about Serb historical suffering and justified the war as a Serb self-defense struggle. "For thirteen months we have been leading a defensive war in which we undertook no offensive actions," he insisted. The VOPP was "catastrophic," he argued. It "denies our right to self-determination [and] our right to our own country that we created and defended on our own." But in the end, he asked the delegates to approve the plan while suggesting that he had been compelled to do so. "I must recommend that you ratify this plan because real dangers hang heavily over us," he said. Gone was the blustery bravado of earlier speeches, replaced by the self-pitying rhetoric of a leader begging for understanding

---

[60] BSA, 26th Session, April 2, 1993, Minutes, BCS 0215–0020.
[61] BSA, 30th Session, May 5–6, 1993, Karadžić, BCS 0215–0119.

that he betrayed his constituents to keep their dream alive. "It is up to you to decide," he told them.

Karadžić failed to show the delegates a way forward, but Milošević then addressed the assembly with a surfeit of reassurance and forcefully urged them to approve the plan.[62] He underlined the favorable concessions that Karadžić had won at Athens. In provinces assigned to Bosniaks and Croats, he asserted, "neither the Berets [Bosniak forces] nor the HVO [Croat forces] can show up in areas where Serbs live, and we shall have local authority, our own police, etc." He told them that they could still eventually achieve their goal after approving the plan. He assured the delegates that clever negotiations could improve the Serb position over time. "They can be overcome through a peaceful process of negotiating exchanges and through other instruments that we have at our disposal," he said, leaving it to his listeners' imaginations what those "other instruments" might be.

Milošević sought to identify with the Bosnian Serbs by using the word "we" to indicate he shared their goals and concerns. He referred cryptically to their hopes for Great Serbia. "[Shall] we give up on our goal?" he asked. "I shall tell you no! The question is whether the plan represents a way toward the final goal.... Of course it does." Serbia would continue to support the Bosnian Serbs, he said. "Let me tell you in the end, do not tell us that you feel abandoned.... We shall continue to help you; that is not in dispute." With Serbia's help, he argued, the Bosnian Serbs could accept the VOPP and eventually achieve a viable state.

The delegates were unmoved by Milošević's argument. They refused to budge from their opposition to the VOPP, and some implied that Milošević had betrayed them. After deferring a vote until the next session, on May 9, the assembly voted to submit the VOPP to an immediate plebiscite, knowing full well that the plan was widely unpopular among Serbs. Going well beyond their leaders' expectations, over 98 percent of voters rejected the plan.

The assembly met again on May 19 and 20 to certify the referendum results and give its final answer to Vance and Owen. Following Karadžić's suggestion, the delegates asserted in their resolution that they wanted to continue the peace process. Stating that all military operations had been halted in accord with a ceasefire, the assembly invited "all prominent personalities of

---

[62] BSA, 30th Session, May 5–6, 1993. Milošević spoke twice during this assembly session. His first speech, meant to appeal to policymakers and the global public using terms they would find attractive, stated that the goal of Serbs in the Balkans was to be "free and equal." BCS 0215–0127–0215–0128. The excerpts here are from his second speech before a closed assembly session that was intended for the Bosnian Serbs and used a vocabulary more familiar to his Serb nationalist audience. BCS 0215–0189–0215–0192.

international political life to engage actively in the resolution of the crises and military conflict in the former Bosnia by providing new peace proposals and solutions."[63] Karadžić rejoiced. The assembly and electorate had redeemed the Bosnian Serbs from Karadžić's capitulation to international pressure at Athens. He ended his silence and candidly told the assembly how much he despised the proposed agreement. "The Vance-Owen Plan is no good," he told the delegates. "Milošević asked me, 'Why did you say that the Vance-Owen Plan is catastrophic?' Because it is catastrophic! In essence, 50 percent of the population stays with the Muslims and Croats, and 50 percent live in a Nagorno-Karabakh in enclaves that they cannot leave."[64]

Karadžić blamed his former allies for pressuring him. "I feel deeply deceived by Milošević and Mitsotakis for Athens," he said. "We cannot say so publicly; I said that secretly.... Everything collapsed after Athens."[65] Given his truculent refusal to admit mistakes, Karadžić could only accuse others of responsibility for his own capitulation and leave it to the assembly to veto the plan. "Last time it saved us to go to a referendum," he said. "America could not shoot at a nation that organizes a referendum.... That's a magical word in the West."[66] Other leaders also viewed the rejection as a triumph of Serb will. "We saved the state then," said RS Vice President Biljana Plavšić in reference to the referendum. "The world has accepted our position, a world that, believe me, recognizes only the law of force."[67]

With no country prepared to enforce the VOPP at gunpoint, international officials abandoned the VOPP a few weeks later. Lord Owen blamed the United States for scuttling his plan, but Karadžić, the Bosnian Serb Assembly, and Serb voters were its true assassins. Remarkably, Karadžić appears to have suffered little if any loss of popularity among his constituents for caving to international pressure and signing the document in Athens. He and other leaders found validation of their view that other countries would eventually acquiesce to Serb territorial conquests and ethnic purification.

[63] BSA, 32nd Session, May 19–20, 1993, BCS 0215–0254.
[64] BSA, 31st Session, May 9, 1993, Karadžić, BCS 0215–0224.
[65] Ibid., BCS 0215–0225.
[66] BSA, 42nd Session, July 18–19, 1994, Karadžić, BCS 0215–3005.
[67] BSA, 39th Session, March 24–25, 1994, Plavšić, BCS 0215–2282.

13

Host in Solitude

With the Vance-Owen Peace Plan relegated to the dustbin of history, Bosnian Serb leaders revived their nationalist project in the summer and autumn of 1993. Karadžić was heartened by international concessions in further negotiations following Serb rejection of the VOPP. He remained personally popular among Serbs and firmly in charge of the RS government, but he began to encounter challenges from other Serbs who found him personally abrasive or found his policy decisions ill-considered. For the first time, his personal standing began to diverge from the movement he had created and led. His relationship with Milošević deteriorated further, he quarreled with Mladić over control of the army, and he watched the assembly become increasingly independent. Unlike his measured responses to earlier challenges, he turned arrogant, self-obsessed, and increasingly isolated in the face of criticism and opposition. In late 1993 he began to become his own worst enemy, just as the Bosnian Serb nationalist movement experienced significant successes in achieving its goals. This chapter examines the slowly developing crisis that beset his diplomatic quest for permanent acceptance of Bosnian Serb territorial gains.

UNION OF THREE REPUBLICS: THE PLAN EVEN
A SERB COULD LOVE

Although international diplomats had threatened Karadžić with grave consequences if the Bosnian Serbs rejected the VOPP, the rejection triggered not retaliation but additional concessions to the Serb side. Only days after the assembly's final rejection, international negotiators revisited their proposals in hopes of tailoring them to win Bosnian Serb approval. On August 21, 1993, they unveiled a proposal called the "Union of Three Republics" (also known as the Owen-Stoltenberg Plan, crediting Vance's replacement, Thorwald

Stoltenberg), that gave the Bosnian Serb nationalists most of what they sought. The new proposal "gave the Serbs their own contiguous area for a republic within a Union of Bosnia-Herzegovina," Owen wrote, acknowledging that negotiators had reoriented their efforts to bring the Bosnian Serbs on board.[1] The Union of Three Republics was a peace plan that even a Serb could love.

The proposed Serb territorial unit was shaped like two irregular saddlebags linked by a strap, but it was pocked in the east with several small, irregular enclaves crammed with Bosniak residents and refugees. In the Union of Three Republics, the negotiators proposed to give a generous 54 percent of the land to the RS, a mere 16 percent to the Croats, and a less-than-generous 30 percent to the Bosnian government.[2] Like the Graz Agreement of May 6, 1992, between Boban and Karadžić,[3] the Union of Three Republics accommodated Serbs and Croats at the expense of the Bosniaks and the Bosnian government, and Owen hoped that all concerned would see it as the product of their own ideas. "It was important that it should have been seen to have come from the Serbs and the Croats,"[4] Owen wrote. As usual, Karadžić sought certain changes in the plan, but he was pleased with most of its provisions and signed it eagerly. He submitted it to the assembly on August 27, 1993,[5] only six days after it was presented to him. Despite the plan's generosity to the Bosnian Serbs, Karadžić expected opposition from strong-willed assembly delegates. He mustered compelling arguments and employed his best persuasive techniques to win approval. "At no prior assembly did Karadžić face a greater task," wrote Koljević, "and never had he expended greater emotive energy in persuading the delegates."[6] In contrast to his dispirited mixed messages to the assembly in May, he delivered a compelling appeal in favor of the Union of Three Republics in August.

Karadžić resurrected many of the arguments that Milošević had made in support of the VOPP a few months before. He urged the delegates to keep in mind their central long-term objective. "We will diminish our territory – diminish it we [already] have," he said, "but we want it to be ours for all time, so that we can organize within it a free, democratic society, economy, culture, and media, a flowering Serb society."[7] That will only be possible, he argued, if "our statehood and our sovereignty are not called into question," and that

---

[1] Owen, *Balkan Odyssey*, p. 190; Burg and Shoup, *War in Bosnia-Herzegovina*, p. 275.

[2] Burg and Shoup, *War in Bosnia-Herzegovina*, p. 276.

[3] Owen, *Balkan Odyssey*, pp. 191–213.

[4] Ibid., pp. 190 and 191.

[5] BSA, 34th Session, August 27, 1993, Karadžić, BCS 0215–0515–0215–0522, 0215–0530–0215–0534, 0215–0567–0215–0571, 0215–0592–0215–0593, 0215–0608–0215–0610, 0215–0621–0215–0622, and 0215–0629–0215–0630.

[6] Koljević, *Republike Srpske*, Vol. I, p. 322.

[7] BSA, 34th Session, August 27, 1993, Karadžić, BCS 0215–0569.

required giving up some valued territory. He described as painful the Serb losses along the Neretva River and in the Ozren area, home to "three monasteries ... with great symbolic and historical significance for the Serb people." Urging the delegates to keep their eyes on the ultimate prize, Karadžić reminded them again of the six strategic goals. "In a certain way it became our task, our obligation to fulfill them," he told the delegates.

Despite Karadžić's best efforts, the delegates seemed unconvinced.[8] They recited the same arguments that Karadžić himself had uttered to denigrate earlier international proposals. They made it clear that Karadžić no longer held a firm grip on their votes, let alone their opinions. Alarmed that the plan might be rejected, Krajišnik took the floor to calm the delegates and urge a "Yes" vote. Speaking authoritatively and bluntly, he praised some plan provisions, criticized others, and told the delegates to anticipate further modifications if they accepted the plan. "I would ask you to keep in mind our first strategic goal, and that is to divide and to withdraw our part from Bosnia and form our state," he told the delegates.

Krajišnik then skillfully whipped the delegates into nationalist fervor in advance of the vote. Resorting to a ruse, he passed over the proposal being voted upon and asked the delegates a simple rhetorical question, "Are you for the Republika Srpska?" Frenzied patriotic fervor broke out in the hall, and Krajišnik called for a vote. Excitedly believing they were simply saying "Yes" to the RS, delegates cast their votes. Sixty-one voted "Yes," 14 voted "No," and 3 abstained. Krajišnik congratulated them, saying, "[Now] you now have the Republika Srpska!" As Koljević described it, "General excitement, celebration and exchanges of kisses followed."[9] No one objected to Krajišnik's deception in presenting the vote as an acceptance of the Union of Three Republics plan. Karadžić was understandably grateful and delighted with the results, but the episode cast doubt on his capacity to get the results he wanted from the obstreperous delegates.

With Bosnian Serb approval, the onus shifted to the Bosnian government. Izetbegović and Bosniak leaders opposed many plan provisions, and they were emboldened by recent U.S. talk of possible air attacks on Serb targets. An assembly of Bosniak leaders voted down the plan on September 27, and the Bosnian Parliament similarly rejected the proposal on September 28.[10] Owen and Stoltenberg, chastened but undeterred, renewed their whirlwind consultations with world leaders and solicited further proposals from the three

---

[8] Koljević, *Republike Srpske*, Vol. I, p. 322.
[9] Ibid., Vol. I, 323.
[10] Burg and Shoup, *War in Bosnia and Herzegovina*, p. 280.

Bosnian belligerents. In the ensuing months, they submitted two more proposals, called the EU Action Plan and the Contact Group Plan, later characterized by Owen as numbers two and three of a "family" of three plans that would have awarded the Serbs their own contiguous area.[11] But even before the Bosnian Parliament voted down the Union of Three Republics proposal, the first of the three plans, a different challenge erupted to threaten the unity of the RS and disrupt the path toward a peace plan favorable to the Serbs.

FEBRUARY 1994: PERIPHERAL POWERS TAKE CENTER STAGE

From the time the Soviet Union began to break into its component republics in 1991, Boris Yeltsin and other leaders of the Russian Federation were preoccupied with domestic affairs. They needed Western aid and freedom from foreign entanglements as they built a new, democratic Russian state, and they could not afford to alienate the Euro-Atlantic powers on whom they relied. Contrary to their inflated historical reputation as heroic saviors of the Serbs, Russia's leaders in the 1990s hewed to neutrality and did little more than lend occasional diplomatic support to their fellow Orthodox Slavs in southern Europe. They voted for Security Council resolutions dealing with the former Yugoslavia until 1995, when they vetoed one resolution at the urging of Owen and Stoltenberg. A few Serb sympathizers in the Russian Ministry of Foreign Affairs urged their superiors to take a more aggressive position and side overtly with the Serbs, but they had little success.[12] Members of the pro-Serb faction in Russia arranged for Karadžić to visit Moscow, but senior Russian officials refused to meet with him during his visit. He was treated as a private citizen and feted with a literary prize for his earlier poetry, but he was otherwise ignored.

Russian Federation diplomats nonetheless assumed roles as mediators and peacekeepers in the Bosnian war. In February 1994, they seized an opportunity to engage in peacemaking diplomacy in the aftermath of a particularly bloody Serb rocket attack on Sarajevo. On February 5, 1992, a single mortar shell slammed into the crowded Markale marketplace in Sarajevo, killing 68 and wounding another 144 persons. The overwhelming weight of evidence pointed to VRS-controlled territory as the likely point of origin, although Karadžić himself and some Serb supporters deny to this day that Serbs fired the fatal shell. The attack further sullied the reputation of Karadžić, Mladić, and the

---

[11] Owen, *Balkan Odyssey*, p. 190.
[12] Konstantin Nikiforov, *Izmedju Kremlja i Republike Srpske* (trans. from Russian by Mira Toholj) (Belgrade: Igam, 2000).

Bosnian Serbs, leading the international community to demand yet again that the Bosnian Serbs withdraw their heavy weapons from a 30-kilometer (20 mile) exclusion zone around Sarajevo.

On February 10, 1994, NATO gave the Bosnian Serbs an ultimatum to withdraw their heavy weapons by February 21 or face air strikes conducted "in close coordination with the UN Secretary General."[13] Karadžić rejected the ultimatum. But on February 17, three days before the ultimatum's deadline, Russian Deputy Foreign Minister Andrei Kozyrev made a surprise visit to Pale. He proposed that Russia would guarantee Serb compliance if Western diplomats agreed to add a battalion of Russian paratroopers to UNPROFOR to monitor the agreement. Karadžić accepted the offer, anticipating friendly, pro-Serb behavior from the Russian contingent, and other diplomats accepted the Russian offer as well. Over the next several days, the VRS halted the shelling of Sarajevo and fulfilled Karadžić's promise by removing tanks and artillery from the exclusion zone.

Karadžić welcomed the Russian troops in a statement, saying, "We are grateful to Russia for its involvement."[14] Since he believed that every nation acted in accord with its national character and geostrategic interests in foreign policy, he fully anticipated that the Russians would show favoritism to the Serbs, just as he believed the Germans and Italians were predisposed to favor Croats. He was soon disappointed. Russian troops carried out their mission with admirable impartiality and oversaw the Serbs' grudging withdrawal of heavy weaponry from the exclusion zone. To the great relief of Sarajevo residents, the February ceasefire and weapons withdrawals inaugurated a fifteen-month hiatus in the use of heavy weapons to shell Sarajevo, although small-arms fire continued intermittently.

The Russians disappointed Karadžić in another way as well. After Owen and Stoltenberg failed to win acceptance of any of their peace plans, the United States took the lead in forming a five-member successor known as the Contact Group, made up of the United States, France, Germany, the United Kingdom, and the Russian Federation. Created in part to bring both the United States and Russia directly into the peacemaking process, the Contact Group met for the first time on April 26, 1993.[15] As a member, Russia actively participated in formulating a plan that denied many Serb ambitions, disappointing Karadžić and his supporters.

---

[13] *New York Times*, February 10, 1994, www.nytimes.com/1994/02/10/world/conflict-in-the-balkans-nato-gives-serbs-a-10-day-deadline-to-withdraw-guns.html, viewed August 11, 2011; and Owen, *Balkan Odyssey*, pp. 262–263.

[14] *New York Times*, February 18, 1994, pp. A1 and A6.

[15] Owen, *Balkan Odyssey*, p. 278.

The Bosnian Serbs, who had been busily seeking further concessions from Vance and Stoltenberg in Geneva, were displeased with the new group's proposal and with the shift in the diplomatic center of gravity to the Contact Group. Summarizing the Serb view, Miroslav Vještica told the assembly, "The Americans, acting like cowboys, put the Geneva [talks] out of business and moved everything to Washington."[16] Although Karadžić had nurtured hopes in February that the Russians would rescue the Bosnian Serbs from their increasing isolation, by summer 1994 he speculated that Russia was allying itself with Germany. He declared himself unable to accept an outline for peace drafted by Russian President Yeltsin.[17]

The United States also increased its involvement in Bosnia in 1994. U.S. diplomats strongly favored a robust response to the mortar attack on the Markale market, and they stepped up efforts to stiffen the resolve of Western countries and the military capabilities of the Croatian and Bosnian governments to fight the Serbs. In Washington's view, the Croats and Bosniaks should resolve the differences that had led to war between them starting in April 1993, leaving their armed forces free to direct their energies against their common Serb foe. With U.S. mediation, the Bosniak and Croat parties agreed to a ceasefire on March 18, 1994, and subsequently established the Federation of Bosnia and Herzegovina.[18] Despite the damage they had inflicted on one another, both Bosniak and Croat forces emerged from their mutual hostilities strengthened, battle-tested, and determined to take the offensive against the VRS. Under U.S. pressure, they eventually coordinated their military operations, although they never merged their armed forces.

The Bosnian Serb nationalists found much to fear from the rapprochement of Croats and Bosniaks, but Karadžić shrewdly perceived a chance to strengthen the Serb bargaining position by advocating the division of Bosnia into two parts instead of three. He rejected the proposal that Serbs join the Federation as its third nation and instead promoted RS parity with the Federation.[19] The RS should be the Federation's equivalent, he argued, thereby justifying a Serb claim to one-half of Bosnia rather than only a third. He further saw the Federation's association with Croatia, authorized in its American-drafted constitution, as legitimizing a Serb demand for the RS to associate comparably with Serbia. In May 1994, the assembly reformulated the

[16] BSA, 39th Session, March 24–25, 1994, Miroslav Vještica, BCS 0215–2258.
[17] BSA, 42nd Session, July 18–19, 1994, Karadžić, BCS 0215–2999 and 0215–2882.
[18] For an account of the negotiations to establish the federation, see Komšić, *Preživljena zemlja*, pp. 345–383.
[19] BSA, 39th Session, March 24–25, 1994, Karadžić, BCS 0215–2280.

Bosnian Serb negotiating position along the lines that Karadžić advocated.[20] As the equal of the Federation, the RS needed "just and defendable borders that will include the Serb ethnic areas," the assembly resolved.

The five-member Contact Group formally presented its new peace proposal in June 1994 and announced a July deadline for the belligerents' acceptance. The group accompanied the offer of peace with threats of armed action against those who refused. NATO jets hovered above Sarajevo, producing ear-shattering screeches and booms that resembled the sounds of air assaults. Karadžić, ensconced in his Pale retreat, was unmoved. He brought the Contact Group Plan before the assembly and roundly criticized its provisions. He complained that the plan left unresolved the status of Sarajevo and failed to provide an outlet to the sea. Assuming that any Serb withdrawal would necessitate population transfers, Karadžić calculated that 400,000 Serbs would require resettlement from territories that the plan proposed to transfer to Bosniak and Croat control.[21] After a lengthy debate, the delegates rejected the plan, employing the coded language of diplomacy by voting to accept the plan as a basis for further talks.

The Contact Group Plan remained on the table unresolved for a full year after it was first presented, but Karadžić and the assembly never accepted it. International actors, although they could agree to threaten bombing, were unable to agree on how and when to begin the actual attacks. Karadžić, for his part, continued his nimble rotation of denials, reinterpretations, and counteraccusations, betting that the bombs would never leave the bays of NATO aircraft. Milošević, on the other hand, was incensed with Karadžić for failing to accept the plan, since Bosnian Serb rejection ruined yet again Yugoslavia's bid to terminate the crippling UN-ordered sanctions. On August 4, 1994, Milošević announced that Yugoslavia was implementing an economic blockade on the Drina River to isolate the Bosnian Serbs. Having again alienated his former patron, Karadžić fell deeper into international isolation. He desperately needed someone to reach out and rescue him from his pariah status.

THE CARTER-KARADŽIĆ SUMMIT

As he nursed his wounded ego, Karadžić found hope in reviving a stalled Milošević initiative from June 1994. Through a French intermediary, Karadžić approached former U.S. President Jimmy Carter (president from 1977 to 1981) and invited him to visit Pale. Carter, who had recently mediated

---

[20] BSA, 39th Session, March 24–25, 1994, Aleksa Buha, BCS 0215–2334.
[21] BSA, 42nd Session, July 18–19, 1994, Karadžić, BCS 0215–2819.

international crises in Haiti and North Korea, commanded immense international respect for his negotiating skills and dedication to peace.

Through two envoys dispatched to Carter's home in Plains, Georgia, Karadžić presented himself as eager for peace but too proud to capitulate to the crude threats of the Contact Group. His utterances betrayed a desire to soothe his own ego as well as to re-enter the peace talks. He sought to convince Carter that only the intransigence of the Western powers stood in the way of peace. Karadžić's French intermediary had first written to Carter that the Bosnia Serbs would find the Contact Group map acceptable "with minor mutually agreeable changes to the map."[22] Assessing the Bosnian Serb leader's approach, Carter's advisors concluded, "Karadžić needed a prominent figure to whom he could make concessions while retaining his 'honor'." Karadžić then dispatched a delegation of three to speak directly with President Carter at his home in Plains. The eclectic group of emissaries consisted of Tom Hanley, a Los Angeles attorney who did work for the Bosnian Serbs; Slavko Lazarević, Karadžić's senior security advisor; and Borko Djordjevic, a naturalized U.S. citizen of Serb origin and plastic surgeon from Rancho Mirage, California, who had attended medical school in Sarajevo with Karadžić. Meeting with Carter's staff, they, too, described Karadžić as eager for peace but holding back because of a wounded ego. They said he "considered Carter an acceptable individual through whom he could make concessions he was previously unwilling to make."[23]

Karadžić was not completely forthright about his own demands for peace as he approached the former American president. Karadžić had already rejected both the Contact Group map and the principles upon which the map was drawn, and he was adamant in rejecting the plan's proposed wholesale dismantling of a compact, contiguous Bosnian Serb state. Karadžić, however, desperately needed recognition from a major global figure and an agreement – any agreement – to break the Contact Group's monopoly on negotiations and discredit its arguments for armed intervention. In the end, Carter accepted the invitation to visit Pale, but he did so only after he had consulted with U.S. officials and demanded that Karadžić clarify his intentions.

---

[22] Joyce Neu and Steven Shewfelt, *Eminent Third Party Mediation: Unofficial Diplomacy in Bosnia* (manuscript, copyright Joyce Neu, Carter Center, 1997), pp. 16–26. This useful report gives the best available account of the Carter mission. Unless otherwise noted, information and quotations concerning the former president's visit in the following pages are taken from this document. Koljević also describes the talks, in less detail but largely consistent with the account of Neu and Shewfelt. Mladić was present at the talks in Bosnia but took only sketchy notes; his account added nothing of substance to the descriptions of other observers.

[23] Neu and Shewfelt, *Third Party Mediation*, p. 16.

President and Mrs. Carter and their party arrived in Bosnia on December 19 and drove from the Sarajevo airport to Pale. As Joyce Neu described their trip, "It was quite sobering to drive through areas on the outskirts of Sarajevo seeing people standing in the doorways of tall buildings looking hungry and sad and to see blankets hanging as we went through the mountains so that snipers could not target them. It was snowing, overcast; the roads were slushy."[24] Although Radovan and Ljiljana Karadžić received them politely in Pale, the mood was somber; Neu wrote, "Both inside the rooms and outside, it was freezing (literally) and tense." The Bosnian Serb leaders, however, were delighted and relieved to have the former president and his party among them, and they found him refreshingly open to communicating and associating with them. Employees of the U.S. government were under orders to avoid being photographed with Karadžić and Mladić, whom Secretary of State Lawrence Eagleburger had publicly proclaimed war criminals in 1992, but President and Mrs. Carter freely posed for photographers in their company. Carter repeated at a press conference his intent to give the Bosnian Serbs a fair hearing. He won approval from his Serb hosts (while raising alarm at the Clinton White House) by declaring to the press, "Americans have heard only one side of the story."

With the opening courtesies completed, the Carters met with Karadžić and presented a proposal that had been crafted with the aid of several advisors. Karadžić accepted the draft after suggesting only minor changes. He then announced the items on his agenda for the talks: a "short history," a "history of the war," and the "general principles for resolution of the crisis."[25] Carter listened politely and intently to Karadžić's history lecture but offered no response. His Serb hosts were impressed. "Carter showed, at least verbally, more understanding than we expected," Koljević wrote of the occasion. "We had the impression that we were speaking with a man of far greater human breadth, and a higher diplomatic caliber, than we had seen before. A blend of good will and pragmatism: that was something completely new for us."[26] After dinner on December 19, Karadžić presented the former U.S. president with a traditional flask and gusle, and he obliged the Carters by playing the gusle for the dinner guests.

Karadžić seemed to other participants to be at ease with the Carters and their advisors. But he soon displayed erratic behavior that seemed calculated to alienate his guests and scuttle the talks. In another meeting with President and

---

[24] Personal communication, Joyce Neu, January 20, 2014.
[25] Koljević, *Republike Srpske*, Vol. II, p. 14.
[26] Ibid., Vol. II, p. 16.

ILLUSTRATION 13.1. Karadžić presents a traditional gusle to former U.S. President Jimmy Carter at dinner on December 19, 1994. Photograph by Joyce Neu.

Mrs. Carter, Karadžić presented his own "Memorandum of Understanding," an alternative to Carter's proposal that he had accepted just minutes before. In his memorandum, he reiterated some provisions of Carter's draft, but he also sought fulfillment of far-reaching Serb expectations as contained in the six Serb strategic goals. The final agreement, stated Karadžić's draft, should include the principle of the "transformation of Sarajevo into two neighboring cities."[27] It should "take into account" the "functionality of two states in a possible confederation; approximately equal distribution of natural resources and infrastructure; natural and defensible borders; access to the sea for the RS; and an end to UN and Yugoslav sanctions against the Serb people in Bosnia during negotiations."

These outlandish demands were far removed from provisions in the Contact Group Plan. Carter, as a private citizen, lacked the authority to either accept or reject them. But Karadžić had already related his high expectations of the talks to *New York Times* correspondent Roger Cohen in an interview. "The [Contact Group] map cuts our territory into Serb enclaves and gives the Muslims continuity," he told Cohen. "We [Muslims and Serbs] both need compact, contiguous land."[28] In reporting the interview, Cohen discerningly noted the radical import of the demands. The mention of natural and defensible frontiers was "a clear reference to doing away with the small Bosniak

---

[27] Neu and Shewfelt, *Third Party Mediation*, p. 23; and Koljević, *Republike Srpske*, Vol. II, pp. 14–15.

[28] *New York Times*, December 21, 1994, p. A6.

enclaves in eastern Bosnia that Dr. Karadžić said were 'totally nonviable',"
Cohen wrote. Indeed, Karadžić's "Memorandum of Understanding" was far
more than a charm offensive to win Carter's favor; it was an effort to lure
the former president into endorsing Bosnian Serb war goals. Cohen rightly
concluded, "In effect, the memorandum seeks to lay the groundwork for the
Bosnian Serbs' long-sought goal of separating themselves definitively from the
Bosnian Muslims."

The mood of the Pale talks darkened as Carter realized the scope of what
Karadžić was asking. Then Karadžić issued a threat: he would not endorse the
agreement with Carter – which he had just explicitly accepted – unless the
Serbs received some relief from international sanctions. Carter explained that
he was only a private citizen with no authority over such matters, but Karadžić
continued to press the issue. Carter, refusing to be intimidated into acqui-
escing to Karadžić's demands, irately threatened to abort the talks and leave
Pale without an accord. Only after his aides intervened did Carter relent and
agree to stay in Pale. But he continued pressing Karadžić to agree to a ceasefire and resume negotiations with the Contact Group. In the afternoon hours
of December 20, Karadžić agreed to a ceasefire running from December 27,
1994, to May 1, 1995. He further promised to begin negotiations during the
ceasefire with the intent of reaching a final peace agreement by January 15.
After consulting with Washington, Carter agreed to acknowledge, but not
endorse, Karadžić's insistence on "negotiations on the basis of the Contact
Group Plan." Karadžić was satisfied, since he had not been forced to "accept
the plan as a starting point" for negotiations, as the United States had been
insisting.

In the evening of December 19, Karadžić and Mladić both signed a
"Comprehensive Peace Agreement." Carter also signed the document, but
only as a witness. The agreement specified timetables for ending hostilities and
starting negotiations, but it included a tightly-worded commitment that "each
side will be responsible on territory under its control for complete elimination
and prevention of firing of any artillery or weapons of any kind that could
damage persons or property."[29] More vaguely, Karadžić pledged the Bosnian
Serbs to "protect human rights in accord with international standards." Absent
from the final agreement was any reference to the specific Bosnian Serb strategic goals that Karadžić had earlier insisted on including.

The Carter party returned that evening to government-controlled Sarajevo
believing the former president had accomplished his mission. The next
day, December 20, Carter met as scheduled with members of the Bosnian

---

[29] Koljević, *Republike Srpske*, Vol. II, pp. 16–17.

Presidency, who had accepted the Contact Group Plan and would not agree to resume negotiations unless the Bosnian Serbs likewise endorsed the plan without conditions. But even before that meeting, members of the Carter party learned from UN briefers that the Serbs had resumed shelling the besieged city of Bihać in northwestern Bosnia, endangering both civilian inhabitants and UN peacekeepers stationed there. Carter considered the Serb shelling a violation of the spirit, if not the letter, of the agreement they had just reached. Showing that he would not countenance Serb defiance of the spirit of the accord, Carter called Pale, complained of the shelling, and demanded that the effective date of ceasefire be moved up. As he had many times before, Karadžić responded by pleading ignorance of Serb violations and blaming others for resuming the fighting.

That evening, Karadžić called Carter from Pale to report that he had not yet succeeded in locating those Serb commanders in the Bihać area with whom he needed to consult. He promised to call Carter again in the morning. The next day, angered by Karadžić's repeated prevarications, Carter and his party raced back to Pale and threatened for a second time to declare the talks a failure and to depart abruptly.

Karadžić, knowing he could ill afford to lose his last hope for regaining entry to peace talks, hastily agreed to move up the effective date of the cease-fire to December 23, only two days later. He then interjected another demand, namely that the Bosnian government withdraw from a demilitarized zone on Mount Igman near Sarajevo, an area government forces had occupied to assure free passage of humanitarian aid into the city. Time ticked down as Karadžić insisted and Carter rejected this last-minute addition to the agreement. Carter very much wanted to be on a flight out of Bosnia before dusk, the UN curfew for air traffic in and out of Sarajevo airport.

Carter finally agreed to mention the Igman occupation in a supplemental agreement, but he secured in return Karadžić's assurance that Serbs would not block humanitarian convoys. Karadžić, although not Mladić, then signed, and Carter witnessed, the "Supplemental Agreement" that included this provision: "On the basis of a guarantee that convoys and humanitarian aid will pass freely, Bosnian forces will withdraw from the Igman demilitarized zone in accord with the existing agreement, before the beginning of negotiations."[30] Having gotten what concessions they could, members of the Carter party hurried down the treacherous mountain road from Pale to the Sarajevo airport late in the afternoon of December 21. Their plane took off at dusk, bearing

---

[30] Ibid., Vol. II, p. 18.

a frustrated peacemaker who had just joined a host of other international diplomats who had experienced Karadžić's maddening negotiating tactics.

REVERBERATIONS OF A PRESIDENTIAL VISIT

Karadžić, seeking to reprise his successful if temporary evasion of international pressures, doggedly urged Carter for months to visit Pale a second time. In letters and verbal messages conveyed by intermediaries, Karadžić flattered Carter and addressed him as a confidant, ally, and friend.[31] In a letter of April 12, Karadžić assured Carter that "the current ceasefire, such as it is, has been by far the most effective one throughout this conflict, and ... it was brought about largely by your efforts.... The [Carter] cessation of hostilities agreement is now dead and buried ... due solely to the recent Muslim offensives."[32]

Seeking to reassure the former U.S. president of his good intentions, Karadžić developed new wording to suggest he was prepared to make further concessions. In a letter dated May 19, 1995, he proposed, as a "condition" for new talks, that "the full catalogue of human rights and fundamental freedoms set out in international instruments will be respected, including the right of refugees and other displaced persons to return to their homes of origin, which has to be an overall process."[33] But built into his pledge was a duplicitous formulation he had used more than a year before. As he explained to the assembly, he advocated characterizing the return of displaced persons as an "overall process," by which he meant that displaced Bosniaks and Croats would only be allowed to return to Serb-controlled areas if Serbs could also return to areas controlled by Croat and Bosnian government forces. He and other Bosnian Serb leaders would then obstruct Serbs who had fled to the RS from returning to areas controlled by hostile forces, making it impossible for the other side to meet the pre-condition for displaced Croats and Bosniaks to return to the RS. "The Muslims and Croats swallowed [the idea of] the comprehensive process," he told the assembly. "When Serbs return from [Serb-held] Zvornik to [government-held] Zenica, then Muslims from Prijedor can return to Prijedor; that means it must be a comprehensive process. Under international law we cannot declare that refugees are forbidden from returning."[34] In

[31] Karadžić to Carter, January 17, 1995, in Radovan Karadžić, *Ratna pisma dr. Radovana Karadžića* (War Letters of Dr. Radovan Karadžić) (Belgrade: International Committee for the Truth about Radovan Karadžić, 2004), vol. 3, p. 285.

[32] Karadžić to Carter, April 12, 1995, in Karadžić, *Ratna pisma.* Vol.3, pp. 340–341.

[33] Karadžić to Carter, May 19, 1995, in Karadžić, *Ratna pisma*, Vol. 3, p. 359.

[34] BSA, 37th Session, January 10, 1994, Karadžić, BCS 0215–2158.

fact he did, however, make it extremely difficult and unlikely that displaced Serbs would return to their homes in the Federation.

Despite the duplicity and evasive language in Karadžić's letters, Carter appeared sympathetic to the Bosnian Serbs and willing to consider another visit. He communicated regularly with the White House, and his staff maintained regular contact with Contact Group officials, UNPROFOR officers, U.S. State Department officials, and with Borko Djordjevic, the California plastic surgeon and long-time Karadžić friend, who had helped arrange the first visit.[35] Carter himself continued to urge his own government and the Contact Group to soften their conditions for resuming talks.[36] But he was not prepared to visit Pale again unless Karadžić made certain key concessions. Karadžić, in turn, experimented with various formulations to lure Carter to Pale without substantively changing his position. "We are ready to negotiate, with the Plan of the Contact Group as the basis for negotiations of all points," he wrote on June 3, adding that he was "prepared to be flexible on the territorial issue."[37] This formulation was far from "acceptance" of the plan, the word on which the Contact Group was insisting.

Karadžić repeatedly urged Carter to come in any case, and he suggested that Carter should engage in deception of his own to lower expectations of his visit. "We cannot make any further concessions," Karadžić wrote on June 3. "Accordingly, at least in public, your visit must not be seen as an ambitious attempt to resolve the conflict, because the possibility of failure is not inconsiderable. Therefore, should you embark on another trip to Pale, we recommend that you should describe it as a fact-finding mission. But, given your contacts with President Clinton, arrangements could be made whereby, 'suddenly,' your visit achieves a breakthrough."[38]

In an editorial note to the letter, written sometime after 2000, Karadžić claimed that his letter of June 3, 1995, "confirms that the Republika Srpska practically accepted the Contact Group's plan as the basis for negotiations on all disputable issues." But even then Karadžić tried to twist the meaning of his wartime language to suggest that he had accepted the Contact Group Plan. Although he had acquiesced, Karadžić claimed in his editorial note, "the Contact Group gratuitously made objections and needlessly prolonged the war so a pretext could be found for NATO's armed attacks."[39] True to form,

---

[35] Personal communication, Joyce Neu, January 29, 2014.
[36] Owen, *Balkan Odyssey*, pp. 310–314.
[37] Karadžić to Carter, June 3, 1995, in Karadžić, *Ratna pisma*, Vol. 3, pp. 366–367.
[38] Ibid.
[39] Ibid., p. 367.

Karadžić continued to blame the Contact Group, arguing that it bore sole responsibility for failure to agree while he himself sought only peace.

In his growing desperation in summer 1995, Karadžić would turn to taunts to convey his bitterness over the many betrayals he ascribed to the internationals. Even the usually thick-skinned Ambassador Richard Holbrooke, sent by U.S. President Bill Clinton in August 1995 to reinvigorate the peace talks, took offense at a Karadžić letter of July 19 that seemed to blame U.S. officials Robert Frasure and Nelson Drew for their own deaths en route to Sarajevo. "If I may suggest, your officials perhaps took unnecessary risks in choosing a most dangerous road,"[40] Karadžić had written. Knowing, however, that the two had been forced to use that treacherous road because Serbs were blocking other passages, Karadžić wrote to Carter, "We therefore offer the use of our territory so that U.S. government officials can in the future safely reach their destinations."[41] Holbrooke was outraged by the implication, calling the letter a "deliberately nasty reference to the Serb offer to use the Kiseljak road."[42]

In a particularly galling letter to President Clinton in July 1995, Karadžić obliquely accused the United States of responsibility for the genocide at Srebrenica (discussed in Chapter 14). "There would have been no battles for Srebrenica and Žepa if peace negotiations had been called as I have been requesting for months," he wrote on July 24.[43] With irony and outrageous disregard for the mass killings at Srebrenica of just days before, Karadžić reiterated his "condition" for further talks, namely that "the full catalogue of human rights and fundamental freedoms as set out in international instruments will be respected."[44]

Increasingly frustrated as his appeals to former President Carter went unheeded, Karadžić's desperation turned to despair. He told the assembly in late August of his futile efforts to reach out. "Last night we got Carter's emissary," he said. "We were on the phone 50 times, sent a fax 50 times, they returned it to us, we co-ordinated, haggled, look[ed] for the traps, the dangers."[45] But Carter never returned to Bosnia. Karadžić was left with the illusion that Carter could have rescued him if only the American government and the Contact Group had not intervened to dissuade him. Karadžić carried that illusion with him into hiding and later into court as evidence of yet another betrayal at the hands of those he had once trusted.

---

[40] Karadžić to President Bill Clinton, July 19, 1995, in Karadžić, *Ratna pisma*, p. 390.
[41] Ibid.
[42] Richard Holbrooke, *To End a War* (New York: Random House, 1998), p. 17.
[43] Karadžić to President Bill Clinton, July 24, 1995, in Karadžić, *Ratna pisma*, Vol. 3, p. 392.
[44] Karadžić to Carter, August 28, 1995, in Karadžić, *Ratna pisma*, Vol. 3, p. 411.
[45] BSA, 53rd Session, August 28, 1995, Karadžić, BCS 0215–4304.

Karadžić possessed all the skills to succeed as a diplomat. Owen praised him as "better than any other Serb except Milošević at negotiating, usually keeping cool, knowing when to give ground to protect a vital interest and on occasions producing imaginative solutions."[46] But as the war dragged on, tact and patience became as important as negotiating skills in achieving diplomatic objectives, and Karadžić possessed little of either. He became increasingly captive to his own megalomania and his apparent inability to separate his personal interests from those of the Bosnian Serbs. His duplicity strained his relations with even his closest allies. Serbs still revered him as the father of the SDS and president of the RS, but other Serb leaders had begun to clash with him, a precursor of impending challenges. With the Carter talks, he won a lengthy reprieve and deferred the punishment that the Contact Group threatened to unleash on the Bosnian Serbs. But the reprieve seemed only to strengthen his delusions that he and the nationalist cause were invincible. Tests of that supposed invincibility were already in the making.

[46] Owen, *Balkan Odyssey*, p. 50.

14

Architect of Genocide

The year 1995 began with relative quiet in Bosnia, as the Carter-negotiated ceasefire took hold in most parts of the country. Karadžić entered the New Year euphoric over his diplomatic triumph in luring Carter to Bosnia, believing that he and his cause had gained much-needed international validation by the former president's visit. Sensing that the fate of his Serb utopian dream hung in the balance, Karadžić redoubled his efforts to win diplomatic recognition of a separate Bosnian Serb state. He feared, however, that his enemies would violate the ceasefire before it expired and renew their military threats to the Republic of Serb Krajina and the Republika Srpska. He and Mladić, like the leaders of other military formations, used the four-month ceasefire to rest their troops, resupply their forces, and develop plans for renewed offensives in the spring. When large-scale fighting resumed in May, the VRS suffered major battlefield losses, alarming Karadžić, Mladić, and assembly delegates. In a final, desperate effort to fulfill a key strategic objective by making eastern Bosnia an all-Serb region, Karadžić turned to planning the deed for which he will be most remembered: the genocide of thousands of Bosniaks around Srebrenica. This chapter relates how the Srebrenica genocide came about.

SREBRENICA

By summer 1995, fear and squalor prevailed in Srebrenica, once a picturesque mountain village with flowering plants on every street-facing balcony. One of three government-held urban enclaves in eastern Bosnia under VRS siege, the town had swelled to 40,000, many times its prewar population of 5,746, with the influx of Bosniak refugees driven by Serb forces from nearby villages.[1]

---

[1] For an account of the struggles of medical professionals during Srebrenica's siege, see Sheri Fink, *War Hospital: A True Story of Surgery and Survival* (New York: Public Affairs, 2003).

Displaced persons and long-time inhabitants alike were malnourished, having become largely dependent for food on UN humanitarian convoys that the besieging Serbs only sometimes permitted to reach the town. Municipal services broke down. The once-pristine streets and apartment buildings were piled with heaps of stinking, rotting garbage. Medical services were strained to the breaking point, and surgeons operated without anesthesia and electricity.

Even worse than physical misery was the constant dread. Every day and hour the inhabitants feared the VRS would launch a full-scale assault and exact brutal vengeance on them. They cowered in anticipation of heavy artillery and mortar fire. They understood that they were trapped in a vise of Serb nationalist ambitions and that their continued survival depended on an irresolute international community. The encircling forces wanted eastern Bosnia to be a land of Serbs only, and the trapped residents doubted that any force would prevent the well-armed VRS Drina Corps from realizing that ambition.

They were, in fact, doomed. Thousands of Srebrenica's inhabitants did not survive the month of July 1995. Unarmed or disarmed, many of them were mowed down in large groups by automatic weapons fire. Their corpses were thrown together into mass graves and bulldozed under the earth, only to be dug up later by Serb operatives and reburied in secondary graves scattered across the countryside. Those who survived the killings would look back on their miserable plight in Srebrenica as better times. They were permanently scarred by grief beyond consolation. Herded into refugee centers, they searched with diminishing hope for family members and friends from whom they had been separated. Some wept for months after losing their entire families; few would ever resume a normal life.[2]

Radovan Karadžić planned, ordered, monitored, and sought to justify the Srebrenica genocide, and afterward he proudly insisted that he was its principal architect. This claim varies from many previous journalistic and scholarly accounts of the event, which attribute the leadership and responsibility for the killings to General Mladić. Most of those accounts accurately spell out Mladić's involvement with the actions,[3] but their authors did not have the

---

[2] Lara J. Nettelfield and Sarah E. Wagner, *Srebrenica in the Aftermath of Genocide* (New York: Cambridge University Press, 2014), describes the Bosniaks' suffering in the aftermath and their memorialization of the killings.

[3] Roger Cohen, *Hearts Grown Brutal: Sagas of Sarajevo* (New York: Random House, 1998), pp. 422–426, offers a succinct, well-researched account of Mladić's role. See also CIA, *Balkan Battlegrounds*, Vol. I, pp. 316–354; Burg and Shoup, *War in Bosnia and Herzegovina*, pp. 324–325; Jan Willig Honig and Norbert Both, *Srebrenica: Record of a Crime* (New York: Penguin, 1996), pp. 30–40.

benefit of the ICTY trove of documents pertaining to planning for the killings. Those documents, combined with the detailed judgments from various trials, reveal Karadžić's primary role in initiating and carrying out the mass atrocity. His strategic vision, authorizations, directives, actions, and claims of personal responsibility make up the bloodiest chapter in his personal story.

THE PATH TO SREBRENICA

In the summer of 1995, Karadžić was a more experienced executioner than was the party president of 1992 who had first orchestrated widespread mass atrocities. But even though his heart was hardened and his conscience moribund, Karadžić did not order the deeds of July 1995 solely out of contempt for Bosniaks. He took action only after an improbable convergence of Serb battlefield defeats, maneuvers of the international community, bitter rivalry with Mladić, and his realization that little time remained to realize his Serb utopian vision in all of eastern Bosnia. Karadžić was not a victim of circumstance, however; he was the master of it. We will never know if he might have ordered the actions in a different set of circumstances or at a different time, but we do know that he acted with forethought, decisiveness, and calm detachment in the circumstances in which he found his movement in July 1995. He acted distressingly methodically in pursuing his goals by putting into action a carefully considered plan.

To be sure, Karadžić did not act alone. He needed an organized military force to prepare and carry out his heinous plan, and he needed a willing and able commander on the scene to lead legions of soldiers to carry out the killings. Mladić eagerly assumed that role, following his superior's orders while simultaneously competing with him for acclaim as the most avid Serb nationalist in Bosnia.

RIFT WITH MLADIĆ

Much of the impetus for the Srebrenica genocide came out of the complex relationship between the two men, bringing us back to events that began when the two first worked together in May 1992. Karadžić and Mladić were very different men. Mladić was a soldier's general, a close-cropped, gruff commander who loved to display reckless bravado before his troops. Karadžić, in contrast, was a polished urbanite who favored designer suits, silk scarves, and roguish long hair. Karadžić once boasted that it was he who had chosen Mladić to command the Bosnian Serb forces in 1992, and the two frequently supported and praised one another in the early months of the Bosnian war.

Starting in summer 1993, however, they began to differ on military policy and to criticize one another in harsh personal terms. Their first serious falling-out took place in August. After the VRS seized the route into Sarajevo over Mount Igman, Karadžić pledged to international negotiators that the VRS would withdraw from those strategic positions from which they had halted traffic into and out of Sarajevo.[4] Mladić, dismayed that his boss would so cavalierly abandon hard-won territory, refused to withdraw his troops and announced at a press conference at the Sarajevo airport that his forces would stay in place.[5] Karadžić, infuriated at his top general's open disobedience, tried to find Mladić but could only locate his second-in-command, Chief of the General Staff General Manojlo Milovanović, on whom he unloaded in two phone conversations. "He will destroy both our country and himself," Karadžić said. "He doesn't have any right to act like that; if I order him to do something, he has to do it."[6] For emphasis, Karadžić called Milovanović again in a few hours and issued a threat. "I delivered that order in my capacity as supreme commander," Karadžić said. "He who does not carry it out will be shot."[7] International diplomats feared that Mladić's obstinacy would endanger peace talks, and Izetbegović did briefly withdraw from negotiations. Even Milošević disapproved of Mladić's insubordinate behavior.

After several days of defiance, Mladić relented and began on August 11 to withdraw his troops from most of the contested locations.[8] The episode left Karadžić determined to bring his disobedient senior general to heel. On August 28, 1993, Karadžić took the bold but ill-advised step of promulgating a comprehensive eighteen-point order to the VRS that intruded deeply into army affairs.[9] In the order, he directed that the VRS be restructured and ordered the VRS generals to form an elite combat brigade in each division and assign the most experienced warriors to it. Those actions alone would have disrupted the existing chain of command throughout the army, but the order also demanded that the army leadership cease tolerating corruption and incompetence. Finally, he directed that most senior generals be stripped of their security details, depriving them of a coveted perquisite.

[4] "Joint statement," Pale, August 5, 1993, ICTY, PMK, Exhibit P67A, ENG 0045–1955.
[5] *Oslobodjenje*, August 5, 1993, p. 2.
[6] Intercept, Karadžić and General Manojlo Milovanović, August 4, 1993, 1425 hours, BCS 0401–0693.
[7] Intercept, Karadžić and Milovanović, August 4, 1993, 1800 hours, ICTY, PRK, BCS 0401–0692.
[8] *Oslobodjenje*, August 12, 1993, p. 8; and *New York Times*, August 15, 1993, p. E5.
[9] BSA, 50th Session, February 13, 1995, Karadžić, BCS 0084–6070.

Mladić and the other generals received the order with disbelief and indignation. They were contemptuous of such ill-considered directives from a man who had never worn a uniform before becoming commander-in-chief. Karadžić, having missed out in youth on Yugoslavia's compulsory eighteen-month military service, had no army experience and only a layman's knowledge of military affairs. Rather than publicly proclaim their defiance, Mladić and the VRS generals ostentatiously professed obedience to their civilian leaders and eschewed public displays of their contempt for Karadžić, while quietly ignoring his offensive order.

Karadžić did not relent. Over the next two years he continued to press for the changes he had ordered, which his civilian allies labeled "reform of the army." He further exacerbated the rift by berating the generals for their disobedience. "I asked for a transformation of the army and it was not carried out in a satisfactory manner,"[10] he complained to the assembly in April 1995. He insisted that the generals were obliged to obey him regardless of their reservations. "My 18-point order of August 1993 may have been an armchair order, and it could have been commented on in feedback," he said, "but it had to be complied with."[11]

SERB REBELLION IN BANJA LUKA: "SEPTEMBER '93"

Shortly after Mladić's insubordination and Karadžić's insulting order in August 1993, another incendiary episode in September re-ignited their feud. During the early morning hours of September 10, about 350 troops of the VRS First Krajina Corps seized control of the city of Banja Luka as their commanders proclaimed a rebellion against the RS government.[12] Equipped with seven or eight tanks and several other armored vehicles, they seized the city hall, major police stations, radio and television stations, and major thoroughfares into the city. Naming their ill-fated movement "September '93," they took hostage several civilian SDS leaders in Banja Luka, although they carefully refrained from harming anyone.

The rebellion laid bare several smoldering sources of discontent within the VRS. The movement's leaders, like other VRS reserve officers, depended for their pay on the largely empty treasury of the RS, while the Republic of Serbia paid generous salaries to its regular officers (almost all of them holdovers from

---

[10] BSA, 50th Session, April 15–16, 1995, Karadžić, BCS 0084–5872.
[11] BSA, 50th Session, April 15–16, 1995, Karadžić, BCS 0084–6070.
[12] "Informacija o dogadjajima u Banja Luci od 10. do 17. Septembra 1993. godine," ICTY, PSM, Exhibit P67A, BCS 0048–0967–0048–0974.

the JNA) through two special payment centers. The rebels demanded better pay and protested war profiteering, but their demands aroused little public support. They organized a rally in Banja Luka's central square that drew only 2,000 supporters, a paltry crowd compared to the many thousands who had packed the square in prewar rallies.

As the revolt was being launched, Karadžić was attending a session of the assembly in Pale. Delegates at that meeting denounced the rebellion as a *coup d'état* directed against the SDS, the RS Presidency, and the assembly.[13] Some delegates speculated that the coup leaders were angry with war profiteers;[14] others saw nefarious foreign influences behind the uprising;[15] and still others blamed Mladić, the VRS General Staff, Milošević, or unspecified "communists."[16] Karadžić held Mladić responsible for the whole incident and archly demanded that he return all his troops to their garrisons.[17] He further bragged of his own role in directing military activities. "I am the Supreme Commander," he asserted. "I don't concern myself with tactics. But whenever I've gotten involved, I've been right." He claimed credit for the success of several operations and asserted that his involvement had saved several areas in Sarajevo and eastern Bosnia from falling to the enemy.[18]

The generals were understandably rankled by Karadžić's claims of omniscience in military matters and his gratuitous humiliation of Mladić before the assembly. But they again cloaked their resentment and proclaimed their loyalty to Karadžić. "You are my boss," Mladić declared, leading off a series of declarations of loyalty. "No officer carried out any task that you had not personally approved for the VRS."[19] He sought to distance himself and his senior commanders from responsibility for the September '93 uprising, while indicating that discontent with the army's financial plight was widespread and justified.

Despite Mladić's conciliatory tone, Karadžić interjected sarcastic retorts as Mladić spoke. The RS president, the better debater of the two, sought to humiliate his top general commander in front of the assembly:

> **Mladić:** The Army and the people, with assistance from the rest of us, and I put myself among the "rest of us," completed most tasks given to us and fulfilled the strategic goals. We created the Republika Srpska –

[13] BSA, 34th Session, September 10, 1993, Sava Knežević, BCS 0215–0791.
[14] BSA, 34th Session, September 11, 1993, Tomo Kovač, BCS 0215–0834–0215–0835.
[15] Ibid., Tomislav Savkić, BCS 0215–0859.
[16] Mladić diaries, September 10–12, 1993.
[17] BSA, 34th Session, September 11, 1993, Mladić, BCS 0215–0817.
[18] BSA, 34th Session, September 10, 1993, Karadžić, BCS 0215–0796.
[19] BSA, 34th Session, September 11, 1993, Mladić, BCS 0215–0821.

Karadžić: There are press interviews.

Mladić: Don't gripe to me about doing press interviews. Unlike some others, I have no private press to organize interviews for me, and I have no journalists here and there.

Karadžić: WHAT others, General – say it!

Mladić: I don't know what others.

Karadžić: Don't speak in allusions, man![20]

Unseemly though these exchanges were, Mladić and Karadžić needed one another to bring the "September '93" rebellion to an end. Over the next few days it became apparent that their bitter competition drove them to cooperate, as each tried to outperform the other in promoting the Serb nationalist utopia. They were to repeat such competition-driven collaboration several times in the subsequent two years. Karadžić eventually abandoned his insistence that Mladić solve the problem on his own, and the two men traveled to Banja Luka simultaneously but separately to calm things down. Karadžić met with civilian leaders while Mladić talked with soldiers. With the benefit of Mladić's forceful bluster and Karadžić's skills of persuasion, they convinced the mutineers to surrender and return the town to civilian authority. A few ringleaders were arrested, but most participants were allowed to return to their units without retribution. "Most importantly, everything took place without shedding Serb blood," said General Milan Gvero, the VRS Assistant Commander for Morale, Legal, and Religious Affairs.[21]

In the end, Karadžić prevailed over the uprising of September '93 using the same tactics that he had employed to defeat the ARK separatists in February 1992. He blamed the revolt on a few key leaders, confronted the miscreants in person, persuaded them to back down, and refrained from significant retaliation against any of them. By isolating the mutineers and treating them firmly but humanely, he bolstered his stature as the pre-eminent civilian leader of the Bosnian Serbs.

Mladić and Karadžić resumed their feud shortly after the revolt ended. They held opposing views on nearly every issue concerning the VRS, but neither man wavered in zealously promoting the fundamental goal of a single Bosnian Serb state. Both of them proclaimed support for the strategic goals adopted in May 1992, but each freely blamed the other for the failure to achieve them. Each accused the other of sowing disunity in the movement. They played out their rivalry before the Bosnian Serb Assembly, most of whose members had come during the war to favor expanded conquests and harsher punishment of

---

[20]   Ibid., Mladić and Karadžić, BCS 0215–0818.
[21]   Ibid., General Milan Gvero, BCS 0215–0936.

their adversaries. In January 1993, members of the assembly had applauded when told that a VRS soldier had pumped five bullets into Hakija Turaljić, a Bosniak and vice president of the Bosnian government, while the latter was in an UNPROFOR armored personnel carrier and under UNPROFOR protection. Even Mladić disapproved of the killing and of the applause.[22] In front of this radicalized audience, Karadžić and Mladić competed for recognition as the most devoted and most effective champion of the Bosnian Serb utopian ideal. Their rivalry did not weaken the Serb nationalist movement, as might have been expected; rather, their fierce competition drove each toward more extreme measures, and energized their followers to do the same.

THE GREAT REVERSAL OF 1995

The Karadžić-Mladić rivalry acquired added significance with a reversal of VRS fortunes in western Bosnia in 1995. As Croat and Bosnian government forces gained territory and fighting strength, Bosnian Serb leaders turned to desperate measures in hopes of simultaneously stanching losses on the western front and completing fulfillment of their strategic aims in eastern Bosnia. Although the route to the final act was circuitous, Serb defeats in western Bosnia contributed to Bosnian Serb nationalist leaders' decisions to commit mass atrocities on the killing fields of Srebrenica in the east.

Unfortunately for the Bosnian Serb leaders, the VRS faced several battlefield contenders in Bosnia: the Bosnian-based Croat Defense Council (*Hrvatska vijeće obrane*, HVO), units of the Army of Croatia (*Hrvatska vojska*, HV); the Army of the Republic of Bosnia and Herzegovina (*Armija Republike Bosne i Hercegovine*, ARBiH), and UNPROFOR, the international peacekeeping force that claimed to be neutral. The various contenders had quite different goals and agendas, but they converged in seeking to halt or reverse VRS advances. Croat commanders hoped to conquer key positions in mountainous western Bosnia from which to attack central territories of the Republic of Serb Krajina, the breakaway state that Serbs had established on Croatian territory three years before. Commanders of both Croat and Bosnian government forces hoped to drive the VRS out of western Bosnia and link up with the ARBiH Fifth Corps that was driving south from the Bosniak enclave at Bihać. To the great dismay of Bosnian Serb nationalists, and after protracted fighting, Croat forces and the ARBiH were poised to achieve their objectives in late summer of 1995.

---

[22] BSA, 24th Session, January 8, 1993, Mladić, BCS 214–9927–0214–9928.

VRS defeats at the hands of Croat and Bosniak-led forces sparked justified fears among many Serb nationalists that their entire utopian project was in jeopardy. As their adversaries drove the VRS out of one municipality after another, long-time Serb inhabitants abandoned their homes and joined an exodus of Serbs fleeing eastward toward the Republic of Serbia. Assembly delegates, led by those representing municipalities lost to Croat offensives, implored the VRS generals to counterattack and recover the lost territories.

The slow deterioration of Serb control in Croatia and Western Bosnia occasioned further acrimony between Karadžić and Mladić. The two aired their differences at a meeting of key civilian leaders and military commanders on March 31,[23] and engaged in further polemics at the fiftieth assembly session on April 15 and 16, 1995.[24] Karadžić complained that the army was exceeding its constitutional powers; Mladić accused civilian leaders of denying the pay and provisions his troops needed to mount effective campaigns. Some delegates questioned Mladić's leadership capabilities; others criticized Karadžić; and still others simply implored both men to reverse the mounting Serb losses in western Bosnia.

A STRATEGY OF DESPERATION: HARASS AND HUMILIATE

Karadžić and Mladić were alarmed by the delegates' discontent and by the accelerating battlefield losses. Remarkably, they were able again to set aside their differences in early spring 1995 and agree on a fundamentally new strategy, identified as "harassment and humiliation" in these pages (although contemporaries gave it no specific name). The shift has not previously been noted in scholarly studies of the war, but it is documented in Karadžić's speeches and evident in calculated provocations carried out by the VRS in the days and weeks afterward. The strategy called for carefully calibrated hostile actions against UNPROFOR to taunt peacekeeping forces, with the intent of persuading the publics of troop-contributing nations to demand UNPROFOR's withdrawal from Bosnia.

Karadžić and Mladić had good reason to believe that harassment and humiliation would hasten a Western capitulation to Bosnian Serb demands. They knew that public opinion in Europe and North America was turning against the deployment of peacekeepers, and they believed, correctly, that

---

[23] "14. sjednica Vrhovne komande oružanih snaga Republike Srpske održane dana 31.03.1995. godine, na Palama, sa početkom u 1700 časova," ICTY, PRK, Exhibit P3149, BCS 0554-2148–0554-2236.

[24] BSA, 50th Session, April 15–16, 1995, BCS 0084-5781–0084-6113.

ILLUSTRATION 14.1. Radovan Karadžić and Ratko Mladić at the Fiftieth Bosnian Serb Assembly Session, April 15, 1995. Corbis Images.

humiliating those troops in public would lead to mounting calls for their withdrawal. They also hoped to force a peace upon the ARBiH and HVO, leaving the VRS in possession of more of its rapidly-vanishing territory than if the war dragged on.

Karadžić first hinted at a new strategy in his Directive No. 7 of March 1995.[25] He did not write the order, but he signed it as "Supreme Commander" and later claimed full responsibility for its contents.[26] In Directive No. 7, he specified the strategy's final objective as a favorable negotiated outcome rather than military victory. He directed the VRS to create "optimum conditions for the state and political leadership to negotiate a peace agreement and accomplish the strategic objectives of the war." He instructed the VRS to "repel all attacks on RS territory by mounting a resolute defense in all sectors of the war front" and particularly emphasized its obligation to "prevent at all costs ... the lifting of the siege of Sarajevo." With Directive No. 7, Karadžić also ordered the VRS to prepare three offensives and, as a contingency, to plan a fourth to "advance deeply into enemy territory, crush and destroy his forces." Like the

[25] "Direktiva za dalja dejstva op. br. 7," March 8, 1995, ICTY, PRK, BCS 0082–3159–0082–3179.
[26] BSA, 54th Session, October 15–16, 1995, Karadžić, BCS 0215–4553.

defensive operations, these offensives had a largely political objective, namely "by force of arms, to impose the final outcome of the war on the enemy, forcing the world into recognizing the actual situation on the ground and ending the war."

Buried in Directive No. 7 lay the phrase that led to mass atrocities at Srebrenica. In prescribing an aggressive offensive strategy for eastern Bosnia, he ordered the VRS to "create an unbearable situation of total insecurity with no hope of further survival or life for the inhabitants of Srebrenica and Žepa." Additionally, should UNPROFOR abandon the UN-designated safe areas in eastern Bosnia, the VRS should attack and conquer those areas. That part of the order was intended to fulfill strategic goal No. 3 established in May 1992, to "establish a corridor in the Drina River Valley."[27] Karadžić did not specify the methods to be used to "create an unbearable situation," but his Directive No. 7 was consistent with his view, shared by other Bosnian Serb nationalist leaders, that Bosniaks were the primary obstacles to realizing Serb strategic goals. By directing his forces to assure "no hope of further survival or life," Karadžić revealed his indifference to Bosniaks and readiness to eliminate them from the Drina Valley.

Mladić, seeking to act in accord with his commander in chief, was not far behind. On March 31, 1995, Mladić issued "Directive 7/1," reiterating almost all elements of Karadžić's Directive No. 7 in identical language.[28] In reiterating Karadžić's instructions over his own signature, Mladić found a way to demonstrate his obedience to Karadžić and retain command of his forces while vigorously advancing Bosnian Serb war aims. But his Directive No. 7/1 differed from Karadžić's directive in one sentence: Mladić conspicuously omitted the sentence directing the Drina Corps to create "total insecurity with no hope of further survival or life" in Srebrenica and Žepa. The omission suggests either that he differed from Karadžić on the wisdom of such an order or that he recognized the folly of stating such a depraved intent in writing. Either way, the slight discrepancy between the two orders shows that Mladić was determined to show himself willing to carry out Karadžić's order. Both men appear to have been competing to be seen as the most ardent implementer of Serb strategic goals.

Karadžić explained why he had adopted the new strategy in addressing the assembly in June 1995. "We decided to opt for an aggravation of the situation,"

---

[27] "Odluka o strateškim ciljevima srpskog naroda u Bosni i Hercegovini," dated May 12, 1992, signed by Momčilo Krajišnik, *Službeni glasnik Republike Srpske*, no. 22, November 26, 1993, p. 866.

[28] "Direktiva za dalja dejstva op. Br. 7/1," March 31, 1995, ICTY, PRK, BCS 0066–8778–0066–8785.

he explained. "The Supreme Command, and I as the Commander, and with the Main Staff, we agreed that the worst for us is a war of low intensity, long duration, etc., and that we have to heat up the situation, take whatever we can, create a fiery atmosphere and dramatize, threaten an escalation, etc.,"[29] he stated. "We noticed that whenever we advance on Goražde, on Bihać or elsewhere, or if the situation escalates around Sarajevo," Karadžić explained, "the internationals come and diplomatic activity speeds up."

HARASSMENT AND HUMILIATION IN ACTION

The VRS began implementing the "harassment" element of the strategy almost immediately after Karadžić signed Directive No. 7. Several civilians were killed as shelling and sniping resumed on March 12, 1995. A plane carrying Yasushi Akashi, the Personal Representative of the UN Secretary General and top UN diplomat for Bosnia, was hit by gunfire as it prepared to land in Sarajevo.[30] Further pressuring vulnerable foreigners in Bosnia, Serb forces detained two Swiss citizens on April 3 at a Serb-manned checkpoint en route to Sarajevo airport.[31] Each of these incidents drew international press attention and provoked strong protests from UN spokesmen. Each implied a challenge to UNPROFOR and demonstrated the force's inability to provide security in the Sarajevo area. The VRS harassment in Sarajevo coincided with attacks on other forces and civilians elsewhere in Bosnia.

The Carter-negotiated ceasefire was scheduled to expire on May 1, but both Croat forces and the ARBiH violated the agreement and launched operations well before it expired. On March 20 the ARBiH attacked Serb forces on Mt. Vlasić in Central Bosnia and eventually captured the summit on April 4.[32] A similar ARBiH assault on Mt. Stolice failed only because superior VRS artillery firepower supported a successful VRS counterattack. The Croats soon resumed their seize-and-hold operations in the west under the name "Operation Leap I."[33] Methodically launching limited attacks every few days, the Croat forces drove a wedge between the Serb forces in Croatia (the Army of the RSK) and those in Bosnia (the VRS). Then, as the oft-violated Carter ceasefire formally expired on May 1, the Army of Croatia launched a large lightning strike and drove Serb forces

---

[29] BSA, 51st Session, June 14–15, 1995, Karadžić, BCS 0215–4145.
[30] *AP News Archive,* March 13, 1995, www.apnewsarchive.com/1995/NATO-Boosts-Overflights-After-Weekend-Attacks/id-b85486448f704dfoa5ba1740e8f6f3e6.
[31] *New York Times,* April 5, 1995, p. A3.
[32] CIA, *Balkan Battlegrounds,* Vol. 1, p. 301.
[33] Ibid., p. 296.

from the Western Zone UN Protected Area (UNPA) in that part of Croatia
known as Western Slavonia.[34] By June 9, Croat units stood poised to take
Bosansko Grahovo in Bosnia, the town widely regarded as the VRS's last
stronghold preventing Croats from advancing on the capital of the RSK,
Knin.[35]

The Army of the Serb Republic of Krajina (RSK), bested by Croatian
forces on the battlefield, responded to their defeats with desperate measures. They avenged their military losses by targeting civilians in an urban
area. Milan Martić, head of the Croatian Serbs and president of the RSK,
ordered an attack on civilian targets in Zagreb with rockets armed with cluster munitions. On May 2, shells fell in several locations in the Zagreb city
center, killing 6 civilians and wounding 180.[36] UN officials and world leaders denounced the assault, and in an unusual admission of responsibility,
Martić publicly boasted of ordering the attack. He earned the scorn of his
fellow Serb nationalists in both Croatia and Bosnia for breaking the code
of silence and owning up to the vicious attacks. Milorad Dodik, leader of
the embryonic opposition in the Bosnian Serb Assembly and later Prime
Minister of the postwar RS, defended the attacks and cynically called for
closer control of the media so that ill-advised confessions like Martić's would
not air publicly.[37]

Karadžić and Krajišnik watched with alarm the gathering storm in western Bosnia, aware that the convergence of the ARBiH and HVO would
form a wedge between the two Serb polities and expose the VRS to further attacks. (Maps 14.1 and 14.2 show how VRS-controlled territory shrank
while the HVO and ARBiH expanded their holdings and converged in
western Bosnia between September 1993 and October 1995.). Much like
Martić had retaliated against Zagreb's civilians, Karadžić and Mladić also
increased their assaults on Sarajevo and its civilian population. They
expanded their repertoire of terror by launching enormous modified
air bombs that floated randomly into the city by parachute. On May 22,
Bosnian Serbs seized several artillery pieces from a UN containment depot
near Sarajevo and redoubled their shelling of the city.[38] Using the royal
"we," Karadžić admitted that the seizures were largely for show and had
little military significance. "We did that around Sarajevo, we took these

---

[34] Ibid., p. 297.
[35] Ibid., p. 300.
[36] *New York Times*, May 3, 1995, www.nytimes.com/1995/05/03/world/rebel-serbs-shell-croatian-
      capital.html; CIA, *Balkan Battlegrounds*, Vol. 1, p. 298; and Reuters, May 2, 1995.
[37] BSA, 3rd Extraordinary Session, May 23–24, 1995, Milorad Dodik, BCS 0410–1827.
[38] Burg and Shoup, *War in Bosnia and Herzegovina*, p. 329; Mark Danner, "Breaking the
      Machine," *New York Review of Books*, February 19, 1998.

MAP 14.1. Areas of Military Control in Bosnia, July 1993.
Original Source: Library of Congress, DI Cartography Center, 753549AI
(R00389) 8–01.

artillery pieces, there were four artillery pieces, maybe they weren't cru-
cial,"[39] he told the assembly.

After Serbs ignored an ultimatum to return the guns to UN control,
UNPROFOR Commander General Sir Rupert Smith on May 25 authorized NATO air attacks on a munitions depot and several bunkers near Pale.[40]
Afterwards, Karadžić told the assembly that Serb seizures of UN-guarded artillery "resulted in the well-known bombing that unfortunately caused us material damage because we didn't disperse these weapons." It could have been
worse, he declared. "Had the depots been full, there would have been massive

---

[39] BSA, 51st Session, June 14–15, Karadžić, BCS 0215–4145.
[40] *New York Times*, June 5, 1995, p. A6; Burg and Shoup, *War in Bosnia-Herzegovina*, p. 329; and
Rupert Smith, *The Utility of Force: The Art of War in the Modern World* (London: Allen Lane,
2005), p. 350.

MAP 14.2. Areas of Military Control in Bosnia, October 1995.
Original Source: Library of Congress, DI Cartography Center 753556AI
(R00389) 8–01.

damage, which was significant anyway." Also on May 25, the VRS lobbed a
single shell into downtown Tuzla that killed 72 people, mostly children and
teenagers out for an evening stroll. The attack set a grim record for the most
people killed by a single shell during the war.

As NATO unleashed air attacks against Serb targets, Karadžić and Mladić
put their new strategy to work, harassing and humiliating UNPROFOR and
Sarajevo's civilians with deadlier attacks. They ordered the VRS to take
UNPROFOR troops hostage and chain them as human shields to potential bombing targets. The VRS took its first hostages on May 26, 1995, and
released a video showing disarmed UNPROFOR soldiers handcuffed to the
door of the damaged Pale munitions depot.[41] Over the next several days,

---

[41] *New York Times*, May 26, 1995, www.nytimes.com/1995/05/27/world/conflict-in-the-balkans-
the-implications-serbs-call-and-raise.html.

VRS soldiers handcuffed 257 UNPROFOR troops to bridges, utility poles, and other strategic objects in the Sarajevo area.[42] As Karadžić and Mladić hoped, the taking of international peacekeepers provoked outrage in the West and led some to call for UNPROFOR's withdrawal. Others called for its reinforcement.

Karadžić claimed credit for initiating the hostage-taking, but his use of the first person plural suggested he had cooperated with Mladić in making the decision. "We ordered the arrest," he later explained. "We didn't go into detail as to when they would be tied up." He relished taunting the global public with the kidnappings. "It had a good effect, it was very shocking for the world," he observed. "Now it's easy, when they ask us if that was a nice gesture, I ask if it's a nice gesture to bomb the Serb rear and frighten our children and old people into fleeing," he said. "Then nobody has a reply."

As images of handcuffed European UNPROFOR soldiers flashed around the world and outrage mounted, the internationals backed down. On May 27 and 28 the United States, France, and Britain quietly withdrew their support for NATO air attacks.[43] UN Secretary General Boutros-Ghali ordered the UNPROFOR Commander to suspend the strikes, effectively giving top priority to the safety of UN troops.[44] In early June, UNPROFOR officials further assured Mladić and Karadžić that airstrikes would not be used against the Serb forces again, although officials of some countries reserved the right to strike later if necessary.[45]

Elated with the success of their new strategy, Karadžić and Mladić intensified their conflict with the UN. On May 30, Bosnian Serb leaders publicly proclaimed the peacekeepers their enemies, declared all UN Security Council resolutions null and void, and warned that UNPROFOR Commander General Rupert Smith might "run into an accident" if he remained in Bosnia.[46] The two leaders were intent on further humiliating the UN and coercing the NATO allies into granting additional concessions.

On June 15, in the midst of the hostage crisis, the ARBiH began its long-anticipated offensive to break the siege of Sarajevo.[47] As Karadžić had anticipated in Directive No. 7, the Bosnian army attacked from the outside, seeking to break the siege by destroying the VRS forces surrounding the city. The VRS, eager to free up all available weapons for use against the ARBiH and

---

[42] *New York Times*, June 5, 1995, p. A7.

[43] U.S. Department of State, *The Road to Dayton: U.S. Diplomacy and the Bosnian Peace Process, May–December 1995* (Washington: U.S. Department of State, 1997), pp. 5–6.

[44] Smith, *Utility of Force*, p. 351.

[45] *New York Times*, June 5, 1995, p. A7; and June 23, 1995, p. A5.

[46] *New York Times*, May 31, 1995, pp. A1 and A8.

[47] CIA, *Balkan Battlegrounds*, Vol. 1, pp. 307–316.

Sarajevo civilians, released their last 26 UNPROFOR hostages on June 18 in exchange for the UN relinquishing the weapons collection points they had occupied earlier.[48] Desperation had led Karadžić to detain UNPROFOR troops in the first place, but even greater desperation led him to release the hostages in exchange for some big guns. The hostage-taking "resulted in a negative effect and a justification for a possible massive military intervention where we would lose our state," he explained. That led the Serbs to release the hostages in stages to "initiate a cool-down process" and optimize concessions from the international community. "[We] couldn't let them all go at once, but in proportions; we even left 15 until the end of this week so we could keep the weapons we have in Sarajevo, knowing about the [Bosnian government] offensive and planning to do something in Sarajevo," he said. On the whole, he was pleased with the results of the RS venture into hostage-taking. "We even somewhat benefited from this entire crisis," he told the assembly.

As the hostage crisis was ending, the ARBiH offensive to break the siege sputtered under relentless VRS artillery bombardment. Facing a stalemate or even possible defeat, the ARBiH broke off the attack and abandoned its final futile effort to break the siege of Sarajevo militarily. Its forces immediately came under further pressure throughout Bosnia. As the summer heat baked Bosnia's besieged cities and towns, the VRS resumed pounding the enclaves with artillery and further constricted the siege lines. The Bosnian government was thrust again into dependence on Croat forces and international actors to end the war. But the VRS was also in a precarious position. The Serb nationalists had played out the short-term benefits of hostage taking and repelled the ARBiH effort to break the siege, but they were still losing territory to the ARBiH and Croat forces in the west and facing increasing threats of intervention from the UN and NATO.

As hostilities escalated, Karadžić repeatedly injected himself into military matters, determined to call the shots in his campaign to taunt and humiliate the peacekeepers. He instructed an entire brigade to transfer from the Drina Corps in the east to the Sarajevo Romanija Corps to suppress the advancing ARBiH offensive against Sarajevo's besiegers.[49] He also ordered formation of a new brigade to defend Pale. Those were audacious, intrusive orders, reminiscent of his harsh directive of August 28, 1993. Mladić and the other offended VRS generals took note and sullenly obeyed, but they were increasingly chafing under Karadžić's amateurish interventions. Even if Karadžić had been right – and it may well be that the additional brigade gave essential assistance to the Romanija Corps – his failure to consult the generals beforehand was stoking resentment among the top brass. Karadžić not only faced resurgent foes on the battlefield; he was losing his grip on his own fighting force.

Realizing he was caught in a downward spiral of unfavorable developments, Karadžić redoubled his efforts to lure Carter back to talks. He even begged the American journalist Mike Wallace to set up a face-to-face meeting with Richard Holbrooke, the US Assistant Secretary of State for European and Canadian Affairs and the top U.S. diplomat for Bosnia. But the Americans held firm. Carter declined to visit again, and diplomats on Holbrooke's negotiating team insisted that they would speak only with Milošević.

In the long run, Karadžić and Mladić sullied themselves with the "harassment and humiliation" strategy and set themselves up to be tried for war crimes at the ICTY. But their initial actions under the new strategy – taking hostages and seizing weapons from UN depots – were but preludes to the outrageous climax of the war: genocide at Srebrenica.

THE DESTRUCTION OF THE SREBRENICA BOSNIAKS

In July 1995, Karadžić conceived and ordered an attack on Srebrenica.[50] The attack and subsequent atrocities bore some resemblance to the conquests of Bosnia's municipalities in 1992, but circumstances had changed dramatically in the meantime. In 1995, VRS forces were reeling from defeats in the west, and the Bosnian Serb strategic outlook was bleak, in stark comparison to the army's triumphant and largely unopposed advances in 1992. The siege of the three eastern Bosnian enclaves – Srebrenica, Gorazde, and Žepa – required continuous deployment of a large number of VRS troops. The entire Drina Corps was devoted to the relatively undemanding task of maintaining the siege of the three eastern enclaves, but those units were desperately needed to help stem HVO and ARBiH advances in western Bosnia. Furthermore, despite the campaign of harassment and humiliation, the Western powers were showing no signs of withdrawing UNPROFOR from the enclaves as Karadžić had hoped. In late June, Karadžić plotted the climactic final act of the "harass and humiliate" strategy in order to free up the Drina Corps for action in the west, remove all non-Serbs from eastern Bosnia, and prevent Bosniaks from ever returning to their homes.

---

[50] For a detailed factual account of developments at Srebrenica, see the judgment in the trial of seven co-defendants at the ICTY, "Judgement," June 10, 2010, pp. 91–306, Paragraphs 242–738, Prosecutor v. Vujadin Popović, et al., IT-05-88, www.icty.org/x/cases/popovic/tjug/en/100610judgement.pdf.

Police from the Republic of Serbia were also involved in security operations in the area. Some served in Serbian MUP units; at least one company consisted of joint police forces from the RS, RSK, and the Republic of Serbia. That unit participated in operations around Sarajevo but was ordered to Srebrenica on July 10, 1995, as Serb forces advanced on the town.[51] The presence of those police units in the RS suggested to some later observers that Milošević may have sanctioned the attack on Srebrenica, but no further evidence has surfaced that either implicates or absolves him of responsibility.

In ordering the VRS to take Srebrenica, Karadžić extended the policies he had outlined in Directive No. 7 with a methodical approach to carrying out mass atrocities. His decision was born in desperation but carried out with businesslike calculation. In the first step, Karadžić, accompanied by Krajišnik and a small entourage, made a surprise visit to the VRS Drina Corps headquarters at Vlasenica in late June 1995.[52] It was an audacious and highly unorthodox step to bypass Mladić and the rest of the VRS Main Staff. He arrived to find that the corps commander was away, so he instead inquired of Colonel Radislav Krstić, the acting corps commander, how long he would need to prepare an attack on Srebrenica. Krstić replied that he would need three to five days; Karadžić told him to do it faster. He directed Krstić to make preparations as quickly as possible and promised to give him all necessary logistical support.

The Drina Corps staff immediately began work on a plan to conquer the town.[53] After completing the plan, the VRS Main Staff issued an operational order "to separate and reduce in size the Srebrenica and Žepa enclaves with surprise attacks, to create the tactical situation of strength deep in the zone, and to create a condition for the elimination of the enclaves."[54] The order cited both Karadžić's Directive No. 7 and Mladić's Directive No. 7/1 as authorizations for the operation, reflecting Mladić's preference for issuing orders nearly identical to those of the RS president. Giving lip service

---

[51] Budimir Babović, "Analysis of Regulations Regarding Responsibility for Control of the Interior Ministry of the Republic of Serbia," Expert Report, April 2, 2003, ICTY, PSM, Exhibit P465a, Paragraphs 160–162, ENG 0306-2523–0306-2524. See also Judith Armatta, "Historical Revelations from the Milošević Trial," *Southeastern Europe* 36 (2012), pp. 23–24; and Emir Suljagić, "Milošević Linked to Srebrenica Massacre," Institute for War and Peace Reporting, April 30, 2005, iwpr.net/report-news/milosevic-linked-srebrenica-massacre, viewed January 1, 2014.

[52] Testimony of Milenko Lazić, ICTY, Prosecutor v. Vujadin Popović, et al., June 4, 2008, pp. 21,727–21,728 and 21,744–21,746; and June 5, 2008, p. 21,862.

[53] Ibid., June 4, 2008, p. 21,728.

[54] "Komanda Drinskog korpusa Strogo pov. Br. 04/156-2, 02.07.1995 godine. Zapovest za aktivna b/d Op.br.1," ICTY, Prosecutor v. Vijadin Popović, et al., Exhibit P00107, paragraph 4, BCS 0084-7290.

to international law, the soldiers were reminded to carry out their actions in accord with the Geneva Conventions.[55] The order otherwise made no mention of killing civilians, although VRS commanders had come to understand that offensives were to include the elimination of non-Serb civilians from conquered areas.

Karadžić later boasted of initiating the action. "As the Supreme Commander, I stood behind the plan for Žepa and Srebrenica," he said. "I personally supervised the plan without the knowledge of the Main Staff, not hiding anything, but I happened to run into General Krstić and advised him to go straight into town and to pronounce the fall of Srebrenica, and later we will chase the Turks around the woods."[56] With his reference to "chasing the Turks around the woods," he suggested that he expected his forces to hunt down fleeing Bosniaks after the VRS had conquered the town. But he refrained from bragging about intentionally bypassing Mladić and instead characterized his meeting with Krstić in Vlasenica as a chance encounter.

The last hope for Srebrenica's approximately 40,000 frightened Bosniaks lay with a battalion of lightly-armed Dutch UNPROFOR peacekeepers, who had neither the ordnance nor the manpower to stave off a VRS attack. UNPROFOR soldiers had been sent there as peacekeepers, but there was no peace to keep; they could do little more than mediate between VRS commanders and the besieged Bosniaks. Owing to a Serb policy that allowed individual UNPROFOR soldiers to leave the enclave but not return or be replaced, by July 1995 the Dutch battalion there had been reduced to 429 soldiers, half of whom were support rather than combat troops.[57] They were dispersed among fifteen locations: one base in the city center, another in an abandoned battery factory at Potočari along the road leading into the city, and thirteen isolated observation posts manned by a total of ninety-five soldiers. Although they had ample vehicles, the Dutch UNPROFOR troops in Srebrenica were short on weapons, ammunition, fuel, and food. They, and the enclave they were tasked with guarding, were hopelessly vulnerable to attack.

The more numerous troops of the 28th Division of the ARBiH present in Srebrenica were even less capable of resisting a VRS assault. The Bosnian government had agreed to disarm its forces in Srebrenica, although

[55] Testimony of Mirko Trivić, ICTY, Prosecutor v. Vujadin Popović, et al., May 21, 2007, pp. 11,884–11,886; and "Glavni stab Vojske Republike Srpske, Komandi Drinskog korpusa, generala Gvere i Krstića, Izvodjenje borbeni dejstava oko Srebrenica," signed by General Zdravko Tolimir, July 9, 1995, ICTY, Prosecutor v. Vujadin Popović, et al., Exhibit P00033, BCS 0086–9096.

[56] BSA, 54th Session, October 15–16, 1995, BCS 0215–4556.

[57] Honig and Both, *Srebrenica*, pp. 5–6.

UNPROFOR had never completely disarmed the 28th Division. VRS estimated that 10,000 men were in the division at the beginning of July, while UNPROFOR put the number at 3,000 to 4,000.[58] In any case, they were disorganized, poorly trained, and equipped only with light weapons or none at all.[59] As Karadžić and Serb apologists were quick to point out, those troops had occasionally conducted hit-and-run raids that resembled guerilla warfare, although these appear mainly to have been cattle-rustling ventures to feed the enclave's starving population. As the VRS prepared to attack, most 28th Division soldiers slipped out of Srebrenica in the days before the assault began, leaving the civilians and the UNPROFOR peacekeepers to fend for themselves.

The VRS began their ground attack on Srebrenica on July 6 with heavy shelling and probing actions on the outer perimeter of the enclaves.[60] The first Dutch UNPROFOR observation post fell on July 8. On July 9, Karadžić issued another verbal order, this time addressing the Main Staff and authorizing the VRS to enter and capture Srebrenica.[61] The Main Staff passed the order along to General Gvero and General Radislav Krstić by telegram. On July 11, the VRS took control of the town of Srebrenica. As chaos and fear gripped Srebrenica's civilians, thousands of them headed toward the single remaining UNPROFOR-controlled installation at Potočari on the outskirts of town, but soon it, too, was in Serb hands.

Later, top VRS generals joined Karadžić in claiming to have authorized the attack. Their claims became another part of the scramble to take credit for mass atrocities. They showed the depths to which the Serb nationalist movement had descended under the pressure of defeat and desperation. Top VRS generals, in collective self-delusion, believed they would be seen as justified in carrying out the Srebrenica genocide immediately after the swift Croat conquests of Serb-inhabited areas of Croatia and western Bosnia. As General Gvero explained, "We did that [the attack on Srebrenica] at a time when we estimated that the international community would not react immediately after the events in Western Slavonia, and we entered [Srebrenica] exclusively because of that. That was one of the strategic decisions of the Main Staff, and

---

[58] "Judgement," Paragraph 246, June 10, 2010, ICTY, Prosecutor v. Vujadin Popović, et al.

[59] U.S. DCI (Director of Central Intelligence), Interagency Balkan Task Force, "The Bosnian Army in Srebrenica: What Happened?" July 18, 1995, pp. 1–2, clintonlibrary.gov/bosniadeclass-docs.html, viewed January 4, 2014. This report was among more than 300 documents declassified in 2013 and made available on the website of the William J. Clinton Presidential Library and Museum, clintonlibrary.gov/.

[60] CIA, *Balkan Battleground*, Vol. 1, pp. 316–354.

[61] "Judgement," paragraph 252, June 10, 2010, ICTY, Prosecutor v. Vujadin Popović, et al.

we achieved it in accord with the greatest possibilities, minimum losses, and maximum rationalization in the use of forces."[62]

On July 11, General Mladić arrived in Srebrenica and assumed command of operations on the ground.[63] Since the military conquest was already complete when he arrived, he can only have gone there to command the final destruction of the frightened and disorganized civilian population. Mladić soon took control with his blunt, decisive leadership style, showing once again that fierce competition could drive both him and Karadžić to functional if fragile cooperation in fulfillment of their shared goals. Mladić basked in the spotlight of the mainly Serb media covering the climactic event. He negotiated in person with a local Bosniak schoolteacher who had been singled out to represent the besieged population, promised him that no one would be harmed, and bullied him into signing a capitulation on behalf of the entire town. He shouted orders to his troops and gave soothing assurances to Srebrenica's civilians as they were being assembled for forced removal from the town. As Karadžić carefully monitored the ongoing operation by phone and closed-circuit radio reports, Mladić pushed the mission forward toward the bloody extermination of the displaced population. He watched approvingly as thousands of Bosniaks were herded into tightly packed warehouses or onto buses heading out of town.

At about midnight on July 11, an estimated 10,000 to 15,000 Bosniak men gathered outside Srebrenica, formed an irregular column, and set out to walk to government-controlled Tuzla, a city of 83,770 about 70 kilometers away. After hearing from many witnesses, ICTY judges concluded that the column was of "mixed ... civilian and military components," and that about one-third of the walkers were armed.[64] At the head of the column were soldiers of the ARBiH 28th Division, followed by the staff of Srebrenica hospital. Besides those two groups, the slow-moving column would be seen by most observers as thousands of ragtag men making a desperate flight to safety; Serb nationalists, however, contended that the entire column was an organized withdrawal of the 28th Division in preparation for counterattacking the VRS. Citing as justification this fabrication that the column was an organized armed force, the VRS and Serb paramilitary forces attacked them. They exterminated much of Srebrenica's male population while "chasing the Turks through the woods," as Karadžić later characterized it. VRS troops shot and killed some of the Bosniak men in flight, but captured most and transported them in buses to holding

---

[62] BSA, 52nd Session, August 6, 1995, General Milan Gvero, BCS 0215–4202.
[63] Honig and Both, *Srebrenica*, p. 30.
[64] "Judgement," paragraph 270, June 10, 2010, ICTY, Prosecutor v. Vujadin Popović, et al.

facilities in warehouses, abandoned factories, and farm buildings where they murdered almost all with automatic rifle fire and hand grenades.

The military operation went beyond a conquest and became a campaign to eliminate all Bosniak males of reproductive age. Very few of them reached Tuzla or any government-controlled territory. One of the few survivors of the massacre, protected witness PW-111, told his harrowing tale in court at the ICTY in February 2007.[65] His story reveals that the VRS troops were systematic in their executions. Himself a former soldier in the JNA, PW-111 was serving in the ARBiH when the VRS attacked Srebrenica. Fearful of Serb reprisals, he had joined the column of desperate men fleeing through the wooded hills toward Tuzla.

PW-111 and a large number of other Bosniaks surrendered to the VRS near the small town of Kravica west of Srebrenica. He and the others were then herded into a meadow. General Mladić briefly visited the prisoners and assured them they had nothing to fear and would be sent unharmed to wherever they wished. PW-111 described being put on a bus packed with other prisoners and told he would be taken toward Tuzla and exchanged for Serbs living there. But instead of heading to Tuzla, the bus delivered PW-111 and the others to a warehouse near Kravica. Serb soldiers ordered the prisoners to leave the buses and enter the warehouse quickly. Soon it was "tightly packed" with as many as 3,000 prisoners, in the estimate of PW-111. As they herded their prisoners into the warehouse, VRS soldiers ordered each prisoner to surrender money, jewelry, watches, and gold.

Shortly after dark, a small group of guards entered the warehouse and began shooting. As the sound of automatic gunfire echoed off the walls, men by the hundreds died where they fell. "I saw they would kill us all," said PW-111. He lay down on the ground and remained still in the dark. "All I could hear were moans and shouts and people calling out the names of their parents, their close relatives, people who were still not dead," he testified. "They had survived, they were alive, but they were heavily wounded, perhaps." During pauses in the firing, guards threw hand-grenades into the warehouse through the windows. One of the grenades injured PW-111.

Inside the warehouse, he made his way in the dark to a large container near a window high on the wall of the warehouse, climbed atop the container to the window and dropped from there onto the grass outside. Wounded, but not gravely, he crawled quietly into a nearby cornfield. As he lay perfectly still on the ground, an alert guard found him and fired a single shot at him, hitting

---

[65] Testimony of Protected Witness PW-111, ICTY, Prosecutor v. Vujadin Popović, et al., February 6 and 7, 2007, pp. 6,971–7,025, and subsequent cross-examination, pp. 7,026, et seq.

ILLUSTRATION 14.2. Memorial and Burial Ground for Victims of Srebrenica Massacre. Photograph by author.

PW-111's right shoulder. Probably believing his target was dead, the soldier moved on to resume searching other areas in the cornfield. Twice injured, PW-111 was able to escape the warehouse area after dawn. But then he made a perfectly logical decision that led him to still more difficulties. Rather than head west toward Tuzla and Central Bosnia, he went east to the besieged enclave of Žepa. When Serb forces conquered that town a week later, after having emptied Srebrenica of its Bosniaks, he was taken prisoner and held another six months until after the war.

With a superb memory and a gift for relating his experiences dispassionately and convincingly, PW-111 riveted the court with his testimony. The key points of his account were verified by other witnesses and corroborated by reams of documentary evidence. He was one of the fortunate few: the VRS slaughtered more than 7,000 Bosniaks, mostly men of reproductive age, in the days following their conquest of the town. Most were captured, concentrated, and executed, just as PW-111's fellow prisoners had been.

Details of the Srebrenica massacre leaked out slowly. At first, international diplomats and observers were more concerned about Dutch UNPROFOR hostages and the audacious violation of the UN safe havens than with the horrific slaughter. The Bosnian Serbs obligingly released their Dutch UNPROFOR hostages after a few days and celebrated their conquest. VRS commanders, seizing the moment, transferred two brigades from the Drina Corps across Bosnia to the Second Krajina Corps in hopes of stemming Croat advances in the west.[66] But they arrived too late to stave off the Croat conquest of the strategically vital towns of Glamoč and Bosansko Grahovo, which Croat forces took on July 28 and 29.[67] On August 4, Croat forces launched Operation Storm, routing the demoralized Serb forces in Croatia, and rapidly conquered most remaining Serb-controlled territory in Croatia.[68] They took Knin the next day and completed Operation Storm by August 7, bringing an end to the Republic of Serb Krajina in all but a small sector in eastern Slavonia.

Those Croat victories shook Bosnian Serb leaders to the core. Karadžić, of course, blamed Mladić and the VRS generals for the catastrophic losses, while he insisted on claiming full responsibility and credit for seizing Srebrenica and Žepa. "I approved that ... radical task and I don't regret it,"[69] he told the assembly. He regarded the operation as successful. "As you know, we had success in Srebrenica and Žepa," he claimed. "There are no objections or remarks on that success." But he complained about unspecified casualties suffered by the VRS during the killing phase of the operation. "Of course, many stupid things were done afterwards," he complained, "because many Muslim soldiers were wandering around in the woods and we suffered casualties then. Still, we did not suffer any casualties during the action itself."[70]

Karadžić insisted that he, not Mladić, had initiated orders to carry out the operation. His rivalry with Mladić thus came down to a contest for bragging rights for the greatest slaughter of human beings in Europe since the Second World War. "All of our decisions, and I stand behind them, were recorded by the High Command," he insisted, "and they all state that I ordered, both verbally and in writing, that we go to Žepa and Srebrenica." He castigated a VRS officer for allowing photographic evidence of the killings to reach foreign media. "Lieutenant Colonel Milutinović has given information to foreign agencies ... pictures that could cost Mladić his life if they were presented in The Hague. They [the Serb media] broadcast whatever they want and they have recorded corpses of women in the streets of Srebrenica after which they broadcast that on foreign media."[71]

Given the aim of freeing up troops to hold western Bosnia against the Croats, the seizure of Srebrenica and Žepa made strategic sense to the Bosnian Serb leaders. But their slaughter of Srebrenica's residents and displaced persons

---

[66] BSA, 52nd Session, August 6, 1995, General Gvero, BCS 0215-4202.
[67] Ibid.; and Burg and Shoup, *War in Bosnia-Herzegovina*, p. 348; and CIA, *Balkan Battlegrounds*, Vol. 1, p. 366.
[68] CIA, *Balkan Battlegrounds*, Vol. 1, pp. 370 and 376–377.
[69] BSA, 54th Session, October 15–16, 1995, Karadžić, BCS 0215-4556.
[70] BSA, 52nd Session, August 6, 1995, Karadžić, BCS 0215-4187.
[71] Ibid., BCS 0214-4234.

was not only a heinous deed but a grave strategic and personal miscalculation. Karadžić seemed unable to grasp the long-term damage he had wrought to the Bosnian Serb cause. He immediately threw up the usual smokescreen of denials and counter-charges to minimize and justify the killings. Seemingly indifferent to the slaughter he had launched, Karadžić looked forward to further Serb conquests. "We could not take Goražde at that moment," he said, "but the time will come for Goražde, just as it did for Srebrenica, to finish it." Further, he said, "we have plenty of other places to conquer."[72]

THE ROOTS OF KARADŽIĆ'S DECISION

In ordering the conquest of Srebrenica, Karadžić descended with deliberation and calm to the worst mass atrocities of the war. Many considerations factored into his decision: his long-simmering anger at Bosniak political leaders; the VRS collapse before the HVO and ARBiH in western Bosnia; mounting uncertainty about international intervention; his rivalry with Mladić; the strategic shift to harassing and humiliating peacekeepers; and most of all, his unbending determination to fulfill the Bosnian Serb utopian dream. In the end, he was swayed by the imminent finality of the struggle. Only by fully and urgently implementing the Serb strategic goals could he assure that the Bosnian Serbs would achieve a separate state. In the previous four years he had sought tirelessly to realize that ideal through means both violent and non-violent, including persuasion, intimidation, diplomacy, and more measured applications of force. Then, hardening his heart and muting his conscience, he was prepared to resort to genocide to rid conquered areas of non-Serbs. He was, after all, not the one who would pay the price for making his utopian dream an earthly reality.

[72] Ibid., BCS 0214–4265.

15

Falling Star

Karadžić fell from power gradually, in stages, unlike many populist leaders who cling to power until death or ouster by angry mobs. In August 1995 he lost his authority to negotiate; in July 1996 he resigned his offices under pressure; in 2000 he was driven from public view; and in 2008 he lost his personal freedom upon his arrest in Belgrade. Karadžić ascribed his fall to a series of betrayals by Western diplomats, but he had also alienated some of his closest supporters and turned once-staunch allies into enemies. The primary source of his undoing was Karadžić himself. The rational Karadžić, a man of immense intellectual resourcefulness and versatility who charmed and bullied his way to power, was pushed aside by his angry, arrogant doppelgänger. Belligerent, tactless, and vain, Karadžić incited former allies and supporters to unite against him, weaken his authority, and force him from office. This chapter describes his protracted descent from power and high office.

THE ROAD TO HELL IS PAVED

In a long-delayed move, the ICTY prosecutor indicted Karadžić and Mladić on July 24, 1995, for dozens of wartime mass atrocities.[1] The sixteen-count indictment charged them with genocide, unlawful confinement of civilians, shelling of civilian gatherings, destruction of sacred sites, appropriation and plunder of property, using hostages as human shields, and other grave crimes. Although it was filed one week after the killings at Srebrenica, the indictment did not mention those events. Not until November 1995 did the ICTY prosecutors amend their indictment to include charges of genocide at Srebrenica. Even so, the initial indictment transformed Karadžić and Mladić into international

---

[1]   "Indictment," ICTY, Prosecutor v. Radovan Karadžić and Ratko Mladić, July 24, 1995, www.icty.org/x/cases/Karadžić/ind/en/kar-ii950724e.pdf.

pariahs and fugitives from the law. Their lives and fortunes changed forever. But at first, each took the indictment in stride, believing there was no realistic prospect of being arrested while remaining in office.

At the same time, international patience – particularly American patience – with Karadžić and the Bosnian Serb nationalists had grown thin. On August 7, 1995, President Clinton selected Richard Holbrooke, Assistant Secretary of State for European and Canadian Affairs, to reinvigorate stalled negotiations for peace in Bosnia.[2] Holbrooke, a tough, seasoned, and energetic diplomat, soon superseded the Contact Group as lead negotiator for the Euro-Atlantic powers. Amid doubts that Karadžić and Mladić would ever be arrested, Holbrooke and his top-flight team of advisors led an international effort to sideline Karadžić and negotiate an end to the war. Holbrooke enjoyed excellent rapport with Milošević and had already decided to make him the linchpin of a strategy to control the intractable Bosnian Serbs.[3]

Citing the ICTY indictment, Holbrooke and his team declared their refusal to meet with Karadžić or Mladić.[4] Karadžić told the assembly that Holbrooke's advance team had asked two questions of RS negotiators on first establishing contact: first, did Karadžić control the situation? And second, with whom could they speak who was not under ICTY indictment?[5] Karadžić's representatives answered the first question in the affirmative. To the second, they directed U.S. diplomats to Momčilo Krajišnik, president of the Bosnian Serb Assembly, and RS Foreign Minister Aleksa Buha. Karadžić would remain the decisive voice behind his negotiators, but U.S. diplomats refused to negotiate with him in person.

In the meantime, Karadžić was making ill-advised moves of his own in his relations with other Serb leaders. On August 4, a few days before Holbrooke assumed the role of chief negotiator, Karadžić issued a directive to demote Mladić. He ordered Mladić transferred to an advisory position and reorganized the VRS General Staff. Other top VRS generals, loyal to a fault to Mladić, were outraged. The next day, August 5, they gathered in Banja Luka, voted to reject Karadžić's directive, and promised thenceforth to obey only orders issued by Mladić.[6]

---

[2] Department of State, *The Road to Dayton*, p. 40.
[3] Ibid., p. 98.
[4] Holbrooke, *To End a War*, p. 90.
[5] BSA, 53rd Session, August 28, 1995, Karadžić, BCS 0215–4402.
[6] Karadžić's order of August 4, 1995, was summarized and assessed in BSA, 52nd Session, August 6, 1995, (speaker identified only as "Minister"), BCS 0215–4224 – 0215–4225. The generals' letter of August 5 was read in full and summarized by General Milan Gvero, in BSA, 52nd Session, August 6, 1995, General Gvero, BCS 0215–4221 – 0215–4223.

In a contentious assembly session on August 6, Generals Gvero, Tolimir,
and Mladić challenged Karadžić's decision to demote Mladić. The assembly,
loath to choose between the two men, adopted a compromise that affirmed
their confidence in the generals yet supported Karadžić's proposed organizational changes.[7] But the exchange cost Karadžić political capital and crippled
his hold on power. Mladić had previously maintained the generals' fictive obedience to Karadžić by transposing his president's orders into Main Staff directives. In announcing Mladić's demotion, Karadžić forced the VRS generals to
choose. They chose Mladić, effectively rebelling against their commander-
in-chief. After the generals' revolt of early August, Karadžić could no longer
plausibly claim to control the VRS.

Within a few weeks, Milošević did as Holbrooke had hoped and moved
against Karadžić. He sought to strip Karadžić of his most important function – leading the Bosnian Serbs in peace talks – without actually removing him from office. Twice in late August, Milošević summoned a group
of top Bosnian Serb leaders to Dobanovci, a camp and conference center near Belgrade once used by Tito as a hunting lodge. At separate sessions on August 25 and 29, he and other Yugoslav leaders were unmoved
by pleas from Karadžić and other RS leaders to continue negotiating as a
separate team.[8] Milošević was unyielding. After many hours of verbal abuse,
Karadžić capitulated late on August 29 and agreed that the Bosnian Serbs
would subsequently negotiate as part of a joint team of three representatives each from the RS and from Yugoslavia. The team leader – Milošević,
of course – reserved the final authority to resolve any disagreement among
delegation members. Karadžić rightly regarded this outcome as humiliating.
By securing Karadžić's proxy to negotiate a peace, Milošević had placed the
entire Bosnian Serb project in receivership and appointed himself as the
sole trustee of their interests.

Despite the pressure from Belgrade, the VRS resumed its gratuitous bombardment of Sarajevo. At about 11 a.m. on August 28, hours before Karadžić
capitulated to Milošević, the VRS fired five shells into Sarajevo's Markale
marketplace, where hundreds gathered daily in a dense throng of buyers and
sellers. Thirty-seven people were killed and at least 75 more were wounded.
Karadžić claimed once again that the Bosniaks were bombing themselves,
but UN personnel found no credible evidence that the shells had come from

---

7 BSA, 52nd Session, August 6, 1995, Minutes, BCS 0215–4167 — 0215–4168.
8 Savezna Republika Jugoslavija, Vrhovni savet odbrane, "Zabeleška sa sastanka predstavnika
   najvišeg političkog i vojnog rukovodstva Savezna Republike Jugoslavije i Republike Srpske ...
   u Dobanovcima," August 25, 1995, and August 29, 1995, ICTY, PSM, Exhibit P469, Tab 20,
   BCS 0115–2319–0115–2334 (August 25) and 0114–1108–0114–1123 (August 29).

outside Serb-controlled territory. This second bloody attack on the market-place (the first was in February 1994) triggered a NATO bombing campaign known as Operation Deliberate Force. Although he deplored the killing of civilians, Holbrooke eagerly seized upon the provocative attack to initiate the campaign against Serb targets. "The brutal stupidity of the Bosnian Serbs had given us an unexpected last chance to do what should have been done three years earlier," he later wrote.[9]

On August 30, the morning after the Bosnian Serbs gave Milošević their proxy to negotiate and the day the bombing started, Holbrooke and his team met with Milošević in the Dobanovci retreat where Karadžić had capitulated the previous evening. Milošević freely boasted to Holbrooke of bringing Karadžić to heel. He proudly showed Holbrooke the final agreement signed by the Bosnian Serbs. He specifically pointed to Patriarch Pavle's signature as witness to the accord, leading the Americans to dub it the "Patriarch Paper." Challenged about his ability to control the Bosnian Serbs, Milošević took offense. "They are not my friends," he snapped. "They are not my colleagues. It is awful just to be in the same room with them for so long."[10] Still, hop-ing to avoid responsibility for Karadžić's behavior, Milošević urged Holbrooke to negotiate directly and personally with the top Bosnian Serbs. Holbrooke declined and pointedly reminded Milošević of his pledge to keep Karadžić under control.

In the first two weeks of September 1995, Karadžić saw his last hopes crushed by an improbable collaboration between Holbrooke and Milošević. On September 3, members of Holbrooke's team dissuaded former President Carter from undertaking a second peacemaking mission to Pale, pointing out that it would undercut the American strategy of isolating Karadžić. Carter reluctantly agreed, closing off Karadžić's last illusory alternative to Holbrooke and Milošević. When Holbrooke returned to Dobanovci on September 13, however, he found that Milošević had stationed Karadžić, Krajišnik, and Koljević in another building only a hundred meters away. Holbrooke should meet with them, Milošević said, again trying to pass the albatross of Karadžic back to the American. He asked Holbrooke's permission to invite the two Bosnian Serbs to join them.

"Yes," said the American diplomat, thereby violating his own policy of no contact with indicted war criminals. But he laid down two conditions. First, he insisted that Milošević lead the discussion and control the Bosnian Serbs. Second, Holbrooke said, "they must not give us a lot of historical bullshit,

---

[9] Holbrooke, *To End a War*, p. 91.
[10] Ibid., p. 106.

as they have with everyone else."[11] The second condition in particular put Karadžić at a disadvantage. In another meeting six months before, former U.S. President Jimmy Carter had listened patiently to Karadžić's historical presentation and long-winded allegations of contemporary Bosniak perfidy and Serb suffering. But Holbrooke would brook no such "self-pitying diatribe," as he called it.[12] Without history, Karadžić was forced to deal with the inconvenient truths of the here and now. He did so in his usual way: in his version of the last few weeks, the Bosnian government had shelled its own people in the marketplace bombing of August 28.

Karadžić then threatened to call Carter and reopen talks with him. Holbrooke pointedly replied that he had once worked for and still admired former President Carter, but that he now represented and reported to President Clinton. He told Milošević that the American team would leave if Karadžić persisted in his weepy sermonizing. His bluff called, Karadžić dropped his truculent tone, shelved his planned history lesson, and invited the Americans to offer a specific proposal for peace. This was Karadžić's prelude to his time-tested tactic of accepting the other side's draft before insisting on a host of modifications that amounted to rejection. But Holbrooke, unexpectedly accepting Karadžić's suggestion, asked his advisors to draft an agreement. As they prepared the draft, he took a long stroll through the grounds with Milošević, who told him sarcastically, "These guys ... are so cut off from the world that they think Carter still determines American policy."[13]

Talks continued, culminating in an agreement that the VRS would lift the Sarajevo siege and honor a ceasefire starting on September 14. The two sides then quarreled about who would sign the agreement. Karadžić, perhaps thinking back to Carter's signature on the agreement of December 1994 as a "witness," wanted Holbrooke to sign in the same capacity. But Holbrooke refused to have any American sign the accord in any capacity. Only Karadžić and Krajišnik signed the document, affixing their signatures at 2:15 a.m. on September 14. Milošević and Yugoslav Foreign Minister Milutinović signed, but only as witnesses. Based on this first encounter with the Bosnian Serb nationalist leaders, Holbrooke concluded that they were "headstrong, given to empty theatrical statements, but in the end, essentially bullies when their bluff was called.... They respected only force or an unambiguous and credible threat to use it."[14]

---

[11] Ibid., p. 148.
[12] Koljević, *Republike Srpske*, pp. 310–312. Koljević and Holbrooke provide similar accounts of this meeting. Elements common to the two accounts are consistent, but each author provides a part of the discussion that the other omits.
[13] Holbrooke, *To End a War*, p. 150.
[14] Ibid., p. 152.

Karadžić remained in office for a time after the cease-fire, but he was no longer in charge. Holbrooke would never again break his self-imposed ban on meeting with indicted Bosnian Serb leaders. In furiously-paced negotiations over the next three weeks, Holbrooke and members of his team shuttled between Zagreb, Sarajevo, and Belgrade, but they stayed away from Pale as though it were a toxic waste dump. On October 8, Milošević summoned Karadžić, Krajišnik, and Mladić to Belgrade to sign another ceasefire; as was the case with previous agreements, Milošević signed only as a witness.[15]

MILOŠEVIĆ PREPARES THE BOSNIAN SERBS FOR DAYTON

Karadžić spent much of the next twelve months denying his own marginalization. On October 16, assembly members authorized a top-level, 22-person state delegation, led by Karadžić, to visit Milošević in Belgrade. Deeply concerned that Milošević would abandon their interests in the imminent peace talks in Dayton, assembly delegates authorized the delegation to "ensure a joint appearance in the peace process and talks at the peace conference, assure the continued defense of the RS, and care for expelled people."[16] Regardless of such formal instructions, the delegation's primary function was to pay homage to their new master. Delegation members pleaded with Milošević to advocate a return to the situation on the ground as of October 8, the date of the latest ceasefire. That would mean the return of twelve municipalities that Croat forces and the ARBiH had seized from the VRS in western Bosnia during the previous few weeks. Milošević knew that no other party to the talks was likely to accept such an ambitious demand in full, but he promised to do what he could to regain part of the territory the Serbs had lost in battle.

In this three-and-a-half-hour meeting, Milošević played to perfection his role as primary patron and protector of the Bosnian Serbs. Milošević went to great lengths to persuade the Bosnian Serbs that he understood their interests and would vigorously defend their cause in the talks at Dayton.[17] At the same time, he was openly contemptuous of Karadžić and other delegation members. He addressed them in blunt and threatening terms, leaving the Bosnian Serbs to wonder if they might soon be dismissed from office.

Speaking at an assembly session after they returned to Bosnia, delegation members differed on Milošević's true intentions. Calling the session "constructive, fair, friendly, [and] brotherly," delegate Dragan Milanović described

---

[15] Department of State, *The Road to Dayton*, p. 145.
[16] BSA, 54th Session, October 15–16, 1995, Minutes, BCS 0215–4443.
[17] BSA, 55th Session, October 22–23, 1995, Dragan Milanović, BCS 0215–4624–0215–4626.

Milošević as "well informed on the problems and positions of this assembly on the priorities, goals, and tasks that need to be accepted by the international community." But he also reported that Milošević had scolded his guests for ignoring his advice in better days when they commanded military superiority. "The president set forth his well-known position that we, unfortunately, gave up a factual situation in our favor," Milanović reported. "He criticized us for being obstinate ... and not accepting all the proposals he put forward."

Another delegate, Slobodan Bijelić, reported with dismay that Milošević had openly criticized top Bosnian Serb leaders in their presence. "The man explicitly ... criticized our leadership," stated Bijelić in a more negative assessment of the meeting. "The man says, 'your obstinate leadership.' I do not have a habit of writing things down, but I wrote this one down." Bijelić concluded that Milošević wanted to oust Karadžić and Mladić. "He literally wants the heads of both Radovan and Mladić." Bijelić perceived that Milošević hoped the assembly would dismiss Karadžić on its own. "He wanted us to shake off our leaders, and our turn would come later," Bijelić said.

Trying to salvage some dignity from Milošević's humiliating dressing-down, Bijelić told the assembly that Karadžić had been the nobler man in the room, in that he had responded to the scolding with protestations of loyalty. According to Bjelić, "President Karadžić ... was intellectually superior when he said, we have taken off our shirts and now we will give ourselves; we have given you everything." Karadžić's pleas must have rung hollow with Milošević, who had long since grown weary of his one-time protégé's haughty defiance. As Bijelić had correctly judged, Milošević would have preferred that others oust Karadžić so he would not need to do it himself. But for the time being, Milošević had communicated to the Bosnian Serbs that, with or without Karadžić, he expected them to acquiesce to whatever he was able to secure for them in Dayton.

From that meeting forward, Milošević negotiated for the Bosnian Serbs and forced the resulting concessions upon their leaders, who either complained bitterly to no avail (the assembly delegates) or sullenly acquiesced to the terms (Karadžić and top RS officials). When Milošević arrived in Dayton for the talks, the Americans greeted him with all the pomp due a head of state, while Holbrooke and Milošević collaborated to relegate the Bosnian Serb representatives – Prime Minister of the RS Vladimir Lukić, Vice President Nikola Koljević, and Foreign Minister Aleksa Buha – to the sidelines.[18] Karadžić, who had conspicuously not been invited to the talks, returned from Belgrade

---

[18] BSA, 56th Session, December 17, 1995, Milovanović, BCS 0215–4803. See also Cohen, *Hearts Grown Brutal*, p. 461.

to Pale and pretended to remain in charge of the RS while following the talks from afar. After the negotiations ended in November with the Dayton Agreement (formally, the General Framework Agreement for Peace in Bosnia and Herzegovina), he meekly endorsed the deal that had been negotiated in his absence, just as Milošević had demanded in August.[19]

A CONTESTED RESIGNATION

Although he was sidelined by the end of 1995, Karadžić clung tenaciously to his two offices as president of the RS and of the SDS for many months, much to the chagrin of Western policy-makers who had forced the Dayton Agreement upon the Bosnian belligerents. As U.S. President Bill Clinton ramped up his re-election campaign, he wanted to eliminate the mortifying situation of the world's most wanted man freely exercising power in Bosnia while some 22,000 U.S. troops were stationed there. In mid-July 1996, Clinton again dispatched his reliable envoy, Richard Holbrooke (by then out of office and working as an investment banker) to force Karadžić from office. The U.S. administration hoped that OSCE-run elections in Bosnia scheduled for September 14 would proceed smoothly as a visible indication that the country had largely returned to normal. But while the Dayton Peace Agreement explicitly banned war criminals from standing for public office, myriad news reports, both in Bosnia and abroad, stoked fears that Karadžić and his network of operatives would intimidate voters and skew the electoral results.

Armed with his mandate, Holbrooke again turned to Milošević for help in bringing Karadžić to heel. Milošević was more than willing to assist, although he sought to leave Holbrooke with public responsibility for the ouster. While meeting with Milošević in Belgrade, Holbrooke phoned Karadžić in Pale and urged him to withdraw unconditionally from office and from public life. At first, Karadžić balked and insisted that Holbrooke guarantee him immunity from arrest and trial. But Holbrooke refused. To break the impasse, Milošević dispatched to Pale his trusted emissary Jovića Stanišić, head of the police (MUP) of the Republic of Serbia, to pressure Karadžić to step down. After several hours of negotiations and phone calls, Karadžić agreed.

On July 18, 1996, Karadžić resigned as president of both the Republika Srpska and the SDS by signing a single-page, three-point declaration. Other signers included Biljana Plavšić, the "temporary acting president of Republika

---

[19] "General Framework Agreement for Peace in Bosnia and Herzegovina," initiated in Dayton, Ohio, on November 21, 1995, signed in Paris on December 14, 1995, in Trifunovska, *Former Yugoslavia through Documents*, pp. 440–456.

Srpska;" Momčilo Krajišnik; and Aleksa Buha, "Bosnian Serb Foreign Minister." Milošević and Yugoslav Foreign Minister Milutinović signed as witnesses, as with previous accords.[20] No other signature or name appears on the document; neither Holbrooke nor any other international official signed in any capacity. "On July 19, 1996, Dr. Radovan Karadžić has relinquished the office of president of the Republika Srpska and has relinquished all powers associated therewith," the document stated. Karadžić also pledged in the document to "withdraw immediately and permanently from all political activities" and not to "appear in public or on radio or television or other media or means of communication, or participate in any way in the elections" scheduled for September 14, 1996.

But there was more – much more – to the agreement than just the official document, and that "more" became the subject of much controversy. The day after his first appearance before the ICTY, Karadžić claimed on August 1, 2008, that he had resigned in exchange for a pledge from the Americans to permit the SDS to participate in the September 1996 elections in Bosnia. "In the name of the USA," Karadžić told the judges, "Holbrooke promised that the SDS would not be prohibited from taking part in the elections and that no more of our officials would be removed from the electoral lists."[21] Furthermore, he claimed, "Mr. Holbrooke undertook on behalf of the USA that I would not be tried before this Tribunal and that I should understand that for a while there would be very sharp rhetoric against me so that my followers would not hamper the implementation of the Dayton agreement." In his submission, Karadžić contended that Holbrooke claimed to have acted under authority of the UN Security Council in promising him full immunity from the Tribunal's prosecution. Therefore, argued Karadžić, the ICTY was violating international law by detaining him. He demanded that he be allowed to leave The Hague a free man.

The judges rejected these claims. Regardless of what he may have promised Karadžić, Holbrooke lacked authority to commit the ICTY to any immunity deal. But the judges' ruling did not quell the controversy. Karadžić had a long history of magnifying the import of promises made to him while ignoring provisions he found inconvenient. Majtaž Klemenčič, a scholar at the University of Durham in England who has studied the diplomacy to end the war, cited U.S. State Department officials in concluding that Holbrooke had

---

[20] CNN, www.cnn.com/WORLD/9607/19/Karadžić.resigns/resign.html, viewed October 31, 2011.

[21] Karadžić, "Irregularities Linked to my Arrival before the Tribunal" (*Neregularnosti u vezi sa mojim dolaskom pred Tribunal*), Submission to the Pre-Trial Chamber, ICTY, PRK, August 1, 2008.

promised only that Karadžić would not be *arrested*, rather than that he would not be *prosecuted* as Karadžić claimed.[22] Charles Ingrao, Professor of History at Purdue University and co-editor of a collection of scholarly essays on controversies related to the Yugoslav wars, found the accounts of Klemenčič's State Department informants to be credible.[23] He pointed out that Holbrooke knew that Clinton had already ruled out the use of IFOR troops to capture war criminals, so Holbrooke had good reason to believe that Karadžić would thenceforth remain at large. That belief could well have led Holbrooke to conclude that a promise of immunity from arrest would never be tested.

Without holding high office, Karadžić could devote more time to his intellectual and literary ambitions. By the time he signed the agreement, he appears to have made arrangements to secure a lifetime livelihood for himself and his family, and he found additional ways to achieve financial security after he left office. By resigning and pledging on July 19, 1996, to remove himself from public life, he established the basis for his claim to be a martyr for the Serb people, sacrificing himself so that the people he served could continue to pursue their Serb utopian ideal.

His final year as president of the SDS and the RS had been a stormy one. He fought a prolonged, uphill, and ultimately futile battle to retain power that did nothing to advance the interests of the Bosnian Serbs who had chosen him. But in the end, the Bosnian Serb nationalists emerged from the contention having achieved their most important goal, the creation of a Serb polity inhabited almost exclusively by Serbs. Holbrooke and his fellow American and Western diplomats had erred in thinking that by driving Karadžić from power, they had removed the source of the grand ambitions and aggressive nationalism that had led Bosnian Serbs to commit mass atrocities. Although Karadžić ceased to hold power, those who succeeded him persisted in following many of his policies for years to come, a tribute to his effectiveness at molding a durable social movement for a Bosnian Serb utopia.

---

[22] Majtaž Klemenčič, "The International Community and the FRY/Belligerents, 1989–1997," in Charles Ingrao and Thomas A. Emmert, eds., *Confronting the Yugoslav Controversies: A Scholars' Initiative*, 2nd ed. (Washington DC: United States Institute of Peace Press and West Lafayette, IN: Purdue University Press, 2013), pp. 189–190.

[23] *New York Times*, March 21, 2009, www.nytimes.com/2009/03/22/world/europe/22hague.html.

16

Resourceful Fugitive

With his indictment by the ICTY on July 24, 1995, Karadžić became an accused international criminal and Europe's most wanted man. But he regarded the indictment with contempt. He refused to turn himself in and took extraordinary measures to avoid capture over the next thirteen years. He audaciously and creatively masterminded his evasion of the law and lived a surprisingly full if unorthodox life on the lam. He owed his success in part to the considerable popularity and influence he retained among Bosnian Serb nationalists, but his ability to adapt and transform his entire persona proved to be his greatest asset. As in his political career, however, the audacity and arrogance that contributed to his success ultimately led to his downfall. Unable to repress his craving for public acclaim, he took inordinate risks as he again entered public life, this time under an alias. This chapter tells of his life, passions, evasions, and deceptions in those years.

FROM OPEN DEFIANCE TO MONASTIC EVASION

The Dayton Peace Agreement not only ended the war, it also imposed an entirely new and untested political structure on the country.[1] A Peace Implementation Council, made up of representatives of 55 countries and headed by a Steering Board, became the supreme decision-making body for the civilian administration. The council supervised the Office of the High Representative (OHR), an appointed senior European diplomat or politician with powers nearly as great as most heads of state. The Dayton agreement provided for an international peacekeeping force led by NATO. That force, consisting at first of about

---

[1] Francine Friedman, *Bosnia and Herzegovina: A Polity on the Brink* (New York: Routledge, 2004), pp. 60–77; David Chandler, *Bosnia: Faking Democracy After Dayton*, 2nd ed. (London: Pluto Press, 2000), pp. 43–51.

65,000 troops, including 22,000 Americans, was called the Implementation Force (IFOR) from December 1995 to December 1996, Stabilization Force (SFOR) until December 2004, and EUFOR (European Union Force, also known as Althea), since then. Over time the force was reduced from 65,000 troops in early 1996 to fewer than 100 in EUFOR. In 1995, many UNPROFOR troops and much equipment were transferred to IFOR, but the new NATO-led force had a broader mandate, more weapons, and many more troops than UNPROFOR. With UNPROFOR's dissolution and the end of fighting, the UN was reduced to a limited role as supervisor of the International Police Task Force and certain advisory functions.

Both the OHR and the peacekeeping force were charged with implementing the Dayton Agreement, but they and their superiors have often differed on what that means. Contention has surrounded the role of both in locating, arresting and prosecuting persons indicted for war crimes (PIFWCs in acronym-laden NATO vocabulary). Both the OHR and peacekeepers stepped up their activities in that sphere during their first decade in Bosnia, even though the signatories to the Dayton Agreement (including Serbia, Croatia, and representatives of the three national parties in Bosnia) are assigned primary responsibility under the treaty to turn PIFWCs over to the ICTY.

On July 24, 1995, the day the indictment was filed, Karadžić held powerful positions as president of both the SDS and the RS and had no reason to fear imminent arrest.[2] Nor was he particularly alarmed when IFOR entered Bosnia in December 1995. Most senior NATO officials, fearing that any casualties would incite a public backlash and force an end to the mission, actively discouraged their subordinates and soldiers in other national units from detaining those suspects.[3] After resigning his state and party posts in July 1996, Karadžić felt even more confident that he would not be detained, believing that Holbrooke had guaranteed that he would never be brought before the ICTY. He adhered scrupulously to his pledge not to re-enter public life as a candidate or office-holder, although he continued to influence RS politics from behind the scenes. Karadžić later recounted that he had been cautious in his movements, "not because of the international forces, whom I used to pass quietly and without demonstration, but because of possible adventurers and glory hunters."[4]

To many, Karadžić seemed to flaunt his assumed immunity by moving freely among the peacekeepers, passing through their checkpoints and appearing

[2] The international manhunt for Karadžić is described in: Nick Hawton, *The Quest for Radovan Karadžić* (London: Hutchinson, 2009).

[3] Klemenčič, "The International Community," in Ingrao and Emmert, eds., *Confronting the Yugoslav Controversies*, pp. 188–190.

[4] Karadžić, "Irregularities Linked to my Arrival before the Tribunal," July 31, 2008, ICTY, PRK, http://www.icty.org/x/cases/karadzic/custom1/en/080822.pdf, viewed May 25, 2014.

unannounced in areas under their control. Charles Ingrao, Professor of History at Purdue University and a frequent visitor to Bosnia at that time, once observed Karadžić sitting in a vehicle parked outside the International Police Task Force station in Pale. When he reported the sighting to United Nations police in their headquarters, they expressed little surprise and no interest in making an arrest. Karadžić drove daily from his nearby family home to Pale and back, the UN police told him. "Our guys are afraid we're going to run into Karadžić," Ingrao quoted one official as saying.[5] Constrained by caution and indifference, the peacekeepers arrested none of the seventy or so indictees known to be in the country during the first eighteen months of their mission.

On July 10, 1997, NATO's indifference ended. Acting as part of SFOR (Stabilization Force, the NATO-led force that succeeded IFOR in December 1996), British troops conducted a raid to capture two ICTY indictees in the northwestern Bosnian city of Prijedor. The raiding party seized one suspect and killed another, while a British soldier was wounded in an exchange of fire during the seizure.[6] Coming just one day after a summit of NATO heads of state, the raid signaled the peacekeepers' more robust policy toward indictees, although NATO commanders insisted publicly that nothing had changed. Behind the shift lay a host of political developments, including the election of the more aggressive Tony Blair as Prime Minister of Britain, Clinton's selection of Madeleine Albright as U.S. Secretary of State, the support of High Representative Carl Bildt (a former Prime Minister of Sweden) for more arrests, and the ICTY decision to issue sealed indictments, so as to avoid alerting the indictees lest they flee before they could be arrested.[7]

Bildt was particularly outspoken in urging IFOR to arrest indictees. He and some other officials were angered by Karadžić's meddling in RS politics, particularly his incessant efforts to undermine Biljana Plavšić, who had been elected president of the RS in an internationally supervised election in September 1996. At a meeting of NATO leaders, Bildt pointed to a map of Pale on the wall and described Karadžić's recent movements in painstaking detail. With so many prominent international officials urging more arrests, some national units of peacekeeping troops became more aggressive and arrested indictees from time to time after the 1997 British raid in Prijedor.

5 Anthony Lewis, "Winking at Karadžić," *New York Times*, October 28, 1996, www.nytimes.com/1996/10/28/opinion/winking-at-karadzic.html, viewed November 30, 2011.

6 *New York Times*, July 11, 1997, www.nytimes.com/1997/07/11/world/nato-troops-kill-a-serbian-suspect-in-war-atrocities.html, viewed November 29, 2011.

7 Richard M. Swain, *Neither War nor Not War; Army Command in Europe during the Time of Peace Operations: Tasks Confronting USAREUR Commands, 1994–2000* (Carlisle, PA: Strategic Studies Institute, 2003), p. 127.

Karadžić was soon forced to take notice of SFOR's more aggressive interpretation of its mission. He had long since decided that remaining free and avoiding capture was his sacred duty to God and the Serb people. "When a man's conscience is clear, when he knows that he worked for the interests of his nation and according to God's commands, he has no complaints," he told an interviewer in 1995.[8] Luka Karadžić summarized his brother's attitude: "My brother made a strategic decision never to surrender to The Hague Tribunal," he said. "If he surrendered, he would betray his people and God, who have protected him from enemies for so long."[9] But Luka's older brother refused to curtail his activities, even those that exposed him to detection and capture. Throughout his life as a fugitive, he seemed to find exhilaration in taunting his adversaries with subtle clues and fleeting appearances in unlikely locales.

With NATO's heightened determination to arrest indictees, Pale was no longer a secure location for Karadžić. Although he probably slipped in and out of the town on numerous occasions, by the end of 1997 he was shuttling among various Serbian Orthodox monasteries and churches near Bosnia's borders with Serbia and Montenegro. In the friendly confines of Serbian Orthodox religious institutions that recalled his youth in Montenegro, Karadžić found protectors and new friends. Most Serbian Orthodox monasteries in the former Yugoslavia are situated in remote locations, usually in hills or mountains, and the monks and priests who tend them are typically Serb nationalists as part of their religious devotion. Most Serbs living near the monasteries and churches regarded Karadžić as a national hero and felt honored to have him among them, so they remained distinctly unhelpful when approached by SFOR patrols or inquiring journalists. Karadžić rightly calculated that any raid on a religious institution would entail unacceptable risks to lives on both sides and create a potential public relations disaster for the peacekeepers.

LIFE ON THE LAM

His friends romanticized Karadžić as a folk hero in flight who drew on his youth in the shadow of legendary Mount Durmitor. His lifelong friend, the poetically inclined Nogo, wrote, "It's enough to hear some rumors about him, that he feels well, namely that he is devoting those Durmitor energies to living like a bandit, and that he is still working."[10] Karadžić had cut back on meetings with friends and given up some other risky practices, but he was not a

---

[8] Milan Stevanović, "Intervju," *Srpska Anarhistička Mreža*, February 14, 1996.

[9] Antony Barnet, "Most wanted: doctor death," *The Observer*, June 25, 2005, www.guardian. co.uk/world/2005/jun/26/warcrimes.focus, viewed October 20, 2011.

[10] Rajko Petrov Nogo, "Staso je kroz krvavu istoriju," in Bulatović, *Radovan*, p. 144.

solitary figure moving furtively among hiding places. In 2001–2002 he wrote
a series of letters from exile to his wife Ljiljana in which he revealed much
about his life as a fugitive, although without disclosing his exact whereabouts.
Karadžić assigned a sequential number to each letter by placing a specific
number of X's at the bottom, much as a bureaucrat would catalogue official
documents. Soldiers from SFOR seized the letters in a raid on the Karadžić
family home in Pale in 2004, and their contents were subsequently published
by a Montenegrin newspaper for all to see.[11] (After a time, SFOR returned the
letters to Ljiljana.)

In each letter, he professed abiding love for Ljiljana and wrote of missing
her desperately. Although he was lonely, he wrote, he suffered few hardships.
He revealed that he lived in comfortable quarters and enjoyed all the con-
veniences of modern urban life. He described working constructively on a
variety of projects, regularly reading each day's newspapers and carefully following political developments in the former Yugoslavia. He spent many hours
at a computer (enough to complain that he needed more disc space on his
hard drive) and kept contact with his family and political associates through
intermediaries.

With time on his hands, Karadžić returned to creative writing. Nogo
reported that Karadžić had completed manuscripts of two novels, a collection of children's poetry, and a comedic play. Karadžić embedded in his new
works a few satirical elements, including cryptic jabs at his pursuers that
he later revealed with pride. He wrote that the play's title, "Sitovacija" in
Serbian, could be read as "small ovation" (*Sit ovacija*) or "This petty CIA" (*sit
ova CI(J)A*). He signed the script of his play "Daba Son," meaning to suggest
the words "Da, baš on" (Yes, it's truly him!). He also gathered materials that
he believed showed his innocence of any wrongdoing during his political
career. He contributed editorial comments and recommendations to a six-
volume collection of his orders, speeches, letters, and interviews assembled
by friends who organized as the "International Committee for the Truth
about Radovan Karadžić." He assembled a trove of newspaper clippings, convinced they would show that the SDA was chiefly responsible for the war and
its mass atrocities.[12]

In his letters, Karadžić told Ljiljana that he controlled the finances of the
clandestine network that supported him in hiding. The Institute of St. John
(*Institut Sveti Jovan*) in Pale was the center of his elaborate support network.
The institute was under the patronage of the Serbian Orthodox Church and

---

[11] *Publika*, March 22–31, 2004, on page 7 of each daily edition.
[12] *Publika*, March 26, 2004, p. 7, quoting from letter of December 24, 2002, Radovan to Ljiljana
    Karadžić.

its head, Patriarch Pavle, he reported, revealing the church's complicity in hiding and protecting its highly-prized fugitive. The headquarters building of the institute's radio station served as an office and occasional meeting place for Ljiljana Karadžić and a few close associates. More important than its public and legal functions, the institute served as a front to launder money, receive donations, disburse funds to the protective network, and hold properties that might have been seized if owned directly by a Karadžić family member. "So it will all be safe, everything must be directed to the 'St. John' Institute,"[13] Radovan instructed Ljiljana in 2001. He also referred in the letters to donations from abroad, from the SDS, from "certain businessmen," and from "the state," apparently referring to the RS government.

With help from his many handlers and protectors, Karadžić was able to arrange a meeting with Ljiljana sometime in 2000. She characterized their time together as "short and moving." Members of Radovan's network escorted Ljiljana through successive evasive maneuvers to shake the omnipresent SFOR surveillants. "I jumped from car to car, led by some people I did not know," Ljiljana related. "Everything was so fast. Our meeting was brief, two hours altogether, but poignant." After meeting Radovan, Ljiljana returned to the solitude of their residence, a two-story home in Pale known as the "pink house," where she was under constant, undisguised SFOR surveillance from a house across the street.

Radovan directed Ljiljana to keep in touch with a certain Tosić (probably assembly member and Pale businessman Momir Tosić) to be sure that money from the SDS and the RS kept flowing. Tosić soon found that Karadžić's mention of his name was no favor. In June 2004, just three months after publication of Karadžić's letters, High Representative Paddy Ashdown removed Tosić from his positions as SDS board member and Deputy Minister of Foreign Trade and Economic Relations of Bosnia. Firing Tosić was part of a broader effort by the High Representative and SFOR to deprive Karadžić of the support and sustenance of his associates. Ashdown denounced Tosić as "culpable for the SDS's failure to purge the political landscape of conditions conducive to the sustenance of individuals indicted."[14]

In addition to funds from the RS government and the SDS, Karadžić drew upon earnings from family-owned businesses. The Karadžić family had

[13] *Publika*, March 30, 2004, p. 7, quoting from letter of June 4, 2001, Radovan to Ljiljana Karadžić.

[14] Office of the High Representative, "Decision removing Momir Tosić from his positions as Member of the Main Board of the SDS and Deputy Minister of Foreign Trade and Economic Relations of BiH and from other public and party positions he currently holds," /www.ohr.int/decisions/war-crimes-decs/default.asp?content_id=32793, viewed November 5, 2011.

accumulated some financial assets during the war, although their resources were modest compared to other wartime political leaders who amassed large fortunes and stashed them in foreign bank accounts. By the early 2000s, the family owned at least seven residential and commercial buildings in the Pale area.[15] In letters to Ljiljana in 2001 and 2002, Radovan spoke of owning two firms: one operated gas stations, and the other distributed foodstuffs and juices.[16] The world's most wanted fugitive wrote optimistically of those two firms as the foundation of a business empire that would eventually provide lifetime livelihoods for Karadžić family members. Life on the lam whetted his appetite for other ventures, and his letters expressed confidence that he would someday enjoy them as a free man. He proposed to construct a building in Belgrade to consist of ten apartments, divided between business purposes and family occupancy. He even engaged in estate planning to provide a lifetime annuity for each member of his family. "My intention is that we don't remain small in business, that we don't remain fruit and vegetable vendors, but that a strong family company is created, a corporation, which will then be able to provide apartments, employment, scholarships for our youth, and everything needed," he wrote.[17]

DILIGENT SFOR PURSUIT, NIMBLE SERB EVASION

SFOR troops further intensified the hunt for their most prominent fugitive after 2000. Dozens of military intelligence analysts, organized into several cells by country, gathered information and planned operations to catch him.[18] Italian Carabinieri, reputedly proficient at surveillance, shadowed Karadžić family members, associates, and friends. With nearly unlimited powers within Bosnia, SFOR intelligence officers tapped the phones of everyone Karadžić might have occasion to contact. SFOR's surveillance capabilities extended into Belgrade, where intelligence analysts believed him to be hiding. Some officers weighed the possibility of a special operations strike into Belgrade to seize him, but they concluded such an intrusion on Serbian soil carried enormous political and military risks and in any case would never win approval from higher ranks.

SFOR escalated its search from undisguised surveillance to periodic searches of the pink house and other Karadžić family properties. The searches

[15] *Publika*, March 24, 2004, p. 7.
[16] *Publika*, March 29, 2004, p. 7, citing letter of December 18, 2002, Radovan to Ljiljana Karadžić.
[17] Ibid.
[18] Interview with former senior NATO officer, August 18, 2011.

were designed to harass the family as much as to discover information about Radovan Karadžić's habits, whereabouts, and associates. In the first extensive raid of the family home in June 2002, SFOR troops seized the letters he had written to Ljiljana, inventoried every item in the house, and generally made life difficult for the residents. At 4:00 a.m. on January 9, 2004, SFOR troops from several countries raided the various Karadžić family properties in Pale. SFOR troops surrounded the family residence and maintained their encirclement for the rest of the night. "They were Slovenes, 30 of them, with six vehicles," Ljiljana recalled. "They entered the house the next day, January 10, about 40 of them, and remained inside until afternoon. The Italian Carabinieri were respectful, the Americans were exceptionally rude. The translators were Bosniaks." The operation was thorough. As Ljiljana sat passively in the living room, the search team rifled through family possessions and seized every piece of paper they could find, including a recipe for pastries, the guest list from their wedding, and wartime photos of Radovan with associates. "They took laptops, computers, mobile phones, and all the photos from the apartments of my daughter and son, including those of my grandchildren," Ljiljana bitterly told a reporter. After SFOR searched their home for a seventh time in 2008, Ljiljana lost her nerve and, for the first time, pleaded publicly with Radovan to give himself up.

Although most of these raids produced no casualties, one British raid on a suspected Karadžić hideout on April 1, 2004, ended in serious injuries. British troops surrounded the home church and residence of Karadžić's parish priest, Jeremija Starovlah, apparently hoping to find their quarry there. The priest had drawn the attention of NATO forces by declaring a week earlier that every Serb cleric had a duty to help Karadžić evade arrest.[19] Aware of the unfavorable response that would inevitably follow an assault on a Serbian Orthodox house of worship, the SFOR raiding party targeted the priest's residential quarters rather than the church itself. Attacking at 1:00 a.m., they used small explosive charges to blow open the doors to the residence. The priest and his son, alerted by a phone call just minutes before the assault, were up and moving about when the attack began. The troops found not Karadžić but the 52-year-old priest, his wife, and their son. The priest and his son sustained multiple fractures and head wounds from the explosions that blew out the residence's doors. They were evacuated by NATO helicopter to a hospital in Tuzla for emergency treatment and later were moved to the Military Medical Academy in Belgrade for further recovery and

---

[19] *Orthodox News*, April 1, 2004, groups.yahoo.com/group/OrthodoxNews/message/599, viewed December 7, 2011.

rehabilitation.[20] The raid generated bitterness and anger among Serbs in the Pale area. Several hundred of them demonstrated in protest in the days after the unsuccessful raid.

Even the invigorated and expanded SFOR quest was often frustrated by Karadžić's protective network. Raiding parties learned that Karadžić's protectors took heed every time an informant told them that box lunches were stacked in the SFOR mess hall, signaling an imminent raid. Intelligence officers observed that local cell phone traffic spiked whenever box lunches appeared as Karadžić's associates flashed word of impending danger. SFOR special units raided several facilities in Bosnia, mainly along the border with Serbia and Montenegro, but failed to find him, often learning that he had just departed. They succeeded to some degree in shrinking his support network and weakening his ties with his family through repeated harassment searches, but their quarry continued to elude them. By late 2004, they had come to believe that he had left the area entirely.

ENTERING THE OCCULT

As SFOR eventually discerned, sometime in early 2003 Karadžić had shifted the locus of his life from the churches and monasteries of eastern Bosnia to Belgrade,[21] a large, sprawling city with a population of over one million. According to his own account, he made the move after growing weary of elaborate ruses, close calls, shifting shelters, and the sheer loneliness of life on the run. "I long stayed away from cities, from family and friends," he stated in his first jailhouse interview in 2009.[22]

When Karadžić was arrested by Serbian police in 2008, many observers were shocked to learn that he had immersed himself in an alternative lifestyle deep in the Belgrade counterculture of medicinal herbs and occult healing. After several years of outsmarting his enemies and evading capture, his restless intellect and fecund imagination turned to activities rooted in the intellectual meanderings of his pre-political life. The occult community in Belgrade offered a venue for Europe's most wanted fugitive to resume his quest of

---

[20] *Serbian Orthodox Church (Srpska Pravoslavna Crkva)* (website), July 20, 2004, www.spc.rs/old/ Vesti-2004/07/20–7-04-e.html, viewed December 7, 2011.

[21] His move to Belgrade was confirmed by Goran Petrović, former head of the Serbian State Security Service, in an interview shortly after Karadžić's arrest. *Blic online,* July 26, 2008, www.blic.rs/Vesti/Tema-Dana/50688/U-Srbiju-je-dosao-iz-Bosne-pocetkom-2003-godine-, viewed November 30, 2011.

[22] *Večernje novosti,* December 27, 2009, www.novosti.rs/vesti/naslovna/politika/aktuelno.289. html:260918-Ne-bi-bilo-rata-da-Alija-nije-mutio, viewed November 30, 2011.

ILLUSTRATION 16.1. Karadžić as Dragan David Dabić, Belgrade, undated photograph. Corbis Images.

two decades earlier to integrate folk poetry and group psychology. His life in Belgrade became a masterly deception, crafted to satisfy his intellectual ambitions, to achieve renewed status as a recognized public figure, and to taunt his pursuers with subtle clues. Radovan Karadžić, architect of genocide, became "Dragan Dabić," guru and master bioenergy healer.

At his core, "Dabić" was yet another iteration of the infinitely mutable Radovan Karadžić. In a studied act that required vivid imaginings and careful planning, Karadžić transformed himself into Dabić by adopting a radically changed appearance, a different body shape, and a strikingly unconventional wardrobe. He cultivated a dense, flowing white beard that outdid even the shaggy growths that adorned the chins of many Orthodox priests. He grew his hair long and tied it in a knot at the top of his head, veiling his head and face in billowing waves of white hair. He further obscured his eyes with large glasses that mellowed his intense gaze. By fasting two days a week and observing a strict diet on other days, he lost considerable heft and girth. He jettisoned his Bosnian accent in favor of speech patterns common in Belgrade, a city he knew well from the time he lived there in the 1980s. With sunken cheeks and slender frame, he became a sepulchral shadow of the bulky and imposing Karadžić of earlier years.

Karadžić attributed the success of his disguise to carefully cultivated inconspicuous behavior. "I was an ideal citizen," he later told an interviewer from his prison cell. "I never crossed the street on a red light and avoided events about which someone had to testify, and I was of interest to no one."[23] His closest associates remembered Dabić as extravagantly courteous, but they also

---

[23] *Večernje novosti*, December 27, 2009.

remembered him for his distinctive iconoclastic attire. Although they never saw him in the business suits and ties earlier favored by Karadžić, they recalled that he was never without a hat and gloves – white gloves in winter, black in summer. Some suggested that his riveting appearance distracted those he met from suspecting that Dabić might be a wanted man, even when a few of them began to doubt the authenticity of his medical credentials. They saw Dabić as physically an anti-Karadžić. He adopted habits designed to draw attention to himself as an eccentric savant, obscuring Karadžić's tell-tale physical features and replacing his coarse, power-driven persona with the genteel courtesy of an offbeat spiritual healer.

At the time of his arrest, Serbian police officials gave conflicting accounts of how Karadžić acquired the name and identity documents of Dragan Dabić. According to one account, the Dragan Dabić they arrested had assumed the identity of a Serb civilian killed in Sarajevo in 1993. Another described the authentic Dabić as a living Serb peasant who never traveled far from home. Whatever the truth, there was no doubt that Serbian security services had provided fake documents to the man they later arrested. Karadžić suggested he had chosen the name himself for its association with the god "Dabog," or "hromi Dab," of pre-Christian Slavic mythology.[24] The name referred in old Slavic tongues to a number of different wild, demonic characters, including a lame shepherd of wolves and an ugly underworld ruler who traveled in disguise among men. With this convoluted explanation, Karadžić again revealed his life-long obsession with outsmarting others with clever linguistic nuances. The Dabić name was simultaneously a deeply embedded clue that his pursuers never detected and a taunt that he and a few friends could mirthfully share.

Although he had been comfortably ensconced in Belgrade earlier in the decade, Dabić did not enter the world of the occult until 2005 (according to a *New York Times* report) or 2006 (according to the Belgrade newspaper *Blic*).[25] He thus had several years to cultivate his disguise, hone his new identity, and develop adequate responses to anyone questioning his authenticity.

In 2006 he knocked on the door of Mina Minić, a practitioner and teacher of the art of "radiesthesia" in Belgrade.[26] Radiesthesia (for those who, like the

---

[24] Ibid.

[25] *New York Times Magazine*, July 22, 2009, www.nytimes.com/2009/07/26/magazine/26karadzic-t.html, viewed November 24, 2011; *Blic online*, english.blic.rs/In-Focus/2585/I-introduced-Radovan-in-the-world-of-bio-energy, viewed November 30, 2011.

[26] *Index.hr*, July 25, 2008, www.index.hr/vijesti/clanak/Karadžića-u-nadrilijecnistvo-uveo-radiestezist-Minić-koji-je-sumnjao-da-je-americki-spijun/396187.aspx, viewed November 8, 2011.

author, did not know) is the human sensitivity to the energy fields emitted by other humans, animals, plants, and objects great and small.[27] A practicing radiesthesiologist uses a pendulum, called a *visak* in South Slavic languages, to divine answers to questions and diagnose various ailments. Minić speculated that Dabić sought him out after consulting the global register of radiesthesiologists. Minić took pity on the sorry-looking soul who landed on his doorstep. Viewing him as a "tired man," Minić took Dabić under his wing, invited him to hang out in his office, and let him sleep there for days at a time.

Dabić, in the role of hapless supplicant, delved deeply into the pseudo-science and discovered the healing power of "special neutralizers" under Minić's tutelage. Minić acknowledged that Dabić, whom he dubbed "David," was an extremely knowledgeable and hardworking student. After completing Minić's rigorous educational and mentoring program, which lasted all of five days, Dabić received a diploma. The wartime leader of the Bosnian Serbs became certified to heal the sick by interpreting the barely perceptible movements of a rock dangling from a string.

A NEW PUBLIC LIFE

Heal Dabić did, and much more. He threw himself into his new vocation with enthusiasm. Having studied and practiced psychiatry for years, Dabić naturally drew on traditional psychotherapy techniques, but he embellished them with the trappings of his new trade. His ambition drove him to claim expertise in a wide range of practices and subfields, and he advertised these claims on websites and in person. His business card gave his name as "D.D. Dabić" and described his field as "Human Quantum Energy," in English. The front of the card listed two mobile phone numbers, a web page, and a slew of e-mail addresses. On the reverse side, Dabić advertised in Serbian that he offered some fourteen different "Programs" including "Psycho and quantum-energetic support in health and in illness, . . . sexual disorders, fertility disorders, renewal of vitality, . . . depression, fears, tension, neurosis, psychosis, autism, epilepsy," and "harmonization of people's vital energy, energetic harmonization of the aura."[28]

He deceived with aplomb. Drawing on his ample prior experiences in inventing and distorting history, he crafted a plausible but unverifiable personal background. Exploiting his year-long U.S. visit in the 1970s, Dabić

[27] "La Radiesthésie," www.systemedecroyances.net/la_radiesthesie.pdf, viewed January 31, 2014.
[28] Robert T. Carroll, *The Skeptic's Dictionary*, updated December 9, 2010, www.skepdic.com/draganDabi?card.html, viewed November 30, 2011.

explained that he had lived in the United States for ten years. He boasted of having obtained a U.S. medical degree. He claimed he had married in the United States but that the short-lived marriage had ended badly. If asked for the physical certificate attesting to his American medical degree, Dabić explained that his vindictive ex-wife kept it and refused to give it to him.[29] Surprisingly, none of his associates appears to have asked Dabić to verify his Serbian license to practice medicine. Like his fictitious American medical diploma, it did not exist.[30]

Dabić gradually took up activities that fulfilled his urge to become again an esteemed public figure but also increased his risk of being unmasked. He wrote five articles for the journal *Healthy Life* (Zdrav život) and joined other contributors in praising health foods, clean living, and spiritual purification. He embraced *tihovanje* ("entering into silence"), the Serbian Orthodox counterpart to meditation, as a path to inner peace. In praising *tihovanje*, he revived the impulses that drove his quest in the 1980s to synthesize psychology and folk poetics. He extolled the possibilities of synthesizing faith, medicine, and culture. "Prayerful meditation establishes equilibrium of inner life by redirecting attention from the sensual to the extrasensual," he proclaimed in an article.[31] "Meditation, and our analogous 'tihovanje,' represent very high spirituality and religiosity." In a cautious, cryptic allusion to Serb nationalism, he wrote that the inner self could develop significantly only in the context of one's own culture – by implication, Serb culture. "The frame of reference and the entire system of beliefs, opinions, and values rest on a cultural foundation, and with the instruments of a distant culture we can complete only a 'beginning level,' while in our own culture we have no limitation on progress," he wrote.

By 2008, Dabić was advancing rapidly in his new career as a spiritual healer and public advocate for radiesthesia, meditation, Oriental herbs, and energy-based healing. No longer content merely to hide in plain sight, Europe's most wanted man transformed himself with verve and finesse into a counterculture personality with a successful alternative medical practice and a growing chorus of admirers. He addressed alternative medicine meetings in several Serbian towns outside of Belgrade, speaking at times to hundreds of listeners.

[29] B92, July 22, 2008, www.b92.net/info/vesti/index.php?yyyy=2008&mm=07&dd=22&nav_id=309674&nav_category=11; *Blic online*, July 23, 2008, www.blic.rs/Vesti/Tema-Dana/50303/Radovan-zaljubljeni-guru.

[30] B92, July 22, 2008, www.b92.net/info/vesti/index.php?yyyy=2008&mm=07&dd=22&nav_id=309674&nav_category=11, viewed November 30, 2011.

[31] draganDabić.blogger.ba/arhiva/2008/07/23/1691765, viewed November 30, 2011.

His talk on healthy living in Kikinda, Serbia, on January 28, 2008, was covered by a local television station.[32] His colleagues at the time later reported that he kept several cell phones which rang incessantly with requests for appointments and talks.

At times, friends or colleagues inadvertently reminded Dabić of his true identity as Karadžić. Dabić employed a fellow biohealer named Zoran Pavlović to design a website that publicized his healing prowess. Pavlović, it turned out, admired the Netherlands and particularly loved the North Sea resort community of Scheveningen in The Hague. A fashionable beach resort town on the North Sea, Scheveningen is also home to the prison that held accused war criminals during their trials at the nearby ICTY. Pavlović once told Dabić his impressions of the place. "I told him I was once in Holland and that I really liked that country," Pavlović told a journalist after Dabić's arrest. "And then I told him, 'David, Scheveningen is one great place – you must visit it. It's full of hotels, beaches, truly one of the great places on earth'." Dabić reacted with indifference, Pavlović related. "He just shrugged his shoulders and said, "Yeah, OK, sure, whatever.'"[33]

After successfully road-testing his disguise, Dabić embarked fearlessly on a social life. He found a girlfriend. Mileva (known by the nickname "Mima") Cicak, a Serbian woman in her early fifties later described as a "mysterious dark-haired beauty," appeared in photos looking more like a twin of Karadžić's wife Ljiljana than a princess of the occult.[34] She and Dabić made no effort to hide their torrid affair from others in the occult community. The two of them regularly appeared in public holding hands and apparently enjoying the same kind of intimacy and friendship that Radovan had once enjoyed with Ljiljana. (Hague prosecutors, who had long feared that their quarry would turn out to be a diminished or gravely ill man unable to stand trial, were relieved to learn of this on his arrest. "At least we knew that something worked well," said one.) In the evenings he often repaired to a bar called the Madhouse, a tiny, one-room dive decorated with the paraphernalia of Serb nationalism. Dabić drank slivovitz, listened to the screeches of traditional gusle music, and occasionally played the instrument himself, to the delight of the other revelers. He sat at a table directly beneath photos of himself and Mladić, a silent taunt to those seeking to identify and arrest him.

---

[32] *Blic online*, July 23, 2008. www.blic.rs/Vesti/Tema-Dana/50303/Radovan-zaljubljeni-guru, viewed November 30, 2011.

[33] *B92*, July 22, 2008,

[34] *Blic.online*, July 25, 2008, www.blic.rs/Vesti/Tema-Dana/50542/Uveo-sam-Radovana-u-svet-bioenergije, viewed December 7, 2011.

VANISHING GURU: DETECTION AND ARREST

In 2008, political changes in Serbia brought to power those who were prepared to arrest Karadžić to win the favor of Western powers. Until then,
Serbian security organs had looked for Karadžić with all the commitment of
O.J. Simpson pursuing the real killer. But after Serbia's ultranationalist Prime
Minister Vojislav Koštunica suffered electoral defeat on May 11, 2008, he was
succeeded by Mirko Cvetković, a moderate who favored Serbia's entry into
the European Union. To be considered for EU membership, Serbia needed
to demonstrate actual cooperation with the ICTY in hunting down and arresting the remaining fugitives. To that end, Cvetković and his coalition partners
named Saša Vukadinović as the new head of the Security Information Agency
(*Bezbednosno-informativna agencija*, BIA), the unit tasked with finding war
criminals. As Vukadinović assumed his new office on July 18, 2008, the hunt
was on in earnest.[35]

In the end, Karadžić's voice did him in. Much as he became an anti-
Karadžić in appearance, attire, dialect, and persona, Dabić could do little to
alter the resonant tones of Karadžić's distinctive voice. In early summer 2008,
an anonymous tipster called the Belgrade police claiming that the counterculture guru Dragan David Dabić sounded just like Radovan Karadžić. It is
possible that the police had already received many such tips, but this time,
with the winds of political change stirring in Serbia, BIA officers located Dabić
and placed him under round-the-clock surveillance. They watched him ride
a city bus from his home to his office and back. Although they saw no sign of
a security detail or indicators of possible violent resistance to an arrest, the
officers remained wary. Dabić lived in a neighborhood known for supporting
national extremists, and they wished to avoid bloodshed when they eventually
apprehended him.

At 9:30 p.m. on Friday, July 18 – the same day that the new BIA director
took office – police arrested Karadžić as he was traveling on bus route no. 73
between his clinic in Batajnica and his home in New Belgrade.[36] Dragan
David Dabić's bogus identity and biography vanished instantly. Karadžić
dropped any pretense of being the occultist Dabić and responded to the officers' first question by affirming that he was indeed Radovan Karadžić. The
officers bundled him off to the detention unit in the building of the Serbian

---

[35] B-92, July 19, 2008, www.b92.net/eng/news/politics-article.php?yyyy=2008&mm=07&dd=
      18&nav_id=52025, viewed November 25, 2011.
[36] *Blic.online*, July 23, 2008, www.blic.rs/Vesti/Tema-Dana/50303/Radovan-zaljubljeni-guru,
      viewed December 7, 2011.

Special Court for War Crimes. When Karadžić requested a haircut and a shave, police found him a barber. In short order, Dabić's signature beard and sculpted white hair fell to the barbershop floor. Dragan David Dabić disappeared, revealing the persona and appearance of a gaunt, austere-looking Radovan Karadžić.

In reverting to his former self, Karadžić showed he had never deceived himself into believing he was Dabić, despite having deceived others so ably. Dabić's friends and associates met his disappearance from their midst with confusion and grief at losing a valued friend. His girlfriend was left to walk her dog alone while seeking to evade prying cameras and reporters' incessant questions. Those who had befriended and worked with him were stunned to learn that the man they had grown to admire was the notorious fugitive and accused war criminal Radovan Karadžić.

Presumably for security reasons, the police kept Karadžić in custody for three days in strict secrecy.[37] On Monday, July 21, they informed an astonished public of Karadžić's arrest and brought him before a judge at the Special Court for arraignment. Serbian extreme nationalists rallied to his defense within hours. A high Serbian Orthodox Church official, Amfilohije Radovic, visited him in jail.[38]

Once it became public, the arrest touched off a swirl of rumors, allegations, and denials. The arrest revealed a deep split within the Serbian government. Police officials from the Ministry of Internal Affairs and military security authorities denied participation in the arrest, while the Security Information Agency (BIA) boasted that it was responsible.[39] Officials and reporters searched for a genuine Dragan Dabić and found sixty-one men of that name in Serbia alone. Meanwhile, Serbian government authorities gave conflicting, self-serving accounts of how Karadžić had acquired the official documents to pass as one of Serbia's sixty-one Dabićes. False rumors flew for days of dubious Dabić sightings in improbable places. Some reports claimed that Dabić had visited and lived in Croatia, and rumors abounded that he had traveled around Europe on a Croatian passport. Police in Vienna reported that they had questioned and released an elderly faith healer who resembled Dabić in 2007, but the next day they identified the man as Petar Glumac (ironically, the last name means "actor"), a 78-year-old resident of Serbia who had practiced alternative medicine in Vienna. Glumac then accused Dabić of

---

[37] *Balkan Insight*, www.balkaninsight.com/en/main/news/12086/, viewed November 25, 2011.

[38] *B-92*, July 27, 2008, www.b92.net/eng/news/politics-article.php?yyyy=2008&mm=07&dd=27&nav_id=52231, viewed November 25, 2011.

[39] *B-92*, July 28, 2008, www.b92.net/eng/news/politics-article.php?mm=7&dd=28&yyyy=2008, viewed November 25, 2011.

stealing his "face and energy," but he was briefly celebrated in his hometown for being Dabić's visual and occupational double.[40]

Encouraged by the extremist Serbian Radical Party (SRS), demonstrators gathered in front of the court building on the evening of July 21 to protest the arrest.[41] Demonstrations grew nightly, moved to the center of town, and turned violent the next week, culminating in a pro-Karadžić demonstration joined by Belgrade's notoriously unruly soccer fans on Tuesday, July 29, 2008.[42] The aggressive demonstrators at the evening rally assaulted and injured two newsmen (one a Serb, the other from Spain).

Despite the plethora of protest demonstrations in Belgrade after he was arrested, Karadžić did not contest extradition to The Hague. His brother Luka and his attorney both indicated their intent to file an appeal, but none was ever lodged. Karadžić was awakened in his cell in the early morning of July 30, 2008, taken to the airport, flown in a Dutch government plane to a small airport in Rotterdam, and transported to Scheveningen Prison in The Hague. As an added security measure, Dutch police drove two vehicles with tinted glass into the prison as a diversion but flew Karadžić by helicopter direct from the airport in Rotterdam into the prison yard. With this subterfuge, officials kept him out of sight of reporters eager for a glimpse of Europe's most wanted man as he was brought to justice.

Karadžić on the lam proved to be very much the same man who had led the Bosnian Serb nationalists for six years, only more so. In exile he was adaptive, innovative, defiant, and resilient, just as he had been in his previous life. At last he had the time and venue in which to pursue the nebulous synthesis of the folk spirit and group psychology that had long eluded him. But as his deceptions grew bolder and his ego drove him further into the drama of public life, he became more vulnerable to detection and capture by the growing number of his pursuers. In the end, he uncharacteristically surrendered without resistance and meekly followed instructions on the way to joining the prison population at The Hague.

The bizarre tale of his life in hiding has a sequel, of course, ongoing as of this writing in 2014. Acting as his own attorney at his trial before the ICTY, he was given hundreds of hours to relive for public display his six years as leader

---

[40] B-92, July 27, 2008, www.b92.net/eng/news/society-article.php?yyyy=2008&mm=07&dd=27&nav_id=52242, viewed November 25, 2011.

[41] B-92, July 23, 2008, www.b92.net/eng/news/society-article.php?mm=7&dd=23&yyyy=2008, viewed November 25, 2011.

[42] B92, July 30, 2008, www.b92.net/eng/news/society-article.php?mm=7&dd=30&yyyy=2008; B92, July 29, 2008, www.b92.net/eng/news/politics-article.php?yyyy=2008&mm=07&dd=29, viewed November 25, 2011.

of the Bosnian Serbs. As described in Chapter 1, he played out in contentious examinations and cross-examinations his self-serving narrative of bold, justified deeds to fulfill the glorious destiny of the long-suffering Serb people. Despite his extraordinary capacity to remake himself on demand, at trial he behaved as much the same bombastic, defiant public actor that he had been since first entering politics in 1990.

Given Karadžić's vigor and resilience, even this seemingly final chapter in his life may have a sequel in later years. If so, it will likely involve yet another attempt to persuade the world of his rectitude and the rightness of his cause.

Conclusion: Radovan Karadžić and the Bosnian War

"Nothing is easier than denouncing the evildoer, nothing more difficult than understanding him."

– Fyodor Dostoevsky

Radovan Karadžić exercised a profound influence on the world around him in the course of his relatively brief political career. He destroyed his adopted home republic of Bosnia by leading the Bosnian Serbs to war and committing mass atrocities against non-Serbs. The path that led him there is neither simple nor linear; it is instructive, however, and its end is particularly disturbing. Because his influence led to such deplorable consequences, it is important to determine how and why he and his Bosnian Serb followers adopted the values and made the decisions that ended in mass atrocities against non-Serbs. This chapter considers those questions and proposes some answers based on Karadžić's life and deeds.

THE MAN

For forty-five years, Radovan Karadžić lived an unremarkable life. Born in Montenegro in the final days of the Second World War, he experienced hardship and deprivation as he grew up, but he benefited from a dedicated, nurturing mother and a hard-working if more distant father. At age 15 he left home and moved to Sarajevo, the capital of the Republic of Bosnia and Herzegovina. There he earned a medical degree, married and started a family, and became a successful psychiatrist at the university clinic. Although he demonstrated many personal qualities that would later make him a successful political leader, he remained distant from politics (except for a brief address at a student demonstration in 1968) and had no public profile as a dissident or nationalist of any kind. He wrote and published poetry that was unconventional in style and stark in tone but devoid of political content. As the 1980s approached their end, he was pursuing his search for a grand intellectual synthesis by bringing together his knowledge of group psychology and the idiom of folklore.

All that changed in 1990. The collapse of communism opened the doors to democratic political involvement throughout the region, and Karadžić joined thousands of others in exploring various options to become politically engaged. After briefly considering joining a green party, he and a small group of fellow Serb literati in Sarajevo dove deeply into politics by forming the Serb Democratic Party (SDS) under the influence of leading Serb nationalist intellectuals in Belgrade. Quite unexpectedly, senior Belgrade Serbs selected him in summer 1990 to head the party, and Karadžić became the new and charismatic voice of Serb nationalism in Bosnia. His firm embrace of Serb nationalism was at once selfish and altruistic: he sensed that advancing the interests of the Serb people would also bring him personal power, rewards, and acclaim that he had never before enjoyed. With uncanny success, he fused his quest for personal benefit with his new-found political cause.

The complex course of Karadžić's political career cannot be understood without recognizing his unparalleled ability to change and adapt. He could alter his entire persona at will, and he did so several times in response to changing circumstances, mostly to his advantage. At one critical juncture in 1993, however, he failed to recognize that the Bosnian Serb nationalist movement had reached its apogee, and he became a political recluse rather than a successful compromiser.

During his early days in politics, although Karadžić harshly denounced Bosnia's incumbent communists, he expressed no particular antagonism to other nations or ethnicities. But after voters removed the communists (relabeled as social democrats) from power in the elections of November 1990, he became ever more critical of Bosniak and Croat political leaders. By September 1991 he had begun to envision the wholesale disappearance of the Bosniaks at Serb hands. His own descriptions of these imagined events are evidence not of a burning hatred, but rather of a chilling indifference to the fate of Bosniaks. Other peoples would pay the ultimate price and disappear if they offended or obstructed the Serbs, he seemed to say, and that would be the fault of their leaders, for whom he harbored true contempt and hatred.

Behind this troublingly dismissive attitude lay not personal hatred, but a grand strategic vision in which Bosnia's Serbs would realize their utopian nationalist dream of a Serb state. His relentless determination to realize Serb dreams, rather than personal hatred, led Karadžić down the path toward extreme and violent measures to create an exclusively Serb political and demographic space. That strategic vision went through several changes. It first centered on keeping all of Bosnia within a Serb-dominated Yugoslav state, then (after October 15, 1991) on a stand-alone Serb state in Bosnia, and finally (as specified in the six strategic goals on May 12, 1992) on creating a separate, compact, and contiguous Serb polity by force of arms. Karadžić was instrumental in defining those successive strategic visions, although many others also contributed. He proved even more able at designing and implementing tactics to realize the Serb utopian ideal. In late autumn of 1991, he began to control his rage that had become a debilitating liability and became the Bosnian Serb planner-in-chief. He crafted a municipal strategy and prepared tactical measures with which local SDS officials could seize power and remove non-Serbs from Serb-claimed territories.

The Bosnian Serbs and the JNA launched their campaign of conquest and atrocities in April 1992 not with the primary intent of slaughtering every living non-Serb, but rather of establishing the political, territorial, and demographic foundations of a permanent separate Serb state purged of non-Serbs. Neither Karadžić nor most other SDS leaders preferred to achieve that goal with war and mass atrocities; they would have preferred to win approval for establishing that state in negotiations. But although they hoped to succeed by persuasion and agreement, they were prepared to use as much violence as they deemed necessary, at whatever administrative level, to establish their state. Karadžić's most consequential contribution to the mass atrocities against non-Serbs in Bosnia was to determine the required level of violence and implement the tactics necessary to accomplish his goals. The first wave of Serb mass atrocities in 1992 proved achievable largely through municipal-level armed conquests and carefully-orchestrated, locally-led elimination of most non-Serbs from conquered land. In 1995, Karadžić determined that it required a carefully planned military assault and the pursuit and killing of those who fled so that they could never return. In both years, and in a host of smaller episodes in between, the overarching goal remained the same, and the means to achieving the goal were chosen for optimum impact and minimum losses of Serb life.

What was it about Karadžić, then, that led him to sanction or order mass atrocities against non-Serbs? It was not hatred of another ethnicity or nation that drove his behavior, nor can we attribute his penchant for mass violence to his impressive leadership qualities, such as his rhetorical eloquence and his broad repertoire of persuasive techniques. Those qualities, widely shared by many political leaders in various lands and different systems of government, have led leaders to do good no less often than evil. It is rather in his overzealous devotion to a vain utopian ideal. He urgently and recklessly drove himself and others to realize that ideal, while gradually erasing non-Serbs from his concerns, seeing them as inconsequential and expendable. His ability to blend self-interest and Serb interests deepened over time and, along with his disregard for the lives of others, led him to authorize and initiate the mass atrocities that will forever define his legacy.

THE MOVEMENT

Karadžić was first and foremost the leader of a social movement. A deeply convinced populist, he felt compelled to lead the Serb people to their utopian destiny, and he saw the people's will as the justification for his leadership. Even though he never ran for office in a multiparty election, he was so popular among Bosnian Serbs that his chieftaincy of their movement was an unassailable assumption throughout the war. Karadžić built consensus, frequently relied on others to carry out plans, and for the most part motivated rather than commanded his followers to carry out his wishes.

He believed in and practiced democracy. In comparative studies, political scientists have challenged the conventional understanding of democracy as inherently virtuous and positive that is based on the observation that no two democracies have ever gone to war. But while noting that democracy can facilitate mass atrocities, they have not agreed on how that happens. Michael Mann, in his study of the "dark side of democracy," suggests that only an extreme, distorted form of democracy leads to ethnic violence: true democracy and its dark side are fundamentally different, he argues. "Regimes that are actually perpetrating murderous cleansing are never democratic, since that would be a contradiction in terms," he wrote.[1] Jack Snyder, in contrast, argues that populist democracy can spur nationalism and nationalist conflict even where it barely existed before.[2]

In the case of the Bosnian Serbs, we may conclude that representative democracy was central to the Bosnian Serb movement from beginning to end, and that mass atrocities were facilitated directly by representative democratic practices. The Bosnian Serb leaders believed strongly in democracy, as long as its results brought the right Serbs to office, and furthermore they were devoted constitutionalists. They submitted every major decision to the assembly for approval and scrupulously observed constitutional procedures. Although one cannot resolve the argument based on one case alone, the Bosnian Serb case

---

[1] Michael Mann, *The Dark Side of Democracy: Explaining Ethnic Cleansing* (New York: Cambridge University Press, 2005), p. 4.
[2] Jack Snyder, *From Voting to Violence: Democratization and Nationalist Conflict* (New York: Norton, 2000), pp. 32–33.

serves to suggest that democracy can facilitate and accelerate mass atrocities. In this case, democracy helped bring about mass murder and genocide, while those countries claiming to champion democracy did too little to prevent or halt those atrocities.

Karadžić's faith in representative democracy was manifest in several institutions and organizations that made up the pillars of his rule. The SDS political party and the Bosnian Serb Assembly were the most significant of these; Karadžić could not have done what he did without them. The SDS became an instrument of power, while the assembly functioned as a legitimizer of authority and a convenient surrogate for what Karadžić saw as the "Serb people." He also found sustenance in a small coterie of close advisors and collaborators, led by Momčilo Krajišnik and Nikola Koljević. The assembly was the most remarkable of these groups. Its continuous existence from October 1991 to the present deserves admiration, but many of the words spoken in its sessions deserve condemnation. The frequency and regularity of its wartime meetings – 55 sessions in four years – speak to a determination to follow democratic, constitutional procedures, but unfortunately those sessions only emboldened RS leaders and sought to legitimize the mass atrocities they carried out. Since assembly sessions rotated among various towns in the RS, delegates traveled considerable distances over sometimes dangerous terrain to attend. Karadžić showed great fealty to the principle of representative government, and he consistently treated the assembly as the final authority on all key decisions.

Unfortunately, the assembly also became with time an echo chamber for many of Karadžić's most radical views and encouraged him to undertake ever more extreme measures. The assembly reinforced the top leaders' sense of urgency to complete their conquests and atrocities. In the fourteen sessions before the war, the assembly reverberated with pronouncements of the ideology and goals of the Bosnian Serb nationalist movement. The assembly went further at the watershed sixteenth session on May 12, 1992, when Karadžić won the assembly's approval for the six strategic goals he proposed to "separate" Serb institutions, land, and people from everyone else in Bosnia.

By embracing the six goals, the assembly committed the Bosnian Serb nationalists to ridding much of Bosnia of non-Serbs, which could only be achieved through a combination of military conquest and mass atrocities. It mattered little that those 1992 goals did not specify the means to achieve the objective of a compact, contiguous Serb state inhabited by negligible numbers of non-Serbs. The six goals thenceforth served as a mandate for delegates to cite and a mantra to be repeated many times in the ensuing four years. Assembly delegates not only endorsed the violence that Karadžić pursued; on many occasions, they called for more. Not until May 1995 did any delegate speak up to offer an alternative to the complete separation of peoples, and even then Krajišnik harshly rebuked him and insisted that the principle could never be violated.[3]

ENABLERS

Slobodan Milošević and Ratko Mladić assumed major roles in guiding the political behavior of the Bosnian Serb nationalists in the 1990s. Karadžić's relationship with each man was complex, multifaceted, and constantly in flux. Much remains to be discovered about those relationships. But Karadžić could not have accomplished what he did without both men, so it is important to assess the impact that each of them had on Karadžić and on the movement he led.

Milošević stepped into Karadžić's life in the fall of 1990 (or perhaps, indirectly, several months before) as his presumptive sponsor and mentor; Karadžić readily accepted him in those roles. Milošević, a master tactician at fomenting unrest and undermining rivals, schooled his acolyte in the Machiavellian variant of power politics, and expected loyalty in return. He rescued Karadžić from some early blunders, including his ill-advised approval of a written agreement among those wishing to merge the two Krajinas in June 1991. He exploited Karadžić's vulnerability by making him the chief Bosnian Serb recruiter and arms dealer for the JNA in Croatia during summer 1991. Milošević's increasingly high-handed approach rankled Karadžić, who began demanding consideration for the military needs of the Bosnian Serbs. Then, in defining a new course of separation in Bosnia in October 1991, Karadžić stepped out on his own. Their relationship cooled and never again became close. But another four years passed before Milošević took the final step of removing Karadžić from power; even then, he did so in stages, removing him first from a role as chief negotiator before stripping him of other powers and eventually sponsoring his removal from all offices and functions.

During those four years, Milošević played a dual role in Bosnia. Politically, he often expressed sharp disapproval of policies pursued by the Bosnian Serb leaders. Sometimes he prevailed; he succeeded, for example, in preventing the VRS conquests of Bihać in December 1994 and of Goražde in summer 1995. But mostly, his jawboning failed, most spectacularly in his vain attempt to persuade the Bosnian Serbs to accept the Vance-Owen Peace Plan in 1993.

---

[3] BSA, 56th Session, December 17, 1995, Grujo Lalović and Krajišnik, BCS 0215–4790 and 0215–4843.

He half-heartedly cultivated other Bosnian Serbs, most significantly Ratko Mladić and possibly Milorad Dodik, in hopes they would persuade or challenge Karadžić and prove loyal to Belgrade. But at the same time that he sought to dissuade or undermine Bosnian Serb political leaders, he oversaw a more or less constant flow of arms and supplies to the VRS so it could wage war. Not until August 1994 did he interrupt his support for the VRS, and then only partially and temporarily. In the grand scheme of things, he proved more effective at fomenting unrest and emboldening the perpetrators of violence than at reining in Karadžić and his supporters. Milošević emerges from this account as ambitious and manipulative, skilled at motivating his acolytes, but willing to betray them when it suited his interests. Still, the results of this study suggest a considerably different view of Milošević than the "butcher of the Balkans" trope that has been advanced by many of his adversaries and critics (including in this writer's earlier works). To a surprising degree, Milošević preferred persuasion over brute force to influence his fellow Serbs west of the Drina. His refusal to force those Serbs to stand down prolonged the war and doomed thousands of Bosniaks to death in the atrocities carried out by Karadžić and his collaborators. By bolstering the Serb military capabilities west of the Drina while giving his political acolytes relatively free rein, the man often described as a tyrannical mass murderer emerges in these pages as an indecisive, weak-willed leader. Although one should not underestimate the mass killings and destruction wrought by the soldiers he recruited and the arms he gave them, Milošević was less able, less resolute, and by his own choice, less autocratic than portrayed in much literature of the time.

He also was not the die-hard promoter of Great Serbia that he was believed to be during the war. He freely exploited Great Serb sentiment to instigate demonstrations and local regime changes during the anti-bureaucratic revolution, but when facing the real possibility that Serb political units would seek to join Serbia, he stepped in and prohibited them from pursuing a Great Serb course. During wartime, he was a Great Serb backer in coordinating military activities, but he consistently denied requests to combine the RS and RSK or attach them to a single Serb state. This study calls for a more nuanced view of Milošević's Great Serb ambitions, distinguishing between his exploitation of those sentiments and his refusal to allow them to be realized.

Ratko Mladić is another story. He ascended rapidly to high command because of his audacity in advancing the Serb cause and his personal bravery on the battlefield, but it should be remembered that he arrived in Bosnia only in May 1992, far too late to be seen as a founder of the Bosnian Serb nationalist project. Although at times he counseled restraint, his measured appeals were often juxtaposed with rousing calls for more aggressive action. Uncomfortable with the Bosnian Serb civilian nationalists from the beginning, he found their criticism of him particularly offensive. Karadžić turned his most demeaning and acerbic rhetoric on his top general, and by summer 1993 the two had become rivals. Each competed to outdo the other as the most avid promoter of the Bosnian Serb project, even as Mladić professed loyalty and obedience to his commander-in-chief and Karadžić strove to maintain the fiction that he was truly in command.

Eventually, their rivalry served as one factor for both to become mass murderers in the summer of 1995. To read their heated exchanges in the assembly during 1995 is to sense how deeply each craved credit for the mass atrocities committed against tens of thousands of non-Serbs during the war. Those verbal confrontations between Karadžić and Mladić or his subordinate generals are chilling evidence that moral restraint had completely vanished in the course of their competition to be the most avid promulgator of a Bosnian Serb utopia. Far from showing even a hint of regret or critical reflection, each man found only virtue as the prime orchestrator of horrific mass slaughter. Although strategic considerations certainly go far to explain the Srebrenica atrocities, the fierce competition between Karadžić and Mladić must be identified as a leading; cause of the Srebrenica genocide of July 1995.

The many interactions described in the preceding chapters and pages allow us to propose a re-characterization of relations among the leading actors in the Bosnian Serb nationalist drama. Karadžić stands at center stage, attended by a handful of loyal supporting actors, performing before an appreciative audience of eighty-three delegate spectators who applaud too long, cheer too loudly, and goad the actors into ever more audacious deeds. Milošević, aspiring to script, cast, and choreograph the performance, provides suitable props for the performance but intervenes only intermittently when his chosen actors stray far from their assigned roles. Mladić joins the performance and seeks to push Karadžić off central stage while still claiming to respect him as the star performer. In the end, the two of them can agree only on the wisdom of shoving a large number of other actors completely off stage into a deep abyss. As the lights go out and the curtain comes down, the prime actors stand alone, proclaiming their innocence to a global public shocked by the bloodshed and by their monumental indifference to human life.

THE MAN AND HIS DEEDS

Karadžić was the central figure in the drama that played out in Bosnia in the 1990s, but he was surrounded by many like-minded persons who influenced, encouraged, or followed him. His achievements were the product of his personal actions and those of his senior aides and colleagues in the Bosnian Serb leadership. Together, Karadžić and his associates adopted policies and made decisions that led them to order and oversee mass atrocities and genocide.

Karadžić, the undisputed principal actor among the leaders, began his journey with an iron-clad, irrevocable commitment to the cause of Bosnian Serb nationalism. He loved his people too much and cared for the rest of humanity not at all. A man of great ability and immense promise, he turned himself into the architect of the worst atrocities in Europe since the Second World War by unequivocally embracing the twisted values of exclusive nationalism. His life thus stands as a stark reminder to every leader and every citizen, that however much we value our own nation, we must also value those of other nations and humanity as a whole.

Chronology of Events

1940s

June 19, 1945. Radovan Karadžić was born to Vuko and Jovanka Karadžić in Petnjica, Montenegro, Yugoslavia.

November 29, 1945. Federal People's Republic of Yugoslavia was proclaimed as a communist federal state.

1950s

September 27, 1950. Vuko Karadžić, Radovan's father, was released from prison after serving nearly five years.

1950 or 1951. Karadžić family moved to Šavnik, Montenegro, owing to lack of work available to Karadžić's father Vuko.

1956. Karadžić family moved to Nikšić, Montenegro.

1960s

1960. Radovan Karadžić moved to Sarajevo to study medicine at the University of Sarajevo.

1967. In Sarajevo, Karadžić married Ljiljana Zelen, a fellow medical student, with whom he had two children, Sonja (b. 1967) and Aleksandar (known as Saša) (b. 1973).

1968. Karadžić published his first book of poetry, *Ludo Koplje*.

June 4, 1968. Karadžić, at the University of Sarajevo, addressed a student protest against communist bureaucracy and the Vietnam War.

1970s

July 19, 1971. Karadžić received diploma from the Medical School of the University of Sarajevo.

July 1971–March 1977. Karadžić worked in Sarajevo at Adult Education Center Djuro Djaković organizing cultural programs.

February 25, 1974. New constitutions promulgated for federal Yugoslavia and each of its six republics and two autonomous regions, awarding greater powers to those eight units at the expense of the federal government.

1974–1975 academic year. Karadžić, accompanied by his wife and daughter, studied at Columbia University on a U.S. government-funded grant.

1977–1992. With a one-year interruption while living in Belgrade, Karadžić practiced psychiatry in Sarajevo at the Koševo clinic and in private practice.

1980s

Early 1980s. Karadžić worked part-time as counselor and morale coach to the "Sarajevo" soccer team in Sarajevo.

March 1981. Karadžić, Momčilo Krajišnik, and a third man from Karadžić's childhood home of Šavnik in Montenegro began construction of homes in Pale.

1983–1984. Karadžić lived in Belgrade and worked as counselor and morale coach to the "Red Star" soccer team.

November 1984–October 1985. Karadžić was imprisoned while being investigated for fraud in obtaining financing for the construction of homes in Pale.

1990

April. Voters in multiparty democratic elections in Slovenia and Croatia chose leaders favoring greater autonomy within Yugoslavia or independence from it.

June. SDS Serbs in Croatia proclaimed associations of Serb municipalities.

July 12. Delegates at founding assembly in Sarajevo established the Serb Democratic Party (SDS) of Bosnia and elected Karadžić the party's first president.

July 25. Jovan Rasković publicly endorsed cultural autonomy for Serbs in Croatia, in effect rejecting territorial separatism of regional associations of Serb municipalities.

August 17. Yugoslav People's Army (JNA) began distributing weapons to Serb civilians in Knin, Croatia.

November 18. Elections in Bosnia produced wins for the three nationalist parties (SDS, SDA, and HDZ) and defeat of social democratic parties and the Reformists.

December 21. SDS Serbs in Croatia formed the Serb Autonomous Region of Krajina (SAO Krajina).

1991

April 25. Community of Municipalities of Bosnian Krajina was proclaimed in Čelinac, Bosnia; in September 1991 it was renamed the Autonomous Region of Krajina (*Autonomna regija Krajine*, ARK).

June 27. Assemblies of the SAO Krajina in Croatia and the Community of Municipalities of Bosnian Krajina met jointly and approved a cross-boundary association of the two regional units.

July 11. At Milošević's urging, Karadžić turned out a large crowd for a pro-Yugoslav demonstration in Sarajevo.

October 15. Karadžić delivered his "road to hell" speech threatening Bosniaks. HDZ and SDA delegates reconvened and approved a memorandum of sovereignty and platform after assembly president Krajišnik had adjourned the session. SDS began a strategic shift from seeking to remain in Yugoslavia to establishing a separate Serb-dominated state within the boundaries of Bosnia.

October 24. Serb nationalist delegates in the Bosnian Parliament gathered as a Delegates' Club and proclaimed a separate Assembly of the Serb People of Bosnia and Herzegovina, referred to in this book as the Bosnian Serb Assembly (BSA).

November 9–10. SDS sponsored plebiscite asking mainly Serb voters if they wished to remain in Yugoslavia.

December 19. Karadžić distributed secret "Instructions" to local SDS officials to form separate assemblies and Serb crisis staffs in every municipality where Serbs lived.

December 20. The Bosnian Presidency forwarded to the European Community a request for recognition of Bosnia's independence; three Bosniak and two Croat presidency members voted "yes," while two Serbs on presidency voted no and protested the move as unconstitutional.

1992

January 8. Bosnian Presidency members Nikola Koljević and Franjo Boras met with Croatian President Franjo Tudjman and his advisors in Zagreb, Croatia, and agreed on advisability of humane population transfers.

January 9. Bosnian Serb Assembly proclaimed the Republic of the Serb People in Bosnia and Herzegovina, a polity renamed the Republika Srpska (RS) in September 1992.

February 29 and March 1. Referendum held on the independence of Bosnia. Following the instructions of the leaders of their respective ethnonational groups, most Croats and Bosniaks voted yes, while most Serbs boycotted the balloting.

February 29. Karadžić, visiting Banja Luka, quelled movement of fellow SDS members for autonomy and separate status for the Autonomous Region of Krajina in Bosnia.

March 2. Karadžić acquired promises of support from JNA and civilian leaders in Belgrade at a meeting of the expanded presidency of federal Yugoslavia.

March 18. Jose Cutileiro achieved agreement in principle, but no signatures or initials, on a plan to divide Bosnia into three ethnonationally determined units, subsequently known as the "Cutileiro Plan."

April 1. Serb paramilitary forces crossed the Drina from Serbia and carried out mass atrocities against non-Serbs in Bijeljina in northeastern Bosnia while seizing control of the town.

April 1–July 30. JNA, VRS, and Serb paramilitaries committed mass atrocities against non-Serbs in dozens of mixed municipalities in Bosnia.

April 6. European Community recognized Bosnia as an independent state.

April 7. United States recognized independence of Bosnia.

May 2. JNA and Serb forces carried out a major attack on Sarajevo resulting in full encirclement of the city and establishment of the siege that lasted nearly four years, until February 1996.

May 6. Karadžić and Bosnian Croat leader met in Graz, Austria, in the absence of any Bosniak or Bosnian government representatives and concluded the Graz Agreement, which was rejected by the EC for leaving out the third party.

May 12. At Sixteenth Session of the Bosnian Serb Assembly, Karadžić introduced the six strategic goals of the Serb people, and the assembly voted to create the Army of the Republika Srpska (*Vojska Republike Srpske*, VRS) and to appoint General Ratko Mladić as Commander of its General Staff.

May 14. U.S. Ambassador to Yugoslavia William Zimmerman accused Karadžić and Koljević of mass atrocities in a heated exchange just days before the departure of the ambassador, who had been recalled.

June 5. Karadžić and Mladić agreed to turn Sarajevo airport over to UN control. Pursuant to agreement with Bosnian government and international negotiators, JNA forces withdrew from Tito Barracks in Sarajevo.

August 26–27. London Conference, chaired by British Prime Minister John Major, established the International Committee for the Former Yugoslavia (ICFY) to lead negotiations to end the Bosnian war.

September–December 1992. Karadžić led negotiating team of RS in intermittently-held talks with ICFY diplomats.

1993

January 2. Co-chairs of the Steering Committee of the ICFY, former U.S. Secretary of State Cyrus Vance and former British Foreign Secretary Lord Owen, formally and publicly presented their peace proposal, the Vance-Owen Peace Plan (VOPP). Croat representatives accepted immediately; Bosnian government representatives and Karadžić, on behalf of the RS, declined.

March 25. Alija Izetbegović signed the VOPP in New York with deep reservations and on condition that Serbs also accept it.

May 2. Karadžić, under pressure from international leaders including Milošević, signed the VOPP in Athens while noting it required approval of the Bosnian Serb Assembly to become effective.

May 9. Despite urging from Milošević and President Mitsotakis of Greece on May 5–6, Bosnian Serb Assembly effectively rejected the VOPP by calling it merely a basis for further talks.

May 20. After decisive rejection by popular referendum, Bosnian Serb Assembly definitively rejected the VOPP.

August. Ratko Mladić disobeyed Karadžić's order to withdraw VRS troops from Mt. Igman near Sarajevo after Karadžić had promised international negotiators the troops would leave, widening the rift between the two men.

August 11–21. Lord David Owen and Thorwald Stoltenberg (replacement for Cyrus Vance, who had resigned May 1) unveiled the "Union of Three Republics" peace plan more favorable to Bosnian Serb nationalists.

August 27. Karadžić and Krajišnik secured the Bosnian Serb Assembly's approval for the "Union of Three Republics" plan.

August 28. Karadžić, intruding deeply into military affairs, issued 18-point directive to reform and reorganize the VRS, offending Mladić and other senior generals.

September 10–17. Junior reservist VRS officers in Banja Luka led a short-lived, unsuccessful uprising called "September '93."

September 28. Bosnian Parliament rejected "Union of Three Republics" plan.

1994

February 5. VRS shelled Markale marketplace in Sarajevo, killing 68 and wounding 144. This became known as the first Markale massacre.

February 10. NATO issued ultimatum to Bosnian Serbs to withdraw heavy weapons from exclusion zone around Sarajevo.

February 17. Karadžić accepted offer of Russian Deputy Foreign Minister Andrei Kozyrev to withdraw heavy weapons from Sarajevo exclusion zone in exchange for Russian troops joining UNPROFOR and patrolling Serb-inhabited areas.

March 18. Bosnian Croats and Bosniaks signed the Washington Agreement, providing for a ceasefire and agreeing to form the Federation of Bosnia and Herzegovina, a two-party power-sharing arrangement that excluded the Bosnian Serbs.

April 26. Contact Group, consisting of the United States, Russia, France, Britain, and Germany, met for the first time, superseding the ICFY as principal convener of talks to end the war.

August 28. After a referendum of RS voters rejected the Contact Group plan, Karadžić and Bosnian Serb Assembly also definitively rejected it.

December 19–21. Former U.S. President Jimmy Carter, his wife Rosalynn, and their staff visited Pale and Sarajevo and mediated a four-month ceasefire agreement intended to last until May 1, 1995.

1995

March 8. Karadžić issued "Directive 7," which included instructions to "create an unbearable situation with no hope of further survival or life for the inhabitants of Srebrenica and Žepa."

March 31. Mladić issued "Directive 7/1," repeating nearly all of Karadžić's language from Directive Number 7 but leaving out the phrase about making life unbearable for residents of Srebrenica and Žepa.

April 15–16. Acrimony between Karadžić and Mladić erupted at 50th session of Bosnian Serb Assembly in Sanski Most, Bosnia.

May 2. Army of the RSK in Croatia launched rockets into Zagreb city center, killing 6 civilians and wounding 180.

May 22. VRS soldiers seized artillery pieces from UN depot near Sarajevo.

May 25. VRS shell struck downtown Tuzla, killing 72 persons, mostly children and teenagers, in greatest loss of life owing to a single shell in the Bosnian war. NATO launched air strikes on VRS munitions depot and bunkers near Pale.

May 26. VRS soldiers began taking hundreds of UNPROFOR troops hostage, forcing NATO to end air strikes.

June 15. ARBiH began unsuccessful offensive to break the siege of Sarajevo from the outside.

Late June. Karadžić visited Drina Corps headquarters in Vlasenica and ordered Colonel Radislav Krstić to prepare for an attack on Srebrenica within a few days.

July 2. VRS Main Staff ordered the Drina Corps to "separate and reduce in size the Srebrenica and Žepa enclaves with surprise attacks ... to create a condition for the elimination of the enclaves."

July 6. VRS began assault on Srebrenica enclave.

July 11–15. VRS completed capture of Srebrenica and carried out genocide against over 7,000 Bosniaks seeking to flee to Bosnian government-held territory.

July 24. The International Criminal Tribunal for the Former Yugoslavia (ICTY) issued an indictment against Karadžić and Ratko Mladić charging genocide, crimes of war, and crimes against humanity.

August 28. At about 11 a.m., five VRS shells hit the Markale marketplace in Sarajevo, killing 37 and wounding at least 90, an attack known as the second Markale massacre.

August 29. Karadžić reluctantly agreed to subordinate Bosnian Serb negotiators to Milošević, effectively giving Milošević a proxy to negotiate for them.

August 30. Triggered by second Markale massacre, NATO commanders commenced Operation Deliberate Force, an aerial bombing campaign that targeted VRS facilities, particularly command and control centers, anti-missile installations, and munitions sites.

September 8. In Geneva, parties to Bosnian war reached an agreement that ended NATO bombing and recognized the RS as a second entity in Bosnia, along with the Federation of Bosnia and Herzegovina. Fighting on the ground continued, mainly with HVO and ARBiH forces making gains against the beleaguered VRS.

October 12. Sixty-day ceasefire took effect, agreed to by all sides after VRS suffered further losses in western Bosnia and ARBiH drove VRS from Sanski Most in northwestern Bosnia.

November 1. U.S.-led peace conference opened at Wright-Patterson Air Force Base in Dayton, Ohio. As an indicted war criminal, Karadžić was not invited and did not attend.

November 21. Presidents Tudjman of Croatia, Milošević of Serbia, and Izetbegović of Bosnia initialed the General Framework Agreement for Peace in Bosnia and Herzegovina, known as the Dayton Agreement for the American city where it was negotiated.

December 14. Dayton Agreement was signed in Paris.

1996–2010

July 18, 1996. Karadžić resigned as president of both the SDS and the RS and pledged to withdraw from public life, believing he had secured a guarantee from U.S. diplomat Richard Holbrooke that he would never be arrested or brought before the ICTY.

July 10, 1997. SFOR raid in Prijedor signaled a more robust NATO policy of raids and arrests in active pursuit of ICTY indictees who refused to turn themselves in.

1998–2003. With the aid of supporters and guards, Karadžić shuttled among Serbian Orthodox religious institutions and other hiding places in Bosnia, Serbia, and Montenegro.

2000S

2003 or 2004. Karadžić moved to Belgrade, Yugoslavia, grew long hair and an untrimmed white beard, and adopted Dragan David Dabić as an alias. Calling on his training as a psychiatrist, he entered the underground cult world and posed as a faith healer who favored herbal medicines.

April 1, 2004. British SFOR troops raided residence of Karadžić's parish priest in Pale, a suspected hiding place, but did not find Karadžić; the priest and his son were wounded by explosions that blew out the doors of the residence.

July 18, 2008. Karadžić was arrested at 9:30 p.m. on a bus in Belgrade, setting off demonstrations by Serb national extremists protesting the arrest.

July 30, 2008. Karadžić was flown to the ICTY's Scheveningen Prison in The Hague, Netherlands, to await arraignment and trial.

July 31, 2008. Karadžić made his initial appearance in Courtroom One of the ICTY in The Hague and listened as the presiding judge read aloud the eleven-count indictment.

March 1, 2010. Karadžić, representing himself, made his opening statement at his trial, which is expected to conclude sometime in 2015.

June 1–9, 2010. Karadžić cross-examined the author, who was called by prosecutors as an expert historical witness in the case.

List of Acronyms and Terms

ARBiH   *Armija Republike Bosne i Hercegovine* (Army of the Republic of Bosnia and Herzegovina).

ARK   Acronym used here for both the *Autonomna regija Krajine* (Autonomous Region of Krajina), formed on April 25, 1991, and its successor, renamed the *Zajednica opština Bosanske Krajine* (Community of Municipalities of Bosnian Krajina) on September 16, 1991.

Assembly   Short title for the Bosnian Serb Assembly (BSA) in this volume; all other legislative bodies are called parliaments.

Bosnia   Name used in this book to refer to the polity of Bosnia and Herzegovina under any of its several names.[1]

Bosniak   Bosnia's most numerous nation, with a plurality but not an absolute majority of the population. Bosniaks were known as the Bosnian Muslims until September 1993, when group leaders voted to refer to members of their group as "Bosniaks" to affirm that they make up a nation, or people, rather than a religious community.

BSA   Bosnian Serb Assembly, name used here for Assembly of the Serb People in Bosnia and Herzegovina (*Skupština srpskog naroda u Bosni i Hercegovini*, October 1991–September 1992) and its renamed successor, the National Assembly of Republika Srpska (*Narodna skupština Republike Srpske*, September 14, 1992–present).

---

[1] Socialist Republic of Bosnia and Herzegovina (*Socijalistička Republika Bosne i Hercegovine*, 1945–1991) Bosnia and Herzegovina (*Bosna i Hercegovina*, December 1995–present), its name as designated in the Dayton Peace Agreement.

FRY	Federal Republic of Yugoslavia, the polity consisting of the Republic of Montenegro and the Republic of Serbia along with its two autonomous regions, Vojvodina and Kosovo, as defined in the constitution of April 27, 1991. It ceased to exist with Montenegro's declaration of independence in 2008.
HDZ	*Hrvatska demokratska zajednica* (Croatian Democratic Union), the main Croat nationalist party in Bosnia, founded on August 18, 1990.
HV	*Hrvatska vojska* (Army of Croatia).
HVO	*Hrvatska vijeće obrane* (Croatian Defense Council), the army of Croat nationalists in Bosnia.
ICFY	International Conference on the Former Yugoslavia, established at the London Conference in August 1992 as an institution to negotiate an end to the war in Bosnia.
ICTY	International Criminal Tribunal for the Former Yugoslavia, an ad hoc United Nations body created by UN Security Council Resolution 827 on May 25, 1993, and located in The Hague, Netherlands.
JNA	Yugoslav People's Army (*Jugoslovenska narodna armija*, JNA).
Left opposition	A coalition of Reformists and social democratic parties formed following those parties' defeat by the three nationalist parties, the HDZ, SDA, and SDS, in elections of 1990.
MUP	*Ministarstvo unutrašnjih poslova* (Ministry of Internal Affairs), the abbreviation and name commonly used throughout the former Yugoslavia for various police forces.
Parliament	Term used in this book to refer to legislative bodies in Yugoslavia and Bosnia with the exception of the Bosnian Serb Assembly.
PMK	Prosecutor v. Momčilo Krajišnik, case IT-00–39-T before the ICTY.
PRB	Prosecutor v. Radoslav Brdjanin, case IT-99–36 before the ICTY.
PRK	Prosecutor v. Radovan Karadžić, case IT-95–5/5/18-I before the ICTY.
PSM	Prosecutor v. Slobodan Milošević, case IT-02–54 before the ICTY.

Reformists	*Savez reformskih snaga Jugoslavije* (Alliance of Reformist Forces of Yugoslavia), founded July 27, 1990 and headed by Federal Prime Minister Ante Marković.
RS	Republika Srpska, name used here for the assembly-proclaimed Republic of the Serb People in Bosnia and Herzegovina (*Republika srpskog naroda u Bosni i Hercegovini*, January 9–August 12, 1992) and its renamed successor, *Republika Srpska* (its formal name in both BCS and English, August 12, 1992–present).
RSK	Republic of Serb Krajina, the breakaway Serb entity in Croatia.
SAO	*Srpska autonomna oblast* (Serb autonomous region), entities created by Serb nationalists in Croatia in 1990 and in Bosnia in September 1991.
SAO Krajina	Serb Autonomous Region of Krajina, a self-proclaimed Serb polity created in Croatia on December 21, 1990, joined on February 26, 1992, by several other SAOs in Croatia to make up the Republic of Serb Krajina (RSK).
SDA	*Stranka demokratska akcija* (Party of Democratic Action), the principal Bosniak nationalist party in Bosnia, founded on May 26, 1990.
SDS	*Srpska demokratska stranka* (Serb Democratic Party), the principal Serb nationalist party in Bosnia, founded on July 12, 1990.
SFRY	Socialist Federal Republic of Yugoslavia (*Socijalističa Federalna Republika Jugoslavija*), 1945–1992.
Social democrats	Members of leftist parties, most of which were renamed successors of the League of Communists or Socialist Alliance
UNPAs	United Nations Protected Areas, consisting of Eastern, Western, Northern, and Southern zones.
VOPP	Vance-Owen Peace Plan.
VRS	Army of the Republika Srpska (*Vojska Republike Srpske*).

Bibliography

BOOKS AND ARTICLES

American Heritage Dictionary of the English Language. 4th ed. New York: Houghton Mifflin, 2009.

Andjelic, Neven. *Bosnia-Herzegovina: The End of a Legacy.* London: Frank Cass, 2003.

Antonić, Zdravko, ed. *Istorija Saveza komunista Bosne i Hercegovine.* 2 vols. Sarajevo: Institut za istoriju and Oslobodjenje, 1990.

Armatta, Judith. "Historical Revelations from the Milošević Trial," *Southeastern Europe* 36 (2012), 23–24.

Arnautović, Suad. *Izbori u Bosni i Hercegovini '90. Analiza izbornog procesa.* Sarajevo: Promocult, 1996.

Arsić, Mirko, and Dragan R. Marković. *'68; Studentski bunt i društvo.* 3rd ed. Belgrade: Istraživačko izdavački centar SSO Srbije, 1988.

Babović, Budimir, "Analysis of Regulations Regard[ing] Responsibility for Control of the Interior Ministry of the Republic of Serbia," Expert Report, April 2, 2003, International Criminal Tribunal for Yugoslavia (ICTY), Prosecutor v. Slobodan Milosević (PSM), Exhibit P465a.

Bećirević, Edina. *Na Drini genocid: Istraživanje organiziranog zločina u istočnoj Bosni.* Sarajevo: Buybook, 2009.

Bennett, Christopher. *Yugoslavia's Bloody Collapse: Causes, Course, and Consequences.* London: Hurst, 1995.

Bethlehem, Daniel, and Marc Weller, eds. *The "Yugoslav Crisis" in International Law: General Issues.* New York: Cambridge University Press, 1997.

Budding, Audrey Helfant. "Nation/People/Republic: Self-Determination in Socialist Yugoslavia," *Collapse in South-Eastern Europe: New Perspectives on Yugoslavia's Disintegration*, edited by Lenard J. Cohen and Jasna Dragović-Soso. West Lafayette, IN: Purdue University Press, 2008, 91–129.

Bulatović, Ljiljana, ed. and comp. *Radovan.* Belgrade: Evro, 2002.

——— ed. and comp. *Zavet majke Radovana Karadžića.* Belgrade: Evro, 2003.

Burg, Steven L., and Paul S. Shoup. *The War in Bosnia-Herzegovina: Ethnic Conflict and International Intervention.* Armonk, NY: M.E. Sharpe, 1999.

Campbell, David. *National Deconstruction: Violence, Identity and Justice in Bosnia.* Minneapolis: University of Minnesota Press, 1998.

Carroll, Robert T. *The Skeptic's Dictionary*. Hoboken, NJ: John Wiley & Sons, 2003.

Chandler, David. *Bosnia: Faking Democracy After Dayton*, 2nd ed. London: Pluto Press, 2000.

Cigar, Norman. *Genocide in Bosnia: The Policy of "Ethnic Cleansing."* College Station: Texas A&M University Press, 1995.

Cohen, Lenard. *Serpent in the Bosom: The Rise and Fall of Slobodan Milošević.* Boulder, CO: Westview, 2001.

Cohen, Lenard, and Jasna Dragović-Soso, eds. *State Collapse in South-Eastern Europe: New Perspectives on Yugoslavia's Disintegration*. West Lafayette, IN: Purdue University Press, 2008.

Cohen, Roger. *Hearts Grown Brutal: Sagas of Sarajevo*. New York: Random House, 1998.

Crnobrnja, Mihailo. *The Yugoslav Drama*. 2nd ed. Montreal: McGill–Queen's University Press, 1996.

Danner, Mark. "Breaking the Machine," *New York Review of Books*, February 19, 1998.

Dizdarević, Raif. *Od smrti Tita do smrti Jugoslavije. Svjedočenja*. Sarajevo: OKO, 1999.

Djilas, Aleksa. *The Contested Country: Yugoslav Unity and Communist Revolution, 1919–1953*. Cambridge: Harvard University Press, 1991.

Djukić, Slavoljub. *Milošević and Marković: A Lust for Power*. Translated by Alex Dubinsky. Montreal: McGill–Queen's University Press, 2001.

Doder, Dusko, and Louise Branson. *Milošević: Portrait of a Tyrant*. New York: Free Press, 1999.

Donia, Robert J., and John V.A. Fine. *Bosnia and Herzegovina: A Tradition Betrayed*. New York: Columbia University Press, 1994.

Donia, Robert J. ed. *From the Republika Srpska Assembly, 1991–1996: Excerpts from Delegates' Speeches at the Republika Srpska Assembly as Evidence for the International Criminal Tribunal at the Hague*. Sarajevo: University Press, 2012.

Sarajevo: A Biography. Ann Arbor, MI: University of Michigan Press, 2006.

Dragović-Soso, Jasna. *"Saviours of the Nation": Serbia's Intellectual Opposition and the Revival of Nationalism*. London: Hurst; Montreal: McGill–Queens University Press, 2006.

Federativna Narodna Republika Jugoslavije, Savezni Zavod za Statistiku. *Konačni rezultati popisa stanovništva od 15. marta 1948 godine*, vol. 9 (*Stanovništvo po narodnosti*).

Friedman, Francine. *Bosnia and Herzegovina: A Polity on the Brink*. New York: Routledge, 2004.

Gelo, Jakov, et al., eds. *Stanovništvo Bosne i Hercegovine Narodnosni sastav po naseljima*. Zagreb: Državni zavod za statistiku Republike Hrvatske, 1995.

Glaurdić, Josip. *The Hour of Europe: Western Powers and the Breakup of Yugoslavia*. New Haven: Yale University Press, 2011.

Gow, James. *Legitimacy and the Military: The Yugoslav Crisis*. London: Pinter, 1992.

The Serbian Project and its Adversaries: A Strategy of War Crimes. Montreal: McGill–Queen's University Press, 2003.

Triumph of the Lack of Will: International Diplomacy and the Yugoslav War. London: Hurst, 1997.

Hadžiomeragić, Maid. *Stranka demokratske akcije i stvarnost.* Sarajevo: Unikopis, 1991.

Hawton, Nick. *The Quest for Radovan Karadžić.* London: Hutchinson, 2009.

Hayden, Robert M. "Recounting the Dead: The Rediscovery and Redefinition of Wartime Massacres in Late- and Post-Communist Yugoslavia," in *Memory, History, and Opposition under State Socialism.* Edited by Rubie S. Watson. Santa Fe, NM: SAR Press, 1994.

Hoare, Marko. *How Bosnia Armed.* London: Saqi, 2004.

Holbrooke, Richard. *To End a War.* New York: Random House, 1998.

Honig, Jay Willig, and Norbert Both. *Srebrenica: Record of a Crime.* New York: Penguin, 1996.

Jackovich, Victor. "Conversations with Karadžić." Typescript, 2008.

Jović, Borisav. *Poslednji dani SFRJ.* 2nd ed. Kragujevac: Prizma, 1996.

Judah, Tim. *The Serbs: History, Myth and the Destruction of Yugoslavia.* New Haven: Yale University Press, 1997.

Kadijević, Veljko. *Moje vidjenje raspada: Vojska bez države.* Beograd: Politika, 1993.

Kahrović, Murat. *Kako smo branili Sarajevo: Prva sandžačka brigada.* Sarajevo: Udruženje gradjana Bošnjaka porijeklom iz Sandžaka, 2001.

Kamberović, Husnija. *Prema modernom društvu: Bosna i Hercegovina od 1945. do 1953. godine.* Tešanj: Centar za kulturu i obrazovanje, 2000.

Kaplan, Robert M. "Dr Radovan Karadžić: psychiatrist, poet, soccer coach and genocidal leader," *Australasian Psychiatry,* 11, no. 1 (March 2003), 75.

Karadžić, Radovan. Collected Works. Belgrade: International Committee for the Truth about Radovan Karadžić, 2004–2005. Six volumes: *Ratna Naredbe dr. Radovana Karadžića* (Wartime orders of Dr. Radovan Karadžić), vol. 1; *Ratna pisma* (Wartime letters), vols. 2 and 3; *Milosrdje i apeli* (Clemency and appeals), vol. 4; and *Intervjui i govori* (Interviews and speeches), vols. 5 and 6.

Kaufman, Stuart J. *Modern Hatreds: The Symbolic Politics of Ethnic War.* Ithaca, NY: Cornell University Press, 2001.

Klemenčič, Mladen. "The International Community," in *Confronting the Yugoslav Controversies.* Edited by Charles Ingrao and Thomas A. Emmert. West Lafayette, IN: Purdue University Press, 2009.

"Territorial Proposals for the Settlement of the War in Bosnia-Herzegovina," in *Boundary and Territory Briefing.* Vol. 3, no. 1 (1994). Edited by Martin Pratt and Clive Schofield.

Kočović, Bogoljub. *Žrtve Drugog svjetskog rata u Jugoslaviji.* London: Naše Delo, 1985.

Koljević, Nikola. *Stvaranje Republike Srpske; Dnevnik 1993–1995.* 2 vols. Edited by Milica Koljević. Banja Luka: Službeni glasnik Republike Srpske, 2008.

Komšić, Ivo. *Preživljena zemlja: Tko je, kada i gdje dilelio BiH.* Zagreb: Promotej, 2006.

Lampe, John R. *Yugoslavia as History: Twice there was a Country.* New York: Cambridge University Press, 1996.

LeBor, Adam. *Milošević: A Biography.* New Haven, CT: Yale University Press, 2004.

Lopušina, Marko. *Radovan Karadžić: Najtraženija srpska glava.* Niš: Zograf, 2004.

MacDonald, David Bruce. *Balkan Holocausts? Serbian and Croatian Victim-centered Propaganda and the War in Yugoslavia.* Manchester: Manchester University Press, 2003.

Mann, Michael. *The Dark Side of Democracy: Explaining Ethnic Cleansing*. New York: Cambridge University Press, 2005.

Meier, Viktor. *Yugoslavia: A History of its Demise*. Translated by Sabrina Ramet. London: Routledge, 1999.

Mesić, Stjepan. "Rasprava," in Branka Magaš and Ivo Žanić, eds. *Rat u Hrvatskoj i Bosni i Hercegovini, 1991–1995*. London: Bosanski Institut, 1999.

Miller, Nick. *The Nonconformists: Culture, Politics, and Nationalism in a Serbian Intellectual Circle, 1944–1991*. New York: Central European University Press, 2007.

Milić, Miloš. *Dogovori u Karadjordjevo o podeli Bosne i Hercegovine*. Sarajevo: Rabic, 1998.

Mojzes, Paul. *The Yugoslav Inferno: Ethnoreligious Warfare in the Balkans*. New York: Continuum Publishing, 1994.

Naimark, Norman. *Fires of Hatred: Ethnic Cleansing in Twentieth-century Europe*. Cambridge, MA: Harvard University Press, 2001.

Nettelfield, Lara J., and Sarah E. Wagner. *Srebrenica in the Aftermath of Genocide*. New York: Cambridge University Press, 2014.

Neu, Joyce, and Steven Shewfelt, *Eminent Third Party Mediation: Unofficial Diplomacy in Bosnia*. Manuscript. Copyright Joyce Neu, Carter Center, 1997.

Nikiforov, Konstantin. *Izmedju Kremlja i Republike Srpske*. Translated by Mira Toholj. Belgrade: Igam, 2000.

Olbina, Dane. *Dani i godine opsade*. Sarajevo: Istorijski arhiv Sarajevo, 2002.

Osiel, Mark. *Making Sense of Mass Atrocity*. New York: Cambridge University Press, 2009.

   Mass Atrocity, Collective Memory, and the Law. New Brunswick, NJ: Transaction Publishers, 1997.

Owen, David. *Balkan Odyssey*. New York: Harcourt Brace, 1995.

Pantić, Miroslav, ed. *Memorandum of the Serbian Academy of Sciences and Arts: Answers to Criticisms*. Belgrade: Serbian Academy of Sciences and Arts, 1995.

Pavković, Aleksandar. *The Fragmentation of Yugoslavia: Nationalism in a Multinational State*. New York: St. Martin's Press, 1997.

Pejanović, Mirko. *The Political Development of Bosnia and Herzegovina in the Post-Dayton Period*. Translated by Borislav Radović. Sarajevo: Šahinpašić, 2007.

   Through Bosnian Eyes: The Political Memoir of a Bosnian Serb. Edited by Robert J. Donia. Translated by Marina Bowder. West Lafayette, IN: Purdue University Press, 2004.

Perica, Vjekoslav. *Balkan Idols: Religion and Nationalism in Yugoslav States*. New York: Oxford University Press, 2002.

Power, Samantha. *"A Problem From Hell": America and the Age of Genocide*. New York: Basic Books, 2002.

Radulović, Srdjan. *Sudbina Krajine*. Belgrade: Dan Graf, 1996.

Ramet, Sabrina. *Balkan Babel: The Disintegration of Yugoslavia from the Death of Tito to Ethnic War*. 2nd ed. Boulder, CO: Westview, 1996.

   Nationalism and Federalism in Yugoslavia, 1962–1991. 2nd ed. Bloomington, IN: Indiana University Press, 1992.

Ramcharan, B.G., ed. *The International Conference on the Former Yugoslavia. Official Papers*. Vol. 1. The Hague: Kluwer Law International, 1997.

Republika Bosna i Hercegovina. *Zemljišna karta sa nacionalnom strukturom Republike Bosne i Hercegovine.*

Republika Hrvatska. *Stanovništvo Bosni i Hercegovine: Narodnosni sastav po naseljama.* Zagreb: Državni zavod za statistiku, 1995.

Rogel, Carole. *The Breakup of Yugoslavia and the War in Bosnia.* Westport, CT: Greenwood Press, 1998.

Rossanet, Bertrand de, *Peacemaking and Peacekeeping in Yugoslavia.* The Hague: Kluwer Law International, 1996.

Roth, Brad R. "Secessions, Coups and the International Rule of Law: Assessing the Decline of the Effective Control Doctrine," *Melbourne Journal of International Law,* vol. 11 (2010), 392–440.

Rujanac, Zijad. *Opsjednuti grad Sarajevo.* Sarajevo: Bosanski kulturni centar, 2003.

Sell, Louis. *Slobodan Milošević and the Destruction of Yugoslavia.* Durham, NC: Duke University Press, 2002.

Shoup, Paul. *Yugoslav Communism and the National Question.* New York: Columbia University Press, 1968.

Šiber, Stjepan. *Prevare zablude istina: ratni dnevnik 1992.* Sarajevo: Rabic, 2000.

Socijalistička Republika Bosne i Hercegovine. *Ustav socijalističke republike Bosne i Hercegovine.* Sarajevo: Službeni glasnik, 1974.

Smith, Rupert. *The Utility of Force: The Art of War in the Modern World.* London: Allen Lane, 2005.

Snyder, Jack. *From Voting to Violence: Democratization and Nationalist Conflict.* New York: Norton, 2000.

Sudetic, Chuck. *Blood and Vengeance: One Family's Story of the War in Bosnia.* New York: Penguin, 1998.

Swain, Richard M. *Neither War nor Not War; Army Command in Europe during the Time of Peace Operations: Tasks Confronting USAREUR Commands, 1994–2000.* Carlisle, PA: Strategic Studies Institute, 2003.

Terrett, Steve. *The Dissolution of Yugoslavia and the Badinter Arbitration Commission: A Contextual Study of Peace-making Efforts in the Post–Cold War World.* Burlington, VT.: Ashgate/Dartmouth, 2000.

Thomas, Robert. *The Politics of Serbia in the 1990s.* New York: Columbia University Press, 1999.

Toal, Gerard, and Carl T. Dahlman. *Bosnia Remade: Ethnic Cleansing and its Reversal.* New York: Oxford University Press, 2011.

Trbić, Jusuf. *Gluho doba: Kolumne reminiscencije, analize i rasprave.* Tuzla: Kujundžić, 2006.

Trifković, Srdja. *The Krajina Chronicle: A History of Serbs in Croatia, Slavonia, and Dalmatia* (Chicago: The Lord Byron Foundation fo Balkan Studies, 2010).

Trifunovska, Snežana, ed. *Former Yugoslavia Through Documents: From its Creation to its Dissolution.* Dordrecht, Boston: Martinus Nijhoff, 1994.

United Nations Commission on Human Rights, "Report on the Situation of Human Rights in the Territory of the former Yugoslavia submitted by Mr. Tadeusz Mazowiecki, Special Rapporteur of the Commission on Human Rights," August 28, 1992.

United Nations Security Council. *Annexes to the Final Report of the Commission of Experts Established Pursuant to Security Council Resolution 780 (1992)*, Volume II, Annex VI, Part 1.

U.S. Central Intelligence Agency. *Balkan Battlegrounds: A Military History of the Yugoslav Conflict, 1990–1995*. Washington, DC: Central Intelligence Agency, 2002. 2 vols.

U.S. DCI Interagency Balkan Task Force. "The Bosnian Army in Srebrenica: What Happened?," July 18, 1995. Available from <clintonlibrary.gov/bosniadeclassdocs. html>, viewed January 4, 2014.

U.S. Department of State. "Karadžić Unrepentant." Zimmerman to U.S. Secretary of State, May 14, 1992.

U.S. Department of State. *The Road to Dayton: U.S. Diplomacy and the Bosnian Peace Process, May–December 1995*. Washington: U.S. Department of State, 1997.

Verdery, Katherine. *The Political Lives of Dead Bodies*. New York: Columbia University Press, 1999.

Vešović, Marko. "Estetizam percepcije," in Radovan Karadžić. *Pamtivek*. Sarajevo: Svjetlost, 1971.

Vuksanović, Mladen. *From Enemy Territory: Pale Diary (5 April to 15 July 1992)*. London: Saqi, 2004.

Woodward, Susan L. *Balkan Odyssey: Chaos and Dissolution after the Cold War*. Washington: Brookings Institution, 1995.

Zanić, Ivo. *Flag on the Mountain: A Political Anthropology of War in Croatia and Bosnia*. Translated by Graham McMaster and Celia Hawkesworth. London: Saqi, 2007.

Žerjavić, Vladimir. *Gubici stanovništva Jugoslavije u drugom svjetskom ratu*. Zagreb: Jugoslavensko viktimološko društvo, 1989.

Zgodić, Esad. *Titova nacionalna politika: temeljni pojmovi, načela i vrijednosti*. Sarajevo: Kantonalni odbor SDP BiH, 2000.

Zimmerman, Warren. *Origins of a Catastrophe: Yugoslavia and its Destroyers – America's Last Ambassador Tells What Happened and Why*. New York: Random House, 1996.

Zulfikarpašić, Adil. *The Bosniak*. London: Hurst, 1996.

PERIODICALS

AP News Archive (New York) <www.apnewsarchive.com>
Balkan Insight Online (Belgrade) <www.balkaninsight.com>
B-92 Online (Belgrade) <www.b92.net>
Blic Online (Begrade) <www.blic.rs>
Bosanski pogledi (Sarajevo)
The European Courier (New York)
Foreign Broadcast Information Service (Rosslyn, VA)
Glas and its weekly insert *Nedeljni Glas* (Banja Luka)
Institute for War and Peace Reporting (London) <iwpr.net>
Javnost (Banja Luka)
Naši Dani (Sarajevo)

New York Times (New York)
Nezavisne novine (Banja Luka)
NIN (Belgrade)
The Observer (London)
Orthodox News (Belgrade) <theorthodoxchurch.info/blog/news/>
Oslobodjenje (Sarajevo)
Publika (Podgorica, Montenegro)
Službeni glasnik Republike Srpske (Banja Luka)
Službeni glasnik Bosne i Hercegovine (Sarajevo)
Srpska anarhistička mreža
Večernje novosti (Belgrade)
Yugoslav Survey (Belgrade)

AUTHOR'S INTERVIEWS

Raif Dizdarević, Sarajevo, May 11, 2004.
Rajko Dukić, Milići, Bosnia, March 21, 2000. Interview conducted by Sinan Alić with
    questions prepared by the author.
Zdravko Grebo, Sarajevo, April 25, 2012.
Josip Istik. Ljubljana, Slovenia, November 9, 2007.
Saša Mlač. Ljubljana, Slovenia, November 9, 2007.

Index